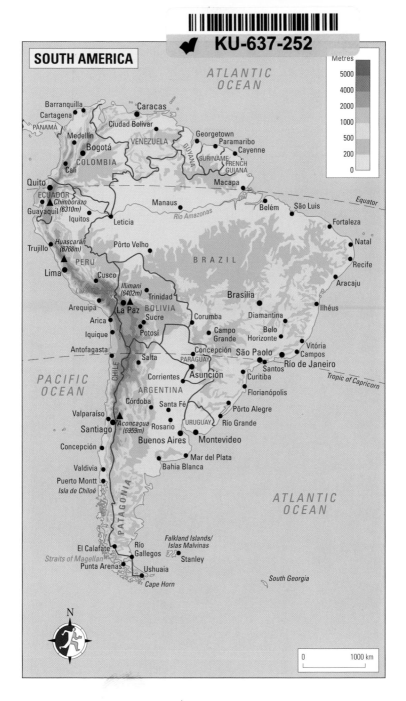

# SOUTH AMERICA

ATLANTIC OCEAN

Metres
5000
4000
2000
1000
500
200
0

Barranquilla
Cartagena
Caracas
PANAMÁ
Ciudad Bolívar
Medellín
Bogotá
VENEZUELA
Georgetown
Paramaribo
Cayenne
SURINAME
FRENCH GUIANA
COLOMBIA
Cali
GUYANA
Quito
Macapa
ECUADOR
Chimborazo (6310m)
Guayaquil
Manaus
Belém
São Luis
Equator
Iquitos
Río Amazonas
Leticia
Fortaleza
Huascarán (6768m)
Pôrto Velho
Natal
Trujillo
BRAZIL
PERU
Recife
Lima
Cusco
Illimani (6402m)
Aracaju
Lake
Trinidad
Brasília
Arequipa
BOLIVIA
Ilhéus
Arica
Sucre
Corumba
Diamantina
Iquique
Potosí
Campo Grande
Belo Horizonte
Antofagasta
Concepción
São Paolo
Vitória
Salta
PARAGUAY
Santos
Campos
Río de Janeiro
CHILE
Corrientes
Asunción
Curitiba
Tropic of Capricorn
ARGENTINA
Córdoba
Santa Fé
Florianópolis
Valparaíso
Aconcagua (6959m)
Rosario
Pôrto Alegre
Santiago
URUGUAY
Río Grande
Concepción
Buenos Aires
Montevideo
Mar del Plata
Valdivia
Bahia Blanca
Puerto Montt
Isla de Chiloé
ATLANTIC OCEAN
PACIFIC OCEAN
PATAGONIA
Falkland Islands/ Islas Malvinas
El Calafate
Río Gallegos
Stanley
Straits of Magellan
Punta Arenas
Ushuaia
South Georgia
Cape Horn

N

0    1000 km

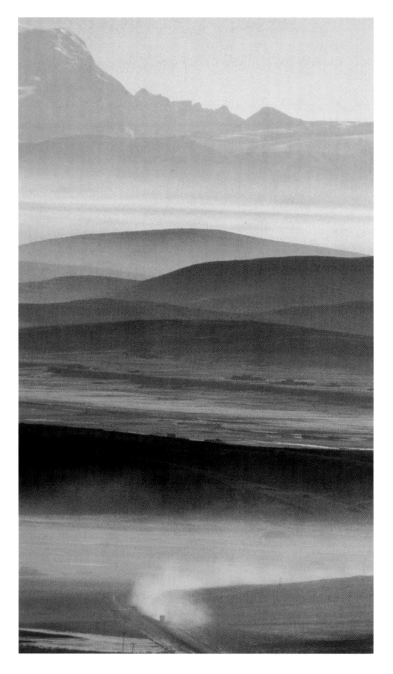

# First-Time
# Latin America

written and researched by

**Polly Rodger Brown and James Read**

www.roughguides.com

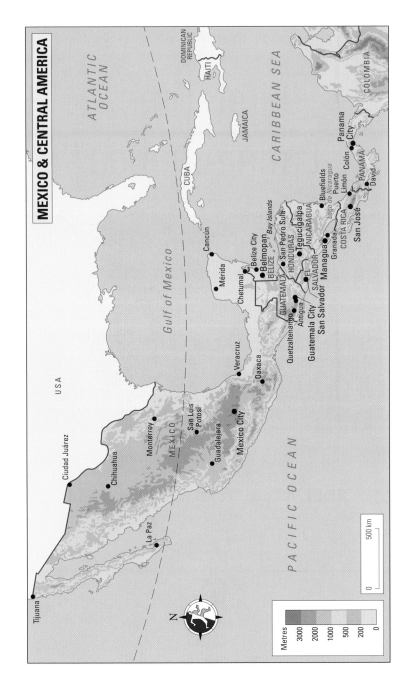

MEXICO & CENTRAL AMERICA

ATLANTIC OCEAN

DOMINICAN REPUBLIC

HAITI

JAMAICA

CUBA

CARIBBEAN SEA

Cancún

Mérida

Chetumal

Belize City
Belmopan
BELIZE
Bay Islands
San Pedro Sula
HONDURAS
Tegucigalpa
NICARAGUA
Bluefields
Lago de Nicaragua
Granada
Managua
EL SALVADOR
San Salvador
Puerto Limón
COSTA RICA
San José
PANAMA
David
Colón
Panama City

GUATEMALA
Quetzaltenango
Antigua
Guatemala City

COLOMBIA

Gulf of Mexico

Veracruz

Oaxaca

USA

MEXICO

Ciudad Juárez

Chihuahua

Monterrey

San Luis Potosí

Guadalajara

Mexico City

La Paz

Tijuana

PACIFIC OCEAN

500 km
0

Metres
3000
2000
1000
500
200
0

N

Introduction to

# First-Time Latin America

**Every year thousands of travellers set off on their own Latin American adventure. Some want to see for themselves the great monuments left by the mysterious pre-Columbian civilizations, such as the spellbinding lost Inca city of Machu Picchu, or join the samba-dancing crowds at Carnaval in Rio de Janeiro, the largest and most spectacular of the region's countless extravagant fiestas. Others are drawn by the stunning scenery: the immense, wildlife-rich rainforests of the Amazon; the soaring snow-capped peaks of the Andes; the idyllic beaches and kaleidoscopic coral reefs of the Caribbean; the dramatic glaciers and fjords of Patagonia.**

But perhaps the greatest attractions are the sheer vitality of daily life in Latin America and the rich and varied lifestyles of its inhabitants. For though from the outside the region may appear to have a relatively uniform culture, in fact each country is made up of a diverse and compelling blend of indigenous, European, African and (to a lesser extent) Asian cultural influences, the product of Latin America's complex and extraordinary history. Even within individual countries, regional differences in human experience can be remarkable, ranging from bankers working in high-rise city centres to semi-nomadic tribes hunting for their supper with bows and arrows. During your travels you may find yourself sipping *caipirinhas* on Copacabana beach or salsa-dancing the night away in the steamy nightclubs of Cali; eating barbecue at a rodeo on the Argentine *pampas* or chewing coca leaves with llama herders in the high Andes; searching for turtles by moonlight on the shores of the Caribbean or watching the sun rise over ancient Maya pyramids in the jungles of Central America.

Nearly all these things are affordable even for travellers on a tight budget, because most of Latin America is inexpensive compared to Europe or the United States (though generally a more expensive place to travel than Africa or Asia). Managed carefully, your money will go much further than it does back home, allowing you to travel for longer and take in sights and experiences you might not be able to afford elsewhere. Unsurprisingly, a growing number of young adventurers from all over the world are visiting the region,

and there's now a well-established "Gringo Trail" linking the main attractions in each country, with many cities and towns home to a lively travellers' scene. This is nowhere near as intense as on the backpackers' trail in Asia, however, and one of the joys of travel in Latin America is that it's so easy to get off the beaten track and visit regions that as yet see few or no tourists. This becomes even easier if you learn a little Spanish (or Portuguese if you're travelling in Brazil). The linguistic uniformity of the region is a massive advantage for travellers: picking up just one European language allows you to speak to and understand almost everyone you meet, making it far easier to get close to the local culture and people in a way that (unless you are a brilliant linguist) you just can't do on a trip to other continents.

However, travel in Latin America can also be a disquieting experience. It's not unusual to be shocked by your first sight of a sprawling slum and upset by your first encounter with a malnourished child begging for change. Many first-timers are distressed by the chaos and squalor of some Latin American cities and by the often appalling poverty and inequality. Some get frustrated by the sometimes labyrinthine bureaucracy that can complicate even the sim-

## The Amazon

Of all the natural wonders of Latin America, none has captured the imagination of the world more than the Amazon Basin. Covering an area almost as large as Australia and extending from its heart in Brazil across the border to cover great expanses of Colombia, Peru, Bolivia, Venezuela and the Guyanas, the Amazon is the largest tropical rainforest and by far the most biologically diverse region on earth, home to a staggering variety of plant and animal life – rare birds and mammals, extraordinary insects and reptiles, and literally millions of plant species – all woven together into a rich and complex natural tapestry. Through this immense forest region, fed by innumerable tributaries, flows the mighty River Amazon itself, a vast river-sea that carries about a fifth of the world's running fresh water. Despite its immense size, however, the Amazon rainforest is disappearing at an alarming rate as a result of logging, mining, oil drilling, cattle ranching, and slash-and-burn agriculture. If current rates of deforestation continue, scientists fear the Amazon rainforest could be completely destroyed within the next few decades, fuelling global climate change and representing the loss of a vast, irreplaceable and largely unexplored repository of genetic resources. For the time being, though, you can still explore the astonishing natural beauty of the forest first hand by visiting one of the numerous national parks in the Amazon – by doing so you may even contribute to their conservation, as ecotourism can help local people to earn a living without destroying the rainforest environment.

plest transaction and by the locals' flagrant disregard for punctuality. Others feel unnerved by suddenly being a relatively wealthy person in a poor country and paranoid about the risks of rip-offs and violent crime that await the unwary. And then there are climatic factors like oppressive heat or extreme altitude to deal with, not to mention the unfamiliar food and strange local customs and attitudes. The truth is,

## Semana Santa

Semana Santa – Holy or Easter Week – is Latin America's biggest festival, even more ubiquitous than carnival, with celebrations taking place in every city, town and village from Mexico to Argentina. Firstly it's a public holiday, when locals head in droves for the beach, national parks and other resorts or else back to their hometowns. Hotels are booked out, buses and domestic flights are crammed full – anyone planning to travel during this period will need to book in advance. More significantly, though, it's a deeply religious occasion with a series of packed masses over the week leading to Easter Sunday and churches lovingly decorated with extravagant flower arrangements. Though ceremonies vary from region to region, they usually include solemn parades of church statues through the town centre and vivid Passion Plays with real blood and suffering – the man playing Christ often wears a genuine crown of thorns, staggers under the weight of a solid cross and is sometimes even nailed to it with real nails. The sanctity of the occasion is lightened with street food stalls, traditional live music and noisy firework displays. The most impressive Semana Santa celebrations in Latin America occur in the colonial city of Antigua, Guatemala, and attract tens of thousands of visitors. Locals spend hours carpeting the streets with elaborate patterns of flowers, coloured sawdust and pine needles for the Good Friday parades where life-sized images of Jesus Christ and the saints are carried through the town on massive cedar platforms to an accompaniment of brass band dirges and thick clouds of incense. Elsewhere, some of the best places to witness the festivities include San Miguel de Allende in central Mexico, Popayán in southern Colombia and Ayacucho in the Peruvian Andes.

every trip involves a degree of hassle, and on reflection travel would be rather dull if everything always went as planned. Adventures are by definition unpredictable affairs, and it's often the dramas and surprises that make for the most memorable experiences.

This book is intended to prepare you for your trip, whether it's a couple of weeks on the beach in Cancún or a twelve-month journey from Mexico down to Tierra del Fuego. It's a book to read before you go rather than an on-the-road guide, a planning handbook to help you decide on the kind of trip you'd like to make and prepare you for your journey. The first thing you'll need to decide is which countries and regions in Latin America you want to visit and which places to skip: the possibilities are outlined in Where To Go, the opening section of the book. The book focuses on the twenty countries of Central and South America plus Mexico, and thus includes several countries – Belize, Guyana, Suriname – that are not strictly speaking part of Latin America, and excludes others – namely Cuba, the Dominican Republic, Haiti and Puerto Rico – that are. We've chosen to do this because travellers visiting several countries on the mainland may well include non-Spanish- or Portuguese-speaking countries on their itinerary, while most people visiting the Caribbean island nations tend to do so without visiting the mainland. If you're intending to visit one of the Latin American Caribbean islands mentioned above, however, you'll find much of the general information and advice we give is also relevant there. For

# The Beautiful Game

Everywhere you go in Latin America you'll find people watching, talking about and playing *futbol (futebol* in Portuguese). Latin Americans are so obsessed with the game that it's often compared to a religion, and across the region it is more of a common language than Spanish or Portuguese. Almost every village has a football pitch, even if it's just the verge of an airstrip carved out of the rainforest or the only flat piece of land in a mountain community, and it's not unusual to come across Latin Americans who are the proud owners of a pair of football boots but possess no other shoes. Even in Central America, where the US influence has made baseball the most popular sport, the passions surrounding football can run high: in 1969 a bitterly contested World Cup qualifying match between El Salvador and Honduras sparked a brief but bloody conflict between the two countries that became known as "The Football War".

First introduced to South America by British engineers and sailors in the nineteenth century, football was quickly adopted by the locals, who began playing with a style and verve that was all their own. The immense skill and flamboyant creativity of Latin American football went on to capture the imagination of the world, as Uruguay, Argentina and Brazil all produced a series of World Cup-winning teams. The region has also produced the two greatest footballers the world has ever seen, in the Argentine Diego Maradona and the Brazilian Edson Nascimiento da Silva, better known as Pelé. The intense carnival atmosphere of big matches in stadiums like the world-famous Maracana in Rio de Janeiro is an experience not to be missed, even if you're not a football fan, while joining in a barefoot game on the beach or a kickabout on the streets is an excellent way of making contact with local people.

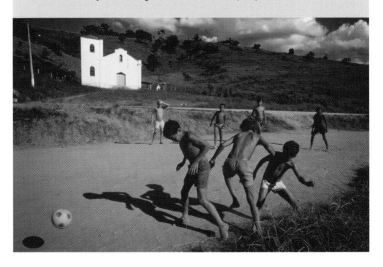

each country covered, you'll find a profile outlining what the destination offers first-timers, including a roundup of the main highlights and suggested itineraries, as well as a selection of personal recommendations and more out-of-the-way attractions.

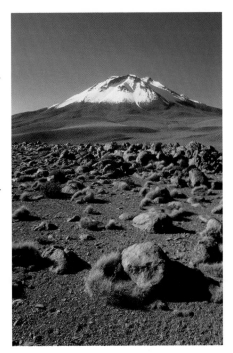

The middle section of *First-Time Latin America*, The Big Adventure, deals with the practical details of travel in the region. This is where you'll find chapters on how to choose the right ticket and which guidebook to use, advice on how long you can afford to stay away and what you need to take with you when you go, and a selection of books and films to inspire your travels, along with lists of useful websites to consult. This section also looks at life on the road in Latin America, giving you an idea of what to expect in terms of transport and accommodation, advice on how to stay safe and healthy while you're away, and tips on how to avoid the potential hassles and hazards that await the unwary traveller. Finally, the Basics section at the back of the book is packed with useful addresses, websites and phone numbers for further information on everything from discount flight agents and specialist tour operators to jungle equipment suppliers and volunteer work opportunities.

Even after you've read through this book, we can't guarantee that you'll avoid every potential pitfall on the road, but hopefully you'll feel well prepared for what awaits you and excited at the prospect of travelling in Latin America. When you return home, be sure to send in your own anecdotes and travellers' tales for inclusion in the next edition.

# things not to miss

*It's not possible to see the whole of Latin America on one trip – and we don't suggest you try. But to give you a taster of where you might go and what you might see or experience, following is a selection of the best that Latin America has to offer. Each entry has a page reference that takes you into the guide, where you can find out more.*

**01 Volcán de Pacaya, Guatemala** Page **53** • The most dramatic of Central America's active volcanoes, whose plume of molten lava is best viewed at night.

| ACTIVITIES | CONSUME | EVENTS | NATURE | SIGHTS

**02** **Scuba diving in the Caribbean** Pages **115–116** • The world's second largest barrier reef and a string of coral atolls make the Caribbean coast and islands of Central America a world-class scuba diving and snorkelling destination.

**03** **Fruit juice** Page **25** • Freshly squeezed *jugo* (*suco* in Brazil) is sold at market stalls all over Latin America, ranging from everyday orange to juices made from rare local fruits.

**04** **Museo Nacional de Antropología, Mexico** Page **65** • Set in the green space of the capital's Chapultepec Park, the museum holds a vast collection of artefacts covering Mexico's pre-Columbian cultures.

**05** **Day of the Dead, Mexico** Pages **65–66** • On November 1 Mexicans honour their dead relatives with an all-night candlelit vigil at their graves. The most traditional celebrations take place on the island of Janitzio on Lago de Pátzcuaro.

**06 Laguna Glaciar San Rafael, Chile** Page **30** • Reached by a spectacular boat journey through labyrinthine fjords, the iceberg-choked Laguna is a great place to observe penguins and other marine wildlife.

**07 Guatemalan markets** Page **53** • Every Sunday indigenous Maya travel to Chichicastenango for Guatemala's largest weekly market, to sell weaving and other crafts, plus fruit and vegetables. Nearby Sololá's market is smaller but more authentic.

**08 Potosí, Bolivia** Page **16** • The highest city in the world, this legendary silver-mining centre also boasts some of Latin America's finest colonial architecture.

**09 Iguaçu Falls, Brazil/ Argentina** Pages **7, 24** • One of the wonders of the natural world, a set of 250 waterfalls straddling the border, which plunge over a 3km precipice in an explosive crash that can be heard long before.

**10** **Machu Picchu, Peru** Page **84** • With a stunning setting in remote, forested mountains, the dramatic lost Inca city of Machu Picchu is one of the world's most remarkable archeological attractions.

**12** **Bay Islands, Honduras** Page **61** • Idyllic Utila, Roatán and Guanaja are renowned for their laid-back Caribbean atmosphere and azure sea.

**11** **Argentine beef** Page **7** • Traditional *parillas* (steak houses) cook whole carcasses over charcoal fires to serve up vast slabs of succulent meat.

**13** **River journeys in the Amazon** Page **84** • A boat trip along the world's mightiest river is a quintessential South American experience – even if at times you can't see either bank.

**14** **Eco-lodges** Page **12** • Staying at eco-lodges such as Chan Chich in Belize is a great way to explore the environment of the region while helping to protect it.

## 15 Brazilian Carnaval Page 23 •

Five days of non-stop music, dancing and drunken revelry, *Carnaval* is held in every Brazilian town but most famously in Rio de Janeiro and in Salvador, left.

## 16 Cartagena, Colombia

Pages **34–35** • Founded in 1533, the magnificent fortress city boasts famously thick walls that enclose a picturesque maze of colonial streets and squares.

## 17 Hiking the Inca Trails Pages

**16, 84** • The high Andes of Ecuador, Peru and Bolivia are crisscrossed by a network of stone-paved pathways built by the Incas and other pre-Columbian civilizations, perfect for trekking.

## 18 Galápagos Islands, Ecuador Page 43 •

More than 170 years after they inspired Charles Darwin to formulate his evolution theory, the Galápagos Islands still teem with an astonishing range of wildlife, much of it virtually tame.

## 19 Tikal, Guatemala

Page **53** • The atmospheric ruined Maya city of Tikal comprises several thousand buildings, dominated by five temples that soar above the treetops of the surrounding rainforest.

| ACTIVITIES | CONSUME | EVENTS | NATURE | SIGHTS

# Contents

## Colour section

## Where to go

## The big adventure

## Basics

# Index ............................337

# First-Time
# Latin America

# Where to go

# Argentina

**Capital** Buenos Aires
**Population** 37.3 million
**Language** Spanish, Italian in Buenos Aires
**Currency** Argentine peso ($)
**Climate** Most of the country is temperate, though it varies from tropical in the northeast to sub-Arctic in southern Patagonia
**When to go** December to May
**Minimum daily budget** US$25

Argentina is an enormous country – the eighth largest in the world – containing within its ample borders attractions ranging from the elegant, European-style boulevards and cafés of Buenos Aires to the sub-Arctic glaciers and mountain ranges of Patagonia in the south. Despite its size, however, Argentina is culturally one of the most homogenous of all Latin American countries – the result of mass immigration from Europe during the late nineteenth century, as well as the almost complete extermination of the native populations – and in the cities, at least, the spirit of Europe is never far away.

Outside the major urban centres, however, a distinctively Argentinian culture has developed, exemplified by the legendary gaucho, or Argentine cowboy, a legacy of the days in the early twentieth century when cattle ranching in the vast pampas of the interior made the country one of the wealthiest in the world. Even now, gaucho culture lives on in the Argentine obsession with meat-eating, while the famous gaucho drink, maté – an invigorating herbal infusion drunk through a metal straw from a colourful gourd – remains the national drink.

For the visitor, Argentina's main attractions, apart from its atmospheric capital, Buenos Aires, are largely outdoors. The southern third of the country, Patagonia, is the principal destination. Here, an extensive series of national parks protects some of the most extraordinary – and extreme – scenery the continent has to offer, including the majestic Andean peaks of the Fitz Roy Massif, site of some of the world's most challenging mountaineering, the extraordinary glaciers of Perito Moreno, and the marine paradise of the Península Valdés – to name just three of the region's main highlights. Bariloche, in Patagonia's Lake District, is the region's busiest holiday resort, with wooden chalet-style buildings, an attractive lakeside setting and skiing nearby at Cerro Catedral.

There are numerous natural attractions in Argentina outside of Patagonia, however. The northeast of the country offers flat swamplands perfect for birdwatching, along with one of Latin America's great natural wonders, the Iguazú Falls. The northwest takes in various types of terrain from jungle-clad cloudforests to high Andean plateaus (known in Argentina as *puna*) and deserts roamed by flocks of llamas. Further south lie the rolling green hills of Argentina's wine region and its lively centre, Mendoza. Most of central

N

BOLIVIA

**ARGENTINA**

BRAZIL

PARAGUAY

Iguazú Falls

Antofagasta
de la Sierra

Salta

PUNA
CATAMARQUEÑA

Tucumán

Corrientes

RESERVA
NATURAL
DEL IBERA

Córdoba

Santa Fe

Rosario

URUGUAY

Mendoza

San Antonio
de Areco

Buenos Aires

PACIFIC
OCEAN

C H I L E

Santa Rosa

Bahía Blanca

ATLANTIC
OCEAN

Bariloche

Península
Valdés

Puerto
Madryn

Argentine
Antarctic
Territory

Perito
Moreno

La Cueva de las
Manos Pintadas

Fitz Roy
Massif

P A T A G O N I A

Glacier Perito
Moreno

Río Gallegos

Punta Arenas

Ushuaia

| 0 | 500 km |

**One week**
- Iguazú–Buenos Aires.
- Patagonia–Buenos Aires.

**Two weeks**
- Buenos Aires–San Antonio de Areco–Antofagasta de la Sierra–Salta–Bolivia.
- Buenos Aires–Ushuaia.
- Buenos Aires–Reserva Natural del Ibera–Salta–Bolivia.

**One month**
- Iguazú–Ibera–Salta–Puna Catamarqueña–San Antonio de Areco–Buenos Aires–Patagonia–Ushuaia–Chile.

Argentina is pampa or cowboy country (see above).

Long considered among the safest, best organized but priciest countries to visit in Latin America, Argentina's recent economic crisis, during which the peso plummeted in value, has seen it become a much cheaper destination.

# Main attractions

● **Buenos Aires** Argentina's capital city is one of the most atmospheric in Latin America. Though its wide tree-lined avenues and architecture were inspired by those of Paris, Buenos Aires is very much its own place, with distinctive barrios – football-crazy La Boca with its bizarrely painted streets, bohemian San Telmo, home to the best tango shows in town, and exclusive Recoleta, site of the magnificently grand cemetery where Eva Perón is buried.

● **San Antonio de Areco, Pampas** 100km west of Buenos Aires, the charming town of San Antonio de Areco, with its cobbled streets and colonial facades, is Argentina's centre of pampa culture. Every November the town hosts a popular gaucho festival, the Día de la Tradición (see p.150), when gauchos parade in their traditional outfits and display their cowboy skills, including *jineteadas* (bronco riding) and horse-breaking. A traditional *asado con cuero* when beef is cooked over an open fire rounds up the festivities.

● **Iguazú Falls** One of the world's most dramatic series of waterfalls, the majestic Iguazú Falls straddle the border between Argentina, Brazil and Paraguay. The statistics are staggering – 275 falls plunging over a precipice 80m high and 3km wide – and you'll hear the deafening noise long before you can see anything. Although the best overall view of Iguazú is from Brazil, the falls' most extensive portion lies in the subtropical Argentinian Parque Nacional Iguazú, a less touristy area with a well-organized system of trails and plenty of wildlife. The most spectacular spot is the Garganta del Diablo (Devil's Throat), where fourteen separate falls merge to form the world's most powerful single waterfall in terms of the volume of water flow per second.

● **Cueva de las Manos Pintadas (Cave of the Painted Hands)** In southern Patagonia, and best approached via a beautiful two-hour trek up the Cañon de Río Pintadas, the *cueva* ("cave", though it's really a series of overhangs in a cliff face) is decorated with 829 black, white and red handprints made by Paleolithic hunter-gatherers and dating as far back as 7300 BC. Probably the best example of rock painting in South America.

● **Glaciar Perito Moreno** Set in the Parque Nacional Los Glaciares in Patagonia, Perito Moreno is one of the few advancing glaciers in the world and offers an enthralling spectacle as it fragments into great chunks of ice, some weighing hundreds of tons, which split off the main body of the glacier in spectacularly noisy fashion.

● **Fitz Roy Massif** A collection of mountain peaks centring on Monte Fitz Roy (3445m) in southern Patagonia, the Fitz Roy Massif is among the most dramatic scenery in South America, its sheer needles of rock set in circles and rising up several kilometres into the Patagonian sky. If you're not an experienced mountaineer, the area still has plenty to offer, laced as it is with lakes, walking trails and spectacular miradors (lookout points).

## Also recommended

● **Reserva Natural del Iberá** A watery network of lakes, marshes and floating islands, the Reserva Natural del Iberá is a vast (13,000 square kilometres) protected area in the northeast of Argentina offering wonderful wildlife-spotting opportunities. Locals in the village of Colonia Carlos Pellegrini take visitors out in small motorboats to see birds, monkeys and caymans at close range.

● **Puna Catamarqueña** The Altiplano of Catamarca province is an eerie and remote place, flanked to the west by the Andes and Chile and dotted with flocks of grazing vicuñas and flamingos on frozen lakes. The region's only settlement, Antofagasta de la Sierra, has a 2000-year-old mummified baby in its museum and a tranquil population of highland farmers and herdsmen. Bring some warm clothes, as temperatures drop at night to −30ºC.

● **Salta** Colonial capital of the beautiful northwest region, Salta is lively and youthful with well-preserved architectural gems (such as the Iglesia y Convento San Francisco) and a surprisingly vibrant nightlife. The town also makes a good base for visiting the nearby Quebrada del Toro, a dramatic gorge sliced into multicoloured rock.

● **Ushuaia and the Beagle Channel** The world's southernmost city, Ushuaia, beautifully situated on the Isla Grande de Tierra del Fuego, is the starting point for a boat trip along the Beagle Channel to the historic Estancia Harberton, a farmstead which gave assistance to shipwrecked sailors and became a refuge for Amerindian tribes Yámana, Selk'nam and Mannekenk.

## Routes in and out

Buenos Aires is easily reached by daily direct flights from Europe (London, Madrid, Rome), the US (New York, Miami and Chicago) and Australasia (Sydney and Auckland). There are principal border crossings to Brazil and Paraguay at Puerto Iguazú; from La Quiaca to Bolivia; and by ferry across the Río Plata to Uruguay. There are many borders with Chile – the scenic Paso Mamuil Malal in Patagonia connects with the popular Chilean backpackers' resort of Pucón, while the equally picturesque Cruce Internacional de los Lagos crossing links with Puerto Montt.

## Itineraries

### One week

● In a country the size of Argentina you won't get very far in a week. The average bus ride from one tourist spot to another is ten hours; if you're pressed for time you should consider taking a domestic flight. You could easily spend seven days in Buenos Aires, exploring its elegant streets and barrios; or combine the city's attractions with several days in the pampa town of San Antonio de Areco.

● If you're coming from southern Brazil or Paraguay, cross the border into Argentina via the Iguazú Falls, where you can explore the surrounding tropical forest as well as visit the falls themselves. Then fly to Buenos Aires (1hr 30min) for a couple of days of city living.

● From Chile, cross the border in Tierra del Fuego and head north into Patagonia to explore the region's dramatic mountains, glaciers and lakes before flying to the capital and onwards to Uruguay or Brazil.

## Two weeks

● From Buenos Aires, travel westwards through the pampas, stopping off for a few days in San Antonio de Areco, and then up through the Argentinian altiplano to Antofagasta de la Sierra, before heading north to the attractive colonial city of Salta and on into Bolivia.

● Travel by bus south from Buenos Aires through the great expanses of Patagonia right to the world's most southerly region, Tierra del Fuego and the city of Ushuaia. On the way, spend some days hiking in the national parks surrounding the Fitz Roy Massif and the Perito Moreno glacier.

● After five or so days in the capital, head northwest to the Puna Catamarqueña and its rural centre, Antofagasta de la Sierra, via the marshes and floating islands of the Reserva Natural del Iberá. After a few days in the pleasant provincial city of Salta, you'll be poised to move on into Bolivia.

## One month

With a domestic airpass (see p.132 you could visit three or four distinct regions of Argentina.

Travel south from Iguazú to the marshlands of the Reserva Natural del Iberá and head northwest towards Salta. From Salta travel south to the Puna Catamarqueña and on to San Antonio de Areco in the pampas, before arriving in Buenos Aires. After a week in Buenos Aires, continue south into Patagonia and Tierra del Fuego for ten days trekking in the mountains and national parks and visiting Ushuaia; from here you can cross into Chile.

# Argentina online

**Argentina Travel Net**
Ⓦ **www.argentinatravelnet.com**
Bilingual tourism portal with several thousand links categorized by region or activity.

**El Sur del Sur**
Ⓦ **www.surdelsur.com** Excellent set of essays on Argentinian history, geography and culture, with links to regional websites.

**Buenos Aires Herald**
Ⓦ **www.buenosairesherald.com**
Website of long-established English-language newspaper, with domestic and foreign news stories, travel features and trenchant opinions on current affairs.

# Belize

**Capital** Belmopan
**Population** 256,000
**Language** English, Spanish, Maya
languages, Garífuna
**Currency** Belize dollar (fixed to US$
at a rate of 2 to1; BZ$)

**Climate** Tropical with a rainy
(May–Nov) season and a dry season
(Jan–April)
**When to go** Late December to
March
**Minimum daily budget** US$25

Belize is one of the smallest countries in Central America and the least densely populated, with a quarter of a million people occupying an area the size of Wales or Massachusetts. Culturally, Belize is distinctively different from the other countries of Central America. A British colony (known as British Honduras) until 1981, Belize has as much in common with the English-speaking islands of the Caribbean as with the Spanish-speaking Latin American mainland (although the presence of immigrants from other Central American countries is gradually eroding this distinction). This Anglo-Caribbean culture, known as creole, is evident in the country's biggest city, Belize City, with its balconied clapboard houses, reggae dancehalls and vibrant carnival, held in September.

Belize's biggest attraction is its offshore cayes, which sit on the largest coral reef in the Americas, stretching from Mexico to Honduras. The whole area is a protected marine park, teeming with hundreds of species of brightly coloured fish and other marine creatures. Crystal clear water means that the scuba diving and snorkelling around the cayes are superb. Of over four hundred islands only two have any kind of tourist infrastructure: Ambergris Caye,

the largest, which attracts over half of all the visitors to Belize, and Caye Caulker, more popular with backpackers.

Away from the coast, Belize is distinctively different. The interior is home to the highest waterfall in Central America, myriad rivers and caves and a network of national parks and reserves – Belizeans are very conscious of their environment and over forty percent of the country is now protected by law. With ecotourism seen by many Belizeans as the country's economic future, it's not surprising that there are some spectacular eco-lodges in Belize. Also in the interior are Belize's ancient Maya ruins, principally Caracol, Xunantunich and Lamanai, which, though less impressive than those in Guatemala and Mexico, are well worth visiting – and Tikal in Guatemala is easily accessed from Belize. In the far south of the country, dotted through the foothills of the Maya mountains, traditional Maya live in small communities, similar to those in Guatemala, where you can stay and in some cases participate in village life.

Belize is one of the safest countries in Latin America – crime against tourists is minimal and its capital city, Belmopan, is one of the safest, though

**BELIZE**

MEXICO

Chetumal

MEXICO

Ambergris
Caye

San Pedro

Caye
Caulker

CARIBBEAN
SEA

RIO BRAVO
CONSERVATION
AREA

Lamanai

St George's
Caye

Belize
City

Turneffe
Islands

Blue Hole

Lighthouse
Reef

BELMOPAN

Xunantunich

Caves Branch River

*Tikal*

MOUNTAIN PINE RIDGE FOREST RESERVE

Dangriga

Glovers Reef

Caracol

Placencia

N

Barrier Reef

**One week**

• Chetumal–Lamanai–Rio Bravo–Belize City–Caye Caulker–
Belize City.
• Belize City–Caye Caulker–Belize City–Mountain Pine Ridge–
Xunantunich–Tikal.
• Puerto Cortés–Placencia–Caves Branch River–
Mountain Pine Ridge–Tikal.

**Two weeks**

• Puerto Cortés–Placencia–Caves Branch River–
Mountain Pine Ridge–Caracol–Xunantunich–Tikal–
Belize City–Caye Caulker–Belize City–Rio Bravo–Chetumal.

Punta
Gorda

Hunting
Caye

GUATEMALA

dullest, in Central America. You should
exercise caution in the former capital,
Belize City, which has a much larger
population. Be warned that prices are

fairly high for the region – if you arrive
from Guatemala you could find your
costs doubled overnight.

# Main attractions

● **Caye Caulker** Laid-back Caye Caulker is much smaller – just over 7km long – and less touristy than neighbouring Ambergris Caye and has long been popular with independent travellers. Most visitors come to scuba dive or snorkel, and day-trips go to top diving spots, such as the Lighthouse Reef and the Blue Hole, a complex network of caves and crevices, made famous by Jacques Cousteau. On the island itself it's possible to bird-watch – there are many bird species and some, like the black catbird or white-crowned pigeon, are rarely seen elsewhere; rent kayaks or swim out to the reef, which lies just 1.5km offshore. There's not much in the way of nightlife, although some of the restaurants in the village have live music in the evenings.

● **Ancient Maya sites at Lamanai, Caracol and Xunantunich** While historically not as important as the Maya ruins in Mexico and Guatemala, the sites in Belize are far less crowded and consequently more atmospheric, with excellent English-language visitor centres and museums on site. Lamanai, in the north of the country, is set in a 950-acre reserve and has wonderful views across the jungle from its temples. In western Belize, Caracol's largest structure, Canaa or the Sky Palace, is still one of the tallest buildings in the country at 42m. Xunantunich's attractions include a restored stucco frieze carved with abstract designs, human faces and jaguar heads, plus its convenient location en route from Belize to Guatemala (and Tikal).

● **Mountain Pine Ridge Forest Reserve** In western Belize, the Mountain Pine Ridge Forest Reserve comprises a range of rolling hills, peaks and gorges. Highlights of the area, which is perfect for hiking and mountain-biking, are the picturesque Río On, which forms a series of natural swimming pools before plunging into a gorge, and the Thousand-Foot Falls, actually 1600ft waterfalls.

● **Rio Bravo Conservation Management Area** In the northwest of Belize, the Rio Bravo Conservation Management Area protects a thousand acres of diverse terrain ranging from forest-covered limestone escarpments through river valleys to palm- and pine-covered plains and swamp. The area has 240 endemic tree species, 70 mammal species including all 5 of Belize's big cats, tapirs, monkeys and crocodiles and 400 kinds of bird. If you're feeling flush, the nearby Chan Chich Lodge is one of the finest eco-lodges in the world.

# Also recommended

● **Belize Zoo** The Belize Zoo, 40km west of Belize City, is widely recognized as the best in Latin America and has achieved international acclaim in the fields of conservation education and captive breeding. Its indigenous collection includes tapirs, jaguars, toucans and crocodiles, all housed in spacious enclosures that replicate their natural habitat.

● **Placencia** One of the few places in mainland Belize with real beaches, Placencia is a laid-back fishing village with a range of inexpensive accommodation and funky live-music venues; it also makes a good base for day-trips to the nearby coral reef and cayes.

● **Caves** Western Belize's (and particularly Cayo District's) limestone hills are home to a spectacular subterranean network, with the Chiquibil cave system in the south of the region ranking as the longest in Central America. All have Maya artefacts inside – ceramics, carvings – and some have underground rivers which you can float down on inner tubes, an activity known as tubing. A good starting point for a caving experience is The Caves Branch Jungle Lodge, 19km from Belmopan, which is run by the founders of the Belize Cave and Wilderness Rescue Team.

## Routes in and out

There are daily flights to Belize City from Miami and Houston. Another convenient way to reach the country is to fly to Cancún in Mexico, served by regular flights from the US and Europe, from where it's a straightforward five-hour bus journey to Belize – the border crossing is at Chetumal, from where there are frequent services to Belize City. The most popular border crossing with Guatemala (for Tikal) is at Benque Viejo. There are boat services from Punta Gordá in southern Belize to Puerto Barrios and Lívingston in Guatemala and, less frequently, from Dangriga and Placencia to Puerto Cortés in Honduras.

## Suggested itineraries

### One week

● Head south from Chetumal in Mexico via the Maya site of Lamanai to the Rio Bravo Conservation Management Area for a few days of wildlife spotting before moving on to Belize City. From here take a boat to Caye Caulker for a long weekend snorkelling and diving and then return to the mainland and catch a boat from the coast to Guatemala or Honduras.

● From Belize City go to Caye Caulker and then loop back across the country to the Mountain Pine Ridge Forest Reserve, then the Maya site of Xunantunich, before crossing the border into Guatemala to visit Tikal.

● Take the boat from Puerto Cortés in Honduras to Dangriga, from where you can catch a bus down the coast to Placencia. Then head west to visit the caves of Cayo district and Caves Branch River, and the forests of Mountain Pine Ridge, before leaving Belize for Guatemala.

### Two weeks

● In two weeks you can see all of Belize's highlights. Arrive in Placencia from Puerto Cortés in Honduras and then travel west to the Caves Branch River, the Mountain Pine Ridge Forest Reserve and the Maya ruins of Caracol and Xunantunich. Briefly cross the border into Guatemala to visit Tikal and then head east to Belize City, and out to Caye Caulker for a few days relaxing on the beach. Then go north from Belize City to the Río Bravo Conservation Management Area and on to Chetumal in Mexico.

## Belize online

**Belizean Journeys**
Ⓦwww.belizejourneys.com An in-depth look into the more remote and unknown parts of Belize.
**Belize News Network**
Ⓦwww.belizenews.net Links to Belizean newspapers, magazines, TV and radio stations, with a changing selection of articles on Belize from international media.
**Belize Tourism Board**
Ⓦwww.travelbelize.org The excellent website of the Belize Tourism Board, with useful advice about travelling in Belize and good essays on history, culture and tourism.

# Bolivia

**Capital** Sucre (official); La Paz (seat of government)
**Population** 8.5 million
**Language** Spanish, Quechua, Aymara, Guaraní, plus thirty other minor indigenous languages
**Currency** Peso boliviano (B/.)
**Climate** Ranging from hot and humid in the tropical lowlands to extremely cold and dry in the highlands
**Best time to go** May–September (dry season); between November and March rains make many roads impassable, particularly in the Amazon lowlands
**Minimum daily budget** US$15

Landlocked and isolated at the heart of South America, Bolivia encompasses everything that outsiders find most exotic and mysterious about the continent. Stretching from the majestic icebound peaks and bleak high-altitude deserts of the Andes to the exuberant rainforests and vast savannahs of the Amazon basin, it embraces an astonishing range of landscapes and climates. The strangeness and variety of the country's natural environment are matched by the ethnic and cultural diversity of its population: the majority of Bolivians are of indigenous descent, and the strength of indigenous culture here is perhaps greater than anywhere else in Latin America.

Indeed, to think of Bolivia as part of *Latin* America at all is something of a misconception. Though three centuries of Spanish colonial rule have left their mark on the nation's language, religion, and architecture, this European influence is essentially no more than a thin veneer. Most Bolivians are conscious inheritors of indigenous cultural traditions that stretch back long before the conquest, and which are rooted in an intimate relationship with the land itself. Though Spanish is the language of business and government, the streets of the de facto capital, La Paz, buzz with the very different cadences of Aymara, one of more than thirty indigenous languages spoken across the country. From the llama-herding settlements and mining camps of the high Andes to the fishing and farming villages of the tropical lowlands, these diverse and distinctive indigenous cultures – alongside the breathtaking landscapes they inhabit – constitute Bolivia's most powerful attraction.

Geographically, Bolivia is dominated by the Andes, which march through the west of the country in two parallel chains, each rising to snowcapped peaks over 6000m, and between which lies the Altiplano, a virtually treeless high-altitude plateau often compared to Tibet. Boasting dramatic mountain scenery, populated by traditional indigenous Aymara and Quechua-speaking farming communities, and with a couple of the finest Spanish colonial cities in the Americas, this highland region encapsulates everything that outsiders

**One week**
• La Paz–Copacabana–Coroico.

**Two weeks**
• La Paz–Copacabana–Coroico–Rurrenabaque.
• La Paz–Copacabana–Coroico–Salar de Uyuni.

**One month**
• La Paz–Copacabana–Coroico–Rurrenabaque–
Potosí–Sucre–Salar de Uyuni.

**BOLIVIA**

PERU

BRAZIL

*PARQUE NACIONAL MADIDI* · Rurrenabaque

*PARQUE NACIONAL NOEL KEMPFF MERCADO*

Trinidad

*Lake Titicaca*

Sorata

Copacabana · Coroico

Tiwanaku · LA PAZ

*CORDILLERA REAL*

AMAZON BASIN

Cochambamba

CHIQUITOS

Oruro

*PARQUE NACIONAL AMBORÓ*

Santa Cruz

Samaipata

Sucre

Potosí

SOUTHERN ALTIPLANO

Uyuni

*Salar de Uyuni*

CHILE

PARAGUAY

*RESERVA DE FAUNA ANDINA EDUARDO AVAROA*

ARGENTINA

0          200 km

think of as quintessentially Bolivian. However, the highlands occupy less than half of Bolivia's territory. The majority of the country is covered by sparsely populated tropical lowlands, including some of the wildest, most pristine and most biodiverse protected areas in the Amazon basin.

Because of its remoteness and isolation, Bolivia is still one of South America's least-visited countries, but for the travellers who do make it here, the fact that the country is not yet on the major tourist routes is an added advantage. Whether hiking an Inca trail or exploring a national park, you're unlikely to find yourself sharing the experience with more than a handful of other foreign visitors, and the attitude of the locals towards you is as yet unlikely to be influenced by the impact of mass tourism. In addition, Bolivia is one of the least expensive countries in the region for travellers – if you're on a tight budget, you'll find costs here a welcome relief after countries like Brazil, Argentina and Chile – and despite its poverty, the country remains one of the safest in the region for the traveller, largely free of the violent crime that blights some of its neighbours.

# Main attractions

● **La Paz** Spectacularly set in a deep canyon at an altitude of over 3500m, Bolivia's de facto capital is the highest in the world. With a largely indigenous Aymara population, it's also amongst the most fascinating: a postmodern crucible where modern banks and government offices coexist with vibrant street markets selling all manner of ritual paraphernalia for appeasing the spirits and mountain gods.

● **The Cordillera Real** North of La Paz lies the Cordillera Real, a jagged ridge of soaring, glacial peaks that forms a barrier between the high Altiplano and the Amazon lowlands. The range offers some of the finest walking in the Andes, including several treks following pre-Columbian stone-paved roads – the so-called "Inca trails" – that plunge down into the humid subtropical valleys of the Yungas. The charming colonial town of Sorata, nestled in a deep valley at the northwestern end of the range, also makes an excellent base for trekking.

● **Isla del Sol** Reached by boat from the pilgrimage centre of Copacabana on the Bolivian shores of Lake Titicaca, the idyllic Isla del Sol is the spiritual centre of the Andean world, revered as the place where the Sun and Moon were created and the Inca dynasty was born. Scattered with Inca ruins, and populated by traditional Aymara communities, it's the best place to enjoy the scenic beauty of the vast, high-altitude lake that straddles the border with Peru.

● **The Salar de Uyuni and Reserva Eduardo Avaroa** The desolate landscapes of the far southern Altiplano are amongst the most extraordinary in all Latin America. From the forlorn railway town of Uyuni jeep tours head across the Salar de Uyuni, the world's biggest salt lake, a vast, perfectly flat expanse of dazzling white surrounded by high mountain peaks. Further south lies the Reserva de Fauna Andina Eduardo Avaroa, a remote region of high-altitude deserts, surreal wind-blasted rock formations, icebound volcanic peaks and half-frozen mineral-stained lakes which is home to a surprising array of wildlife, including great flocks of pink flamingos and herds of vicuña, the highly endangered wild relative of the llama.

● **Potosí** Set at an altitude of over 4000m, the legendary silver-mining centre of Potosí is the highest city in the world, and at once one of the most interesting and tragic cities in Latin America. The city's magnificent colonial architecture reflects the fabulous wealth it once generated, but a visit to see the almost medieval working conditions endured by indigenous miners in the labyrinthine mineshafts that honeycomb the mountain overlooking Potosí reveals something of the horrific price in human lives paid for that wealth.

● **The Bolivian Amazon** The Bolivian Amazon is relatively undeveloped and boasts some of the most pristine and biodiverse protected areas in the region. The laid-back jungle town of Rurrenabaque is one of the cheapest and easiest places to organize trips by motorized canoe deep into the Amazonian wilderness. From here you can explore the rainforests of Madidi National Park (where you can also stay at the excellent Chalalán eco-lodge, operated by the local indigenous Tacana community) or along the Río Yacuma, which flows through savannah-like pampas and supports an astonishing density of wildlife including cayman, capybaras and pink river dolphins.

● **The World's Most Dangerous Road** Linking La Paz with the Yungas town of Coroico, this infamous road descends 3500m over a distance of just 64km, plunging down from the high peaks of the Andes through dense cloudforest. The road clings to steep mountainsides above hair-raising precipices, with views so spectacular that many travellers choose to go by mountain bike rather than by bus, an exhilarating downhill ride that's easy to organize with tour companies in La Paz.

## Also recommended

● **Sucre** Known as the White City, Bolivia's official capital is a jewel of colonial architecture and a lively university city that combines serene dignity with an easy provincial charm. The beautiful highland region surrounding the city is populated by traditional Quechua-speaking communities famous for their exquisite weavings, which are best seen (and bought) at the Sunday market in the nearby town of Tarabuco.

● **The Jesuit Missions of Chiquitos** Spread across a vast, sparsely populated region in the tropical lowlands of eastern Bolivia, the Jesuit mission churches of Chiquitos offer a splash of incongruous splendour in the midst of the wilderness, a reminder of the time in the eighteenth century when a handful of European missionaries organized the indigenous Chiquitanos into utopian agricultural communities where music, art and sculpture flourished.

● **Parque Nacional Noel Kempff Mercado** Occupying the far northeast-ern corner of Bolivia on the border with Brazil, this is Bolivia's finest national park, with abundant wildlife, exuberant Amazonian rainforest and magnificent waterfalls tumbling down from the plateau that supposedly inspired Sir Arthur Conan Doyle's *The Lost World*.

● **Oruro Carnival** Of all Bolivia's innumerable religious fiestas, the Carnival celebrations in the otherwise dour Altiplano mining city of Oruro (late Feb or early March) are the country's most colourful and dramatic. The celebrations combine Catholic and indigenous religious beliefs, with thousands of dancers in extravagant costumes parading through the streets accompanied by massed brass bands, while revellers indulge in heavy drinking and indiscriminate water fighting.

● **Samaipata** Set amid the lush eastern foothills of the Andes, the idyllic town of Samaipata is home to the mysterious ruined temple complex of El Fuerte and a perfect base for hiking and exploring the cloudforests of the Parque Nacional Amboró. It's also not far from Vallegrande, the town where the Argentine revolutionary hero Che Guevara was secretly buried after being killed in nearby La Higuera.

## Routes in and out

La Paz and Santa Cruz are both served by direct flights from Miami in the US and major South American capitals, though flights to Bolivia are considerably more expensive than to neighbouring countries like Peru. Bolivia can be reached overland from Peru via Puno on the shores of Lake Titicaca, and is well connected to Argentina and Chile by road and rail. The railway journey between Uyuni and Calama in Chile in particular passes through spectacular high Andean scenery, and you can also travel between Uyuni in southern Bolivia and San Pedro de Atacama in Chile at the remote border crossing at Laguna Verde as part of an organized jeep tour of the Reserva de Fauna Andina Eduardo Avaroa. The main border crossing with Brazil is in the far east of Bolivia at Quijarro, opposite the city of Corumbá in the Brazilian Pantanal, from where there's a direct train link to Santa Cruz: this is the best route to take if you're travelling overland between Brazil and the Andean countries on the western side of South America. There are also several remote road border crossings between Bolivia and Brazil along the northern frontier in the Amazon. In the May to September dry season you can travel between Santa Cruz and Asunción in Paraguay by bus or lorry along a rough road that runs through the heart of the great thornbrush wilderness of the Chaco.

# Itineraries

Remember that you'll need a few days to acclimatize to the altitude in highland Bolivia, especially if you want to do any trekking.

## One week

● Spend a day or two in La Paz, and use the city as a base to visit Copacabana and the Isla del Sol on Lake Titicaca, and to make the journey by bus or mountain bike down the spectacular Yungas road to Coroico.

## Two weeks

● Spend the first week in and around La Paz as described above, then fly north to Rurrenabaque in the Amazon and go on an organized tour into the rainforests of Madidi National Park or down the wildlife-rich Río Yacuma.

● Spend the first five days exploring La Paz and visiting the Isla del Sol, then travel by bus and train down to Uyuni and take a four-day jeep tour of the Salar de Uyuni and the Reserva de Fauna Andina Eduardo Avaroa, stopping off for a couple of days in Potosí on the way back to La Paz.

● Spend the entire two weeks based in La Paz and trek one of the Inca trails that link the Altiplano with the Yungas.

## One month

● Spend a week in and around La Paz as described above, then either trek, mountain-bike or take the bus down to Coroico in the Yungas. From there either return to La Paz and take a flight or continue overland by road to Rurrenabaque and take a three- or four-day organized tour into the rainforest or the pampas along the Río Yacuma. If you return to La Paz by plane, you should then have a couple of weeks to explore the southern Altiplano, visiting the legendary mining city of Potosí and taking a jeep tour of the far southwest from Uyuni. If you've time, you can also visit Sucre for two or three days from Potosí.

● Spend the first five days or so exploring La Paz and visiting the Isla del Sol, then head south to Uyuni and take a jeep tour of the Salar de Uyuni and Reserva Eduardo Avaroa in the far southwest. From Uyuni, head northeast to Potosí and then on to Sucre, spending a couple of days in each city. From Sucre, travel by bus to Santa Cruz, possibly stopping off in Samaipata for a day or two, then either visit Parque Nacional Noel Kempff Mercado by plane or, if you're heading to Brazil, travel overland through the Jesuit mission towns of Chiquitos and cross the border at Puerto Quijarro.

# Bolivia online

**Boliviaweb** Ⓦ www.boliviaweb.com
Good general Bolivian site with links to
many other Bolivia-related web pages
and general background information on
subjects such as Bolivian art, history
and food.

**Latin America Network Information
Center, Bolivia**
Ⓦ lanic.utexas.edu/la/sa/bolivia An
excellent resource, with links to a massive range of Bolivia-related sites divided
into themes including art and culture,
environment, government, indigenous
peoples and news, as well as other portals, directories and search sites.

# Brazil

**Capital** Brasília
**Population** 172 million
**Language** Portuguese, Spanish in border areas, plus around 180 indigenous languages
**Currency** Real (R$)
**Climate** Mostly tropical with distinct rainy seasons (south, southeast and north Nov–March; northeast April–Aug) and a temperate zone in the south with winter chills and occasional snow
**Best time to go** February (for *Carnaval*) to June or September to December
**Minimum daily budget** US$25

Brazil is vast, the fifth largest country in the world, occupying half the entire landmass of South America and encompassing all its diverse terrains – bar any mountains that can match the height of the Andes. Its enormous interior (which takes four days and nights to cross) consists of sparsely populated scrub, swampland and Amazon rainforest, with two-thirds of Brazilians living on or close to its 8000-kilometre coast and over half in cities.

It isn't just its size which sets Brazil apart from the rest of South America. The country was formerly part of the Portuguese empire, and consequently Brazilians speak Portuguese rather than Spanish (although Spanish is widely understood). The Portuguese built attractive colonial towns much like those of the Spanish colonies – some of the prettiest are in the state of Minas Gerais. Virtually nothing is known of Brazil's indigenous culture before the Portuguese arrived in 1500 – there were no cities built in stone like those of the Inca, Aztecs and Maya, no metal or flint artefacts – although it is reckoned that 5 million pure-blooded Amerindians were scattered across the country in various tribes. Of these some 300,000 remain, most living deep within the Amazon where it's believed that some tribes remain undiscovered by the outside world.

The Amazon rainforest, the world's largest at six million square kilometres, covers over half of Brazil's landmass and extends into neighbouring Venezuela, Colombia, Peru and Bolivia. With 6000 known species of plant (and thousands more yet to be identified), one in five of all the earth's birds and one-fifth of the planet's fresh water, the Amazon is a vital part of the earth's biosphere. Increasingly, though, large tracts have been felled by loggers and cattle ranchers and deforestation is a real and continuing threat to the Amazon. The rainforest is still a highlight of many tourists' visit to Brazil and there are a growing number of eco-lodges close to the region's capital, Manaus.

Brazil's other natural attractions are impressive, too – the Pantanal swampland, which borders Bolivia to the west, is one of the best places to see wildlife in Latin America, with jaguars, rare blue macaws, armadillos and anacondas all commonly sighted. The Foz do Iguaçu waterfalls in the south of Brazil are another of Latin America's most visited attractions, a truly spectacular series of cascades surrounded by subtropical forest. Brazil's long Atlantic coastline has some lovely beaches, too, which remain mostly unspoilt with surprisingly little mass-market tourism.

Thanks to rapid postwar growth, Brazil is one of the most industrialized countries in Latin America, although most of the wealth is concentrated in the southeast region around Rio de Janeiro and São Paulo, the biggest city in Brazil – and South America – with over 17 million inhabitants. Though it lacks the spectacular setting of Rio de Janeiro, São Paulo has long surpassed it as the cultural powerhouse of the country and its international contemporary art exhibition or bienal, held every two years, is rivalled only by Venice's in prestige. The capital of Brazil is neither of these cities but Brasília, a planned city in the interior built in the 1950s, and interesting only on an architectural level – the Brazilian politicians and bureaucrats who work there arrive on Monday morning and leave on Thursday for the weekend.

Brazil is celebrated for its vibrant music and dance forms, the most diverse in South America – bossa nova and samba are two of the best known, but there are dozens of others. Brazilians are famously hedonistic too, with tolerant attitudes to sexuality and a gregarious openness unsurpassed even in Latin America. The annual carnival brings all these things together in five days of relentless partying.

Unfortunately Brazil is not always safe to travel in. Opportunistic theft is rife in larger towns and cities – particularly São Paulo, Rio de Janeiro and Salvador. You should only go out at night with enough money for the evening, never leave your bags unattended or wear an expensive watch or jewellery. Public transport is surprisingly reliable with a network of comfortable modern coaches, though distances are huge (24-hour journeys are not uncommon); if you have limited time, consider buying an airpass.

# Main attractions

● **Rio de Janeiro** Cariocas (residents of Rio) say that God made the world in six days and on the seventh he created Rio, the *cidade marvilhosa* (marvellous city). One of the world's most exciting cities, Rio is spectacularly set between jungle-covered mountains and beach-lined Guanabara Bay. Don't miss the towering statue of Christ the Redeemer at Corcovado, a cable-car ride to Sugar Loaf Mountain, a ferry across the bay to Niterói and Oscar Niemeyer's Museu de Arte Contemporanea, the leafy bohemian suburb of Santa Teresa and – most importantly – the vibrant beach culture at Copacabana, Ipanema and Leblon.

● **Salvador da Bahia** The oldest city in Brazil with fine examples of colonial architecture, Salvador was once the country's main slave port and still retains a strong African feel. As well as a largely black population, Salvador boasts the best music scene in Brazil, a uniquely spicy cuisine and cultural activities dating from the slave era – *capoeira* (an elegant non-contact martial art) and *candomblé*, an Afro-Brazilian religion with a large cast of gods and goddesses (*orixas*) and ritual ceremonies which induce wild, reeling trances through drumming and dancing.

● **Bahia State** It isn't just its regional capital Salvador which makes the state of Bahia worth visiting. The lush green plains of the surrounding Recôncavo countryside have two pretty colonial towns, Santo Amaro and Cachoeira. Inland, the arid plains of the *sertão* have

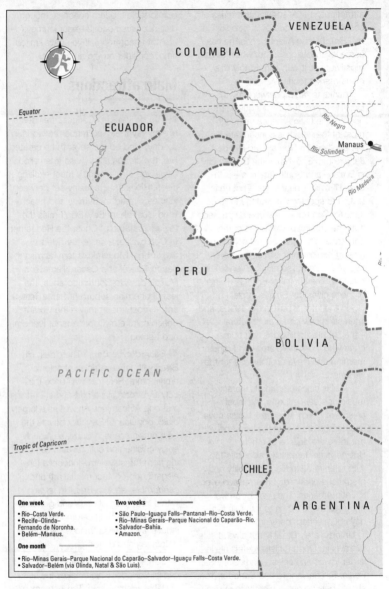

**One week**

- Rio–Costa Verde.
- Recife–Olinda–Fernando de Noronha.
- Belém–Manaus.

**Two weeks**

- São Paulo–Iguaçu Falls–Pantanal–Rio–Costa Verde.
- Rio–Minas Gerais–Parque Nacional do Caparão–Rio.
- Salvador–Bahia.
- Amazon.

**One month**

- Rio–Minas Gerais–Parque Nacional do Caparão–Salvador–Iguaçu Falls–Costa Verde.
- Salvador–Belém (via Olinda, Natal & São Luis).

an outback cowboy culture best seen during Monday's leather market in Feira de Santana and in the friendly mining town of Jacobina. Further inland are the

waterfalls, strange rock formations and rivers of Parque Nacional Chapada Diamantina. Bahian beaches include Porto Seguro, famous for its dancehalls,

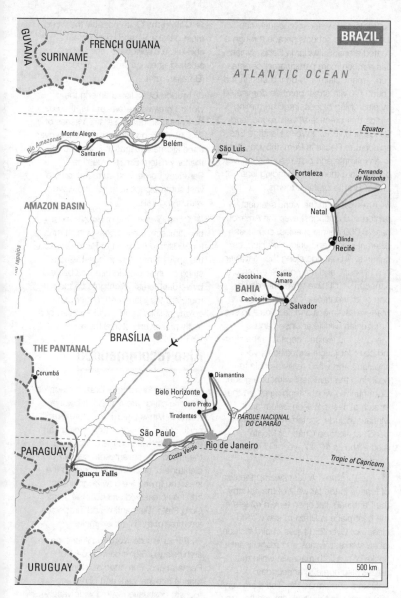

and Morro de São Paulo, located on the island of Tinharé and reached by boat.

● **Carnaval** Justifiably recognized as the biggest party on the planet, *Carnaval* takes place all over Brazil, for five non-stop days from the Friday (usually in February) before Ash Wednesday. There are three renowned *Carnaval* hotspots: Rio, where gorgeously costumed samba schools parade through a seated arena; Salvador in Bahia, which has a much more participatory celebration – many claim it to be the best in the country – with street parades dominated by electrifying *blocos*, large drumming bands that practice all year round; and Olinda (a UNESCO World Heritage Site adjacent to Recife in Pernambuco), host to an intimate and picturesque *Carnaval* packed into the narrow winding lanes of one of Brazil's prettiest towns.

● **Amazon** Both the world's largest rainforest and longest river, the Amazon has 15,000 animal species, countless different plants and unique indigenous cultures. A boat ride along the vast river is a hypnotic and memorable adventure, although you'll have to venture down one of its tributaries – the rios Negro, Madeira, Solimões and Tapajós – to see Amazonian wildlife at close hand. Manaus, the region's capital, is the starting point for jungle expeditions; you shouldn't and won't really be able to head into the rainforest without a guide. Communities worth stopping off on the stretch of river between Belém and Manaus include Santarém, with a river beach at Alter do Chão, or Monte Alegre and its 10,000-year-old rock paintings.

● **The Pantanal** A vast swamp the size of France in the far west of the country, the Pantanal's flat open terrain makes it the best place in Brazil to see wildlife close-up. Over 250 types of bird include jabiru storks, toucans and magnificent flocks of hyacinth macaws, while the area is also home to anacondas, anteaters and armadillos. There are very few roads into the Pantanal and its size makes it inaccessible and even dangerous to enter alone – you'll need to take an organized tour from Corumbá or Cuiabá.

● **Caipirinha** Quite possibly the world's most delicious – and most potent –- cocktail, a *caipirinha* is made from crushed limes, sugar and *cachaça* (Brazilian rum).

● **Iguaçu** Often listed among the world's greatest natural sights, the Foz do Iguaçu or Iguaçu Falls is a series of 275 interlinking waterfalls stretching over three kilometres. Iguaçu is located on the far western Brazil–Argentina–Paraguay border and surrounded by a vast subtropical nature reserve woven with hiking trails.

● **Costa Verde** One of Brazil's most beautiful stretches of coast which runs for 300km to the west of Rio de Janeiro, the aptly named "green coast" is a string of undeveloped beaches backed by verdant forest. Highlights on the route are the island and former penal colony of Ilha Grande, and Parati, a perfectly preserved colonial town.

# Also recommended

● **Cidades historicas** Brazil's so-called "historic cities" are a string of colonial towns in Minas Gerais, the state directly north of Rio. Once bustling mining communities, created on the discovery at the end of the seventeenth century of a plenitude of gold and diamonds in the area, the towns are now tranquil and carefully preserved architectural gems. Ouro Preto, Diamantina and Tiradentes are three of the finest examples.

● **Fernando de Noronha** A pristine archipelago 350km off the coast of Pernambuco, Fernando de Noronha is a marine national park and prime ecotourism destination with a wide variety of birds and sea creatures to spot, including turtles, sharks and whales.

● **Football** Football is ubiquitous in Brazil and you shouldn't miss the opportunity to see a stadium match with all its attendent hysteria, live samba and fireworks. Rio's Maracaña Stadium is the world's largest, holding 200,000 people, and during November and December matches are held here three times a week. Otherwise fishermen and other locals play together, usually at dusk, on almost every beach in the country. Gringos are very welcome to join in, though the standard is always high and the game is played barefoot.

● **Parque Nacional do Caparão** In the east of Minais Gerais state, the Parque Nacional do Caparão has some of Brazil's most spectacular scenery, divided into two ecological zones: thickly forested valleys, hills and streams in its lower section give way to craggy mountains and treeless alpine landscapes. Brazil's highest peak, Pico da Bandeira (2890m), is not difficult to climb and on a clear day those who reach the top will be rewarded with a panoramic view over Espírito Santo and Minas Gerais states.

● **Fruit juice** Freshly squeezed fruit juice or *sugo* is found everywhere in Brazil, particularly at dedicated juice stalls where drinks are made to order. As well as the common orange, mango and passionfruit (and dozens of others), juice is made from fruits only found in Brazil – graviola, bacuri and cupuaçu.

## Routes in and out

Direct international flights usually land in Rio or São Paulo, although from Miami you can also fly straight to Brasília, Recife, Manaus and Belém. Brazil borders every country in South America apart from Chile and Ecuador, so there are myriad spots to arrive and leave the country. Overland border crossings are fairly straightforward, though the only

direct access to Suriname is via plane from Belém (very expensive) or through its neighbours, Guyana or French Guiana.

Another option is to take a boat into and out of Brazil via the Amazon river. Standard routes link to Iquitos in Peru or, less popularly, Leticia in Colombia.

## Itineraries

### One week

● Visit Rio de Janeiro and then spend the weekend relaxing on the Costa Verde south of the city.

● From Recife take a short bus ride to Olinda for a couple of days wandering through the steep cobbled streets, then fly to the Fernando de Noronha marine park for bird and shark spotting.

● Travel from Belém to Manaus (or vice versa) along the Amazon and stop off halfway for a day or two.

### Two weeks

● Fly into São Paulo and spend a day or two enjoying the city's sophisticated cultural scene before travelling to the Iguaçu waterfalls, where you'll need at least three days to fully explore. From there, head to the Pantanal for an organized trip into the swamplands. Depart from Rio after you've enjoyed all the city sights and spent a day or two on one of the beaches of the Costa Verde.

● Head north from Rio to the mining towns of Minas Gerais and then to the Parque Nacional do Caparão before looping back to Rio.

● Fly into Salvador and after a few days in the city explore the colonial towns, beaches and Afro-Brazilian culture of Bahia, one of Brazil's most fascinating states.

● Explore the river and rainforest in some depth with an initial trip down the Amazon and then take further boat trips along the river's tributaries, where you'll have a much greater opportunity to spot wildlife, learn about the complex Amazonian biosphere, and visit remote jungle towns.

## One month

● From Rio and its environs, travel north to several of the colonial towns of Minas Gerais, and east to the Parque Nacional do Caparão. From Minas Gerais head to the city of Salvador and visit the various highlights of Bahia. Fly south to the Iguaçu Falls for a few days. Finish your trip on one of the beaches of the Costa Verde, between São Paulo and Rio de Janeiro.

● Travel from Salvador around the Atlantic coast to Belém, which sits at the mouth of the Amazon, spending several days each at a string of beach resorts and various other points of interest along the way: Chapada Diamantina in Bahia, Olinda and Recife, Fernando de Noronha marine park, the beaches of Natal (take a dune buggy ride), Canoa Quebrada and Jericoacoara and the faded charm of the Afro-Brazilian city São Luis.

# Brazil online

**Brazilian Embassy in London**
Ⓦ**www.brazil.org.uk** The British Brazilian embassy website which doubles up as the English-language version of the Brazilian Tourist Board website. It gives an excellent overview of the country as well as information on topics such as business, culture and sport.
**Gringoes.com**
Ⓦ**www.gringoes.com** Brazil's first portal for its ex-pat community, this website combines folksy articles on various aspects of Brazilian culture with hard facts on living and working in the country.
**Maria-Brazil**
Ⓦ**www.maria-brazil.org** Written by an American smitten with the country, this has entertaining features on such essentials as Brazilian bikinis and other light-hearted but important aspects of Brazil.
**Sonia-portuguese.com**
Ⓦ**www.sonia-portuguese.com** An excellent website, written in English by a Brazilian, for learning a little Portuguese before you arrive in Brazil.
**BrazilMax**
Ⓦ**www.brazilmax.com** Billed as "The hip gringo's guide to Brazilian culture and society", this internet magazine is written by American journalist Bill Hinchberger and has an excellent selection of articles and further links.

# Chile

**Capital** Santiago
**Population** 15.5 million
**Language** Spanish, plus minority indigenous languages
**Currency** Peso Chileno (CH$)
**Climate** Temperate, with warm days and cool nights in the north and centre, colder in the south, particularly during the winter months from June to September
**Best time to go** November to March (summer) is the best time, though the north can be visited at any time; avoid June to September, which is winter in the centre and south
**Minimum daily budget** US$25

The first thing most people notice about Chile when they look at a map is its utterly implausible shape. A narrow strip of land running down the west coast of South America, it measures over 4000km in length – the same distance as that from Scotland to Nigeria – though its width rarely exceeds 180km. Absurd as it may seem, however, this bizarre shape makes perfect sense geographically: hemmed in by the South Pacific to the west, separated from Argentina to the east by the Andes, and divided from Peru to the north by the arid expanse of the Atacama Desert, the country is a geographically self-contained unit.

The historic isolation brought by these natural barriers has helped create a nation very distinct from the rest of Latin America. Of all the countries in the region, Chile is the one where European cultural influence is strongest, a result both of the Spanish colonial period, subsequent waves of immigration from elsewhere in Europe, and major British commercial involvement in the nineteenth and twentieth centuries – until the arrest of the former Chilean dictator Augusto Pinochet in London in 1998, the Chilean upper classes liked to think of themselves as the English of South America, and would hold formal tea parties every afternoon. It's for Pinochet's brutal military regime, which ruled the country between 1973 and 1989, that Chile has become best known internationally, but in fact that dictatorship was an aberration from a long tradition of political stability, civilian government and the rule of law. Compared to the rest of the continent, Chile is a modern and relatively affluent society, and is without doubt one of the safest and easiest places to travel in South America. The police are generally helpful and efficient, the infrastructure is well developed and – most amazingly for Latin America – the buses run on time.

In terms of cultural interest, Chile can't really compete with other Andean countries like Peru and Bolivia, with their extremely diverse populations and deep-rooted indigenous traditions. (Chile's largest remaining indigenous group, the Mapuche, number a million but are largely confined to reservations in the Lake District, while their ancestral lands are farmed by the descendants of European colonists.) What it lacks in culture, however, it more than makes up

CHILE

PERU

Arica

BOLIVIA

PARAGUAY

Calama

San Pedro
de Atacama

Antofagasta

A R G E N T I N A

Viña del Mar
Valparaíso    Santiago

Concepción

Temuco

LAKE DISTRICT

P A C I F I C

O C E A N

Puerto Montt

Isla de Chiloé

PARQUE NACIONAL
LAGUNA SAN RAFAEL

PARQUE NACIONAL
TORRES DEL PAINE

Tierra
del Fuego

Punta
Arenas

Cape Horn

**One week**

• Santiago–Valparaíso–San Pedro de Atacama.
• Santiago–Valparaíso–Lake District.

**Two weeks**

• Santiago–Lake District–Chiloé–Puntas Arenas–Torres del Paine–
Santiago–Valparaíso.
• Santiago–Lake District–Chiloé–Laguna San Rafael–Santiago–Valparaíso.

**Four weeks**

• Santiago–Lake District–Chiloé–Puerto Montt–Laguna San Rafael–
Torres del Paine Santiago–Valparaíso–San Pedro de Atacama/Easter Island.

Easter Island (Rapa Nui) 4000km

0          500 km

for with its astonishing variety of dramatic landscapes, which range from the Atacama desert, the driest in the world, to the glaciers and icefields of Patagonia. And between these extremes are beautiful beaches; fertile valleys where vineyards and orchards flourish; huge temperate forests and dazzling emerald lakes; stunning fjords and bleak Patagonian steppes; and, towering above it all and running the length of the country, the jagged spine of the Andes, with its icebound peaks and smouldering volcanoes. Moreover, with a population of fewer than sixteen million, largely confined to a few cities in a country three times the size of Britain, much of its stunning expanse is virtually uninhabited wilderness. Coupled with a well-organized tourism industry, this makes Chile an excellent country for the outdoor enthusiast, whether your preference is for skiing, bird-watching, sea kayaking, whitewater rafting, trekking, mountaineering, horse-riding or fly-fishing. As if all this wasn't enough, Chile also includes the far-flung Easter Island, lost in the vastness of the Pacific Ocean almost 4000km from the mainland, which was home to one of the world's most mysterious and remarkable prehistoric cultures, best known for the enormous stone idols that still dot the island's shores.

Chile's climate is much closer to that of Europe or the US than to most other Latin American countries, ranging from an almost Mediterranean climate in the centre of the country to much colder conditions in the far south. The further south you travel, the more seasonal variation in climate there is, so while the southern hemisphere winter between June and September brings extremely cold weather in the far south, with heavy snow blocking access to many of the best national parks, the summer months from November to March enjoy good weather and long sunny evenings, meaning you can fit much more into a day, all of which makes it the perfect place to escape from the winter back home.

# Main attractions

● **Parque Nacional Torres del Paine** Situated in the far south of Chilean Patagonia, this remote park encompasses Chile's single most famous attraction, the stunning Torres del Paine, a small mountain range of magnificent near-vertical granite pinnacles that soar more than 2000m above the surrounding plains, amidst a pristine wilderness of glaciers, lakes and primeval forests – a paradise for walkers and mountaineers.

● **Lake District** Stretching some 340km between the towns of Temuco and Puerto Montt in the south of the country, the Chilean lake district is a beautiful region of lush farmland, dense forest and deep, clear lakes which sit at the foot of a series of spectacular snow-capped volcanoes. Much of the stunning wilderness scenery of the region is protected by national parks such as Puyehue, which offer excellent hiking opportunities, with the added bonus of numerous volcanic hot springs where you can relax and sooth tired legs after a hard day's walking.

● **Chiloé** Just south of the Lake District and reached by boat from Puerto Montt, Chiloé is a peaceful and isolated archipelago famous for its traditional rural culture and rich folklore and mythology. The windswept west coast of the main island, Isla Grande de Chiloé, is covered with dense forest, much of it protected by the Parque National Chiloé, while the more sheltered east coast is dotted with quiet fishing and farming communities, with ancient wooden churches and traditional wooden houses built on stilts.

● **The Carretera Austral** Stretching over a thousand kilometres south from Puerto Montt to the remote settlement of Yungay, the Carretera Austral – the Southern Highway – is one of the most dramatic roads in Latin America, carving its way through great tracts of untouched wilderness between soaring, snow-capped mountains, ancient glaciers, narrow fjords, emerald rivers and swathes of temperate rainforest.

● **Parque Nacional Laguna San Rafael** Reached from the port of Chacabuco by a spectacular 200km boat journey through labyrinthine fjords, the iceberg-choked Laguna San Rafael, at the foot of the glacier of the same name, is one of the most awe-inspiring sights in Chile. It's also a great place for observing penguins, sea-lions, albatrosses and other marine wildlife, and is the centre of a vast national park that encompasses huge ice fields, high mountain peaks, primeval forests and hundreds of glacial lakes.

● **Valparaíso and the Litoral Central** The coastal city of Valparaíso, about 120km northwest of Santiago, is Chile's biggest port and a wonderfully atmospheric place, with labyrinthine cobbled streets lined with ramshackle, brightly painted houses that cover the steep hillside down to the seashore. Known as the Litoral Central (the Central Coast) or the Chilean Riviera, the stretch of coast either side of Valparaíso boasts bay after bay lined with beautiful white sand beaches and twenty or so resort towns, the largest and most famous of which is the upmarket Viña del Mar.

## Also recommended

● **Atacama Desert** Stretching over 1200km south from the Peruvian border,
the Atacama Desert is the driest desert in the world, a desolate plain of rock and gravel that contains areas where no rain has ever been recorded. The region also boasts a spectacular coastline, geysers, ancient petroglyphs and abandoned nitrate-mining ghost towns.

● **Skiing** Chile boasts arguably the best skiing in South America: some skiers believe that the very dry powder snow (known as "champagne snow") found on the country's high-altitude slopes is of a quality found nowhere else. The season runs from June to September and the best slopes and resorts – El Colorado, La Parva and Valle Nevado – are conveniently close to Santiago. Prices, however, are high, with a one-week all-inclusive package costing around $800 in the low season, and twice that in the high season.

● **The Central Valley** Many travellers speed through Chile's Central Valley – the rich agricultural heartland stretching from Santiago 400km or so south to the Río Bio Bio – without stopping as they head to more spectacular attractions further south, but with its lush, pastoral landscape dotted with orchards and vineyards, its splendid colonial haciendas and tranquil villages, and its deeply traditional rural culture, the region rewards those who stop off and explore away from the main road.

● **Easter Island (Rapa Nui)** Isolated in the vastness of the Pacific Ocean almost four thousand kilometres west of the Chilean mainland, tiny Easter Island – known to its indigenous Polynesian inhabitants as Rapa Nui – is one of the most remote places on earth, and home to the extraordinary monuments left by one of the world's most enigmatic prehistoric cultures. The coast of the island – which measures just over 20km across at its widest point – is dotted with huge, ancient monolithic stone statues of squat human torsos and heads, the origin and meaning of which remain deeply mysterious.

# Routes in and out

The Chilean capital Santiago is served by regular flights from major European capitals and cities in the US, and from Australia via New Zealand, Papeete and Easter Island in the Pacific; it also has regular flights to all the main South American capitals. By land, it's easy to enter and leave Chile across the northern border with Peru and at many points along the long eastern frontier with Argentina – if you visit Patagonia you may well find yourself crossing the border between Chile and Argentina several times. There's a good road link between Arica in northern Chile and La Paz in northern Bolivia, but you can also cross into Bolivia by train from Calama to Uyni – a route that passes through spectacular high Andean scenery – or by jeep as part of an organized tour from San Pedro de Atacama, passing through the stunning Reserva de Fauna Andina Eduardo Avaroa in the far southwest of Bolivia.

# Itineraries

The huge distances involved mean that if you've only got a short time to explore Chile but want to travel widely, you'll need to take one or more internal flights, so consider buying LAN Chile's Explore Chile airpass, which gives you three internal flights for around $350 (less if you fly into Chile with the same airline), with each additional flight costing $80 or so.

## One week

● From Santiago head to Valparaíso or one of the nearby beach resorts for two or three days (or, if you're there in the winter, spend a couple of days skiing near the capital), then either head north by road to San Pedro de Atacama and spend your remaining time exploring the Atacama Desert and the Altiplano, or head south overland and spend the time in the Lake District.

## Two weeks

● Travel south by road from Santiago through the Central Valley and spend the first week or so exploring the Lake District and Chiloé, then either fly down to Punta Arenas in Patagonia to visit the Parque Nacional Torres del Paine, or take a four-day boat trip from Puerto Montt via Chacabuco to the Laguna San Rafael, returning to Santiago by road from Chacabuco along the Carretera Austral. With any luck you'll have enough time at the end of the trip to spend a day or two in Valparaíso and one of the nearby beach resorts, or skiing near Santiago.

## One month

● Spend ten days or so working your way south from Santiago, passing through the Central Valley and visiting the Lake District and Chiloé, then take a boat tour down from Puerto Montt to the Laguna San Rafael. Next, head to Patagonia to visit the Parque Nacional Torres del Paine, either by disembarking at Chacabuco as you return north from Laguna San Rafael and travelling by road down the Careterra Austral and through Argentina, or by returning to Puerto Montt and catching the weekly ferry to Puerto Natales. Return by plane to Santiago, then either fly out to Easter Island for a week, or spend the time visiting Valparaíso and some of the surrounding beaches and heading up into the Atacama Desert.

# Chile online

### Easter Island
ⓦ**www.netaxs.com/~trance /rapanui.html** A good introduction to the history and culture of Easter Island, with plenty of good pictures, practical information and lots of useful links.

### Latin America Network Information Center, Chile
ⓦ**lanic.utexas.edu/la/chile** Comprehensive listing of Chile-related links, including everything from universities and tour companies to media and government departments.

### Sernatur
ⓦ**www.sernatur.cl** National Tourist Board site with good general information on the main attractions, and links to online hotel bookings and other government websites.

### Visit Chile
ⓦ**www.visit-chile.org** Excellent general tourist information site with information on all the main attractions and activities from skiing to wine tours, as well as links to airlines, hotels and car rental companies and a wealth of other practical information.

# Colombia

**Capital** Bogotá
**Population** 43 million
**Language** Spanish, plus over a dozen indigenous languages and English Creole
**Currency** Colombian peso (Col$)
**Climate** Large variations in temperature: tropical along coast and eastern plains with wet (April–May & Sept–Nov) and dry (Nov–March) seasons; cooler in the Andean highlands
**Best time to go** November to March (dry season)
**Minimum daily budget** US$15

To most people, Colombia means only three things: coffee, cocaine and civil war. The country has been blighted by over fifty years of fighting between left-wing guerrillas and right-wing paramilitaries, with hundreds of thousands of Colombians losing their lives and many more being made homeless. As if this wasn't already enough, the country also reels under the influence of the billion-dollar cocaine trade – Colombia is both the world's largest grower of coca (the raw material of cocaine) and the world's leading processor of the drug – whose economic and social consequences permeate all levels of society, from peasant farmers coerced into growing coca to corrupt politicians in the pay of drugs cartels. Not for nothing is Colombia nicknamed *Locombia*, or "Mad Country".

Sadly, Colombia is currently more dangerous than ever to travel in, with over three thousand kidnappings a year and high levels of guerrilla and paramilitary activity. If you decide to visit the country, make sure you check the latest political situation with the government travel advisories listed on p.328. At present, the entire country east of Bogotá is effectively out of bounds to tourists, and overland travel isn't currently safe at night or in remote areas – it's best to take internal flights between cities or travel with major bus companies on main routes during the daytime only.

These warnings aside, there are still parts of Colombia which are no more dangerous to visit than anywhere else in Latin America, and those travellers who do make it to Colombia often cite it as their favourite country in South America. Certainly, Colombia has a lot to offer, including one of the most geographically diverse landscapes of any Latin American country, with the Andes stretching right through its western side, unspoilt Caribbean and Pacific coastlines, and a large area of remote Amazon basin. Uniquely in South America, it's possible to see the ocean from the snow-capped Sierra Nevada de Santa Marta (rising to 5800m), while the lower Andes are dotted with a series of pretty colonial towns and traditional highland villages, along with several unique pre-Columbian sites: the *Cuidad Perdida* of the Tayrona people in northern Colombia and San Agustín and Tierradientro in the south of the country. Additionally, you'll have most of Colombia's beauty spots to yourself – almost nowhere in the country is overrun by tourists.

**One week**

• Bogotá–Leticia–Brazil/Peru.
• Santa Marta–Ciudad Perdida.
• Medellín–Nuquí–El Valle.

**Two weeks**

• Ecuador–San Agustín–Bogotá–Cartagena–
Parque Nacional Tayrona.
• Bogotá–Nuquí–Cali–Popayán–San Agustín.

**Three weeks**

• Cartagena–Parque Nacional Tayrona–Ciudad Perdida–
Villa de Leiva–Bogotá–Cali–Popayán–San Agustín–Ipiales.

But the country's greatest attraction is perhaps the Colombians themselves, a more homogenous people than that of most other South American countries, with over 75% of the population mixed (both mestizo and mulatto) race. Renowned for their exuberance and friendliness, they celebrate life in the midst of civil war with noisy parties whenever possible, and welcome the few tourists they see wholeheartedly. In spite of its continuing violence and criminality, Colombia remains a spontaneous, vibrant and remarkably open society.

## Main attractions

● **Cartagena** Founded in 1533, the great walled city of Cartagena de Indias, on the Caribbean coast, was the main Spanish port in northern South America for several hundred years. Cartagena's thick walls and ring of outer forts, built to protect the city from pirate attacks, are part of the unique character that makes it Colombia's main tourist attraction and one of the finest colonial cities in the Americas. You could easily spend days wandering through its maze of narrow streets, arcaded squares, grand buildings and ruined forts. Adjacent to the old city is a vibrant modern beach resort, and at night Cartagena comes alive with a mixture of live music, salsa and beachfront discos.

● **Parque Nacional Tayrona** The most popular national park in Colombia, Tayrona protects a 35-kilometre stretch of Caribbean coast, with glorious sandy beaches set in palm-fringed bays and backed by lush rainforest. A well-known hippy hangout, it's the perfect place to take a break from travelling, though if you feel energetic you could make the five-day trek from the park to the *Ciudad Perdida* ("Lost City") or Teyuna – its indigenous name – of the Tayrona Indians, dating back to 500 AD, which occupies a spectacular location at 1100m on the northern slopes of the Sierra Nevada de Santa Marta.

● **Chocó region** This remote and unspoilt region encompasses the northern half of Colombia's Pacific coast, with virgin rainforest running down to miles of empty beach, a tropical backwater atmosphere and traditional communities of Chocó and Emberá Indians. The region's capital is the ramshackle riverside city of Quibdó – it's better to head straight for the coastal resorts of Nuquí, El Valle and the Ensenada de Utría National Park. Highlights of the area include tiny Isla de Salomon, which has the prettiest white-sand beach in the area, and the small village of Tribugá, both stopoffs on the boat ride from Nuquí to El Valle.

● **San Agustín** Principally known for a number of mysterious carved statues in a series of nearby sites, San Agustín is a pretty market town in the rolling green foothills of the Andes, with locals on horseback and a thriving backpacker scene. The surrounding countryside is known for its natural beauty, and there are several impressive waterfalls close to the town.

● **Salsa in Cali** Salsa is one of Colombia's most popular forms of music and dance and nowhere in the country is it more popular than in the *salsatecas* (salsa clubs) of Cali, an inland city with tropical temperatures and an atmosphere to match. Cali's citizens, *caleños*, are among Colombia's friendliest locals – try and persuade them to take you to the authentic *salsatecas* in the barrio of Juanchito, which can be dangerous if you go alone. If not, there are salsa clubs dotted along Avenida Sexta, the city's main street for nightlife.

## Also recommended

● **San Andrés y Providencia** A small archipelago in the Caribbean (it's actually closer to Nicaragua than Colombia), San Andrés y Providencia has a unique culture, a fusion of Jamaican and Colombian, marked by soca music and Creole-speaking inhabitants, while the islands' clear blue waters and coral reefs make them a great destination for snorkelling and scuba diving.

● **Popayán** Situated in the southwest of the country, Popayán is one of Colombia's most perfectly preserved colonial towns, boasting cobbled streets and several noteworthy colonial churches and hosting spectacular Semana Santa (Easter) parades. It's a small, tranquil place with a mild climate, and there's little to do here other than wander through the pretty squares and streets, though it makes a good base from which to visit the Tuesday market at Silvia, where the local Guambiano Indians can be seen weaving textiles in their colourful blue and fuchsia costumes.

● **Mud volcanoes** Arboletes and El Totumo are the two most impressive of the series of natural mud lakes that stretch along the Caribbean coast of Colombia. Both have craters filled with the warm, thick stuff, in which you can bathe: the mud has beneficial healing properties and leaves your skin baby smooth – a weird and unforgettable sensation.

● **Bogotá** Colombia's noisy, grid-locked and exciting capital is well worth a visit, despite its (largely unde-served) reputation for danger. The city's lovely colonial quarter, La Candelaria, makes an atmospheric retreat from the city bustle, while other highlights include the world-famous Museo de Oro and the monastery of Montserrate, perched high above the city and boasting wonderful views – not to mention one of the best club scenes in Latin America.

● **Leticia** A small town in the south-eastern tip of Colombia, Leticia is the tourist centre of the country's remote Amazon region. The town itself is fairly ordinary but the surrounding area is dense rainforest dotted with Ticuna and Yagua settlements. Popular trips go to Amacayucu National Park, 75km upstream, where there are walking trails through the forest, and the Lago de Tarapoto, a beautiful lake featuring the famous *Victoria Amazonica* waterlily and occasional sightings of pink dolphins. From Leticia (which you'll have to fly to from within Colombia) it's possible to get a boat down the Amazon river to Brazil and Peru.

# Routes in and out

There are direct daily flights to Bogotá from several cities in the USA (principally Miami and New York), plus direct flights from Miami to Cartagena and Medellín. From Europe there are flights from London via Caracas to Bogotá thrice weekly, and direct flights from Madrid, Paris and Frankfurt to the capital. Overland border crossings from Venezuela to Colombia are at Cúcuta and the less popular Maicao, on the northern Guajira Peninsula. The border between Colombia and Ecuador is at Ipiales. Boats go irregularly from Colón in Panamá to Puerto Obaldía (2–4 days), from where you can take an *expreso* or speedboat to the Colombian resorts of Capurganá and Acandi. The famous over-land crossing of the Darién Gap (see p.113) is extremely dangerous and should on no account be attempted at present.

# Itineraries

## One week

● Spend four days in Colombia's capi-tal and then fly to Leticia in the Amazon for some jungle exploration. From Leticia move on by boat to Brazil or Peru.

● Take an organized five-day trek from Santa Marta to the *Cuidad Perdida* and then spend your last two days relaxing on the Caribbean beaches of the Tayrona National Park.

● Fly from Medellín to Nuquí in the Chocó region. Travel from Nuquí to El Valle by boat with an overnight stay on the Isla de Salomon and forays into the Ensenada de Utria National Park.

## Two weeks

● Cross the border from Ecuador to San Agustín. Spend several days relaxing in this small rural town before moving on to Bogotá for some big city life. Travel north to Cartagena for a few days and then go east to the Parque Nacional Tayrona for a long weekend or fly to the Caribbean island of San Andrés, from where you can fly on to Costa Rica or Panamá.

● Head west from Bogotá to the seaside town of Nuquí in the Chocó region for several days on the Pacific coast. Head south from Chocó's regional centre, Quibdó, by bus to Cali and its salsa dance clubs. From there make your way to San Agustín and then on to one of Colombia's colonial highlights, Popayán, and the market town of Silvia.

## Three weeks

● Fly into Cartagena from Panamá and spend ten days on the coast exploring Cartagena, trekking to the *Cuidad Perdida* and relaxing in the Parque Nacional Tayrona. Travel south to Bogotá for four or five days and then on to Cali to check out its dance clubs. Visit San Agustín, Popayán and Silvia before crossing the border into Ecuador at Ipiales.

# Colombia online

### Colombia Report
ⓦ**www.colombiareport.org** Excellent analysis and history of civil unrest in Colombia and the drugs trade from a left-wing perspective.

### Colombia Support Network
ⓦ**www.colombiasupport.net** Website of the largest grassroots organization in the USA working to improve human rights in Colombia, with articles and background information on the current political crisis.

### Poorbuthappy.com
ⓦ**www.poorbuthappy.com** Excellent homepage set up by an ex-pat now living near Medellín with useful and upbeat advice on travel in Colombia and articles by other travellers on their experiences.

### El Tiempo
ⓦ**www.eltiempo.com** The well laid-out and comprehensive site (in Spanish only) of Colombia's best daily newspaper, *El Tiempo*.

# Costa Rica

**Capital** San José
**Population** 3.8 million
**Language** Spanish, Creole English on the Caribbean
**Currency** Colón (¢)
**Climate** Tropical on the coast, cooler in the mountains, with distinct dry (Dec–April) and rainy (May–Nov) seasons
**When to go** November, April and May
**Minimum daily budget** US$30

In a region synonymous in many peoples' minds with civil war and natural disasters, Costa Rica stands out as a beacon of prosperity and stability – not for nothing is the country often described as the Switzerland of Central America. Today, as Costa Ricans will proudly tell you, the country has no army, more teachers than policemen, free and compulsory primary education, and a literacy rate of ninety percent. For the visitor, Costa Rica's overwhelming draw is its outstanding range of natural attractions, from stunning landscapes to rare and colourful birds and wildlife. Around a quarter of the country is now protected by a widely admired system of national parks and reserves which cover a fascinating diversity of terrains, from mysterious cloud- and rainforests to active volcanic peaks and stunning stretches of palm-fringed coast. And found within these parks is a remarkable array of biodiversity, some five percent of the world's total – an astonishing figure given the country's tiny dimensions – and including (to give just one example) some 850 species of bird, more than in the US and Canada combined.

All of which natural attractions have made Costa Rica one of the finest places in Latin America for ecotourists, bird-watchers and wildlife enthusiasts, with the result that Costa Rica is now Central America's most popular tourist destination, attracting around a million visitors annually – quite an achievement for a country whose entire population numbers less than four million. The large number of North Americans who come to visit (or, increasingly, to live in) the country means that many Costa Ricans now speak at least a little English and are used to dealing with foreigners. In sum, if you're nervous about culture shock, Costa Rica is the best place in Central America to ease into your Latin American adventure. Conversely, if you prefer to travel off the beaten track, Costa Rica isn't the place to go.

Away from the nation's national parks and reserves, there are outstanding beaches to be found on both coasts, some world-class surfing and white-water rafting. Man-made and cultural attractions are few, however, although the Jamaican-descended black population which lives around Puerto Limón on the Caribbean coast supplies a welcome splash of cultural diversity (and nightlife) in the country's overwhelmingly mestizo population.

As the visitor numbers would suggest, Costa Rica has a well-developed tourist infrastructure, including some of

Peñas Blancas

NICARAGUA

COSTA RICA

PARQUE
NACIONAL
VOLCÁN
ARENAL

Liberia

CARIBBEAN
SEA

Tortuguero

RARA AVIS
NATURE RESERVE

RESERVA
SANTA ELENA

San Carlos

SAN JOSÉ

OROSÍ VALLEY

Puerto
Limón

Puerto Viejo

Sixaola

PACIFIC OCEAN

Bahía
Drake

OSA PENINSULA

PANAMÁ

N

**One week**

- San José–Tortuguero–Puerto Limón–Puerto Viejo.
- San José–Volcán Arenal–Santa Elena–Liberia.
- San José–Osa Peninsula–Bahía Drake.

**Two weeks**

- San José–Rara Avis–Orosí Valley–Tortuguero.
- Sixaola–Puerto Viejo–San José–Orosí Valley–Osa Peninsula.

**One month**

- Peñas Blancas–Liberia–Santa Elena–Volcán Arenal–San José–Orosí Valley–Osa Peninsula–San José–Puerto Viejo.

0    50 km

Latin America's most memorable eco-lodges and an efficient public transport network, even though some of the country's roads remain pretty appalling. This development comes at a price, however: Costa Rica is perhaps the most expensive country in Central America to travel in, with daily costs being twice those in neighbouring Nicaragua. On the plus side, it's still amongst the safest countries in the region, though levels of crime against tourists are unfortunately rising, and parts of San José should be avoided at night.

## Main attractions

● **Parque Nacional Tortuguero** Most visitors come to Tortuguero to see hawksbill, green and leatherback turtles laying their eggs on the beach (March–May & July–Oct), but the park's network of inland waterways also teems with other forms of wildlife, particularly birds, while the village itself is extremely pretty, with pastel-coloured wooden houses and lots of rakish charm.

● **Puerto Viejo** Situated on the southern end of Costa Rica's Caribbean coast, the funky fishing village of Puerto Viejo has possibly the liveliest nightlife in the whole country, with several good beach-side discos. By day, there are miles of clean sandy beaches to lounge about on, plus excellent surfing and snorkelling.

● **Volcán Arenal** One of the western hemisphere's most active volcanoes,

Arenal spews out rivers of molten red lava on an almost nightly basis, although you'll need a clear night to see this amazing pyrotechnic display. During the daytime it's possible to hike on one of several trails around the volcano and across its solidified lava fields.

● **Reserva Santa Elena** In northern Costa Rica, the Reserva Santa Elena comprises a small area of virgin cloud-forest with dense walls of dripping vegetation and brightly coloured birds and flowers. Though it's only a third the size of the famous Monteverde Cloudforest just down the road, it's also much less visited – and more tranquil – and profits go to local schools. The surrounding area was colonized by a group of US Quakers (a progressive and pacifist Christian movement) escaping the draft in the early 1950s, and now offers a rural idyll of small dairy farms and mountain scenery.

● **Osa Peninsula** Much less well-known than other parts of Costa Rica, the Osa Peninsula is difficult to reach – getting to both the village of Aguijitas in Bahía Drake and Carate on the edge of the Corcovado National Park entails lengthy uncomfortable boat or bus rides – but rewards the few travellers who make it here with stunning scenery. Corcovado, with its series of rainforest-fringed beaches populated by flocks of scarlet macaws, is one of Costa Rica's most beautiful national parks, and there's wonderful marine life and snorkelling at Bahía Drake.

## Also recommended

● **Orosí** The peaceful Orosí river valley, 25km southeast of San José, is little visited by tourists but has much to offer, with a dramatic setting in a deep bowl of steep forested hills. There's a series of lovely walks and waterfalls in the area, and a very pretty village, Orosí, which has two outdoor swimming pools fed by hot springs and one of the oldest churches in Costa Rica, an attractive adobe and red-tiled structure built in 1735.

● **Rara Avis** A private rainforest reserve and research station 80km northeast of San José, Rara Avis offers one of the best ecotourism experiences in the country. Getting to the forest is half the adventure – its remoteness means that it's only accessible by tractor-drawn cart from the nearest village along a muddy track, with great views over the surrounding countryside and toucans in the trees. Once there you can walk one of several excellent trails through the forest, check out the abundant flora (including rare palm species and orchids) or swim in a waterfall pool.

● **Liberia** In the northern province of Guanacaste, calm Liberia is Costa Rica's most attractive town, with wide streets of whitewashed houses lined with mango trees, while the town's main street, the Calle Real, has been restored to its original nineteenth-century glory and is now the best example of colonial architecture in Costa Rica. The town is also a good jumping-off point for the popular beaches of Guanacaste, several national parks and the Nicaraguan border.

## Routes in and out

There are direct flights daily to San José from Miami, Houston and Dallas. The border between Costa Rica and Nicaragua is at Peñas Blancas, close to the Pacific coast, and has direct bus routes on to Managua; it's also possible to cross the Río San Juan from Los Chiles to San Carlos. There are two main borders with Panamá: Paso Canoas on the Panamerican Highway, and Sixaola on the Caribbean, convenient for the popular Panamanian resort of Bocas del Toro.

# Itineraries

## One week

● Take a bus or boat from San José to Tortuguero and then travel by boat down the Caribbean coast to the region's capital, Puerto Limón, and on to seaside party town Puerto Viejo.

● Head north from San José to Volcán Arenal and the Santa Elena cloudforest before stopping off in laid-back Liberia for a few days.

● Travel from San José to the Osa Peninsula, do the popular five-day trek in Corcovado National Park and then recover on the beaches of Bahía Drake.

## Two weeks

● Travel from San José to Rara Avis and spend a few days bird-spotting, followed by a few days relaxing and exploring the tranquil Orosí valley before heading east to Tortuguero.

● From Panamá, cross the border into Sixaola and then head to Puerto Viejo. Head right across the country to the Orosí valley and then on to the Osa Peninsula, where you can hike through the Corcovado National Park or go snorkelling at Bahía Drake.

## One month

● If you're travelling south through Central America, cross the border from Nicaragua to Peñas Blancas and head on to the cowboy city of Liberia – a pleasant introduction to Costa Rica. Continue on to the Santa Elena cloudforest and the Quaker communities of Monteverde, visit Volcán Arenal and then head south to the Osa Peninsula. Loop back to the centre of the country and Orosí, then cross over to the other coast and Puerto Viejo before moving on to Panamá.

# Costa Rica online

**Cocori.com**

Ⓦ **www.cocori.com** Excellent series of well-written articles on all aspects of life in Costa Rica including food, scuba diving and spelunking amongst others.

**Costa Rican National Chamber of Tourism**

Ⓦ **www.tourism.co.cr** The website of the Costa Rican National Chamber of Tourism with interesting and informative features on the country's history, geography and highlights.

**Info Costa Rica**

Ⓦ **www.infocostarica.com** Well-organized portal with hundreds of good links as well as in-house articles and a messageboard.

**Tico Times**

Ⓦ **www.ticotimes.net** Website of the award-winning weekly English-language newspaper, with a focus on national news as well as folksy columns on cooking, fishing and expat life in Costa Rica.

# Ecuador

**Capital** Quito
**Population** 13 million
**Language** Spanish, Quechua, plus minority indigenous languages
**Currency** US dollar ($)
**Climate** Hot and humid in the tropical lowlands of the coast and the Amazonian Oriente, cooler in the highlands
**Best time to go** June to August in the highlands, December to April on the coast, and any time outside the June-to-August rainy season in the Amazon lowlands
**Minimum daily budget** US$15

Sitting on the equator between Peru and Colombia, Ecuador is the smallest of the Andean republics, covering an area only slightly larger than the United Kingdom. But despite its diminutive size, the country is packed with dramatic scenic contrasts, encompassing snow-capped volcanic peaks, palm-fringed beaches lapped by the warm Pacific, and the steaming tropical rainforests of the Amazon basin. Ecuador is also home to a diverse population, including a wide range of indigenous groups, while many of its towns and cities boast magnificent colonial architecture. As if this wasn't enough, Ecuador's attractions are crowned by the Galápagos Islands, the famous archipelago whose unique and extraordinary wildlife played a key role in shaping Charles Darwin's theories on evolution.

In many ways, Ecuador is a kind of pocket-sized South America, making it the ideal destination for travellers who want to experience a wide range of the continent's manifold attractions but only have a relatively short time in which to do so. Unlike larger South American countries, where moving between different regions involves travelling vast distances, Ecuador's compact size means

that getting around is straightforward and relatively quick, with few destinations more than a day's journey from the capital Quito. It also has a relatively well-developed tourist infrastructure, making it easy to arrange guided tours and treks, rainforest expeditions, or climbing and mountain-biking trips.

Like the other Andean countries, Ecuador suffers from chronic political instability – in 1997 it went through three presidents in a year, including the infamous Abdalá Bucaram, known as "El Loco" ("The Mad"), who was removed from office on grounds of mental incompetence. Fortunately, these periodic political upheavals are rarely violent, although they do often involve mass protests and road blockades that paralyze the country and make travel virtually impossible, so it's important to check on the current political situation before you arrive. In recent years the economy – dependent largely on oil and banana exports – has also been in deep crisis, bringing increased poverty and unemployment and leading to the abandonment of the national currency in favour of the US dollar. Crime levels have also increased, ending Ecuador's reputation as one of the

ECUADOR

COLOMBIA

Galápagos Islands (980km)

Esmeraldas
Atacames

Equator

Otavalo · Ibarra
Lago Agrio

QUITO
Coca

RESERVA
FAUNÍSTICA
CUYABENO

Volcán Cotopaxi

THE CENTRAL SIERRA · Tena

Isla de
la Plata

THE ORIENTE

Baños

PARQUE NACIONAL
MACHALILLA

Riobamba

Guayaquil

0    50km

Equator

Cuenca

Galápagos Islands

Loja

PERU

Vilcabamba

0        100 km

**One week**

• Quito–Otavalo–Cotopaxi–Riobamba.

**Two weeks**

• Quito–Lago Agrio–Quito–Otavalo–Cotopaxi–Riobamba.

**One month**

• Quito–Lago Agrio–Quito–Otavalo–Cotopaxi–Riobamba–
Cuenca–Quito–Galápagos Islands.
• Quito–Lago Agrio–Quito–Otavalo–Cotopaxi–Baños–
Riobamba–Cuenca–Vilcabamba.

safest countries for travellers in South America. But for all that, the overwhelming majority of Ecuadorians remain remarkably cheerful, courteous and welcoming to foreign visitors.

## Main attractions

● **Galápagos Islands** Lying almost 1000km east of the Ecuadorian mainland, the extraordinary Galapagos Islands – which inspired Charles Darwin to formulate his theory of evolution – are Ecuador's best-known attraction, home

to a unique, abundant and virtually fearless range of wildlife including marine iguanas, giant tortoises, whales, dolphins, sea lions, penguins and boobies. Visiting the islands is relatively expensive – flights from the mainland, the national park entrance fee and the cost of a seven-night cruise around the archipelago will set you back well over $1000 – but few travellers who come here regret splashing out to experience one of the most astonishing nature-tourism destinations in the world.

● **Quito** Set at an altitude of 2800m in a valley at the foot of the soaring

Pichincha volcano, the Ecuadorian capital has a beautiful old colonial quarter of narrow streets lined with exquisite churches, monasteries and mansions that warrants a day or two of exploration. The modern new town is packed with hotels, restaurants, tour companies and other useful facilities, and makes a convenient place to recuperate between trips around the country. There are also a number of good excursions from the city, including to the town of Otavalo, which on Saturdays hosts a rather touristy but still excellent market where you can buy beautiful textiles and other indigenous handicrafts.

● **Avenue of the Volcanoes** South of Quito, the two parallel chains of the Andes that run the length of Ecuador rise to their most dramatic and spectacular, forming a double row of soaring, snowcapped peaks. The fertile basin between the two chains is the indigenous heartland of Ecuador, dotted with traditional farming villages and peaceful market towns, many of which can be visited in a 200-kilometre loop known as the Quilotoa circuit.

● **Reserva Faunística Cuyabeno** Though the ravages of oil development mean it's generally not as pristine as similar regions in Peru or Bolivia, Ecuador's Amazon lowland region – known as the Oriente – is fairly easily accessible from the highlands, making it an easy place to experience the Amazon rainforest. The best place to head for is the wildlife-rich Reserva Faunística Cuyabeno, in the northern Oriente, which you can visit on an organized tour from the oil town of Lago Agrio or by staying with one of several indigenous Amazonian communities that accept visitors.

● **Cuenca** Set amid the gentler mountain scenery of the southern Sierra, Cuenca is Ecuador's most captivating city, graced with elegant colonial architecture including magnificent churches and monasteries. It's also within easy striking distance of the ruins of Ingapirca, Ecuador's only major Inca site, as well as the starkly beautiful wilderness of Parque Nacional El Cajas, which offers excellent hiking and trout fishing.

# Also recommended

● **Parque Nacional Cotopaxi** Surrounding the perfectly symmetrical cone of Volcán Cotopaxi – at 5897m the highest active volcano in the world – the beautiful Parque Nacional Cotopaxi is an excellent place for hiking, with numerous trails, campsites and mountain refuges. Even if you've little or no technical mountain-climbing experience, if you're fit and acclimatized you can reach the summit with a guide.

● **Baños** With a warm, subtropical climate and a spectacular setting amid lush green hills streaked with waterfalls, the tranquil spa town of Baños is deservedly popular with Ecuadorian and foreign tourists alike. It's a good base for hiking, horse-riding, mountain-biking and whitewater rafting in the surrounding mountains, after which you can relax in the natural thermal baths that gave the town its name. Check the latest information before travelling here, however, as Volcán Tungurahua, which towers above the town, has been particularly active in recent years.

● **Parque Nacional Machalilla** Away from the unappealing industrial port cities of Guayaquil and Esmeraldas, Ecuador's varied Pacific coastline boasts some glorious beaches, dense mangrove swamps and peaceful Afro-Ecuadorian fishing villages, and several lively resort towns. One of the highlights of the coast is Parque Nacional Machalilla, northeast of Guayaquil, which combines stunning unspoiled beaches, pristine tropical forests and, on the offshore Isla de la Plata, an inexpensive alternative to the Galápagos for viewing boobies, frigate birds and albatrosses.

● **El Nariz del Diablo** From the pleasant city of Riobamba in the Central Sierra, a dramatic train line runs down to the village of Sibambe, zigzagging down a near-vertical wall of rock known as *El Nariz del Diablo* – "The Devil's Nose".

● **Vilcabamba** Set in an idyllic valley surrounded by crumpled mountains, the village of Vilcabamba first came to international attention in the 1950s, when it was hailed as the "Valley of Eternal Youth" after researchers claimed its inhabitants enjoyed unusually long life spans, with many living well over a hundred years. These days, it's an archetypal gringo hangout popular for its beautiful scenery and laid-back atmosphere, as well as for the widely available – and highly illegal – hallucinogenic San Pedro cactus. It's also a good base for exploring the cloudforests of the nearby Podocarpus National Park.

# Routes in and out

Quito and Guayaquil are served by regular flights from most major South American capitals, several cities in the US, and Amsterdam and Madrid in Europe. The main land crossing with Colombia is at Tulcán on the Panamerican Highway north of Quito. For Peru, the main border crossing is at Huaquillas on the southern coast; if you're heading to or from the highlands, it's much more convenient to cross the border at Macará in the Southern Sierra – you can travel on this route on direct

buses between the southern Ecuadorian city of Loja and Piura in Peru. Following the resolution in 1998 of a longstanding border dispute with Peru it is – in theory at least – possible to cross the border at Nuevo Rocafuerte in the Oriente, travelling by irregular riverboat along the Río Napo – check with the immigration authorities and the Peruvian Embassy in Quito, however, before attempting this rarely travelled route.

# Itineraries

## One week

● Spend a couple of days in Quito, including if possible a day-trip to Otavalo for the Saturday market, then head south into the Central Sierra through the Avenue of the Volcanoes, stopping off in whichever town that has a market day coinciding with your trip and hiking for a day or two in the Parque Nacional Cotopaxi. Finally, continue south to Riobamba and take the *Nariz del Diablo* train ride.

## Two weeks

● Spend two days in and around Quito, then head down to Lago Agrio in the Oriente by road and spend three or four days visiting the rainforests of the Cuyabeno Reserve on an organized tour or staying in a jungle lodge. Return to Quito, and head down into the Central Sierra, following the same route as described in the one-week itinerary.

## One month

● Follow the two-week itinerary, then continue south and spend three or four days in and around Cuenca. If you can afford it, return to Quito and fly to the Galápagos Islands and take a week-long cruise around the archipelago. If the Galápagos is outside your budget, take a little more time to cover the Central Southern Sierra, perhaps visiting El Cajas National Park, Baños or Vilcabamba for a few days. Then head down to the coast for a week or so, taking in one or two of the beach resorts west of Esmeraldas on the northern coast, and Machalilla National Park on the southern coast.

# Ecuador online

**Ecuador Explorer**
Ⓦ**www.ecuadorexplorer.com**
Excellent tourist information site with plenty of background information on Ecuador's main attractions, practical advice for travellers, and details of an extensive range of tour operators and hotels.

**Galápagos Islands**
Ⓦ**www.darwinfoundation.org**
Website of the Charles Darwin Research Station on Santa Cruz island, with masses of information on the ecology and biology of the Galápagos, the latest conservation and research news, details on volunteering opportunities, and good links to related sites.

**Latin American Network Information Centre, Ecuador**
Ⓦ**lanic.utexas.edu/la/sa/ecuador**
Comprehensive research resource with links to a massive range of Ecuador-related sites, including news media, tour companies and government agencies.

**Volcanoes**
Ⓦ**vulcan.wr.usgs.gov/Volcanoes /Ecuador/framework.html**
Comprehensive links to sites with information and photos of Ecuador's major volcanoes.

# El Salvador

**Capital** San Salvador
**Population** 6.2 million
**Language** Spanish, Nahua
**Currency** US dollar ($)
**Climate** Tropical on the coast and temperate in the highlands with two distinct seasons, rainy (May–Oct) and dry (Nov–April).
**When to go** November to April
**Minimum daily budget** US$15

El Salvador is the smallest country in Central America, the most densely populated and one of the least visited, largely as a result of the violent civil war which raged from 1980 to 1992, and whose memory still colours outside perceptions of the country. Even now, a decade after the end of the conflict, the country is struggling to rebuild itself, a process which wasn't helped by the series of massive earthquakes which devasted the coastal and central regions of the country in 2001, during which a thousand people died and 145,000 homes were devasted, leaving the country with a clean-up bill of US$2.8 billion – a sum which El Salvador can ill afford.

Nevertheless, El Salvador is a beautiful place, a land of mountain peaks and rolling green hills studded with no fewer than 25 volcanoes, not to mention a long swathe of palm-fringed beaches on the Pacific – one of the loveliest stretches of coastline in the region. Salvadorans, though sometimes initially wary of foreigners (particularly if you're North American), are known throughout Central America for their wry humour, vivacity and industriousness, and if you do venture into the country, you'll have the advantage of being one of very few foreign tourists to visit the country: apart from a small surfing community at La Libertad, El Salvador remains almost completely unvisited.

Not surprisingly given its recent past, there's little tourist infrastructure, although a government-run network of *turicentros* – largely patronized by locals on holiday rather than by foreign visitors – at least provides basic eating and camping facilities in some places of particular natural beauty. Otherwise, there's a shortage of decent budget accommodation and almost no nightlife to speak of, while security is also a concern – extreme levels of poverty (a quarter of the population lives on less than US$1 a day) have led to rising levels of crime, particularly in the frenetic capital, San Salvador.

## Main attractions

● **Suchitoto** Set amidst beautiful rolling countryside on the shores of Lago de Suchitlán, Suchitoto (the Nahuatl name means "city of birds and flowers") is the finest colonial town in the country, with low, red-tiled adobe houses, a tranquil and friendly atmosphere, and stunning views over the lake (where you can swim or fish). Attractions include the Museo de Alejandro Cotto, which is housed in a restored colonial mansion and includes

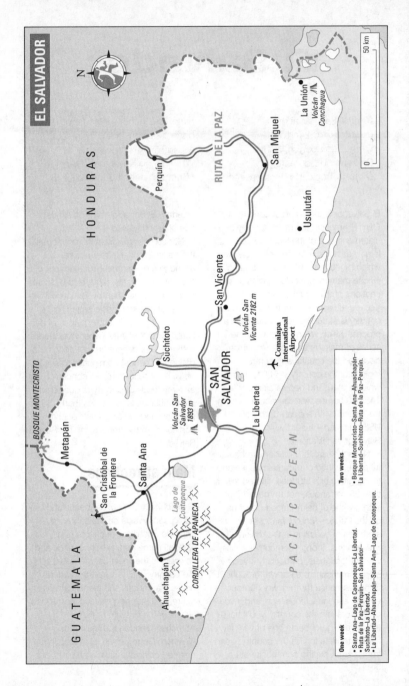

EL SALVADOR

N

HONDURAS

GUATEMALA

BOSQUE MONTECRISTO

Metapán

San Cristóbal de
la Frontera

Santa Ana

Ahuachapán

Lago de
Coatepeque

CORDILLERA DE APANECA

Volcán San
Salvador
1893 m

SAN
SALVADOR

La Libertad

Suchitoto

Volcán San
Vicente 2182 m

San Vicente

Comalapa
International
Airport

PACIFIC OCEAN

Perquín

RUTA DE LA PAZ

San Miguel

Usulután

La Unión
Volcán
Conchagua

0        50 km

**One week**
• Santa Ana–Lago de Coatepeque–La Libertad.
• Ruta de la Paz–Perquín–San Salvador–
  Suchitoto–La Libertad.
• La Libertad–Ahuachapán–Santa Ana–Lago de Coatepeque.

**Two weeks**
• Bosque Montecristo–Santa Ana–Ahuachapán–
  La Libertad–Suchitoto–Ruta de la Paz–Perquín.

collections of local paintings, indigenous artefacts and musical instruments.

● **Montecristo cloudforest** The remote and pristine Bosque Montecristo "El Trifinio" straddles the borders between El Salvador, Honduras and Guatemala. The reserve rises through two climatic zones to its peak at Cerro Montecristo (2418m), surrounded by an expanse of virgin cloudforest which is home to orchids, huge oak and cypress trees, monkeys, jaguars and quetzals.

● **Pacific beaches** El Salvador has a long sweep of undeveloped Pacific coastline, with palm-fringed beaches, dramatic cliffs, mangrove swamps and unspoilt islands. Two of the prettiest beaches are Playa El Espino, towards the border with Honduras, and Playa Barra de Santiago, in the far west; neither has any facilities, although it's fine to camp. The coast's main settlement is the rather shabby fishing town of La Libertad, which has plenty of budget accommodation and café life catering to visiting surfers – beaches on both sides of the town have good, uncrowded waves.

● **Ahuachapán and the Cordillera Apaneca** Ahuachapán, close to the Guatemalan border, was one of the first Spanish settlements in El Salvador and is now a comfortably bourgeois city with quiet streets, a lively market and several attractive churches. The surrounding area, the Cordillera Apaneca, is studded with mountain peaks laced with pine forest and coffee plantations, which are at their most picturesque when their white flowers blossom in May.

## Also recommended

● **Perquín civil war museum** The friendly mountain town of Perquín in the northeast of the country is home to the moving Museo de la Revolución Salvadoreña, which was set up by ex-guerrillas in the wake of the 1992 peace accords. Photographs and personal effects from those who died fighting have been collected from all over the country, along with weapons, propaganda and the equipment used by the guerrilla radio station, Radio Venceremos ("We Will Triumph").

● **Santa Ana** El Salvador's second city is a relaxing place with some lovely colonial architecture and a magnificent neo-Gothic cathedral. Set in the verdant Cihautehuacán valley, the city is close to three volcanoes, including the highest in the country, Volcán Santa Ana (2365m).

● **Ruta de la Paz** Part of a major project to develop tourism in the northeast of El Salvador, the so-called Ruta de la Paz ("Peace Route") encompasses a beautifully mountainous region dotted with small villages and a series of caves with pre-Columbian wall art.

● **Lago de Coatepeque** This stunning crater lake lies in the west of the country, shadowed by the volcanic peaks of Cerro Verde, Santa Ana and Izalco. The lake's deep blue waters are fed by hot springs (access to the water is easiest if you stay in one of several pleasant lakeside hotels) and ringed by walking trails offering panoramic views over lush green slopes.

## Routes in and out

There are flights daily to San Salvador from various cities in the US, including Los Angeles, Miami, Houston and New York, as well as daily flights from all the other Central American capitals and Mexico City. There are no direct connections from Europe or Australasia. You can cross overland into Guatemala at La Hachadura, near the Pacific (which is used by international buses heading to Mexico and is closest to Guatemala's Western Highlands); Las Chinamas, an hour from Ahuachapán, which has buses to Guatemala City; and, if you're visiting the Montecristo cloudforest, Anguiatú, which has connections to Esquipulas. The main crossings between El Salvador and Honduras are at El Amatillo, on the Panamerican Highway, and at El Poy in the north.

# Itineraries

## One week

● From Guatemala, cross the border to San Cristóbal and head south to the mellow city of Santa Ana for a few days, making day-trips to Lago de Coatepeque and its surrounding volcanoes before moving on to the Pacific coast.

● From Honduras, enter El Salvador and travel the pretty Ruta de la Paz to the civil war museum at Perquín. Then loop eastwards to San Salvador and make day-trips to the Maya ruins at Joya de Cerén and the colonial lakeside town of Suchitoto before finishing your week by the sea at La Libertad – the airport is close by.

● From El Salvador's airport go directly to the coast and, after a couple of days relaxing, head west to Guatemala via Santa Ana with a trip to the Lago de Coatepeque and its surrounding volcanoes and a stopover in Ahuachapán.

## Two weeks

● Two weeks is long enough to visit all the country's main attractions. From Guatemala go first to the Bosque Montecristo and then on to the relaxing cities of Santa Ana and Ahuachapán and their volcanoes. Take the seaside road to La Libertad and then head inland to Suchitoto before going east to the highlands of the Ruta de la Paz and the civil war museum at Perquín. Then cross the border into Honduras.

# El Salvador online

**Committee in Solidarity with the People of El Salvador (CISPES)**
Ⓦ www.cispes.org Website of a left-wing organization which supports the FMLN or Frente Farabundo Martí de Liberación Nacional, campaigns against the introduction of CAFTA (Central American Free Trade Agreement) and has some volunteer projects.

**El Diario de Hoy**
Ⓦ www.elsalvador.com Spanish-only website of the national daily paper, with local and international news, features and listings of cultural and sports events.

**El Salvador Tourist Board**
Ⓦ www.elsalvadorturismo.gob.sv The official El Salvador tourist board site, with essays on history and Maya culture, regional details and listings of cultural events.

**Republic of El Salvador**
Ⓦ www.sv.com Official government website (in Spanish and English), with details of the constitution, an extensive photo album of the country's beauty spots and links to other websites.

# Guatemala

| | |
|---|---|
| **Capital** Guatemala City | and Xinca) |
| **Population** 13 million | **Currency** US dollar ($) |
| **Language** Spanish, although 40% | **Climate** Hot and humid in the |
| speak one of twenty indigenous | lowlands; cooler in the highlands |
| languages (most widely Quiché, | **When to go** February to May |
| Cakchique, Kekchi, Mam, Garífina | **Minimum daily budget** US$15 |

After decades of civil war, Guatemala has in recent years transformed itself into one of Central America's most popular tourist destinations, drawing visitors with its memorable natural landscapes, outstanding archeological sites and, especially, by the strength of its indigenous Maya culture. Compared to the overwhelmingly mestizo populations of other Central American countries, Guatemala remains quintessentially Amerindian: almost half the country's population is pure-blooded Maya, speaking their own languages and living in small rural communities which have barely changed in centuries. The strength of this culture is everywhere apparent, most obviously in the colourful traditional costumes worn across the highlands and in the country's absorbing markets and riotous fiestas, less obviously in the society and beliefs which continue to sustain Guatemala's indigenous communities in the face of constant change and challenges to their traditional way of life.

The strength and longevity of Maya culture is also witnessed by Guatemala's outstanding Maya ruins, including not only Tikal, perhaps the single most impressive archeological site in the whole of Latin America, but also in dozens of less well-known but intriguing sites, many of them atmospherically buried in the pristine rainforests which cover much of the country's eastern lowlands.

Maya culture apart, Guatemala also boasts some of Central America's most memorable landscapes, from the towering volcanoes which surround magical Lake Atitlán in the highlands to the vast expanses of rainforest which cover much of the eastern part of the country, the Petén. In addition, Guatemala is home to Antigua, Central America's loveliest and liveliest colonial city, which is also one of several excellent places in the country in which to study Spanish.

Thankfully, Guatemala has now largely shaken off its turbulent past and put its long and bloody civil war behind it. The country is now relatively safe to visit, although incidents of armed robbery and even rape are still reported, especially around Lake Atitlán – don't walk alone, especially at night. In common with other Central American countries, Guatemala's climate varies between the temperate highlands and the hot and sticky regions along the coast and in the Petén. The rainy season runs from May to October, when jungle trails in the remoter parts of the country get very muddy.

**One week**

- Antigua–Lake Atitlán.
- Livingston–Río Dulce–Tikal–Belize.
- Guatemala City–Sololá–Chichicastenango–Ixil triangle–La Mesilla.

**Two weeks**

- Corinto–Puerto Barrios–Livingston–Río Dulce–Tikal–Antigua–Lake Atitlán–Ixil triangle–Mexico.

**One month**

- El Salvador–Antigua–Lake Atitlán–Sololá–Chichicastenango–Ixil triangle–Guatemala City–Río Dulce–Tikal–Belize.

# Main attractions

● **Antigua** Formerly the capital of Guatemala, and probably the most beautiful colonial city in Central America, Antigua retains its tranquil atmosphere despite a vibrant gringo scene, based around the city's dozens of language schools. Dating back to the Spanish conquest, the city's Easter Week (Semana Santa) celebrations are the most extravagant in the country.

● **Lake Atitlán** In the highlands, a hundred kilometres north of Guatemala City, Lake Atitlán is hemmed in by three soaring volcanoes and surrounded by a string of intriguing lakeside Maya villages, where traditional life continues more or less unchanged, despite the hordes of tourists who now descend on the lake. It's possible to walk round the lake in four or five days – the less energetic will also find plenty of day hikes, while boats regularly travel across the lake from village to village. Panajachel is the lake's principal community and the main base for most tourists to the area, with an abundance of cheap hotels and a long-established gringo scene.

● Sololá market Set high up on a hill-side overlooking Lake Atitlán, the village of Sololá is home every Friday to one of Central America's finest markets, with thousands of Maya traders in colourful woven clothes descending at dawn from the surrounding hills to sell their wares.

● Tikal Considered by many to be the finest of all Maya sites, the ruined city of Tikal – which at its height around 500 AD was one of the most powerful and populous cities in the region – lies in the far east of the country, its ruined temples soaring majestically out of undisturbed rainforest which is home to monkeys, toucans and parakeets.

● Volcán Pacaya Just south of Guatemala City, Pacaya is one of Central America's most active and spectacular volcanoes, with dramatic night-time eruptions of molten orange lava. Pacaya is easily reached by public transport and has impressive views from its summit, which can be climbed in a day – but check on the volcano's current state of activity first.

## Also recommended

● Río Dulce Starting in Lívingston on Guatemala's Caribbean coast, the spectacular journey along the Río Dulce passes through a steep, narrow gorge, hemmed in by sheer walls of tropical vegetation, before opening out into tranquil Lake Izabal, which has some lovely beaches to swim from and boat trips around its shores.

● Ixil triangle Set in the verdant Cuchumatanes mountains at the northern edge of the Western Highlands, the remote Ixil region is one of the most tra-

ditional areas in Central America's most traditional country, whose Maya inhabitants speak a rare language and maintain their traditional way of life. The area has some beautiful walking trails, while its three main towns – Nebaj, Chajul and Cotzal – are made of up picturesque white adobe houses and cobbled streets.

● Fiesta in Todos Santos A famously traditional village in the Cuchumatanes mountains, Todos Santos hosts a riotous annual fiesta on November 1 (All Saints or Todos Santos day) with all-day horse races, marimba music and relentless drinking.

● Santo Tomás, Chichicastenango The attractive small town of Chichicastenango is home both to a famous (though touristy) market and also to one of Guatemala's most intriguing churches, Santo Tomás. Originally built in 1540 on the site of a Maya altar, the church offers a fascinating glimpse into the unique world of Maya religion, with its strange mix of indigenous and Catholic beliefs, with a fascinatingly bizarre mix of Christian saints and indigenous shamans.

## Routes in and out

There are direct daily flights to Guatemala City from cities in the USA including Miami, Houston, Chicago and Los Angeles. Many travellers from Europe fly directly to Mexico City or Cancún and make their way overland. Travelling overland, Guatemala has frontiers with four countries – Mexico, Belize, Honduras and El Salvador. The border at Florido is conveniently close to the ruins of Copán in Honduras. A bus from Flores (near Tikal in the Petén) goes to Belize City and straight through Belize to the Mexican border town of Chetumal. There are numerous other borders between Guatemala and Mexico. The most popular crossing to El Salvador is at Asuncíon Mita on the Panamerican Highway.

# Itineraries

## One week

● Spend a few days in Antigua and then move on to Lake Atitlán.

● From Honduras, cross into Guatemala on the Caribbean coast and travel upriver from Lívingston along the Río Dulce to Lake Izabal. Continue from here by road, to Tikal, before moving on to Belize.

● From Guatemala City, head west to the Ixil triangle via the market towns of Sololá and Chichicastenango. Spend a few days hiking in the Cuchumatanes mountains, and then cross into Mexico at La Mesilla.

## Two weeks

● From Antigua, go to Lake Atitlán and spend five days walking round the lake. Then travel north to Tikal and explore the rainforests of the Petén and some of the lesser-known Maya sites nearby.

● Cross the border from Honduras at Corinto and go by boat to Lívingston. Take a trip down the Río Dulce and then travel by road to Tikal. From Tikal head south to Antigua and Lake Atitlán and spend several days in each place.

Visit the Ixil trangle for some trekking and then head west into Mexico.

## One month

● From El Salvador, travel west to Antigua (you could stop for a week of Spanish study in one of the town's language schools), Lake Atitlán and the market towns of Sololá and Chichicastenango. Loop back to Guatemala City for the main cross-country route to Río Dulce. Take a boat trip down the river, then travel by road to Tikal and the Petén, before moving on to Belize.

# Guatemala online

**Guatemala Travel**
Ⓦ**www.guatemala.travel.com.gt**
Tourist website with brief facts and more detailed information split into regions or themes, as well as listings and a chatroom.

**Guatemala Web**
Ⓦ**www.guatemalaweb.com** Excellent website created by the owner of the *Posada Belén* hotel in Guatemala City, with articles and links on everything from visa requirements, the locations of cash machines, and the current government, to Guatemalan charities, festivals and cuisine.

**Siglo Veintiuno**
Ⓦ**www.sigloxxi.com** The website of the daily newspaper, with crisp articles on domestic and foreign news and features on sport, culture and lifestyle.

# The Guianas

**Guyana**
Capital Georgetown
Population 697,000
Language Creole English, Hindi, Urdu
Currency Guyanese dollar (G$)
Climate Tropical – hot all year round, with two rainy seasons (Dec –Jan and April–July)
Best time to go February and March and August to November
Minimum daily budget US$20

**Suriname**
Capital Paramaribo
Population 405,000
Language Dutch, Hindi, Javanese, Chinese
Currency Euro (€)
Climate As Guyana, above
Best time to go As Guyana, above
Minimum daily budget US$20

**French Guiana**
Capital Cayenne
Population 177,500
Language French, Hindi, Chinese, some indigenous languages
Currency Euro (€)
Climate As Guyana, above
Best time to go As Guyana, above
Minimum daily budget US$45

Perched on the northern coast of South America, the three small countries known collectively as the Guianas (Guyana, Suriname and French Guiana) are the least visited in Latin America, with a complex blend of races and cultures that makes them different to any other part of the region.

The three countries share an early history, all originally inhabited by Arawak and Carib peoples. In the sixteenth century, they were settled by the Dutch, English and French, rather than by the Spanish and Portuguese. Slaves were brought in from West Africa until slavery was abolished, after which indentured labourers were imported from other colonies, especially India and Indonesia. Today, Guyana and Suriname reflect this racial history with Creole, Hindi and Javanese spoken alongside the official languages, and temples and mosques almost as common as churches.

This is not the case in French Guiana, however, which is still a department of France – and the only remaining colony in mainland South America – with European living standards and prices to match. That said, it's only the urban areas that have the infrastructure, as well as what little French culture exists (notably restaurant cuisine).

Away from the coast – home to capital cities Georgetown, Paramaribo and Cayenne – all three countries comprise a largely unsettled wilderness, with vast tracts of unspoilt rainforest. (Suriname alone is said to contain more virgin jungle than almost all of Central America put together, and 85 percent of the country is classified as inaccessible.) Not surprisingly, ecotourism is beginning to take off in all three Guianas, and there are wonderful opportunities for wildlife spotting, trekking off the beaten track and bush camping – either in a

THE GUIANAS
& SURINAME

**One week**
• Cayenne–Kourou–Îles du Salut.
• Georgetown–Lethem–Iwokrama Rainforest Programme–Georgetown.
• Paramaribo–Raleighvallen/Voltzberg Nature Reserve.

**Two weeks**
•Georgetown–Lethem–Iwokrama–Georgetown–Paramaribo–Raleighvallen.
•Paramaribo–Cayenne–Kourou–Îles de Salut.

ATLANTIC OCEAN

N

VENEZUELA

Shell Beach

Georgetown

GUYANA

Kaieteur Falls

Paramaribo

Îles du Salut

Kourou    Cayenne

Iwokrama

RALEIGHVALLEN/
VOLZBERG
NATURE PARK

FRENCH
GUIANA

SURINAME

Lethem
RUPUNUNI
SAVANNAH

BRAZIL

0          300 km

spartan tent or at one of many swanky eco-lodges.

Infrastructure in the Guianas is still very basic and exploring these countries is not for the faint-hearted. Travelling might mean taking a horrendously bumpy truck journey on one of the few roads in existence or, more likely, an uncomfortable boat ride down one of many rivers. For the most part, the Guianas are relatively crime-free, with the exception of Georgetown, Guyana's capital – even during the day, some areas of the city are best avoided.

## Main attractions

● **Kaieteur Falls (Guyana)** The Kaieteur waterfalls, situated on the upper Potaro river and surrounded by unspoilt forest, are one of the world's most spectacular, plunging down a sheer drop of 228m. Most people fly in on a day-trip from Georgetown – January, June and July are the best months to see the falls at their fullest.

● **Iwokrama Rainforest Programme (Guyana)** This 3880-square-kilometre conservation project is home to an exceptionally wide range of wildlife and is one of the best places in Latin America for spotting jaguars. You can also take guided treks through the forest to Mount Iwokrama and boat trips along the Burro-burro and Essequibo rivers.

● **Paramaribo (Suriname)** Suriname's lively capital is a melting pot of the country's diverse cultures – a wooden cathedral rubs shoulders with one of the biggest mosques in the Caribbean, with several Hindu temples nearby. There's some fine Dutch colonial architecture to boot, while on Sundays you can witness the unusual spectacle of the locals taking their pet birds to Independence Square for the weekly birdsong competition.

● **Raleighvallen/Voltzberg Nature Reserve (Suriname)** On the Coppename River, this rainforest park includes the Voltzberg peak, which is usually climbed at sunrise for spectacular views. It's also possible to arrange a tour of the Maroon villages and rapids in the area.

● **Cayenne (French Guiana)** One of the prettiest capital cities in South America, with balconied wooden houses reminiscent of New Orlean's French Quarter. The city's street life centres on the Place des Palmistes, home to lots of outdoor cafés, while the city's Village Chinois has the best nightlife – live reggae – though you shouldn't go there alone. Also worth a visit is the Musée Départemental, an eccentric collection of assorted wildlife, butterflies and paintings of life in the country's penal colonies.

● **Îles de Salut (French Guiana)** These tiny islands were the location of the notorious penal colonies which Henri Charrière made famous in *Papillon*. Popular with visitors because of their atmospheric ruins, they also have abundant wildlife and wild, palm-fringed beaches.

## Also recommended

● **Shell Beach (Guyana)** Stretching for some 140km along the coast of Guyana, Shell Beach is an important nesting ground for turtles (April–June) and has a profusion of birds, including macaws and toucans. Occasionally it's possible to see rare river dolphins nearby, too.

● **Lethem (Guyana)** In the far southwest of Guyana, Lethem is the gateway to a number of wildlife adventures and several of the country's best eco-lodges. Here, the Rupununi savannah, a large area of flat grassland, has great birdspotting; there are waterfalls at Moco-Moco; and the Amerindian villages of Annai and Surama have set up ecotourism projects that take visitors on night trekking, boating and Land Rover trips. The town itself is friendly and hosts a rodeo at Easter which attracts cowboys from all over the savannah.

● **Surinamese food** Suriname's food is richly varied, showing a range of culinary influences that mirrors the country's history, with Indonesian dishes such as *bami goreng* (fried noodles) served up alongside Indian rotis and samosas and West Indian-inspired *pinda soep* (peanut soup with plantain dumplings).

● **Kourou (French Guiana)** Kourou is the location for a large space station that houses the European Space Agency's Ariane programme. With advance reservations, it's possible to tour the site – and maybe even watch one of the annual rocket launches.

● **Carnival (French Guiana)** Carnival in French Guiana is Afro-Caribbean in style, with four days of unique and colourful parades, including Lundi Gras, which mocks the institution of marriage with men dressed as brides and women as grooms, and Mardi Gras, the next day, which sees locals dressed as devils in red outfits with horns and pitchforks.

## Routes in and out

There are daily flights to Guyana from both New York and Miami; from Europe you'll have to go via Antigua, Port of

Spain or Barbados in the Caribbean. To Suriname, there are direct flights from Amsterdam several times a week, as well as from Miami, Port of Spain and Curaçao in the Dutch Antilles. There are daily flights to French Guiana from Paris, Guadeloupe and Martinique, plus four times weekly from Miami.

It's not possible to travel by land between Guyana and Venezuela. Border crossings between the Guianas are complicated and because smuggling is rife, you may be checked several times – many tourists prefer to fly from one capital to another. Between Guyana and Brazil there's just one remote border crossing by ferry near Lethem in the Rupununi savannah (not always accessible in the rainy season). Between Guyana and Suriname, a ferry runs from Corriverton to Niew Nickerie, both coastal towns. Suriname and French Guiana are connected by frequent ferries from Albina to St Laurent-du-Maroni and a good connecting road to Cayenne. To reach Brazil from French Guiana, you'll need to hire a motorized canoe to take you across the Oiapoque river (15min) from St-Georges de L' Oiapoque (which is only accessible by plane from Cayenne) to Oiapoque and onto Macapá – it's much easier to fly all the way.

## Itineraries

### One week

● Guyana (dry season only) Take a truck from Georgetown to Lethem in the Rupununi savannah and then on to the Iwokrama Rainforest Programme, returning to Georgetown by air. Alternatively, use the capital as a base for day-trips to the Kaieteur Falls and Shell Beach.

● Suriname Soak up the atmosphere of *Carnaval* in Paramaribo and then

recover at the Raleighvallen/Voltzberg Nature Reserve.

● French Guiana From Cayenne, go west to Kourou, tour the space station and then take a boat to the Îles de Salut.

### Two weeks

● After a week in Guyana (see above) cross into Suriname and go from Paramaribo to Raleighvallen/Volzberg Nature Reserve.

● Or start your fortnight in Paramaribo, explore the interior of Suriname and then go south to Cayenne in French Guiana and follow the itinerary above.

### One month

● In a month it's possible to visit the main attractions of all three Guianas and then either fly north to Venezuela from Georgetown or head down into the Brazilian Amazon overland.

## Guianas online

Guyana News and Information
Ⓦ www.guyana.org Large US-based website with an emphasis on politics and diplomatic issues and good links.
Guyana: Land of Six Peoples
Ⓦ www.landofsixpeoples.com Comprehensive and informative, with articles on Guyanese history, society, politics, economics and ethnography
Surinam.net
Ⓦ www.surinam.net Online visa applications, concise general article on Suriname and some listings of tour operators/hotels.
French Guiana Tourist Office
Ⓦ www.guyanetourisme.com Official site of French Guianese Tourist Board with short essays on folklore, history and seasonal events.

# Honduras

**Capital** Tegucigalpa
**Population** 5.6 million
**Language** Spanish, Creole English, Garífuna
**Currency** Lempira (L)
**Climate** Subtropical in the lowlands and temperate in the mountains; the rainy season runs from May to November, while hurricane season is in October and November
**When to go** March to May
**Minimum daily budget** US$10

Honduras is the original Banana Republic. From the late 1800s until the 1950s it was largely run by powerful US fruit companies who controlled not only the national banana trade (which accounted for no less than seventy percent of the country's foreign exports), but also its railways, banks and factories. The US influence lasted well into the twentieth century – while neighbouring El Salvador and Nicaragua suffered years of civil war, Honduras infamously served as the training ground for CIA-funded counter-revolutionaries, and was consequently kept stable by US investment and support throughout the 1980s. Nevertheless, it remains one of Latin America's poorest nations, one of its least developed and least visited.

In October 1998, Hurricane Mitch ripped through Central America, causing most of its destruction in Honduras, where it killed seven thousand people. Large parts of the capital, Tegucigalpa, were flattened and the river valleys of the western highlands turned into rivers of mud. Although international aid and experts helped to repair much of the damage, Honduras is still reeling from the aftershock, with widespread poverty and soaring levels of street crime.

Geographically, Honduras boasts similar terrain – a cool, mountainous interior fringed by a humid Caribbean coastline – to neighbouring Guatemala and Nicaragua. Much of the country is protected by an extensive network of national parks and reserves, including the eastern cloudforest of Sierra de Agalta and the Río Plátano Biosphere Reserve in the remote wetlands of Mosquitia, which protect two of the largest stretches of pristine forest in Central America. The country is also sparsely populated, with fewer inhabitants than El Salvador despite being five times as large, while foreign tourists are also pretty thin on the ground – if you go to Honduras you'll have the place pretty much to yourself, apart from at the backpacker hotspots of Copán and the Bay Islands.

The bad news is that Honduras isn't the safest country in Central America – you'll need to be particularly careful in the Caribbean towns – Tela, La Ceiba, Trujillo – after dark, while the country's second city, San Pedro Sula, is now very dangerous, with rife crack cocaine usage and gang warfare. You should also avoid walking on deserted beaches. Honduras is, however, very cheap, with daily costs among the lowest in Latin America.

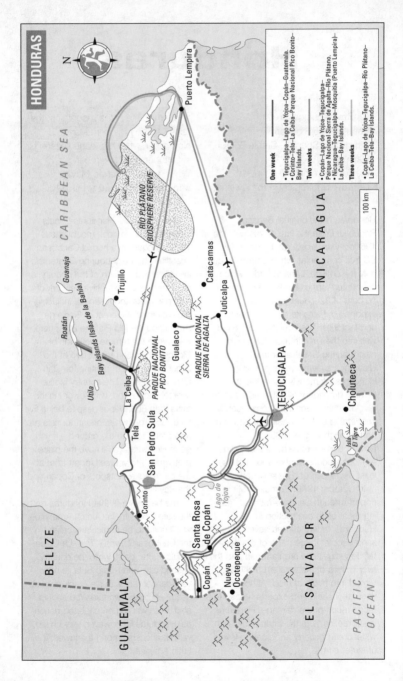

HONDURAS

N

CARIBBEAN SEA

Guanaja

Roatán

Bay Islands (Islas de la Bahía)

Utila

Trujillo

RÍO PLÁTANO
BIOSPHERE RESERVE

Puerto Lempira

La Ceiba

PARQUE NACIONAL
PICO BONITO

Gualaco

PARQUE NACIONAL
SIERRA DE AGALTA

Catacamas

Juticalpa

Tela

San Pedro Sula

TEGUCIGALPA

Corinto

Choluteca

Santa Rosa
de Copán

Lago de Yojoa

Isla
El Tigre

Copán

Nueva
Ocotepeque

BELIZE

GUATEMALA

EL SALVADOR

NICARAGUA

PACIFIC
OCEAN

**One week**
- Tegucigalpa–Lago de Yojoa–Copán–Guatemala.
- Corinto–Tela–La Ceiba–Parque Nacional Pico Bonito–
  Bay Islands.

**Two weeks**
- Copán–Lago de Yojoa–Tegucigalpa–
  Parque Nacional Sierra de Agalta–Río Plátano.
- Nicaragua–Tegucigalpa–Mosquitia (Puerto Lempira)–
  La Ceiba–Bay Islands.

**Three weeks**
- Copán–Lago de Yojoa–Tegucigalpa–Río Plátano–
  La Ceiba–Tela–Bay Islands.

0    100 km

# Main attractions

● **Copán** Copán is one of the most impressive of all Maya sites. Although not large – it's dwarfed in scale by Tikal and Chichén Itzá – the site boasts some of the Maya region's most magnificently carved sculptures, as well as the remarkable Hieroglyphic Stairway. There's also the outstanding on-site Museum of Maya Sculpture, featuring a full-scale replica of the stunning Rosalia temple, along with many original sculptures from the Copán valley. The nearby town, Copán Ruinas, is an attractive and relaxing place to spend a few days.

● **Bay Islands** Honduras's biggest tourist attraction comprises three small Caribbean islands set on a coral reef. The scuba diving is superb and the Bay Islands' calm turquoise waters have become a mecca for divers, with some of the world's cheapest scuba courses on offer. Utila is the most popular of the islands with backpackers and has a firmly entrenched gringo party scene with the occasional rave and regular full-moon parties. The largest island, Roatán, is much quieter, with good hiking trails and more upmarket accommodation.

● **Río Plátano Biosphere Reserve, La Mosquitia** Northeast Honduras is covered with remote and marshy wetlands, known as La Mosquitia after the Miskito Indians who still inhabit it. La Mosquitia is rarely visited – you'll have to fly in – but is home to the most significant nature reserve in Honduras, the Río Plátano Biosphere Reserve, which hosts eighty percent of the country's animal species.

● **Parque Nacional Sierra de Agalta** In the eastern Olancho region of Honduras, the Parque Nacional Sierra de Agalta protects a vast area of pristine and rarely visited cloudforest which is home to many rare animals including tapirs, jaguars and ocelots, as well as over 400 species of birds, including no fewer than 33 different kinds of hummingbird alone.

● **Garífuna villages** Surrounding Tela on the Caribbean coast is a string of sleepy villages with palm-thatched huts which are populated by friendly Garífuna people – the descendants of African slaves brought to the Caribbean to work on banana plantations. Weekends are the best time to visit, when you'll have the chance to hear the seductive drum rhythms of Garífuna music performed by local musicians.

# Also recommended

● **Nightlife in Tela and La Ceiba** These two Caribbean towns are home to the country's wildest nightlife, with vibrant dancehalls, patronized both by locals and foreign tourists, which churn out Garífuna punta rock music, reggae and Latin sounds. The best time to visit is during La Ceiba's carnival in May, during which 200,000 revellers descend on the town and dance until dawn.

● **Lago de Yojoa** Set among the mountains and coffee plantations of Honduras's western highlands, the expansive Lago de Yojoa boasts sparkling blue water and hundreds of bird species. Busy at weekends with wealthy Hondureños, during the week the lake is calm and peaceful.

● **Parque Nacional Pico Bonito** South of La Ceiba, the Parque Nacional Pico Bonito protects a remote expanse of broadleaf, cloud- and pine forests that's crisscrossed by twenty rivers and dominated by the dramatic peak of Pico Bonito (2435m). There is an abundance of wildlife – including armadillos, monkeys and pumas, while the Río Cangrejal has some of the best Class III and IV rapids for whitewater rafting in Central America.

## Routes in and out

There are direct international flights daily from the US (Miami and Houston) to Tegucigalpa, as well as to Honduras's second city, San Pedro Sula, and Roatán. There are no direct flights from Europe or Australasia. The most popular and useful overland border crossing into Guatemala is at El Florido (close to Copán), and there are also several others; you can also cross overland from Honduras into El Salvador and Nicaragua. A weekly boat goes from the Caribbean town of Puerto Cortés to Belize; you may also be able to find a boat leaving from one of Honduras's Caribbean towns to Puerto Cabezas in Nicaragua. Large groups might be able to charter a boat from Omoa to Lívingston in Guatemala.

## Itineraries

### One week

● Travel from the capital Tegucigalpa to the tranquil Lago de Yojoa. From here, continue towards Guatemala via Copán and its pretty village, Copán Ruinas.

● Cross the border from Guatemala to Corinto and then down the Caribbean coast to the lively coastal towns of Tela and La Ceiba. Make a day-trip to Parque Nacional Pico Bonito and then take a boat to the Bay Islands.

### Two weeks

● From Copán and Copán Ruinas travel to Lago de Yojoa. Go eastwards via

the capital, Tegucigalpa, to the Parque Nacional Sierra de Agalta and then north to La Mosquitia and the Río Plátano Biosphere Reserve.

● Cross the border from Nicaragua and travel on to Tegucigalpa. From here, fly to Mosquitia and then on to La Ceiba and the Caribbean coast before heading out to the Bay Islands for a week's scuba diving.

### Three weeks

● In three weeks you can visit all the highlights of Honduras. Travelling from Guatemala, cross the border at El Florido for Copán and then head on to Lago de Yojoa. From Tegucigalpa, head north to La Mosquitia. Fly from here to La Ceiba, visit Tela and the Garífuna villages before taking a boat to the Bay Islands.

## Online

**Honduras This Week**
Ⓦ **www.marrder.com/htw** Award-winning website of the English-language newspaper, with national news coverage, tourist information and listings.
**Honduras Tips**
Ⓦ **www.hondurastips.honduras.com** Website of the free magazine, which has useful tourist information divided into regions and includes town maps marked with hotels and restaurants.
**In-Honduras.com**
Ⓦ **www.in-honduras.com** Comprehensive portal with hundreds of links to media, arts and entertainment, political and tourist websites – and also to personal websites featuring the travel journals of people who have visited Honduras.

# Mexico

**Capital** Mexico City
**Population** 100 million
**Language** Spanish and various indigenous languages including Maya languages and Nahuatl
**Currency** Peso ($)
**Climate** Varies widely, from tropical to desert, with most of the country having two distinct seasons, wet (June–Sept) and dry (Oct–April)
**Best time to go** November to February
**Minimum daily budget** US$25

Mexico's distinctive character and culture have had a powerful effect in shaping outside perceptions of what Latin America is like, and even those who don't know anything about the region probably will have seen poncho-clad Mexican cowboys at the movies, will have tasted the country's spicy, chilli-based cuisine, and perhaps will have heard the unmistakeable strains of mariachi music – all clichés, but all still very much part of Mexican life.

Even so, while to the rest of the Western world Mexico seems to embody all that's most Latin in Latin America, the country does have a distinct identity. Geographically, it's the only Latin American country in North America and it has strong ties with that region, both historic – Texas and California were both once part of Mexico – and modern, through the North American Free Trade Agreement and the fact that so many Mexicans go to the US to work, often illegally. It's partly this tension – between the desire for US-style consumerism and material prosperity on the one hand, and traditional Latin American values on the other – which gives the country so much of its particular character.

For visitors, however, it's the longevity and diversity of Mexican culture that's likely to make the strongest impression. It is home to two of the greatest of Latin America's pre-conquest civilizations, the Aztec and Maya, as well as countless others, and the country's indigenous populations – among them Maya, Mixtec, Zapotec – live much as they have done for hundreds of years, speaking their own languages and cultivating their land in the same way as their forebears did. The monuments of these ancient cultures can be seen everywhere – at the great Maya sites of Chichén Itzá, Uxmal and Palenque (to mention only the most famous) in the Yucatán; at the Zapotec sites of Monte Albán, Yagul and Mitla in Oaxaca state; and at the majestic Aztec sites of Tenochtitlán and Teotihuacán, in and close to present-day Mexico City. The country also boasts one of Latin America's richest legacies of colonial architecture, including florid churches and perfectly preserved cities, ranging from the Zócalo (main plaza) in Mexico City to the picturesque silver-mining towns to the north. All of which offers the visitor a heady mix of cultures – Mexico City, for instance, boasts Aztec ruins, atmospheric Spanish-colonial architecture and ultra-modern architecture within the space of a few miles.

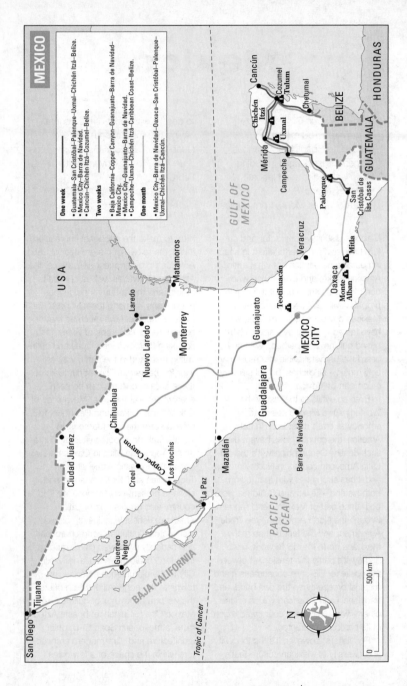

**One week**
- Guatemala–San Cristóbal–Palenque–Uxmal–Chichén Itzá–Belize.
- Mexico City–Barra de Navidad.
- Cancún–Chichén Itzá–Cozumel–Belize.

**Two weeks**
- Baja California–Copper Canyon–Guanajuato–Barra de Navidad–Mexico City.
- Mexico City–Guanajuato–Barra de Navidad.
- Campeche–Uxmal–Chichén Itzá–Caribbean Coast–Belize.

**One month**
- Mexico City–Barra de Navidad–Oaxaca–San Cristóbal–Palenque–Uxmal–Chichén Itzá–Cancún.

Geographically, too, Mexico offers an embarassment of riches, from the arid canyons and cactus-strewn badlands of the north to the tropical rainforests of the south – not to mention the thousands of kilometres of Pacific and Caribbean coastline, dotted with beach resorts ranging from brash Cancún on the Gulf of Mexico (from where it's a short trip out to the world's second longest barrier reef) to Bahía Concepción on the wild peninsula of Baja California.

Mexico's comparatively well-developed economy means that the country has a good infrastructure, with decent roads and decent public transport. There are many holiday resorts on both coasts, and accommodation is widespread and of every conceivable type. Costs are relatively high, although they vary enormously between established tourist resorts and traditional inland regions. Most of Mexico is safe to travel in, with the inevitable exception of Mexico City – take care at night.

## Main attractions

● **Mexico City** The country's capital and the world's second largest city (with a staggering 19 million inhabitants), Mexico City sits at the spiritual and geographical heart of Mexico and is a fascinating blend of pre-Columbian, colonial and modern architecture and culture. Its long list of attractions includes the impressive colonial Zócalo, the world-famous Museo Nacional de Antropología, and Diego Rivera's celebrated murals of historic events, not to mention fascinating markets and frenetic streetlife.

● **Oaxaca** Some 500km southeast of Mexico City, Oaxaca is a colonial town of enduring charm in one of the country's most traditional regions. The city's main square is one of the most atmos-

pheric in the country, with live music in the evenings and local Zapotec and Mixtec Indians in indigenous costumes selling textiles, accessories and clothes. Don't miss the lavish gilded interior of the Santo Domingo church or the Saturday market for locally made shawls, leatherwork, pottery and (most famously) fried grasshoppers.

● **Guanajuato** To the north of Mexico City, in the fertile hills and valleys of the Bajío, are the country's finest colonial remnants, cities founded by the Spanish on the wealth brought by silver- and gold-mining. Perhaps the loveliest of these is Guanajuato, for centuries the wealthiest city in Mexico and declared a UNESCO World Heritage Site in 1988. A maze of steep narrow streets and leafy squares surrounded by the grand colonial mansions of the mine-owners, Guanajuato also has a unique network of subterranean streets running under the city. Other attractions include the macabre Museo de las Momías (mummy museum), which displays over a hundred mummified bodies; the *callejoneadas,* walking tours led by student minstrel groups; and a superb café life.

● **Maya sites in the Yucatán** Mexico has one of the most diverse and impressive collections of pre-Hispanic ruins in Latin America and the most spectacular are the Maya cities situated on the plains of the Yucatán peninsula in south-eastern Mexico. Chichén Itzá is the most impressive with its vertiginous temple, snail-shaped observatory and distinctive reclining statues or Chaac-Mools. The smaller site of Uxmal is celebrated for its decorative style and stone mosaic friezes. Palenque, while not strictly in the Yucatán but rather in neighbouring Chiapas, has the loveliest setting, surrounded by jungle-clad hills.

● **Day of the Dead** (Día de los Muertos) Taking place annually on All

Souls Day and its eve (November 1 & 2), this is the occasion for Mexicans to honour their dead family members and friends. Although a deeply religious ceremony, with all-night vigils held in cemeteries and shrines built in every home, it's also an incredibly picturesque event – papier-mâché skeletons, sweets shaped like skulls and banks of chrysanthemums abound. The place to aim for is Lago de Pátzcuaro, 200km west of Mexico City in the state of Michoacán, and particularly the island of Janítzio.

● **Yucatán's Caribbean coast** In the far southeast of the country, the Yucatán peninsula's Caribbean coast offers long beaches of white sand and azure sea. Although much of the coast south of Cancún is now lined with ugly resorts, there are still pockets of relative tranquility, like Puerto Morelos, Xpu-ha and Tulum. The "Riviera Maya", as this stretch of coast has been named by the Mexican Tourist Board, also gives access to the world's second largest coral reef, which extends as far as Honduras and makes for wonderful scuba diving and snorkelling. The otherwise nondescript island of Cozumel is a mecca for scuba diving, with a world-class series of drop-offs, walls and coral gardens.

● **Food and drink** Mexico is probably the only country in Latin America which you might visit for its food. The country's imaginative cuisine ranges from street snacks of tacos (corn pancakes or tortillas rolled around strips of meat or fish, and served with avocado dip and tomato salsa) to more refined dishes like *mole*, a classic sauce made from chilli and chocolate, all the way through to more outlandish offerings like fried grasshoppers and maggots. The country's drinks are no less irresistible, including the famous spirit tequila.

Mexican beer is excellent, too, with several brands of bottled lager (*cerveza clara*) and dark beer.

## Also recommended

● **Whale-watching in Baja California** The scruffy town of Guerrero Negro in Baja California is the base for Mexico's best whale-watching excursions. During January and February California gray whales arrive from Alaska to give birth in the relatively warm waters of the Laguna Ojo de Liebre, and it's possible to see them swimming calmly alongside their newly born calves from very close quarters.

● **The Copper Canyon** The thirteen-hour train journey from the Pacific town of Los Mochis to Chihuahua is one of the most scenic in the Americas, crossing the Sierra Madre and offering breathtaking views over the 2000-metre deep Copper Canyon. The best stopping point for tourists keen to explore the area on foot is Creel, with its nearby canyons, pine forests and the Basaséachic Falls, claimed as North America's highest single cascade at 254m.

● **San Cristóbal de las Casas** The attractive and relaxing mountain town of San Cristóbal, at the centre of Chiapas state, makes a perfect base for exploring the indigenous Maya communities which dot the surrounding hills, notably the nearby village of San Juan Chamula, whose famous church offers a rare insight into the unique forms of indigenous Christianity, with rituals and imagery drawn freely from both Catholicism and pre-conquest indigenous beliefs.

● **Campeche** The capital of Campeche state, on the Yucatán peninsula, is a lovely walled city with immaculately kept narrow streets and pastel-coloured houses. One of the best ways to see the city is on a picturesque tram ride – trams run along the seafront to the city's archeological museum, housed in an old fort, which numbers jade death masks from the Calakmul Maya site among its treasures.

● **Bahía de Navidad** Bahía de Navidad is one of the most beguiling stretches of Pacific coast in Mexico, directly west of Mexico City. Neither deserted nor overdeveloped, the entire length of the large bay is edged by fine sand and has two small communities, Barra de Navidad and San Patricio-Melaque, which are Mexican rather than gringo in feel and great places to chill out.

## Routes in and out

Mexico is one of the easiest countries in Latin America to reach, with daily flights from the USA to a range of cities and resorts, including Mexico City, Cancún, Acapulco, Monterrey and Veracruz. There are also daily flights from Madrid to Mexico City and Cancún, and thrice weekly flights from London to Mexico City. By land there are dozens of border crossings between the USA and Mexico, the most popular being between San Diego in California and Tijuana; El Paso in Texas and Ciudad Juárez; and Brownsville on the Gulf of Mexico and Matamóros. The most popular land frontiers between Mexico and Guatemala are from Tapachula to either Talismán or Tecun Umán on the Pacific coast of Guatemala. Hourly buses leave from Chetumal in southern Quintana Roo state to Corozal in Belize and on to Belize City. There are also several river crossings in northern Chiapas to the Petén region of Guatemala: Frontera Corozal–Bethel (30min by boat) and La Palma–El Naranjo (4hr) are the least complicated.

## Suggested itineraries

### One week

● Explore Mexico City, with a day-trip to the enormous pyramids of Teotihuacán, and then spend the weekend relaxing in laid-back Barra de Navidad on the central Pacific coast.

● From Cancún, visit the inland Maya ruins at Chichén Itzá and then head south to the island of Cozumel for the region's best scuba diving and snorkelling before moving on to Belize or returning to Cancún.

● Travel overland from Guatemala to San Cristóbal and then on to the Maya sites at Palenque, Uxmal and Chichén Itzá, before looping south again into Belize and to its offshore cayes.

### Two weeks

● Travel south from the US border at San Diego to Baja California and take a ferry across the Sea of Cortez to the mainland to connect with the train through the Copper Canyon. Head south for a few days relaxing on the Pacific coast, before moving on to Mexico City.

● Spend some time in Mexico City, then head north to Guanajuato before making your way across to the Pacific coast and Barra de Navidad for a few days' relaxation.

● Spend a fortnight on the Yucatán peninsula visiting the attractive state capital, Campeche, and the Maya ruins at Chichén Itzá and Uxmal. End your trip relaxing on the Caribbean coast south of Cancún, from where you can easily head into Central America through Belize.

## One month

● After a week in Mexico City take a bus to the Pacific coast and relax for several days in one of the smaller beach towns. Then travel on to Oaxaca and spend five days exploring the attractive market town and its surrounds. Travel south to Chiapas and visit the mountain town of San Cristóbal and the Maya ruins at Palenque. Spend a final week in the Yucatán peninsula sunbathing on the Caribbean beaches and visiting the Maya sites of Uxmal and Chichén Itzá. Then you can either fly out of Cancún or cross into Belize.

# Mexico online

**Mexico Travel Guide**

ⓦ**www.go2mexico.com** Online travel guide with features and articles on culture, the environment and living in Mexico.

**Mexico Connect**

ⓦ**www.mexconnect.com** Monthly e-zine providing information on all aspects of Mexico.

**Mexican Tourist Board**

ⓦ**www.visitmexico.com** The official website of the Mexican Tourist Board has comprehensive listings for each region of the country, with background information, maps, attractions and activities covered in impressive detail.

**Mexicanwave**

ⓦ**www.mexicanwave.com** Excellent English-language website with book reviews, articles on Mexican culture and life, shopping and links.

**The News**

ⓦ**www.thenews.com** Online version of the English-language daily, with news plus features on Mexican food, culture and travel.

# Nicaragua

Capital Managua
Population 4.9 million
Language Spanish, Creole English
on the Caribbean coast, plus
indigenous languages including
Sumo, Rama and Miskito

Currency Córdoba (¢)
Climate Tropical in the lowlands,
cooler in the highlands; rainy season
June to October
When to go December to March
Minimum daily budget US$15

Despite over a decade of peace, Nicaragua is still associated in many people's minds with the long civil war between the left-wing Sandinistas and the US-backed Contras which devastated the country from 1979 to 1990 and in which some 30,000 died. Indeed, whatever has changed in the last ten years, Nicaragua is still paying the price for that war – as well as for the 45 years of brutal dictatorship which preceded it – and currently has the lowest per capita income in Latin America, along with eighty percent unemployment.

Despite the lack of basic infrastructure (some of the roads are memorably appalling, while there's a real paucity of decent hotels, hostels and restaurants), the country is finally starting to realize its potential as a tourist destination – one of the last countries in Latin America to do so. Not that Nicaragua lacks its fair share of compelling attractions: two long coastlines, picturesque highland scenery and a landscape dotted with lakes and volcanoes, including the vast Lake Nicaragua (the largest in Central America) and the beautiful colonial city of Granada that sits on its shore.

Nicaraguans are famously friendly and have yet to become blasé or cynical about tourists in the way that the inhabitants of more visited countries can

be. With so much unemployment, some families (particularly in touristy areas) are happy to take in visitors as paying guests for as little as US$10 a day, with all meals included. This is a great way to gain an insight into daily life, to contribute directly to the local economy and to practise your Spanish.

Nicaragua doesn't have the most temperate of climates – it's very hot and very dry some of the year and very hot and wet the rest – nor does it offer luxurious or even comfortable travel. It is, however, among the cheapest countries in Latin America to visit, as well as being one of the safest and most unspoilt. If you want to step off the Gringo Trail, this is the place to come.

## Main attractions

● **Granada** Granada is one of the oldest and most attractive colonial cities in Latin America and Nicaragua's premier tourist attraction. Founded in 1524, the city's position on the shores of Lake Nicaragua meant that it was formerly an important commercial centre, though it's now subsided into a peaceful somnolence, with wide streets of imposing mansions and an attractive Parque Central.

**One week**
- Granada–Masaya–San Juan del Sur.
- Granada–San Carlos–Solentiname–El Castillo.
- Managua–Matagalpa–Selva Negra–Honduras.

**Two weeks**
- Northern Highlands–Masaya–Granada–Managua–Bluefields–Corn Islands.
- Los Chiles–San Carlos–El Castillo–Solentiname–Ometepe–Granada.

H O N D U R A S

**NICARAGUA**

Puerto Cabezas

*NORTHERN HIGHLANDS*

Estelí  Jinotega

Matagalpa

*CARIBBEAN SEA*

León

MANAGUA

*Little Corn Island*

Masaya  Granada

Bluefields

*Corn Island*

*Lago de Nicaragua*

*PACIFIC OCEAN*

*Isla de Ometepe*

N

San Juan del Sur

*Solentiname Archipelago*

San Carlos

El Castillo

0        100 km

C O S T A R I C A

Los Chiles  *Río San Juan*

● **The Corn Islands** Two tiny islands in the Caribbean, Big Corn and Little Corn are a world apart from the rest of Nicaragua, with a largely black population of Jamaican descent. The islands make a perfect place to kick back for a few days, with sandy, unspoilt beaches, a laid-back pace and locally caught (and mouthwateringly cheap) lobster on every menu; there's also superlative snorkelling around Little Corn.

● **Northern highlands** The cool green hills around Matagalpa and Jinotega in the north of the country offer the perfect escape from the searing heat of the Nicaraguan lowlands, a pine-studded landscape dotted with attractive coffee plantations and highland ranch-

es. There are also several patches of cloudforest in the area, the most accessible being in the grounds of the *Hotel de la Montaña Selva Negra*, a popular eco-lodge with over a dozen walking trails into the forest and great bird-watching.

● **El Castillo** Situated on the Río San Juan roughly halfway between Lake Nicaragua and the Atlantic, the village of El Castillo sits like a mirage in the midst of the remote and scarcely inhabited wetlands that line the river. It's a pretty little place, with wooden houses on stilts over the water and a ruined Spanish fort on a grassy knoll – a perfect place to relax, eat locally caught fish and watch boats sail down the river.

# Also recommended

● **San Juan del Sur** Set on a bay surrounded by towering cliffs, with a string of smaller, undeveloped beaches stretching down the coast nearby, San Juan del Sur is a laid-back seaside town with a growing gringo scene, largely thanks to the surfers who come here in search of uncrowded Pacific waves.

● **Masaya** The market town of Masaya is home to several beautiful churches and a continuing tradition of skilled craftsmanship; the locally produced hammocks are particularly good – you can watch them being woven and even have one custom-made. The best time to visit is during October and November when the town stages a two-month festival to celebrate its patron saint, San Jerónimo. This kicks off with two colourful processions (Sept 30 & Oct 7), when the saint's image is borne on a gaily decorated plinth round the town. Every Sunday until the end of the festival is marked by fireworks, dancing and live marimba music.

● **Solentiname** Situated in the southern corner of Lake Nicaragua, the tiny islands of the Solentiname archipelago represent one of the country's most remote, peaceful and picturesque destinations. Home to an artistic community established by Nicaraguan poet Ernesto Cardenal, Solentiname has three inhabited islands where you can stay and watch the locals painting in their distinctive primitive style, or simply swim in the calm waters of the lake.

● **Ometepe** The island of Ometepe, in the middle of vast Lake Nicaragua, takes its name (originally Ome Tepetl, or "the place of two hills") from the two perfectly conical volcanoes, Volcán Concepción and Volcán Maderas, which tower over it. Most visitors come to climb the volcanoes – it takes seven strenuous hours to ascend and descend Maderas, the smaller of the two, but the view from the top over the lake is stunning.

# Routes in and out

There are several direct flights daily to Nicaragua's capital, Managua, from Miami, as well as a once-daily service from Houston. If you're travelling from Europe, there's a well-priced Martinair flight four times weekly from Amsterdam to San José in Costa Rica, from where you can make your way overland (around 9hr by bus). There's one land crossing between Nicaragua and Costa Rica at Peñas Blancas; you can also cross by river from San Carlos to Los Chiles. There are several land borders between Nicaragua and Honduras – the most popular is El Guasaule in the north of Chinandega province.

# Itineraries

## One week

● From Managua head north to the highlands of Matagalpa and the Selva Negra cloudforest before moving on into Honduras.

● Spend a few days in Granada, visit the market in Masaya and then head south to San Juan del Sur on the Pacific coast.

● Cross Lake Nicaragua by ferry from Granada to the town of San Carlos (16hr), and then visit the islands of Solentiname and El Castillo on the Río San Juan, both accessible by motor boat from San Carlos.

## Two weeks

● Coming south from Honduras, spend several days in the northern highlands, then visit Masaya and Granada. Fly to the town of Bluefields, on the Caribbean coast, from where you can catch a boat to the Corn Islands to relax for a few days before flying back to Managua and moving on to Costa Rica via the border at Peñas Blancas.

● Take the boat from Los Chiles in Costa Rica to San Carlos in Nicaragua, then head down the Río San Juan to El Castillo. Return to San Carlos and visit the Solentiname archipelago for a few days, then take the ferry from San Carlos to Granada across Lake Nicaragua, with a few days' stopover on the island of Ometepe. Spend your last few days exploring Granada.

# Nicaragua online

Nicanet

Ⓦ**www.nicanet.org** Website of a US organization committed to social and economic justice for the people of Nicaragua, with information on current campaigns and issues.

Nicaragua Guide

Ⓦ**www.guideofnicaragua.com** Glossy online tourist magazine, with decent features on where to go and things to do, plus background on Nicaraguan culture.

Nicaraguan Tourist Board

Ⓦ**www.intur.gob.ni** Official website of the Nicaraguan Tourist Board, with well-organized information on each region of the country.

# Panamá

Capital Panamá City
Population 2.9 million
Language Spanish, English and
minority indigenous languages
Currency US dollar ($), also
referred to as Balboa (B)

Climate Tropical
Best time to go December–April
(dry season)
Minimum daily budget US$25

Occupying the narrow, S-shaped isthmus that links Central and South America, Panamá is arguably the most underrated and overlooked country amongst travellers to Latin America. In part, this is because the land border between Colombia and Panamá across the Darién Gap (see p.113) is virtually impassable, making Panamá a dead end for those heading south from Central America, but mainly it seems that Panamá suffers something of an image problem: known only for its interoceanic canal and for its longstanding dominance by the US, it's still seen by many outsiders as a virtual North American colony, even though the last US troops left in 1999.

In fact North American cultural influence, though strong, is only one among many to affect this vital thoroughfare of international trade: Spanish, African, West Indian, Chinese, Indian, European – all have contributed to a compelling cultural mix, creating a society which is surprisingly cosmopolitan, open-minded and outward-looking. At the same time, Panamá is also home to some of the most fascinating and unassimilated indigenous cultures in Central America, such as the indigenous Emberá communities, who still hunt and practise traditional subsistence agriculture in the

rainforest within just 30km of the high-rise banking district of Panamá City.

Obviously, the mighty Panamá Canal remains the country's defining feature and the main attraction for visitors, but Panamanians rightly insist their country is "much more than just a canal". Most travellers who make it to Panamá are surprised by its outstanding natural beauty. With 1600km of Pacific and 1280km of Caribbean coast, Panamá boasts unspoiled beaches and coral reefs to match almost any in the region, making it a great place for snorkelling, diving, surfing or just lying around on the beach. And although it is Costa Rica that has achieved world renown as an ecotourism destination, in terms of pristine wilderness and ecological diversity, Panamá has little reason to envy its neighbour. Over half the country is covered by dense tropical forest, and large areas are protected by a system of nature reserves and national parks. With little tourist development, the infrastructure for visiting these protected areas is as yet limited, but while this may put some people off, to others it just adds to the attraction: whether watching turtles laying their eggs by night on pristine beaches or searching for resplendent quetzals in the high cloudforest, visitors to Panamá's national parks are unlikely

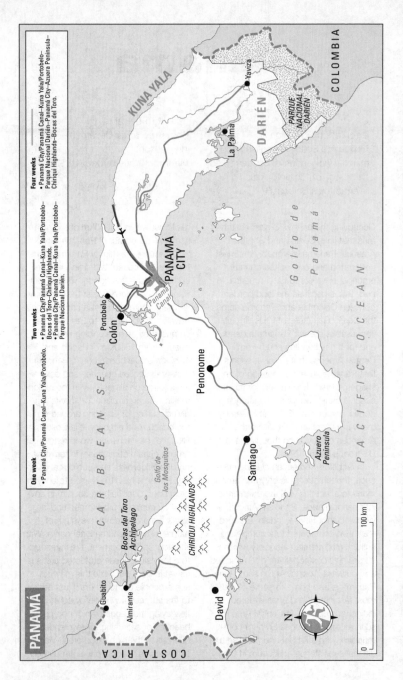

PANAMÁ

**One week**
• Panamá City/Panamá Canal–Kuna Yala/Portobelo.

**Two weeks**
• Panamá City/Panamá Canal–Kuna Yala/Portobelo–Bocas del Toro–Chiriquí Highlands.
• Panamá City/Panamá Canal–Kuna Yala/Portobelo–Parque Nacional Darién.

**Four weeks**
• Panamá City/Panamá Canal–Kuna Yala/Portobelo–Parque Nacional Darién–Panamá City–Azuera Peninsula–Chiriquí Highlands–Bocas del Toro.

to share the experience with more than a handful of other people, and with little mass tourism, Panamanians have not yet become jaded with foreign visitors, though the fact that it's now often described as "like Costa Rica twenty years ago" suggests Panamá is finally catching on with travellers to Central America keen to escape the crowds.

# Main attractions

● **Panamá City** Cosmopolitan and contradictory, Panamá City combines the intrigue and energy of its modern high-rise banking district with the laid-back street life and Spanish colonial architecture of the historic city centre and the antiseptic order of the former US-controlled canal-zone suburbs. With a spectacular setting on the Pacific coast, it's close to some beautiful beaches and surrounded by some of the best-preserved and most accessible tropical rainforest in the Americas. It's also the best base from which to explore the rest of Panamá, including the canal.

● **Panamá Canal** Almost a century after its construction, Panamá's most famous landmark remains one of the greatest engineering feats of all time, impressive both for its sheer magnitude and its unexpectedly rugged beauty. Linking the Pacific and Atlantic oceans, the canal cleaves a narrow path through pristine rainforest and can easily be visited on a day-trip from Panamá City, either by taking a cruise through the canal, riding the train that runs alongside it, or simply by catching a bus or taxi up to the Miraflores locks, where you can watch massive ships being raised and lowered.

● **Kuna Yala** Stretching almost 400km along the northeastern Caribbean coast, Kuna Yala – also known as the San Blas Archipelago – is the self-governing homeland of the indigenous Kuna, who live in splendid isolation on a series of tiny palm-fringed coral atolls strung out along the densely forested coast. Best known for the distinctive costumes worn by the women, the Kuna enjoy almost total autonomy, a status that has helped them maintain their unique and compelling traditional culture and way of life. This wildly beautiful region can easily be reached by light aircraft from Panamá City, and basic accommodation and other services – run by the Kuna themselves – are available on several islands.

● **Bocas del Toro** Long one of the best-kept travellers' secrets in Central America, the remote and beautiful Bocas del Toro archipelago on Panamá's northwestern Caribbean coast is now the scene of growing tourist development. However, this has yet to change the laid-back approach to life adopted by the region's indigenous, English-speaking Afro-Antillano population, and the archipelago's richly varied ecosystems – tropical forests, deserted beaches, coral reefs, crystalline waters teeming with marine life – are still largely unspoilt.

● **Chiriqui Highlands** In the far west of Panamá on the Costa Rican border, the Chiriqui Highlands are a beautiful region of cloudforest-covered peaks, fertile valleys dotted with orange groves and coffee plantations, and peaceful mountain villages. From the town of Boquete you can walk or drive up to the peak of the 3475-metre Volcán Barú, from where (on a clear day at least) you can see both the Pacific and Atlantic oceans, while the pristine cloudforests of nearby Parque Nacional La Amistad are perhaps the best place in all Central America to see the rare resplendent quetzal.

# Also recommended

● **Portobelo and the Costa Arriba**
Though the infamously poor and dangerous Caribbean port of Colón should be avoided at all costs, the nearby Costa Arriba, which stretches northeast of the city, covers an isolated and enticing region of palm-fringed beaches, coral reefs and laid-back fishing villages, while the historic town of Portobelo preserves its formidable colonial fortifications, built to protect Spanish treasure fleets from pirate attack.

● **Azuero Peninsula** Jutting out into the Pacific west of Panamá City, the dry and scrubby Azuero Peninsula is considered the cradle of Panamanian rural traditions and folklore and is home to many vibrant religious fiestas. It's also fringed with huge deserted white-sand beaches and boasts two offshore nature reserves: Isla Iguana, which is excellent for diving and snorkelling, and the rarely visited Isla Cañas, where sea turtles nest in large numbers.

● **Darién** Though guerrillas, drug traffickers and bandits mean that the adventurous journey overland across the Darién Gap to Colombia (see p.113) is now strictly off-limits, the splendid wildlife-rich rainforests of Parque Nacional Darién – one of the most biodiverse regions on earth – remain largely safe to visit, either independently or on an organized tour from Panamá City.

● **The Canopy Tower** Set amid the lush rainforests that protect the watershed of the Panamá Canal, the Canopy Tower is one of Latin America's best and most unusual eco-lodges: a former US military radar station that's been stripped and refitted with comfortable rooms and galleries overlooking the rainforest canopy in one of the world's best bird-watching locations.

# Routes in and out

Panamá City is a major transportation hub and is well connected by plane to other Latin American capitals, the US and Europe. Travelling overland, there are road crossings between Panamá and Costa Rica on both the Pacific and Caribbean coasts – as a consequence, western Panamá sees more backpackers than the rest of the country combined. Overland travel between Panamá and Colombia is virtually impossible, however. Drug trafficking and guerrilla and bandit activity have made the famous crossing of the Darién Gap (see p.113) extremely dangerous – several travellers have been kidnapped and killed in recent years. The ferry service between Colón and Cartagena in Colombia no longer operates, but private yachts often carry travellers on this route, passing through the beautiful San Blas archipelago, for about the same price as a flight – ask around at the yacht clubs in Balboa (Panamá City) or Cristobal (Colón), or at the *Voyager International Hostel* in Panamá City.

# Itineraries

## One week

● Spend a couple of days exploring Panamá City, another day or two visiting the Panamá Canal and the surrounding rainforest – possibly staying at the Canopy Tower – and then either fly to one of the islands of Kuna Yala or head up to Portobelo on the Caribbean coast for a few days – at a push you could just about manage to do both.

## Two weeks

● Cover the same ground as in the one-week itinerary at a more leisurely pace, then either fly or take a bus up to Bocas del Toro in the northwest for a few days' snorkelling and beachcombing. Finish your trip by travelling west to explore the Chiriqui Highlands.

● Do the one-week itinerary, then head east for a rainforest adventure in Darién.

## One month

● A month will give you enough time to visit all Panamá's main attractions. Spend ten days or so taking in the attractions listed in the one-week itinerary, and four or five days making a trip down to the Parque Nacional Darién. Return to Panamá City and head west by road to the Chiriqui Highlands, stopping off on the way for a few days in the Azuero Peninsula, and then continue across the continental divide to Bocas del Toro.

# Panamá online

### ANCON
Ⓦ **www.ancon.org** Website of the National Conservation Association, Panamá's biggest and most influential environmental group, with general information on Panamá's national parks, ecology and endangered species and voluntary work opportunities.

### ANCON Expeditions
Ⓦ **www.ecopanama.com** The website

of ANCON expeditions, the highly rated commercial arm of the National Conservation Association and Panamá's foremost ecotourism operator, with information and booking details for guided tours throughout the country and of their exclusive lodges in Darién.

### IPAT
Ⓦ **www.ipat.gob.pa** The site of the Panamánian Tourist Institute, IPAT, with plenty of basic information on Panamá's many attractions and good links to hotels, airlines and tour agencies.

### Panamá Tours
Ⓦ **www.panamatours.com** One-stop resource for travel to Panamá, with plenty of general information on tourist attractions and links to all kinds of related sites.

### Panamá Canal Authority
Ⓦ **www.pancanal.com** Official site with plenty of information and news, a history of the canal in English and Spanish, plus pictures of the canal and a live webcam.

### Latin American Network Information Centre, Panamá
Ⓦ **lanic.utexas.edu/la/ca/panama** An excellent resource, with links to a massive range of Panamá-related sites divided into themes including art and culture, environment, government, indigenous peoples and news, as well as other portals, directories and search sites.

# Paraguay

| | |
|---|---|
| **Capital** Asunción | hot and humid in the east, hotter |
| **Population** 5.5 million | and semi-arid in the west |
| **Languages** Spanish and Guaraní | **Best time to go** May to September |
| **Currency** Guaraní (G/) | **Minimum daily budget** US$20 |
| **Climate** Subtropical to temperate; | |

A remote backwater in the centre of the continent, Paraguay is one of the least-known and least-visited countries in South America. Very few travellers come to Paraguay, and those that do tend to pass through only briefly as part of a multi-country trip. The reason for this is simple: in terms of conventional tourist attractions, Paraguay has little to offer, especially when compared to neighbouring countries like Brazil and Argentina. There are no soaring mountain ranges, beautiful beaches or lost cities here, and the lack of infrastructure and limited tourist development make the more interesting wilderness areas difficult to reach. That said, Paraguay is not without appeal, and just coming here takes you firmly off the beaten track, offering a far more authentic (if much less dramatic) experience of Latin America than many more popular destinations.

Paraguay's geographical isolation has combined with a history of traumatic wars (in 1865–70 almost half the population died when Paraguay took on the combined might of Brazil, Argentina and Uruguay in the disastrous War of the Triple Alliance) and long-running military dictatorships (the last military ruler, General Stroessner, ruled for 34 years until he was deposed in 1988) to create an inward-looking society with a strong sense of national identity that can feel totally cut off from the outside world. Although few Paraguayans would describe themselves as indigenous, almost all speak the indigenous language Guaraní as well as Spanish, making Paraguay the most bilingual country in the region. Both are official languages, but outside the cities Guaraní is far more widely used, and even in the capital, Asunción, you'll hear its musical lilt every time you pass Paraguayans gathered to share a chat and sip the ubiquitous yerba mate', a stimulating herbal tea drunk from gourds through metal straws that is both the country's favourite pleasure and one of its main exports.

Paraguay is one of the poorest countries in South America, its economy based largely on agriculture and smuggling (or "re-exporting") goods to neighbouring Brazil and Argentina – contraband flourished under Stroessner's corrupt military regime and the black economy is still thought to account for up to half Paraguay's gross domestic product.

Geographically, Paraguay is divided into two distinct regions by the river that gives it its name. East of the Río Paraguay is the country's traditional rural heartland, a rich agricultural region of rolling hills covered by well-watered grasslands and patches of subtropical

One week ─────

• Asunción–Parque Nacional Ybicuy.
• Asunción–Jesús–Trinidad.

Two weeks ─────

•Asunción–Parque Nacional Ybicuy/Jesús–Trinidad–
Concepción–Filadelfia/Parque Nacional Defensores del Chaco.

forest. North and west of the river stretches the Gran Chaco, a harsh wilderness
region of low plains covered by swamp,
scrub and impenetrable thorn scrub
stretching north to the Bolivian border, an
area rich in wildlife and home only to scattered indigenous groups and remote settlements of German-speaking Mennonite
farmers. In neither region is the scenery
particularly spectacular, but travelling
across the Chaco is still one of the great
wilderness journeys in South America,
particularly if you're heading to or from
Bolivia, while the more populous agricultural region east of the Río Paraguay, with
its deep-rooted cultural traditions and
sleepy towns and villages, has an under-
stated but timeless rural charm.

# Main attractions

● **Asunción** Though it's the political
and commercial heart of Paraguay,
Paraguay's riverside capital retains the
sedate atmosphere of a provincial backwater and an old-fashioned feel, with
elegant nineteenth-century public buildings and some interesting – though
rather militaristic – monuments and
museums, dedicated above all to former
dictators and the fallen heroes of
Paraguay's catastrophic wars. The pretty countryside and traditional farming
towns of the surrounding rural heartland
– including the lace-making centre of
Itaugúa – can be visited on day-trips

from the city, following a route known as the Circuito de Oro.

● **Parque Nacional Ybicuy** About 150km southeast of Asunción, this easily accessible region of rainforest-covered hills dissected by tumbling streams with numerous waterfalls has plenty of good hiking trails.

● **Gran Chaco** Covering more than half of Paraguay, the wildlife-rich Gran Chaco is one of the last great wilderness regions of South America, a vast plain covered by swamp, savannah and scrub and inhabited only by indigenous tribes and hardy colonies of Mennonites, a German-speaking religious sect. The easiest way to visit the Chaco is by making the arduous journey by bus or truck through the heart of the region and on into Bolivia. With more time and money, you can visit the remote Parque Nacional Defensores del Chaco by jeep with an Asunción-based tour company.

● **Jesuit missions** In Trinidad and Jesús, close to the southern city of Encarnación on the Argentine border, stand the ruined churches and other buildings of the utopian Jesuit mission settlements established here in the eighteenth century, their well-preserved stone structures a vivid testimony to the artistic heights reached by the indigenous Guaraní under the tutelage of a handful of European priests.

## Also recommended

● **Río Paraguay** Travelling on one of the irregular passenger boats that ply the mighty Río Paraguay between Asunción and Concepción is one of the best ways of seeing the tranquil rural heartland of Paraguay.

● **Itaipú Dam** Close to the unattractive smuggler's paradise of Ciudad del Este on the Brazilian border lies the massive Itaipú Dam, one of the world's biggest hydroelectric projects. Completed in 1984, it's a monumental sight – though apparently nowhere near as spectacular as the dramatic waterfalls drowned by the reservoir after it was built.

● **Turismo Rural** A number of farms and *estancias* or ranches accept paying guests, rather like "dude ranches" in the US, allowing you to experience at first hand the traditional way of life in Paraguay's rural heartland.

## Routes in and out

The international airport at Asunción has frequent direct flights to most other South American capitals and to the US. By land, you can cross the border from Brazil between Foz de Iguaçu and Ciudad del Este in the east and between Ponta Porã and Pedro Juan Caballero in the northeast. From Argentina there are road crossings between Asunción and Clorinda and between Encarnación and Posadas in the south, and you can also enter Paraguay from Puerto Iguazú via Foz de Iguaçu in Brazil. The overland route to and from Bolivia is along the Trans-Chaco Highway, an adventurous journey through the heart of the great Chaco wilderness. Alternatively, you can also enter and leave Paraguay on one of the irregular river boats that travel the Río Paraguay between Asunción and Corumbá in Brazil.

## Itineraries

### One week

● Spend a couple of days in Asunción, explore some of the surrounding countryside, and then either visit the Jesuit missions of Jesús and Trinidad or head out to the Parque Nacional Ybicuy for a couple of days hiking.

## Two weeks

● Follow the one-week itinerary, then (erratic schedules allowing) travel up the Río Paraguay to Concepción and continue into the Chaco, either by taking a bus to the Mennonite centre of Filadelfia (and, if you're heading that way, on to Bolivia), or by joining an organized tour from Asunción into the Parque Nacional Defensores del Chaco.

# Paraguay online

### Ecotours
Ⓦwww.ecotour.com.py Information on rural tourism in Paraguay, including details of numerous traditional *estancias* (ranches) that accept paying guests.

**Latin American Network Information Centre, Paraguay**
Ⓦlanic.utexas.edu/la/sa/paraguay
Links to an extensive range of Paraguay-related sites divided into themes including art and culture, environment, government, indigenous peoples and news, as well as other portals, directories and search sites.

**Senatur**
Ⓦwww.senatur.gov.py Official Paraguayan tourist office site with good general information on the country's attractions and links to other relevant sites.

**Yagua.com**
Ⓦwww.yagua.com Comprehensive Paraguayan internet directory with links to all manner of Paraguay-related sites, including tourist information and the media.

# Peru

**Capital** Lima
**Population** 27.5 million
**Language** Spanish, Quechua, plus over thirty other indigenous languages
**Currency** Nuevo Sol (S/)
**Climate** Tropically hot and humid in the Amazon lowlands, drier along the desert coast and much cooler with altitude in the Andes
**Best time to go** May to September (dry season for the highlands and Amazon), December to March for the coast
**Minimum daily budget** US$15

Peru is one of the most varied and fascinating countries in Latin America, a place to which even seasoned travellers return again and again, drawn back by the promise of endless new experiences. It's best known as home of the Incas, the rulers of the largest and most powerful of Latin America's pre-Columbian empires, and as the location of Machu Picchu, the original lost city in the jungle that encapsulates much of what outsiders find so mysterious and intriguing about South America. But though Machu Picchu and the Inca heartland around the unforgettable city of Cusco are rightly the main draws for visitors, their fame sometimes obscures the manifold attractions of the rest of the country. The Incas were just the last and best known of many civilizations that rose and fell in Peru before the Spanish conquest, and the whole country is dotted with magnificent archeological sites, with major new finds – from lost cities in the Andes to golden tombs in desert pyramids – being regularly discovered.

The country's astonishing archeological heritage is set amidst fabulously varied scenery, ranging from the deserts of the Pacific coastal strip through the high peaks of the Andes to the seemingly endless expanse of the Peruvian Amazon rainforest. This astounding range of different ecosystems and climates makes Peru one of the most biodiverse countries on earth, home to 84 of the 104 different life zones on the planet and to an incredible variety of plant and animal life. It also makes it an ideal setting for all kinds of adventure sports, including trekking, mountaineering, whitewater rafting and mountain-biking.

This huge range of landscapes is more than matched by the diversity of the population, an intriguing blend of indigenous, Spanish, African and Asian peoples. The most distinctive of these cultures is found in the Andes, where the majority of people are of indigenous descent and speak Quechua, the language of the Inca empire, as their first language. Their Inca heritage is also evident in deep-seated cultural traditions and beliefs, which are manifested most vibrantly in their music and dance and in the many colourful fiestas that combine Catholic and traditional indigenous beliefs and customs.

PERU

COLOMBIA

ECUADOR

Piura

PARQUE NACIONAL
PACAYA-SAMIRIA

Iquitos

Río Amazonas

N

Chachapoyas

Tarapoto

BRAZIL

Cajamarca

Juanjui

Contamana

CORDILLERA BLANCA

Trujillo

Huaraz

PACIFIC
OCEAN

Huancayo

PARQUE
NACIONAL
MANU

Puerto
Maldonado

LIMA

Ayacucho

Machu
Picchu

Islas Ballestas

Pisco

Cusco

**One week**
• Cusco–Machu Picchu.

**Two weeks**
• Cusco–Machu Picchu–Puerto Maldonado.
• Cusco–Puno–Arequipa–Colca Canyon.
• Cusco–Machu Picchu–Lima–
  Trujillo/Isla Ballestas–Nazca Lines.
• Lima–Huaraz–Lima–Islas Ballestas–Nazca.
• Lima–Huaraz–Lima–Iquitos.

**One month**
• Lima–Ayacucho–Cusco–Machu Picchu–
  Puerto Maldonado/Parque Nacional Manu–
  Puno–Arequipa–Colca Canyon–Nazca–
  Islas Ballestas.

Nazca Lines

Lake
Titicaca

BOLIVIA

Colca Canyon

Arequipa

Puno

0          250 km

Tacna

CHILE

Peru's complex ethnic make-up, along with the legacy of conquest and underdevelopment, has produced a volatile political mix, but thankfully the violence of the 1980s and 1990s – when a bloody war between the state and the Maoist rebel group Sendero Luminoso (Shining Path) made large areas of the country too dangerous to visit – is largely a thing of the past. The political situation is now fairly stable (by Peruvian standards, at least), though some remote areas should still be avoided. Peru also has an unfortunate reputation for theft and other scams which, though not entirely undeserved, is exaggerated and shouldn't put you off visiting this fascinating country.

# Main attractions

● **Cusco** The ancient heart of the Inca empire, Cusco is Peru's most famous attraction and one of the most compelling destinations in all Latin America. A beautiful colonial city built amidst the magnificent ruined temples and palaces of the Incas (and still largely inhabited by their Quechua-speaking descendants), Cusco is surrounded by spectacular mountain scenery and remarkable Inca archeological sites, including the monumental fortress of Sacsayhuaman, which towers above the city, and the numerous temples and palaces of the nearby Sacred Valley of the Incas. Cusco is also a great base for trekking, climbing, mountain-biking and whitewater rafting trips and for expeditions into the rainforests of the southern Peruvian Amazon. With all this plus good tourist infrastructure, a lively nightlife scene and some of the most colourful fiestas in the Andes, it's no wonder many travellers end up staying here much longer than they originally planned.

● **Machu Picchu and the Inca Trail** Of all Peru's archeological attractions, the most famous and dramatic is the lost city of Machu Picchu, set amid the dense forests north of the Inca capital, Cusco. You can reach the ruins either by taking a stunning train journey from Cusco or by hiking the Inca Trail, a well-preserved (though increasingly crowded) stone-paved Inca road which passes through spectacular high mountain scenery and numerous Inca sites before plunging down through the cloudforest to Machu Picchu.

● **Huaraz and the Cordillera Blanca** Nestled in the deep valley of the Callejon de Huayllas, Huaraz is the perfect base for trekking and climbing in the spectacular Cordillera Blanca, the highest tropical mountain range in the world, much of which is protected by the Parque Nacional Huascaran. It's also close to Chavín de Huantar, an ancient complex of ruined temples and underground labyrinths decorated with stylized stone carvings that was a major Chavín religious centre more than 2500 years ago.

● **Nazca Lines** Set in the arid coastal strip south of Lima, the Nazca Lines are one of the most mysterious and dramatic ancient sites in South America, a series of massive geometric shapes and animal figures drawn into the ground over some five hundred square kilometres of stony desert – their origins and meaning remain unknown, despite endless speculation.

● **Peruvian Amazon** Covering over half the country, the rainforests of the Peruvian Amazon are amongst the best preserved and least explored in South America. They're also amongst the least accessible, so you may want to save time by flying to one of the Amazon towns from where you can organize a rainforest expedition rather than make the arduous journey by land down the eastern slopes of the Andes. The best place to visit in the region is undoubtedly the stunning Parque Nacional Manu in the southern Peruvian Amazon (accessible on organized tours from Cusco), arguably the most pristine, biodiverse and wildlife-rich national park in all South America. A cheaper alternative in the south is the more accessible Tambopata-Candamo Reserve, reached by boat from Puerto Maldonado, while in the northern Amazon the city of Iquitos, on the banks of the mighty Amazon itself, is the best-organized and established tourism centre, with plenty of companies offering everything from luxury cruises and eco-lodges to rugged survival expeditions and trips into the vast and virtually untouched Parque Nacional Pacaya-Samiria.

● **Arequipa** Set at the foot of the snow-capped El Misti volcano, the city of Arequipa boasts a lovely climate and some of the finest colonial architecture in Peru, including the beautiful Monastery of Santa Catalina. From the city it's easy to organize trips into the surrounding mountains, with the main attraction the spectacular Colca Canyon, the world's deepest, which is an excellent place for trekking, whitewater rafting and condor-spotting.

## Also recommended

● **Lima** With its sprawling shantytowns, chaotic traffic, high crime rate and dismal, fog-bound climate, Lima can seem a pretty daunting and unattractive place. But beyond these first impressions the capital has much to offer, including excellent museums, like the Museo de Oro, and an elegant colonial city centre that's gradually being restored. It also boasts perhaps the finest cuisine in Latin America and a vibrant nightlife scene, and if you stay out in the wealthy seaside suburb of Miraflores you can avoid the worst aspects of the city centre.

● **Lake Titicaca** Though the lakeside city of Puno is a drab, unexciting place, it's the perfect base for exploring the magical scenery of the Altiplano, the high Andean plateau, and above all for making boat trips out across Lake Titicaca to the idyllic islands of Taquile and Amantani, where you can get a real taste of traditional rural Andean culture by staying with an indigenous family.

● **Chachapoyas** Set in the northern highlands, which are usually overlooked in favour of the more famous attractions of the Cusco region, the remote town of Chachapoyas is the centre of a beautiful region of cloudforest-covered mountains dotted with scarcely explored pre-Inca ruins, including the spectacular walled city of Kuelap.

● **Ayacucho** Long off-limits to travellers as the centre of Sendero Luminoso guerrilla activity in the 1980s and 1990s but now safe to visit, the highland city of Ayacucho boasts fine colonial architecture and strong indigenous cultural traditions, making it an excellent place to break the tough overland journey between Cusco and Lima, especially during Easter, when it stages fabulous Semana Santa celebrations.

● **Trujillo** The handsome colonial city of Trujillo on the north coast is surrounded by beautiful deserted Pacific beaches, peaceful fishing villages, and an amazing collection of ancient archeological sites, including the massive earthen pyramids of the Huaca del Sol and Huaca de la Luna, and the monumental ruined adobe city of Chan-Chan. It also boasts Peru's finest regional cuisine, based above all on the excellent local seafood.

● **Islas Ballestas** From the pleasant fishing town of Pisco on the south coast you can take boat trips to the Islas Ballestas, a group of offshore islands, known as the "Poor Man's Galapagos", which teem with sea lions, penguins and other marine birds.

## Routes in and out

Lima is connected by frequent international flights to Europe, the US and most major Latin American capitals. Entering or leaving Peru overland by road across the Bolivian, Chilean and Ecuadorian borders is easy. You can travel to and from Colombia and Brazil by boat along the Amazon River from Iquitos, and there are also several more remote Amazon border crossings with Brazil and Bolivia.

# Itineraries

Taking a local flight – particularly from Lima to Cusco or to Iquitos or Puerto Maldonado in the Amazon – is a good and relatively inexpensive way of maximizing your time. If you're flying into Lima and don't have much time, it can be worth booking a connecting onward internal flight in advance, so you can head on to Cusco without having to leave the airport and go into the city. On longer trips, you're likely to have a day or two in Lima at the beginning and end of your visit – more than enough to get a feel for the capital and take in its main attractions. Remember that you'll need several days to acclimatize to the altitude in the highlands, especially if you're planning to do some trekking.

## One week

● Fly straight up to Cusco and spend the week exploring the city and the surrounding region, including a visit to Machu Picchu and the Sacred Valley of the Incas.

● Travel south along the coast from Lima, visiting the Islas Ballestas and the Nazca Lines before heading inland to Arequipa, from where you can return to Lima by air or continue overland to Chile.

## Two weeks

● Fly to Cusco and spend at least a week in and around the city, or longer if you to walk the Inca Trail or one of the many other trekking routes in the region, then fly down to Puerto Maldonado in the southern Amazon and spend a few

days in a rainforest lodge on the Tambopata River.

● Spend a week in the Cusco region, then take a train down to Puno on the shores of Lake Titicaca and visit one of the islands on the lake. From Puno, take another train to Arequipa and spend a few days exploring the city and visiting the Colca Canyon before taking a bus or plane back to Lima.

● Spend a week in the Cusco region, then return to Lima by plane and head either up the north coast to Trujillo or down the south coast to visit the wildlife-rich Islas Ballestas and the Nazca Lines.

● From Lima, head up to Huaraz for a week or so trekking in the Cordillera Blanca, taking in the ruins at Chavín de Huantar while you acclimatize, then either head to Trujillo on the north coast or return to Lima, from where you can either head south to Nazca and Arequipa or fly up to Iquitos and spend a few days at a rainforest lodge or on an Amazon river cruise.

## One month

● Starting in Lima, travel to Cusco by plane or overland via Ayacucho, spend ten days or so in the Cusco region, including time to trek the Inca Trail and visit all the major Inca sites, then either go on an organized tour down into the rainforests of the Parque Nacional Manu or travel by plane to Puerto Maldonado for a shorter stay at a rainforest lodge. Return to Cusco, then head by train to Puno for a day or two on Lake Titicaca, continue by train to Arequipa and spend a few days taking in the city and exploring Colca Canyon. If you flew to Cusco and didn't visit Manu, you should then have a few days left to return to Lima overland from Arequipa along the south coast, visiting the Nazca Lines and the Islas Ballestas along the way.

# Peru online

### Latin American Network Information Centre, Peru
Ⓦ lanic.utexas.edu/la/sa/peru
Links to an extensive range of Peru-related sites divided into themes including art and culture, environment, government, indigenous peoples and news, as well as other portals, directories and search sites.

### Machu Picchu
Ⓦ www.machupicchu.org Links to all kinds of websites related to Machu Picchu, the Incas and Andean culture in general.

### PromPeru
Ⓦ www.peru.org.pe Official tourist promotion site with comprehensive information on everything from history and archeology to food and fiestas, as well as details on all the major attractions, practical advice on travel in Peru, and links to all manner of related sites.

### Rumbos
Ⓦ www.rumbosperu.com Peruvian environmental and travel magazine with good photos, travel articles, background information and practical tips on visiting a huge range of different sites.

# Uruguay

| | |
|---|---|
| **Capital** Montevideo | **Climate** Temperate, with long warm |
| **Population** 3.2 million | summers and mild winters |
| **Language** Spanish | **When to go** September to April |
| **Currency** Peso Uruguayo (U$) | **Minimum daily budget** US$25 |

Squeezed in between the vast expanses of Argentina and Brazil, diminutive Uruguay is usually overlooked by travellers to South America. It is, however, an oasis of stability in the fluctuating fortunes of the region, with moderate politics, an educated and tolerant population and a beguiling atmosphere of old-fashioned elegance reminiscent of neighbouring Argentina, whose neo-European culture Uruguay shares. There is no mass tourism in Uruguay and the country remains unspoilt and hospitable.

Given Uruguay's modest dimensions, its characterful capital, Montevideo, looms large in the national psyche – almost half the country's three million-plus inhabitants live here, and the capital is very much the economic, cultural and political heart of the country. Not that Montevideo is Uruguay's only attraction. Close to hand is the country's alluring Atlantic coastline, centred on the ritzy resort of Punta del Este, but also boasting more low-key seaside villages in which to loll on the beach and enjoy Uruguay's pleasantly Mediterranean climate. What really defines Uruguay, however, is its gaucho culture, which is even more ubiquitous and traditional than neighbouring Argentina's – you're still more likely to see farmhands wearing *bombachas* (loose trousers), bandanas and felt hats

than jeans. The colourful three-day "Fiesta de la Patria Gaucha", held in the town of Tacuarembó in late March, is a good place to see fine displays of gaucho horsemanship and other skills like horse-breaking and cattle herding.

Although parts of Montevideo aren't entirely safe at night, Uruguay is an otherwise safe place to travel, with reasonably priced accommodation and an efficient network of public transport.

## Main attractions

● **Montevideo** Like nearby Buenos Aires, Montevideo's passions are tango, football and maté, although the city is more laid-back and relaxing than its brasher Argentine cousin. Along with elegant European-style coffee houses and boulevards, the city also boasts a small colonial centre, the Cuidad Vieja, and one of the most atmospheric markets in South America, the Mercado del Puerto, housed in a large, nineteenth-century wrought-iron building and known for its delicious *parilla* (barbecues) – eating here on Saturday afternoons is a popular pastime with Montevideans.

● **Punta del Este** On the Atlantic coast, 85km east of Montevideo, the glitzy seaside resort of Punta del Este

URUGUAY

One week
• Montevideo–Colonia.
• Punta del Este–Aguas Dulces.

Two weeks
• Colonia–Montevideo–Punta del Este–Aguas Dulces–Chuy.

N

BRAZIL

Tacuarembo

Paysandú

Río Uruguay

Mercedes

Durazno

Carmelo

Chuy

PARQUE FORESTAL
CABO POLONIA

Aguas Dulces

Colonia del
Sacremento

La Paloma

Río de la Plata    Montevideo    Punta del Este

ARGENTINA

0    200 km

is popular with wealthy Brazilians, Argentinians and, from December to February, European clubbers in search of winter sun. While Punta's beaches are broad and sandy, most visitors come for the best nightlife south of Rio de Janeiro, with world-class DJs flown in from Europe and the US. Punta is far from cheap, though – costs are equivalent to those in the south of France.

● **Colonia del Sacramento** Founded by Portuguese settlers from Brazil in 1680, Colonia sits directly opposite Buenos Aires on the Río de la Plata. It's a charming town, Uruguay's prettiest, with whitewashed buildings, narrow cobbled streets and squares lined by plane trees, as well as the ruins of the seventeenth-century Convento de San Francisco and a nineteenth-century lighthouse, from where there are lovely views over the town.

● **Gaucho culture** Many Uruguayan *estancias* (ranches) offer comfortable home stays during which you can ride, rope steers and learn about farm life. You might also be encouraged to join in with daily tasks performed by ranch hands like branding cattle, shearing sheep or milking cows, or be taken out for a ride in a traditional horse-drawn carriage.

# Also recommended

● **Dunes of Cabo Polonio** On the Atlantic coast 200km east of Montevideo, the Cabo Polonio offers one of Uruguay's wildest and most dramatic vistas, with a ten-kilometre stretch of shifting sand dunes, some of them reaching 30m in height, making for an invigorating coastal hike.

● **Candombe** Montevideo's Barrio Sur is home to the country's colourful Afro-Uruguayan population, whose unique ceremonial form of music and dance, known as *candombe*, can be seen most weekends in the city's cabaret venues or, more authentically, outside on the barrio's Calle Carlos Gardel. As well as drumming and dancing, *candombe* events involve a fixed cast of characters including a matriarch, a medicine man and El Bastonero – a man with a magic wooden stick.

● **Aguas Dulces** If you fancy a quiet beach holiday, head for the quaint fishing village of Aguas Dulces, 120km east of Punta del Este, which has several good seafood restaurants and few tourists. The surrounding area has undeveloped sandy beaches, while 30km further north is the Parque Nacional Santa Teresa, which incorporates an eighteenth-century hilltop castle, pine and eucalyptus forests and marshes with abundant bird life.

# Routes in and out

There are no nonstop flights from the US, Europe or Australasia to Uruguay, although there are flights from Miami via Bolivia and Argentina to Montevideo four times weekly. The easiest way to reach the country is to fly directly to Buenos Aires from the US or Europe (London, Madrid and Amsterdam) and take the ferry across the Río de la Plata to Montevideo or Colonia. Alternatively, fly to São Paulo in Brazil and get one of several daily flights to Montevideo. There are a number of land crossings into Brazil – the most popular goes between Chuy at the northern end of Uruguay's Atlantic coast and twin city Chui in Brazil. There is also a land crossing to Argentina at Gualeguaychú, though this is less convenient than crossing the Río de la Plata.

# Itineraries

## One week

● Visit two of Uruguay's most interesting cities, Montevideo and Colonia.

● Explore the country's coast, varying the pace from the party town of Punta del Este to the tranquil fishing village of Aguas Dulces.

● Stay on an inland ranch and learn how to become a cowboy.

## Two weeks

● Take the ferry from Argentina to Colonia and then move down the coast to Montevideo and the Atlantic beaches before crossing the border into Brazil at Chuy.

● Head inland from Colonia to the rolling hills and lowlands of the country's interior, stay on a ranch, and then end your trip with a few days relaxing on the beach at Aguas Dulces.

# Uruguay online

**Uruguay Aktuell**
Ⓦ www.uruguayaktuell.com
The enthusiastic homepage of two Germans living in Montevideo. Available in three languages (German, English and

Spanish), and with an interesting range of features and hundreds of photographs.

**Uruguay Total**

ⓦ**www.uruguaytotal.com** Uruguay's main internet portal, with hundreds of links on business, politics, the media and much more.

**Uruguay Turismo**

ⓦ**www.turismo.gub.uy** Official tourist website with useful listings of *estancias* and detailed information on resorts and beauty spots – it's only in Spanish though.

# Venezuela

| | |
|---|---|
| **Capital** Caracas | **Climate** Hot and humid in the |
| **Population** 24 million | lowlands, cooler in the Andes |
| **Language** Spanish, plus minority | **Best time to go** November to June |
| indigenous languages | (dry season) |
| **Currency** Bolívar (B) | **Minimum daily budget** $25–35 |

Venezuela is the fifth biggest country in South America and, like the continent's other Andean nations, encompasses a stunning variety of dramatic landscapes, ranging from Andean peaks to the immense, wildlife-rich plains, swamps and rainforests of the Amazon and Orinoco basins. With almost three thousand kilometres of Caribbean coastline, Venezuela also boasts some glorious beaches, as well as numerous idyllic offshore islands surrounded by coral reefs. In addition, the country is home to two of South America's most outstanding natural wonders: Angel Falls, the world's highest waterfall, with a drop of almost a kilometre; and the stunning, flat-topped sandstone mountains known as *tepuis* that rise almost vertically from the plains of the remote Gran Sabana – the biggest of these, Mount Roraima, is said to have provided the inspiration for Sir Arthur Conan Doyle's epic adventure novel, *The Lost World* (though a similar claim is made for the Parque Nacional Noel Kempff Mercado in Bolivia)

Given all these attractions, Venezuela receives surprisingly few travellers, other than the package tourists who fly in to enjoy the beautiful beaches and duty-free shopping of the resort island of Margarita, and the smaller numbers who come specifically to see Angel Falls. Many budget travellers are put off by the country's relatively high costs, by the fact that you have to pass through Colombia to get here from Ecuador or Peru, and by the visa requirement for travellers entering the country overland. Above all, though, it seems that despite its natural wonders Venezuela somehow lacks the romantic allure evoked by places like Brazil and Peru.

Economically, Venezuela depends overwhelmingly on its massive oil industry (it's the world's fourth biggest exporter, often referred to as *Saudi Venezuela*), which has funded a good road network and relatively modern infrastructure that make travel fairly easy. But the oil industry has acted as a disincentive to the development of tourism, and has also had a profound cultural impact. Uniquely in South America, Venezuelans prefer baseball – introduced by US oil workers – to football, and most of the country's cities, though modern, somehow lack the exotic appeal and excitement you expect from Latin America. The capital, Caracas, has a dramatic setting in a deep valley surrounded by rugged forested mountains that rise sharply from the coast, but otherwise it's a rather unattractive place, with a modern high-rise city centre ringed by depressingly poor shantytowns in a juxtaposition that encapsulates the deep inequal-

VENEZUELA

Coro
Maracaibo
PARQUE NACIONAL
MORROCOY
Colonia
Tovar
Caracas
Archipelago
Los Roques
Isla de Margarita
Grenada
Tobago
Trinidad
Maturín
Orinoco
Delta
Mérida
Ciudad
Bolívar
Ciudad Guayana
San Fernando
de Apure
Puerto Páez
Angel Falls
LA GRAN
SABANA
COLOMBIA
GUYANA
BRAZIL
N

**One week**

• Caracas–Parque Nacional Morrocoy–Mérida.
• Caracas–Parque Nacional Morrocoy–Angel Falls.

**Two weeks**

• Caracas–Parque Nacional Morrocoy–Coro–
Mérida–Angel Falls.

**One month**

• Caracas–Parque Nacional Morrocoy–Coro–
Mérida–Angel Falls–Orinoco Delta–Gran Sabana.
• Caracas–Parque Nacional Morrocoy–Coro–
Mérida–Angel Falls–Orinoco Delta–
Archipelago Los Roques.

0        300 km

ities created by the oil boom, and levels of violent crime which are high even by Latin American standards. You shouldn't let this put you off, though, as however unappealing the urban centres may be, the enormous and diverse natural beauty of the country's immense coastline and interior – much of it still sparsely inhabited wilderness – make Venezuela a fantastic travel destination. Moreover, the fact that it attracts relatively few visitors means that it's easy to get off the beaten track, and even in the more popular destinations you'll rarely find yourself surrounded by crowds of other tourists.

Because of its massive oil exports Venezuela ought to be one of the richest countries in Latin America, but in fact the enormous oil revenues have largely been squandered through decades of inefficient and corrupt gov-

ernment, leaving the vast majority of the population in poverty. Frustration with this led to the election in 1999 of President Hugo Chavez, a populist left-wing leader and self-proclaimed champion of the poor. Unsurprisingly, President Chavez's radical policies have alienated the traditional political elites and the US, which imports huge quantities of Venezuelan oil, leading to growing political tension and violent clashes on the streets. In 2002, Chavez was briefly overthrown in a military coup, allegedly supported by the CIA, before mass protests by his supporters forced his reinstatement. Tensions remain high, however, and though the political situation is unlikely to affect your travel plans, it's worth checking the media for the latest developments and steering clear of political demonstrations.

# Main attractions

● **Angel Falls** Set amid pristine rainforest inside the remote Canaima National Park in the southwest of the country, the Angel Falls (Salto Angel, named after Jimmy Angel, the US bush pilot who stumbled across them in the 1930s) are Venezuela's most famous attraction. Plummeting almost 1km – around fifteen times the height of Niagara Falls – this is by far the highest waterfall in the world, an amazing spectacle made all the more alluring by its remote wilderness location. Getting to the falls is no easy matter: you have to fly into the village of Canaima, from where you can either fly over the falls in a light aircraft or travel to their foot by motorized canoe. This latter option is only possible during the June to December rainy season, which is in any case the best time to visit, since the high water levels mean that the falls are at their most spectacular.

● **Gran Sabana** South of Angel Falls and set within the same massive Canaima National Park, the beautiful and remote Gran Sabana is a vast, rolling plateau covered with savannah grassland and tropical rainforest, from which rise over a hundred flat-topped mountains known as *tepuis*. Inhabited by scattered indigenous groups, the region is rich in wildlife, and the tops of the *tepuis*, where plant species have evolved in isolation, are amongst the most unique natural habitats in Latin America. The largest of the *tepuis* is the 2810-metre Mount Roraima, which sits on the three-way border with Guyana and Brazil and can be climbed on a tough five- to six-day trek.

● **Parque Nacional Morrocoy** With its clear blue waters, near-deserted beaches and islands, and extensive coral reefs, Parque Nacional Morrocoy covers an idyllic stretch of the Caribbean coast west of Caracas, and is an excellent place for snorkelling, diving or just chilling out on the beach. It's best visited by taking day-trips by boat from the towns of Tucacas and Chichiriviche, though if you take your own camping equipment and supplies you can arrange to be dropped off on one of the deserted islands and enjoy a few days of blissful isolation.

● **Mérida** Set at an altitude of 1640m within sight of Venezuela's highest mountain peaks, the friendly city of Mérida is the best base for exploring the Venezuelan Andes, which stretch for some 400km along the western side of the country. From the city you can take the world's longest and highest cable car ride up to the 4765-metre summit of Pico Espejo for fabulous views of the mountains all around. Mérida is also home to a well-developed tour industry which makes it easy to organize trekking, mountain-biking, whitewater rafting and horse-riding trips into the surrounding mountains, large areas of which are protected by the Sierra Nevada National Park.

● **Orinoco Delta** The Orinoco Delta is a massive wetland region of swamp and rainforest where the waters of the mighty River Orinoco – the third biggest in South America – weave their way through an intricate system of waterways before reaching the sea. The delta supports a rich and varied range of wildlife, and is also home to the indigenous Warao, who reside in houses raised on stilts on many of the innumerable forested islands, and live largely by fishing from dugout canoes. You can visit this great wilderness on organized tours from the riverside town of Tucupita.

# Also recommended

● **Archipelago Los Roques** Situated some 160km off the mainland north of Caracas, the Los Roques archipelago comprises a beautiful collection of coral atolls with white-sand beaches, fringed by extensive coral reefs which support a great density and diversity of tropical marine life, making for fantastic snorkelling and diving.

● **Coro** Set on the Caribbean coast about 180km west of Parque Nacional Morrocoy, the peaceful little port town of Coro was one of the first Spanish settlements in South America, and is home to the finest colonial architecture in Venezuela.

● **Colonia Tovar** Set in the forested mountains west of Caracas, the Colonia Tovar was founded in 1843 by a group of German settlers who proceeded to live in near total isolation from the rest of Venezuela for almost a century, marrying only amongst themselves and maintaining their German cultural traditions and language. This isolation faded from the mid-twentieth century with the introduction of Spanish and the construction of a road link with the rest of the country, and the colony has since become a major tourist attraction, but its distinct cultural background is still very much evident in the Aryan looks and German accents of most of the inhabitants, and in their rich agricultural produce.

● **Isla de Margarita** The Isla de Margarita is Venezuela's biggest island and a major holiday resort, attracting large numbers of package tourists with its combination of beautiful beaches, modern hotel complexes and duty-free shopping. Despite the impact of mass tourism, however, the island's many beaches are so extensive that you can still find relatively peaceful stretches, especially if you avoid the main Venezuelan holiday periods (around Christmas and Easter), making it an excellent place to relax by the sea for a few days after some hard travelling elsewhere.

# Routes in and out

Caracas is a major regional hub for air travel, with regular flights to most South American capitals, and is also generally the cheapest place to reach in South America from Europe or the US, with regular flights from major cities in both continents. By land, there are four major crossings between Venezuela and Colombia, the easiest, safest and most scenic of which runs through the Andes between Cúcuta and San Antonio del Táchira. You can travel between Venezuela and Brazil along the recently opened road through the Gran Sabana, across the border at Santa Elena de Uairén and south to Boa Vista and Manaus in Brazil. There are no land crossings between Guyana and Venezuela; the only way to travel overland between the two is to go via Brazil. You can also enter and leave Venezuela by ferry between Isla Margarita and Trinidad and Tobago. Note that though you generally don't need a visa if you're flying into Venezuela, most nationalities do need one to enter the country overland, so check to make sure you can get one in a neighbouring country, or ideally pick one up before you leave home.

# Itineraries

## One week

● Head west from Caracas to Chichiriviche and spend a few days exploring the beaches and islands of Parque Nacional Morrocoy, then either travel up into the Andes to Mérida and spend the remainder of the week exploring the city and taking the cable-car up into the high mountains, or fly down to the village of Canaima in Parque Nacional Canaima and take a one-day trip by plane to the Angel Falls.

## Two weeks

● Follow the one-week itinerary at a slightly more leisurely pace, perhaps continuing further west along the coast to Coro, before heading up to Mérida or taking a couple of extra days once there to trek in the mountains, then return to Caracas and fly down to the village of Canaima in Canaima National Park and take a three-day canoe trip to Angel Falls.

## One month

● Follow the two-week itinerary and arrange to be dropped off in the historic city of Ciudad Bolívar on the banks of the Orinoco River on the way back from Angel Falls. From there, head east by road via the new city of Ciudad Guayana to Tucupita to take a two- or three-day tour into the Orinoco Delta. Return to Ciudad Bolívar, then either head south by road to San Fransisco de Yuruaní in the Gran Sabana and spend

your last week trekking up Mount Roraima, or return to Caracas and fly out to the Archipelago Los Roques and spend the week snorkelling or diving on the coral reefs and relaxing on the beach. If you have a couple of days left over at the end of the month, visit Colonia Tovar from Caracas before you leave.

# Online

**Think Venezuela**
Ⓦ**www.think-venezuela.net**
Comprehensive online tourism directory, with excellent information on Venezuela's main attractions and on practical details like accommodation, transport and tour companies, plus a good selection of links to other relevant sites.
**Latin America Network Information Centre, Venezuela**
Ⓦ**lanic.utexas.edu/la/venezuela** An excellent research site, with links to a massive range of relevant sites divided into themes including art and culture, media, environment and government, as well as other portals, directories and search sites.
**Vheadline.com**
Ⓦ**www.vheadline.com**
Good English-language online news site for Venezuela, with a directory of other Venezuela-related sites.

# First-Time
# Latin America

# The Big
# Adventure

# 1

# Planning your route

I t's extremely unlikely that you'll be visiting every country in Latin America, and built-in constraints like time and budget will help you to whittle down the myriad possibilities, but there are other factors to consider. Try to make your itinerary as varied as possible: spend time in the mountains, the rainforest and by the sea, as well as mixing the experience of rural indigenous life with peaceful colonial towns and big-city bustle. But don't make the mistake of trying to see too much in a limited time, or you'll end up racing through countries, which will leave very little impression.

Try to be as flexible as possible when planning your route. Until you arrive you won't really know how much you're going to like (or dislike) the places you're visiting, so build enough time into your itinerary so that you're able to extend your stay if somewhere particularly takes your fancy.

See "When to Go" (p.138) for more detailed information on climate and specific holiday seasons.

## A shared experience?

Once you've decided to travel to Latin America you need to think about whether you want to go on your own, with friends or a partner, or even on an organized tour. Don't make this decision lightly, because the people you travel with will greatly affect the kind of experience you have and the success of your trip.

There are obvious advantages in going with other people. Travelling in a couple or a group is cheaper than travelling alone, since you're able to share the cost of hotel rooms, taxi fares and many other expenses. Travelling with a friend means you'll always have someone to eat with and talk to, offering some protection against loneliness and homesickness. You'll feel safer and possibly more adventurous with people you know by your side, and you'll also have someone to look after you if you get ill. And at the end of it all you'll have someone who was also there to share in the memories. Having said that, travelling with people from back home can insulate you somewhat from the countries you've come to visit, so that you're less tempted to explore, and you might meet fewer locals. There's also always the possibility that you might fall out with each other.

## Going solo

Travelling alone in Latin America is still uncommon. If you do go solo, your trip will be more expensive and more challenging, and you'll also be seen as an oddity by gregarious Latin people (and, if you're a woman, as very perverse indeed). Nevertheless, if you're brave enough to take the plunge, the rewards are huge. You'll be much more deeply immersed in local culture than if you're travelling with someone else from back home, while the locals will find you much more approachable, and may well take you under their wing. You might even find that the greater challenges you face will uncover previously unknown reserves of ingenuity, strength and courage, so that you return as a much more confident and self-aware person.

## Travelling with friends

If you've decided to visit Latin America with friends, take a long hard look at the people and personalities involved: travel in Latin America is often uncomfortable, chaotic and stressful, and you'll be asking a lot more from your friends than is customary back home

– and they in turn will expect support from you. Ask yourself if your friendship is strong enough to withstand the occasional disagreement, the extra time spent together, whether you'll be able to share responsibilities and decision-making, and whether you trust them to look after you should the need arise. It's important to establish whether or not you have similar expectations and goals – there's no point in going trekking in the Andes with a friend whose ideal trip is a couple of weeks clubbing in Ibiza or lying on a beach in Hawaii. Be wary, too, about travelling with someone who has a significantly different budget – if you don't agree similar budgets right from the start, you'll find yourselves rapidly parting ways. Finally, consider how many of you are going together: three is an awkward number unless you all know each other very well, while larger numbers are difficult to manage and usually split up into smaller groups.

There are lots of ways of finding a travel companion if you don't want to travel alone but don't know anyone who's able to come with you. Your best bet is to check out the numerous internet bulletin boards or forum sections of

## Single white female

"Sola?" (alone?) ask fellow passengers in amazement, shock even. "Solita?" (really alone?) – they say it again, with more emphasis. Travelling alone as a woman in Latin America is still uncommon enough to elicit curiosity from the locals, who wouldn't consider it. Questions come thick and fast – where's your husband? Why would he let you travel alone? Are you divorced, perhaps, or a widow? Haven't you any friends? Aren't your family worried about you? Far from being marked out as a victim, I find travelling alone as a woman is a positive experience – Latin Americans feel less threatened by the presence of a solo female tourist, more willing to talk and invite you into their lives. They also feel more protective. In Colombia, a busload of macho guys heading for the city were appalled at my lone state and insisted the driver re-route the bus so that I could reach the main terminal safely rather than being dumped on the edge of town as they were. In Nicaragua I chatted long into the night with three sisters who had dozens of children between them and errant husbands – were men as feckless in England? they wondered. In Brazil a woman who ran a food stall warned me against walking down a dangerous street and from then on kept an eye out for me, offering large plates of food whenever I passed by. Even the prostitutes in one Brazilian city, unafraid of the night, made sure I got to my hotel door safely. The downside is that the local guys assume you're available – I can't remember how many times puzzled men in Latin America have said to me, "if you're not with anybody why don't you want to be with me?" – but if you've the right attitude (say "no, thank you" with conviction and humour) they soon leave you alone. For me and increasing numbers of women, the greater sense of adventure and freedom that travelling alone brings makes it the only way to go.

Polly Rodger Brown

travel websites (see pp.330–31 for details) and perhaps post a message yourself. Alternatively, the classified ads in travel magazines often have sections dedicated to finding travel companions – *Wanderlust* (⊛www.wanderlust.co.uk) is particularly extensive. Make sure that you meet potential fellow travellers as many times as possible before you set out, and discuss your expectations about the trip with them in detail.

If you don't manage to find anyone to travel with before you set out, don't despair. Once in Latin America, there's a good chance of hitching up with other travellers – popular travellers' cafés, hostels and resorts are all good places to meet up with like-minded people. Though of course, the same rules apply as when travelling with people from home.

## Travelling with partners

Although lots of things are taken for read with couples travelling together – budgets, common goals, mutual levels of trust and care – the intensity of the experience and an unexpected sense of isolation that many couples feel as a self-contained unit on the road can cause irreparable damage to even the strongest of relationships. Go on a brief, less challenging holiday together at least once before you set off and try to remain open to meeting others, and even occasionally spending time apart on your trip. On a positive note, travelling in Latin America can be incredibly romantic: you'll have time together that you won't have at home and, assuming all goes well, you'll possibly be much closer.

## Travelling with kids

Latin Americans love children, and if you're travelling with kids you're likely to be the object of special attention and care. Locals will ensure you get a place on the bus, women will talk to you in regions where they're otherwise wary of tourists, and waiters and shopkeepers will coo and flirt. And of course, the children will come back with unforgettable memories.

Bear in mind, though, that if you're flying from anywhere other than the US, you'll have to endure a long-haul flight. Additionally, conditions in Latin America are often less than comfortable and sanitary; if you're travelling on a tight budget, it may not always be easy to find somewhere that feels clean and safe enough. You'll also need to be careful to make sure your children stay healthy in the face of risks ranging from contaminated water to obscure tropical diseases.

## Organized tours

Dozens of travel companies run trips to Latin America (see the list of specialist tour operators on pp.323–24), with endless variations in terms of destinations, length, theme and style of travel. Many of these tours are imaginative and well organized, accompanied by guides who have in-depth knowledge of the area, offering a painless and potentially insightful introduction to the region without any of the hassles suffered by independent first-time visitors.

If you do decide to go on an organized tour, choose the company you go with very carefully – as always, the best recommendations are via word of mouth. Bear in mind, also, that the majority of these tours are much more expensive than travelling independently, and much of what you'll see is on well-established tourist trails. Don't be afraid to ask lots of questions before booking a tour – in particular, try to get some idea of the size (8–10 is a good number) and average age of your group, the pace of the trip (many organized tours run at breakneck speed) and the exact details of your itinerary.

## Getting there

Once you've chosen your travelling companions (if any), you'll need to think about where in Latin America your trip will begin, since this will obviously have a major role in shaping your itinerary. For more advice on buying a plane ticket to Latin America, see pp.133–34.

## By air

There are plenty of options when it comes to flying into Latin America – major gateway cities include Mexico City, San José in Costa Rica, Caracas in Venezuela, Lima in Peru, Buenos Aires in Argentina, and São Paulo and Rio de Janeiro in Brazil. Major cities across the US – notably New York, Miami, Houston and Los Angeles – have a wide range of connections to Latin America; Miami offers the greatest choice, with several daily flights not just to capital cities, but to smaller destinations as well, and Houston has almost as many. In Europe, there are direct flights to most South American capitals and to Mexico City from London, Paris, Frankfurt and, especially, from Madrid. There are also direct flights from Australia (Sydney) and New Zealand (Auckland) to major Latin American air-hubs (Mexico City, Buenos Aires, São Paulo and Rio de Janeiro).

Bear in mind that if you've arrived on a long-haul flight you'll be suffering from jet lag and may not be ready to face the full force of culture shock. If you want to ease yourself into your trip gently, choose a relatively safe and easy-going city or a well-established resort town to arrive and acclimatize in. Good starting points include Cancún in Mexico, San José in Costa Rica, Santiago in Chile and Buenos Aires in Argentina. Quito in Ecuador is also relatively small and trouble-free, although its high altitude may mean that you suffer from headaches and nausea for your first few days.

## Overland from the US

If your home country is the USA (or, less practical given the vast distances involved, Canada), you might consider travelling overland to Mexico and beyond – though there aren't as many advantages to this as you might think. Greyhound bus services (⬤www.greyhound.com) run to all the main border crossings (there are more than twenty in total between the US and Mexico) and some of these will take you right into Mexico and drop you conveniently at the local bus station for onward routes. Additionally many Mexican bus companies cross the border into the USA, so that you can now pick up a bus back into Mexico as far north as Houston or Los Angeles. Distances can be huge, though – 60 hours travel time from New York to the Texas–Mexico border and 15 hours from San Francisco to the Baja California border – and you'll need a further day to get from the border to Mexico City. You might save some money travelling overland since bus journeys are generally slightly cheaper than flights (New York to Texas return, for example, costs US$198 by bus and around US$290 by plane), you'll get to see a lot of both countries from the bus window, and have plenty of time to acclimatize to your new surroundings.

# By sea

Travelling to Latin America by sea may sound exciting, but in reality it's usually expensive (costing at least three times as much as flying) and time-consuming – if you're coming from Europe, voyages across the Atlantic take three weeks or more. Cargo ships take a limited number of passengers, though the fares are high and the journey long.

It might also be possible to reach Latin America across the Atlantic for free by working your passage as a crew member. In Europe the best place to hitch a ride is Gran Canaria in the Canary Islands, where lots of commercial shipping stops en route to the Caribbean islands or the Venezuelan coast. Once in the Caribbean, there are plenty of boats between islands and over to Central America (particularly Panamá, a good place to find onward rides and yachting work in general: visit the Panamá Canal Yacht Club in Colón) and the coasts of Colombia and Venezuela. Ask around at any major port or large marinas. If you're keen on setting up lifts before you set off, you could check the classified ads sections of boating magazines or one of a number of crewfinding websites (ⓦwww.crewfinders.com, for example).

# Itineraries

The following itineraries describe some of the classic Latin American journeys, and will hopefully give you some idea of how you might structure your trip, whether you want to hike up Andean peaks, explore the ruined cities of the Maya or Inca, or simply lounge around on a Caribbean beach. More detailed itineraries for individual countries are given in the country profiles on pp.5–96; many of these can be connected into longer, multi-country trips.

## Ruta Maya

One of the world's most fascinating ancient cultures, the Maya civilization left behind the often spectacular remains of hundreds of cities – the majority still unexcavated – across southern Mexico, Belize, Guatemala, Honduras and El Salvador. While the Ruta

△ Uxmal, Mexico, part of the Ruta Maya

First-Time Latin America | planning your route

Maya (or Mayan Route) is essentially a tourist board invention, it makes an excellent itinerary for exploring parts of Mexico and Central America. The most important – and magnificent – sites are at Palenque, Uxmal and Chichén Itzá in Mexico, Tikal in Guatemala and Copán in Honduras; it's possible to see all five in three or four weeks, as well as explore the surrounding region, which includes the gorgeous Caribbean coast of the Yucatán peninsula in Mexico, the coral reefs and islands of Belize and Honduras, and the dense jungle surrounding Palenque and Tikal.

A good starting-point for visiting the Maya region is Cancún, on the northeastern tip of Mexico's Yucatán peninsula, partly because you can fly there direct from the US, partly because it's close to two of the most significant Maya sites – Uxmal and Chichén Itzá. From the Yucatán, you can cross the border at Chetumal into Belize, whose Caribbean cayes make an idyllic spot for some welcome relaxation after exploring a few ruins, before continuing on to Tikal in northern Guatemala, perhaps the most impressive of all Maya sites. From Tikal, head southwest into the highlands of Guatemala, still largely inhabited by pure-blooded descendants of the ancient Maya, who preserve their traditional customs and colourful costumes. From Guatemala, you can cross the border into Honduras to visit Copán, the last of the big five Maya sites, renowned for its carvings. Finally, if you'd rather venture a little way off the well-trodden trail, there are plenty of less touristed but rewarding Maya sites to visit, such as Caracol, Lamanai and Xunantunich in Belize, Ceibal and El Mirador in Guatemala's Petén region, San Andrés in El Salvador, or the vast site of Calakmul in Mexico.

## Central America

The seven countries that make up Central America are much smaller than those of South America and, conveniently linked in a long narrow isthmus, form an easily negotiated, ready-made itinerary. Essentially a bridge between the temperate climate of North America and tropical South America, Central America is incredibly diverse, its terrain ranging from the cloudforests of Costa Rica and Panamá to the swampy flatlands of Mosquitia in Honduras and Nicaragua and the Caribbean coral atolls of Belize, with a central chain of volcanoes – over 250 in all, a number of them active – running the length of the region. This geographical diversity also means the region has much to offer nature enthusiasts, with a wide variety of environments (and countless wildlife species) within easy reach of one another; visitors are well catered to with a network of national parks and a host of ecotourism projects, particularly in Belize and Costa Rica. Culturally, too, Central America is rich in diversity, its peoples ranging from the deeply traditional Maya groups of the Guatemalan highlands to the English-speaking African-descended population of the Caribbean coast.

It's possible to travel through the whole of Central America, north to south, in two or three months. Belize is a good starting point, especially since it's easy to reach overland from Cancún in Mexico, which has direct flights from the US and Europe. From Belize City, you can head out to Caye Caulker in the Caribbean for some great snorkelling, then cross the country westwards towards Guatemala and the magnificent Maya site of Tikal, before heading southwest into Guatemala's Western Highlands. Cross the border into tiny El Salvador then travel on to Honduras, where there's superb snorkelling and diving in the Bay Islands, before crossing the border to visit Lake Nicaragua. From Nicaragua, head on into Costa Rica, in many ways the most developed of Central American countries, with a range of ecotourism opportunities and over 850 species of birds, then finish off in Panamá, which has similar natural attractions but fewer tourists. Panamá City is one of the most vibrant of Central American capitals, a melting pot of different immigrant and domestic cultures; you can fly from here to Colombia in South America.

## The Amazon

Covering over half of Brazil and significant parts of The Guianas, Venezuela, Colombia, Ecuador, Peru and Bolivia, the Amazon basin is one of the defining landscapes of South America. It's the largest rainforest on earth with the greatest biodiversity: over 6000 known species of plant (and many more unknown), 15,000 animal species and a fifth of the planet's birds can be found in the Amazon; the river itself extends 6500km from source to mouth and has over a thousand tributaries; and the basin also supports hundreds of thousands of indigenous peoples, living deep within the forest and resistant to outside influence. That said, it's not easy to penetrate the jungle – you're most likely to visit the region as part of a guided tour or on a boat trip along the river.

Popular starting points for organized trips into the Amazon are Iquitos in Peru, Tena and Misahuallí in eastern Ecuador, and Rurrenabaque in Bolivia – the last is the base for the cheapest trips into the Amazon region (from US$20–25 a day). All these towns are easily reached by land, offer accommodation in jungle lodges and established routes down rivers and into the forest. With less infrastructure and fewer tourists but similar environments to explore are Leticia in Colombia (which you'll have to fly to within Colombia – there's no road) and Puerto Ayacucho on the Venezuelan border with Colombia.

A classic Amazon journey is the Brazilian trip from the mouth of the River Amazon at Belém to Manaus, right in the heart of the rainforest, a boat journey of five days. Because of the massive width of the river between these points (you can't see both its banks when you're on it), you won't see a lot of wildlife, but it's a great adventure all the same, with accommodation in hammocks, river dolphins playing in the boat's wake (if you're lucky), and local people paddling past in canoes, selling jungle fruit. From Manaus you can make boat trips on the Amazon's tributaries – such as the Rio Negro, which winds northwards to Colombia, or the Rio Madeira, which makes its way down towards Brazil's border with Bolivia – many of which are sizeable rivers in their own right but offer better opportunities for spotting river wildlife.

## Caribbean coast and islands

From the Yucatán peninsula of Mexico south through Central America and curving east along the northern edge of South America, Latin America forms the western edge of the Caribbean sea. If you're looking for palm-fringed beaches or coral-fringed islands, this is the place to come. With clear aquamarine waters and the world's second largest barrier reef, the scuba diving and snorkelling are excellent; for those who'd rather just lie in the sun, there are endless little beach communities; and in terms of culture, the Latin American Caribbean has its own distinctive atmosphere – thanks to a mixture of the Afro-Caribbean (descendants of slaves brought in by the Spanish to work on plantations) and mestizo (European-Amerindian) populations of the interior. Which means you're as likely to hear reggae and soca rhythms as Latin American salsa, English is widely spoken in some places, and the region's cuisine is often spiced up with ingredients like coconut milk and chilli.

There are two strands to this itinerary, which can be joined together if you've several months' travelling time. The first is to fly to Caracas in Venezuela, a major air-hub with direct connections to the US and Europe, and then make your way along a stretch of Venezuela's 2800-metre coastline (the longest in the Caribbean) to Colombia. Travelling west from Caracas brings you to the travellers' hotspot of Choroní, reached via a spectacular bus ride through the cloudforest of the Parque Nacional de Henri Pittier. Other highlights of this coastline include the paradisical islands of the Parque Nacional de Morrocoy – you can charter a boat here without breaking the bank and even camp overnight on some islands.

Once over the border in Colombia, you'll want to make your way to the city of Cartagena via the popular Parque Nacional Tayrona, a collection of white sandy beaches where you can hang a hammock or camp. From here you could also make the spectacular five-day trek to the Cuidad Perdida in the Sierra Nevada de Santa Marta mountain range. Cartagena itself is one of the loveliest colonial cities in Latin America and probably the most interesting destination on the coast, with remnants from its past as the biggest port in northern South America. From here you could either head south into Colombia towards Ecuador, or fly to Colón in Panamá to explore Central America.

The second strand of the itinerary encompasses the Caribbean coast of Central America and especially its offshore islands. These include the San Blas archipelago of Panamá, home to the traditional Kuna people, the Bay Islands of Honduras, one of the most popular spots for learning to scuba dive, and the cayes of Belize, which lie right on the edge of a lengthy coral reef. It's not possible to hop from one chain of islands to another, though – you'll have to return to the mainland and travel to the next departure point (see above for details of the Central America itinerary). Points worth exploring inland are Costa Rica's Parque Nacional Tortuguero, especially in turtle-hatching season, and surfing spot Puerto Viejo; the wild swamplands of the Mosquitia region in Nicaragua; and the Afro-Caribbean Garífuna villages of Honduras.

# The Andes

The longest chain of mountains in the world at 7200km, the Andes run the length of western South America, from the southern tip of Chile to Venezuela, and include some of the highest peaks outside the Himalayas. Made up of dozens of parallel mountain ranges or *cordilleras*, the Andes provide some of the most spectacular scenery in Latin America. These mountains were home to the great Inca race and to others before them – Chavín, Nazca and Tiahuanuco, to name three – who left behind a string of dramatic ruined cities and trading routes that now form memorable hiking trails. Today, the rural highlands are still inhabited by indigenous peoples, principally the Quechua and Aymara, who wear traditional costume, farm the terraced slopes much as their ancestors did and come together to trade in colourful weekly markets.

The classic Andean itinerary runs between Quito in Ecuador and La Paz in Bolivia via Peru – this is the most visited region in Latin America and accordingly known as the Gringo Trail. It's easy to escape other travellers, though – apart from the resorts and attractions on the well-worn route (listed below), the Andean region is still largely undisturbed by tourists.

Quito, capital of Ecuador, is an attractive colonial city that, with its easy-going charm and good tourist facilities, makes an excellent starting point. The country's central sierra, site of the so-called Avenue of the Volcanoes, has some spectacular trekking and climbing opportunities and is also the indigenous heart of the country. Heading south towards Peru, highlights include Baños, a small thermal spa town with a subtropical climate; Cuenca, an even finer example of colonial architecture than Quito – and without the traffic; and Vilcabamba, a gringo hangout set in a beautiful valley and close to the cloudforests of Parque Nacional Podocarpus. Crossing into Peru, head for the Cordillera Blanca, the highest tropical mountain range in the world with spectacular scenery, glacial lakes and pre-Inca ruins, before making for Cusco. A delightful colonial city with a lively backpacker scene, Cusco is the gateway to the Inca ruins of Machu Picchu, Latin America's biggest tourist attraction, set on a terraced plateau between two prominent mountain peaks; one of the most popular ways of reaching it is the Inca Trail, a strenuous five-day hike. Bolivia's Andean highlights include the clear blue waters of Lake Titicaca, which straddles the border between Bolivia and Peru, the legendary silver-mining city of Potosí, and La Paz, Bolivia's de facto capital and a bustling cultural melting pot situated at an altitude of over 3500m. Close to the city, the Huayna Potosí mountain is one of the few peaks in South America over 6000m that can be climbed by people with no mountaineering experience. To cover this whole stretch of South America, you should allow two to three months.

## Patagonia and Tierra del Fuego

Patagonia, a huge and remote wilderness in the far south of South America, encompasses more than a third of Argentina along with the southern tip of Chile. Of its several distinct landscapes, the central region is a vast dry steppe with little of interest for tourists; western Patagonia, however, comprises the dramatic terrain punctured by the huge Andean peaks, glaciers and lakes commonly associated with the region, while the eastern coast boasts a rich marine wildlife. There are almost no indigenous peoples in Patagonia: the native Tehuelche tribes, nomadic hunter-gatherers, were wiped out by European settlers in the nineteeth century. Bizarrely, though, Patagonia's Chubut Valley became home to a Welsh Nonconformist community in 1865, whose descendants continue to farm the land today.

In this scarcely populated region, distances between areas of interest are immense – you'll either have to fly from place to place or be prepared to spend days sitting on a bus. Still, with its world-class trekking, mountains and national parks – and no large cities to speak of – Patagonia is the perfect destination for hardy outdoors types.

This also goes for the archipelago of Tierra del Fuego to the south, again split between Argentina and Chile and quite literally the end of the earth. Tierra del Fuego's principal island, the Isla Grande de Tierra del Fuego, has one main tourist destination, Ushuaia, a town dramatically wedged between the mountains and the sea. From here the Parque Nacional Tierra del Fuego is easily accessible, with its diversity of landscapes ranging from subantarctic tundra to intricate lakes and swampy marshland, all offering some great trekking. The island's central landscape comprises rolling hills covered with beech woodland, at its prettiest in autumn (late March to late April), while the north of the island consists mainly of pasture grazed by sheep – though it does have some superlative flyfishing on the Río Grande.

An exhaustive trip starts with flying into Buenos Aires, then heading south to Chile, a journey of over 1500km. Other highlights of the region not listed above include (from north to south) the Península Valvés, with its colonies of penguins, killer whales and other marine wildlife; the 10,000-year-old handprints on the walls of the Cueva de los Manos Pintadas; and the Perito Moreno Glacier, with its sixty-metre cliffs of ice. Cross the border into Chile at Tierra del Fuego and take the two-day ferry ride from Puerto Natales, conveniently near to Parque Nacional Torres del Paine, through the Chilean fjords to Puerto Montt and on up the scenic Carretera Austral to points north in Chile and the other Andean countries.

You'll need several weeks to fully explore the region. Bear in mind that during the winter months of June and July temperatures drop to as low as -25°C.

## Crossing the Darién Gap

Connecting Central and South America, the so-called **Darién Gap** is the name given to the region of jungle wilderness that straddles the border between Panamá and Colombia. There are no roads across it – the Panamerican Highway, which runs the length of the Americas from Alaska to Tierra del Fuego – here suffers its one and only interruption (hence the "gap"), meaning that travel from Colombia to Panamá is by plane, boat or on foot only. Previously, the overland crossing of the Darién Gap was one of the classic Latin American adventures (although risky at the best of times), whereas these days the presence of Colombian guerrillas, paramilitaries and drug traffickers means it's now extremely dangerous, with a significant risk of kidnap or murder, and should on no account be contemplated.

Nowadays, most visitors cross the gap by plane – you can fly from Panamá City to various cities in Colombia, with Cartagena being the most popular option. A more adventurous crossing is by sea, most easily done by travelling on one of the private yachts that sail regularly between Colón and Cartagena, a three- to four-day trip. The *Voyager International Hostel* (Ⓦwww.mipagina.com/pmahoste) in Panamá City usually has up-to-date information on which yachts are carrying passengers on this route; otherwise ask around at the yacht clubs in Colón or Panamá City.

# Themed trips

If you've a particular interest, be it wildlife, language and culture, or activities such as whitewater rafting or scuba diving, there's the option of planning your trip around a theme instead of basing it on a strictly geographical itinerary.

## Adventure sports

Latin America has a wide range of adventure sports on offer, many of which are far more reasonably priced than at home; bear in mind, though, that safety standards may not be what you'd expect at home either. If you have your own equipment, consider bringing it along, in case the quality of gear available isn't up to scratch.

- **Mountaineering and rock-climbing** There are superb climbing opportunities in the Andean countries of South America, ranging from some of the world's most challenging ascents to relatively easy ones that can be tackled by anyone with a reasonable level of fitness (remember, though, that you'll need to be properly acclimatized, or you risk developing the potentially fatal acute mountain sickness – see p278). John Biggar's *The High Andes: A Guide for Climbers* is an excellent comprehensive climbing guide to the region. Amongst specific destinations, Bolivia's spectacular Cordillera Real, close to La Paz, has six peaks over 6000m, one of which, Huayna Potosí (6088m), can be climbed by people with absolutely no mountaineering experience. For experienced climbers, *Bolivia: A Climbing Guide* by Yossi Brain, is an essential read. Ecuador's Avenue of the Volcanoes, south of Quito, also offers a wealth of climbing opportunities (see *Climbing and Hiking in Ecuador* by Rob Rachowiecki, Mark Thurber and Betsy Wagenhauser for further details). In Argentina, the main climbing centres are the city of Mendoza, close to South America's highest peak, Aconcagua (6962m); the holiday resort of Bariloche in the Patagonian Lake District; and western Patagonia, particularly the Fitz Roy Massif in the Parque Nacional Los Glaciares and the Volcán Lanin (3776m).
- **Skiing** Argentina's main resort is Las Lenas in the southwest of Mendoza province, which attracts a chic South American crowd as well as northern hemisphere skiers looking for some summer (June–Oct) action. Chile has the best skiing in South America, with very dry powder snow; the main resorts – El Colorado, La Parva and Valle Nevado – are all roughly 40km from Santiago.

- **Whitewater rafting and river kayaking** Latin America has some championship-level locations for whitewater rafting and river kayaking. In Chile there are two world-class rafting rivers (graded III–IV) in spectacular settings with volcanoes, waterfalls and lush forest: the Bío Bío on the southern edge of the Central Valley; and the Futaleufu down by the southern Carretera Austral, occasional venue of the Rafting World Championships. Gentler waters can be found on the Río Maipo near Santiago, the Río Trancura near Pucon and Río Petrohue near Puerto Varas. Peru also offers some of the best whitewater rafting in the world, the main centre being Cusco, from where you can organize trips to the Urubamba and Vilcanota rivers; the Cotahuasi and Colca river canyons close to Arequipa are also popular. For a thrilling account of a 1986 journey by kayak from the Amazon's source to its mouth (2500km later), read *Running the Amazon* by Joe Kane.
- Other adrenaline highs include **bungee-jumping** in Costa Rica, from a bridge over the Río Colorado in the Central Valley, and also in Guatemala, over one of the ravines near Guatemala City or on the Río Dulce; **hang-gliding** from the Parque Nacional de Tijuca in Rio de Janeiro, where a spectacular tandem flight takes you 520m down to the beach at São Conrado; and **mountain-biking** on the road which runs dramatically from the mountains of La Paz to the jungle lowlands around Coroico in Bolivia.

## Scuba diving and snorkelling

The Caribbean coast and islands offer the best scuba diving and snorkelling in Latin America, with great visibility. The year-round warmth and calm of the water make this region a good place to learn to scuba dive. Courses range in price from fairly expensive in Mexico to very cheap in Honduras. There are various isolated snorkelling and diving spots in South America, too, principally the Galápagos Islands.

- **Mexico, Belize and Honduras** Lying offshore from the Caribbean coast of the Yucatán peninsula in Mexico is a huge coral reef which offers some world-class scuba diving, particularly around the island of Cozumel and further south around the pristine Banco Chincorro. The cayes of Belize and Bay Islands of Honduras, set on the same 290-kilometre-long coral reef that begins in Mexico, also have wonderful diving, along with idyllic island settings. The Bay Islands are especially popular with backpackers – Utila has the cheapest diving courses in Latin America. Recommended specialist guidebooks are: *Diving and Snorkeling Guide to Cozumel* by George S. Lewbel, *Diving in Belize* by Ned Middleton, and Cindy Garoute's *Diving the Bay Islands*.

- **Colombia** The tiny coral islets called the Islas del Rosario, just off the Caribbean coast at Cartagena, are teeming with brightly coloured fish – dive operators in Cartagena take trips out to the islands. Further out in the Caribbean, the island of Providencia also has wonderful scuba diving and snorkelling in pristine turquoise sea.
- **Ecuador** The Galápagos Islands are home to unique marine species and offer some of the world's best diving (and snorkelling), although colder water and testing conditions mean that this is for experienced divers only, and rates are not cheap.
- **Brazil** The Atlantic coast of South America has crystal-clear waters and good scuba diving around the marine park island of Fernando de Noronha in northeastern Brazil.

## Surfing

The entire Pacific coast of Latin America is dotted with surfer communities, with a high concentration in Mexico and Costa Rica, and several in El Salvador and Nicaragua – these are populated mostly by well-organized and friendly US surfers. In South America the scene is much more homegrown, with large domestic surf scenes in Peru and Brazil. Renting reasonably priced boards and equipment is possible in all these places. Check websites ⊛www.surfline.com and ⊛www.surflink.com for detailed reports on the best breaks.

- **Mexico** The Pacific coast has the best waves and the most established surfer communities, notably the laid-back town of San Blas and the larger resort of Puerto Escondido. The Baja California peninsula also has lots of more remote surfing beaches.
- **Costa Rica** With some famous breaks on both coasts, Costa Rica has a big surfing scene. The Pacific side attracts more visitors – with a whole series of top spots including Boca Barranca, Jaco and Dominical – while Puerto Viejo on the Caribbean is home to the *salsa brava*, one of the country's few really big waves.
- **Peru** Peru has some of the longest waves in the world, with quality surf spots around Lima, particularly Punta Hermosa, 50km south of the city, and also in the far north of the country.

● **Brazil** The best surfing in South America is on the southern beaches of Brazil, though Brazilian surfers have a terrible reputation for aggressive riding and stealing waves. The island of Santa Catarina in the state of the same name is famous for its waves and hosts the Brazilian national championships every January.

# Wildlife

Latin America is one of the world's leading destinations for ecotourists and wildlife enthusiasts. Of course, the Amazon rainforest holds by far the largest number of animal, plant and bird species, but wildlife can be spotted just as easily in other environments, from flat grasslands to mountain forests, lakes and seas. There are good opportunities for spotting wildlife in every Latin American country, but some – notably Belize, Costa Rica and Argentina – have better organized networks of national parks and reserves, which can make a wildlife-themed trip a lot easier and more rewarding. Animals you might see include anteaters, tapirs, pumas and jaguars; howler monkeys and sloths; giant turtles, caymans and anacondas; poison dart frogs and leafcutter ants. The region is also a paradise for bird-watchers: there are more species of bird in Brazil and Colombia than in any other country in the world, while Guatemala and Costa Rica aren't far behind. Condors, scarlet and hyacinth macaws, toucans and quetzals are among Latin America's most colourful and exotic birds. *Andes to Amazon: A Guide to Wild South America* by Michael Bright and John C. Kricher's *A Neotropical Companion: An Introduction to the Animals, Plants and Ecosystems of the New World Tropics* are recommended guidebooks to the flora and fauna of Latin America. There are also dozens of specialist books on birds – *A Field Guide to the Birds of Mexico and Central America* by Meyer de Schauensee and L.I. Davis's *A Guide to the Birds of South America* are the most comprehensive. Below are just a few of the best destinations – other than the Amazon (covered on pp.108–9) – for spotting wildlife in Latin America.

● **The Petén** In northern Guatemala, the Petén comprises a mixture of low-lying swamp, savannah and rainforest, and includes the Maya Biosphere Reserve, the largest tropical forest reserve in Central America. The most accessible area is that surrounding the Maya site at Tikal.

- **The Darién Gap** Straddling the border between Panamá and Colombia, much of the Darién Gap is currently off-limits thanks to the activities of guerrillas and drug runners (see p.113). However, parts of this great untouched natural wilderness can be explored from the Panamanian side, where large tracts of forest are protected by the Parque Nacional Darién.
- **Los Llanos** A vast area of plains between the Andes and the Río Orinoco basin in Venezuela, Los Llanos is flooded annually in October and November, when wildlife spotting is at its best.
- **The Pantanal** The open swampland of the Pantanal in western Brazil is not easily reached independently, but there are dozens of tour operators in Corumba running trips into the area. The flatness of the Pantanal (and its lack of inhabitants) means that sighting wildlife is more likely than almost anywhere else in Latin America – species you might see include anteaters, armadillos, rare blue macaws, toucans, jaguars and anacondas.
- **The Galápagos Islands** In one of the world's pre-eminent wildlife destinations, the abundant marine fauna of the famous Galápagos Islands, 950km off the coast of Ecuador, leaves an unforgettable impression, even if the cost of reaching the islands (US$500–1500 for an eight-day boat tour) is enough to put a serious hole in your budget.
- **Península Valdés** The waters around the arid Península Valdés in Argentinian Patagonia are protected as one the most important marine reserves on earth. Highlights include elephant seals (which weigh three tonnes and measure up to five metres) and the killer whales that prey on them.

## Learning a language

One of the strongest bonds between the countries of Latin America is their shared linguistic inheritance, with most of the region's nations having **Spanish** as their main language. If you don't already speak a bit of Spanish and haven't attempted to learn it at home (see the chapter on "Guidebooks and other resources", p.166, for details), you could arrange your trip around taking a language course in Latin America itself. This has long been a popular way to begin travelling in Latin America, and most towns on the Gringo Trail have at least one language school, while some have become specialist centres with dozens of establishments to choose from.

While language courses in Latin America will invariably cost less than at home, they're not all good, and some are actually pretty shoddy. Do some research before you choose your school (many now have websites), check out the classes before you sign up or, best of all, get a personal recommendation. Language courses usually take the form of four hours a day, five days a week and last anywhere from a week to several months according to your needs (and budget). Some schools will arrange extracurricular activities in your spare time, and almost all will be able to place you with a local family for the length of your course, so that you can practise what you've learned.

Though by no means the only place in Latin America to learn Spanish, Guatemala is by far the most popular and consequently has the widest range of options, with well-established schools and very reasonably priced courses. What's more, Guatemalan Spanish is spoken slowly and clearly.

If you're visiting Brazil for any length of time and want to study Portuguese, your best bet is to contact the universities of the large cities, like São Paulo or Rio de Janeiro, in advance, since there is no well-established network of language schools in the country.

Should you be interested, it's also possible to study several indigenous languages in Latin America. In Bolivia, which has the largest indigenous population in South America, you can study Aymara in La Paz and Quechua in Cochabamba. The small town of Joyabaj in the Western Highlands of Guatemala has a language centre where you can learn Quiché.

- **Mexico** The attractive colonial city of Cuernavaca, 50km south of Mexico City, makes a good base for exploring the capital, the pyramids of Teotihuacán and the silver town of Taxco. *The* place for learning Spanish in Mexico, particularly popular with young Americans, it has lots of language schools and teaching of a high standard.
- **Guatemala** Antigua, one of the most impressive colonial cities in Latin America, is now one of the most popular places in Latin America to learn Spanish, although you may not be able to see (let alone practice on) the locals for the crowds of tourists. Further west, the city of Quetzaltenango is less pretty but boasts some equally good schools in a far less touristed environment.
- **Costa Rica** The country's capital, San José, is the centre for Costa Rica's language schools: they're mostly US-owned and comparatively expensive, though very well organized.

- **Nicaragua** Although the colonial cities of Granada and León have several language schools, the pleasant university town of Estelí in the north has the longest established and most professional places, originally set up in the 1980s for the visiting supporters of the Sandinista revolution.
- **Ecuador** Ecuador's capital, Quito, is easily the most popular place to study in South America, with over sixty language schools. Spanish is spoken more slowly and clearly here than in many other parts of Latin America, and courses are cheap.
- **Peru** Backpacker hot spots Cusco and Arequipa both have several language schools, as does the more commercial city of Huancayo in the foothills of the Andes.

## Trekking

Even if walking and outdoor activities are normally anathema to you, you'll probably be tempted by the dramatic beauty of Latin America's mountains and rainforests to do some trekking on your trip. Try always to stick to established paths and, if you're walking in an area with a guerrilla or paramilitary presence (such as Colombia or Chiapas in Mexico), check first with the locals about the current situation and err on the side of caution. Never go trekking alone – even a sprained ankle could prove hazardous if you're stuck on your own in a remote region.

If you're planning on doing several long treks (three or more days), consider taking your own camping and water filtration equipment. Detailed topographical maps can be purchased from the relevant Instituto Nacional Geográfico/Militar (normally located in capital cities). Several well-worn routes in Latin America (notably the Inca Trail, see opposite) can only be done in organized groups with registered guides – these regulations are to protect you as well as the landscape and should be respected. Even if a guide is not strictly necessary, you should always consider the option when trekking in lesser known areas and particularly in the jungle, where dense vegetation makes getting lost a real possibility. If you're planning to walk for several days in a national park you may have to book your place well in advance. And finally, if you're trekking in the Andes, bear in mind that at high altitudes there's an enormous difference in temperature between sunny and shady areas during the daytime – and once the sun sets it gets very cold indeed.

Guidebook publishers Bradt are experts in trekking and have some excellent guides to climbing and trekking in Latin America. There are opportunities for trekking in every country in 'Latin America – listed below are just a few of the best.

- **Guatemala** The Western Highlands of Guatemala provide a variety of trekking experiences through lush green hills dotted with traditional Maya villages and volcanoes. The Ixil triangle in the Cuchumatanes mountains is another of the region's picturesque walking areas, while the northern Petén region offers an arduous two-day trek with pack horses through remote jungle to the remote Maya ruin of El Mirador.
- **Costa Rica** Costa Rica's many national parks and nature reserves are home to numerous excellent, well-organized walking trails. Some of the most popular include those in the famous Monteverde Cloudforest Reserve (and in the less touristed Santa Elena Reserve nearby), the trek along the coast of the pristine Osa peninsula in the Parque Nacional de Corcovado, and the challenging climb to Costa Rica's highest point at 3819m in the Parque Nacional Chirripó.
- **Colombia** Starting from the Caribbean coast, the five- or six-day trek to the Cuidad Perdida of the Tayrona Indians in the Sierra Nevada de Santa Marta is one of the country's highlights, while the mountainous Parque Nacional de Puracé, in southern Colombia, offers a rewarding day's trek up Volcan Puracé, with the possibility of spotting condors, bears and tapirs.
- **Venezuela** Climbing the *tepui* or flat-topped mountain of Roraima at the eastern edge of the Gran Sabana is strenuous and takes at least five days, but the eerie landscape at its summit makes the climb worthwhile.
- **Bolivia** Bolivia's most popular trekking region is the Cordillera Real, which is blessed with high Andean scenery and easily reached from La Paz. Three different Inca trails run from close by La Paz across the mountains and down to the tropical valleys of the Yungas – the most spectacular, the Takesi Trail, takes two to three days and is easily done by less experienced hikers without a guide.
- **Peru** The Peruvian Andes are home to Latin America's most popular trek, the three- to five-day Inca Trail to the legendary ruined city of Machu Picchu. There are many other good trekking opportunities in the surrounding Sacred Valley, while Huaraz in the Cordillera Blanca, north of Lima, is the starting point for serious mountain-hiking.

- **Brazil** The Parque Nacional de Chapada Diamantina in Bahia, northeastern Brazil, is laced with caves, waterfalls and dramatic rock formations rising from flat grasslands. The full day's trek from the colonial mining town of Lençois to the hamlet of Capão is one of many spectacular walks in the park.
- **Chile** The meadows, lakes and forests of the Chilean Lake District make it the most popular trekking region of the country, along with the spectacular mountain peaks of the Parque Nacional Torres del Paine in Chilean Patagonia.

## Volunteering

A good way to give purpose to your trip is to work as a volunteer. You'll be getting directly involved in local communities and experiencing Latin America in ways you won't as a tourist, as well as giving something back to the countries you're travelling in. Volunteering opportunities usually follow one of two themes: working with nature (generally conservation or scientific research) or working with people (for example, building homes, caring for the homeless, sick or drug-addicted, or teaching). In most cases volunteers have to commit themselves for a certain amount of time (at least one to three months). Once you've enrolled, you'll be expected to work hard, even though you won't be paid – volunteer organizations don't take kindly to their workers choosing their own hours, partying all night and sleeping the day away. Some volunteer schemes will cover your basic living expenses (though rarely your flight), while you'll have to pay to take part – and it's not cheap, the average cost running to several thousand dollars.

Dozens of international volunteer organizations have programmes in Latin America (see pp.324-26 for more details), while there are many more local community and government-sponsored projects. Although in theory you could just turn up while in Latin America and offer your services to a suitable organization, it's much better to organize work in advance. Some projects require volunteers with specific skills (teaching, medical and engineering skills are always in demand); others will take on anyone with enthusiasm and energy. The *International Directory of Voluntary Work* (Vacation Work) will give you lots of ideas on what kind of work is available, while the Lima-based South American Explorers Club (Ⓦwww.samexplo.org) has a free online service called Explorers

Volunteer Resource, which hooks up organizations and potential volunteers, as well as providing up-to-date feedback from people who've taken part in various projects. Amerispan (❀www.amerispan.com), chiefly a language school organization, also has a section on volunteer opportunities in Latin America. Finally, check your guidebook – many have sections on voluntary work, complete with listings.

Listed below are a few of the volunteer projects in Latin America that you could get involved in.

- **Belize** Green Reef ☏026/2838, ❀www.ambergriscaye.com. Based in San Pedro on Ambergris Caye, Green Reef helps protect the caye's marine environment and also runs bird sanctuaries.
- **Costa Rica** ASVO (Association of Volunteers for Service in Protected Areas; contact the Fundación de Parques Nacionales, Av 15 C 23/25, San José ☏506/257-2239, ❀www.minae.go.cr/asvo). Government-run scheme which places volunteers in Costa Rica's national parks for a minimum of two months.
- **Ecuador** AmaZOOnico ❀www.amazoonico.com. Animal refuge and rehabilitation centre on the Río Napo which accepts volunteers to help tend rescued forest animals and show visitors around.
- **El Salvador** CIRES (Comité de Integración and Reconstrucción Para El Salvador), 2a C Pte #2137 at 41a Av Sur, San Salvador ☏298 9410. Development agency which sets up agricultural cooperatives, builds houses and potable water networks, and runs primary health-care schemes all over the country.
- **Peru** The Cusco Weekly ❀www.cuscoweekly.com. English-language newspaper which occasionally hires volunteers to help out in the office, with some editorial duties.

# 2

# Visas, tickets and insurance

Once you've decided where you're going, there are several essential documents you'll have to organize, including a plane ticket, insurance, and any visas you might require. You'll also need to make sure your passport will remain valid for the entire length of your stay and beyond – officially, all countries in Latin America require you to hold a passport which still has at least six months before it expires. Renewing your passport is fairly straightforward – in most cases you can apply for a new one at your local post office or online. Don't leave it to the last minute, though, or you may have to pay much more than the standard fee for rapid processing.

## Visas

Very few Latin American countries now require visitors to get a visa before arrival. Current entry regulations are given in the box opposite, but bear in mind they do change, and it's always worth contacting the relevant embassy or consulate (see pp.316–20) to check the latest situation. If you do need a visa, you'll have to apply to the relevant embassy or consulate in your country – which can mean hours of queueing, armed with photos, a return air ticket and proof of funds. Don't leave this until the last minute: well before you set off, find out how long your visa will take to process (although it rarely takes longer than two weeks). Occasionally there won't be a consulate in your country, so you may have to write to one abroad – the only European consulates for Suriname, for example, are in Holland and Germany.

Visas usually have a time limit: you'll have to use them within three to six months of their being issued. If you're planning a long trip, this might make it impossible to collect all your visas in advance, in which case you'll have to wait until you arrive in a neighbouring country and apply for a visa there (take all the necessary documents with you, including passport photos). If you do have to do this, remember that Latin American bureaucracy is notoriously inefficient and frequently corrupt. You might be given incorrect information, the office may have run out of the relevant pieces of paper, or its staff might not know how to deal with you. Always give yourself plenty of time to cope with any problems that might arise. It's also probably worth applying for a multiple-entry visa if you think you might want to leave and re-enter a particular country; though this usually costs more than a single-entry visa, you could save yourself a lot of time and paperwork.

## Entry cards and stamps

On arrival, your passport will be stamped and you may also be given an entry card – known variously as a *tarjeta de turismo* (tourist card), *tarjeta de embarque* (embarkation card) or *tarjeta de ingreso* (entry card). To obtain your entry card, you'll have to fill out a form. Although you may not know where you'll be staying it's always best to fill in the destination address box on the form (a blank space can make officials nervous) – if you don't have a hotel, pick one, preferably well-known, from your guidebook; no one will check whether or not you actually stay there.

On arrival you'll have to present your completed form to an immigration official who, all being well, will stamp your passport and give you one half of the entry card, if you're being issued one (he'll keep the other half). In several Central American countries you'll have to pay a fee on arrival; this will be in dollars (or local currency), so keep at least $10 to hand. Take special care of your entry card – it's regarded as being as important as your passport, and officials will not take kindly to you being without it if you're asked to show your documents whilst in the country (although they won't bother to tell you this at immigration). You'll have to surrender it on departure, so have it ready when leaving.

Although in theory there are complicated regulations regarding the length of your stay according to your nationality, in practice the decision is left to individual officials. It's always worth asking, as politely as you can, for the standard maximum of ninety days, although you may not get it – it's infinitely preferable to have more days than you'll need rather than to have to extend your stay, which is generally a costly and time-consuming procedure.

## Extending your stay

In theory, it's almost always possible to renew your entry stamp if you decide to stay longer. The procedure involves going to the nearest immigration office (*migrácion*) or police station (*policia*) with your documents – passport, return ticket, proof of funds – and asking for a *prórroga* (extension) *de turista*. Bear in mind that although extensions are nearly always granted, you're not guaranteed to be given one – dress smartly and be polite. In many cases, it's possible to add an extra ninety days to your original ninety (though you'll never get more than 180 days in total); however, you may only be given another month or two. Extensions cost anything from a few dollars up to $100 – as a rule of thumb, the more expensive the country generally, the more expensive a visa extension is liable to be.

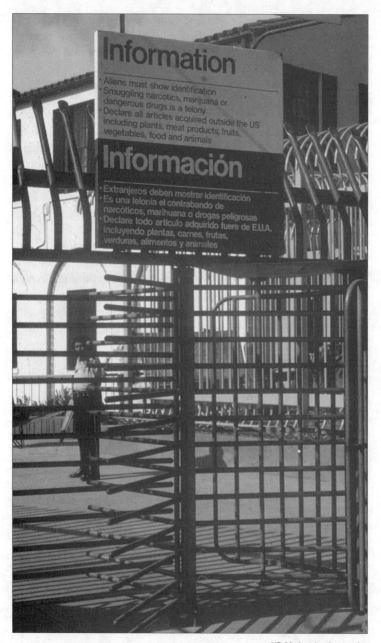

△ US–Mexican border crossing

An alternative way of prolonging your stay – especially in Central America, where distances are relatively small – is simply to cross briefly into a neighbouring country and then return over the border, where you'll be given a brand-new entry stamp.

## Overstaying

If you stay beyond the date stamped in your passport or written on your tourist card, you'll have to pay a fine when you leave the country. This is usually calculated on a daily basis of a few dollars per day, though some countries operate a fixed fine ($38 in Costa Rica, and $50 in Argentina, for example) irrespective of how long you've overstayed. If you know you're going to overstay your visa, make sure it's not going to cost an arm or a leg first – if the fine is cheap it may be worth paying it rather than going through a costly extension process or having to leave and re-enter the country. Bear in mind, though, that overstaying your welcome is a risk – although most Latin American countries will just fine you and let you go with no problems at all, there's always the possibility that you might be refused entry to that country in the future.

## Tickets

In all likelihood, your biggest single expense will be your **airline ticket** to Latin America. Whichever country you're planning to fly into, there will be a variety of routes and fares, so give yourself plenty of time to shop around and make sure you do your homework: a few hours' research should give you a good idea of current prices and routings. It's also best to adopt a flexible approach so that you're able to take advantage of any special deals which crop up, even if this means, say, starting your trip in a city or country other than the one you had in mind – for example, there are cheaper and more frequent connections to Lima in Peru or Santiago in Chile than to La Paz in Bolivia. As a rule of thumb, more affluent cities with well-established tourist attractions or business links with Europe, North America and Australasia will have better plane services and therefore potentially cheaper deals. These include Mexico City, São Paulo and Rio de Janeiro, Buenos Aires and Santiago.

Fares vary according to the season. High season in Latin America runs from mid-November to mid-January (fares are particularly high over Christmas), Easter, July and August. If you're determined to fly at Christmas or Easter, be prepared to pay premium prices and book months in advance. By contrast, flying in low season can knock as much as $150 off the cost of your flight. The most direct flights are faster but usually more expensive, and you can save cash by taking an indirect flight.

Finally, remember that it's best to avoid arriving in Latin America at night. Banks, bureaux de change and tourist information desks may well be closed and if you don't have a hotel or hostel booked you won't want to start wandering through a strange city in the dark. Always check landing times of any flights. It's also possible to reserve particular seats on some airlines when booking your ticket – ask your travel agent.

## Types of ticket

### One-way

The idea of a **one-way ticket**, leaving you completely free to decide when and from where you're going to return (if ever), might sound romantic, but in real terms it's not very practical. For starters, one-way tickets usually cost around two-thirds of the price of a return ticket, so aren't very economical. Then you'll have to deal with immigration on arrival: without an onward or return ticket, proving that your stay is temporary will be virtually impossible, and you might even be refused entry. Additionally, when you do eventually decide to return you'll find that your flight will cost much more than you would have paid back home – there are none of the discounted ticket deals you'll find in the UK or North America, so you'll be paying full fare, and with Latin America's often exorbitant departure taxes on top.

### Return

Mile for mile, **return tickets** are a much more economical option than one-way fares. However, flying in and out of the same city does restrict your movements, and you may find yourself either having to take a local flight to get back to where you started or wasting valuable days retracing your steps.

The following sample fares are for flights during low season.

**To Mexico City**

| | |
|---|---|
| From London | £488 |
| From Los Angeles | US$450 |
| From New York | US$362 |
| From Toronto | C$854 |
| From Sydney | A$1761 |
| From Auckland | NZ$2455 |

**To Lima**

| | |
|---|---|
| From London | £515 |
| From Los Angeles | US$722 |
| From New York | US$795 |
| From Toronto | C$1451 |
| From Sydney | A$1990 |
| From Auckland | NZ$2020 |

**To Rio de Janeiro**

| | |
|---|---|
| From London | £506 |
| From Los Angeles | US$1295 |
| From New York | US$1345 |
| From Toronto | C$1527 |
| From Sydney | A$1551 |
| From Auckland | NZ$1910 |

## Open-jaw returns and circle tickets

A useful alternative to a straightforward return, especially if you're on a longer trip, is an **open-jaw return**, which allows you to fly into one city and return from another – ticket prices aren't much more than a standard return. A slight variation on an open jaw is a **circle ticket**, which involves flights linking more than one destination – for example London–Caracas–Bogotá–London. This may sound ideal if you want to travel large distances and on specific stopover routes, but choosing several cities to fly between months in advance really does set your itinerary in stone, and a certain amount of backtracking is required on each leg, since you'll have to return to the city you arrived in to fly on to the next.

## Round-the-world (RTW) tickets

If Latin America is part of a longer trip, you might consider a **round-the-world (RTW) ticket**, which is often excellent value for money. Unfortunately, the countries of Latin America aren't included on many standard RTW itineraries – which tend to focus on Asia and Australasia – and where they are, they tend to be on the more expensive routings. The most frequently featured Latin American cities are Mexico City, Lima, Buenos Aires and Rio de Janeiro.

## Charter flights

There are almost no charter flights to Latin America from the UK, although there's a reasonable selection from North America. Virtually all charters go to tourist resorts in Mexico or Costa Rica; although they're often much cheaper than scheduled flights, tickets are only valid for a maximum of three weeks. One possibility, if you can manage to find a charter return which is less than half the price of the standard fare (not as unlikely as you'd imagine), is to buy two and ditch the half of each you won't be using – your local high-street travel agent may be able to come up with a good deal.

## Courier flights

On a **courier flight**, you'll get a deeply discounted ticket – always at least half the price of an average return ticket, and often considerably less – in exchange for accompanying business cargo (which means checking freight in as excess baggage and carrying the relevant shipping documents). Unfortunately, despite their obvious attraction courier flights aren't very practical for long-haul flights, since couriers can only take hand luggage and tickets are usually only valid for a fortnight (and never more than a month). Even so, you may be able to save money by organizing a courier flight out to your destination and then purchasing another ticket when you want to come home. For more information, read the *Courier Air Travel Handbook: Learn How to Travel Worldwide for Next to Nothing* by Mark I. Field (Perpetual Press) or *Winning the Airfare Game* by Charles McCool (Hawk Ridge Press). Alternatively, check out ⓦwww.aircourier.co.uk or ⓦwww.aircourier.org.

## Airpasses

Given the size of Latin America, at some point you might want to take an internal flight. Most Latin American airlines offer **airpasses**, either covering a single country or a particular region – these are more economical if you're planning a series of short flights within a single country or region of Latin America. Airpasses usually include a set number of flights for a certain fee, plus the option of buying a limited number of additional flights at a reduced rate. Airpasses must always be purchased outside the country they serve, and in conjunction with an international air ticket: routes and dates must be fixed on purchase, although they can later be altered for a fee ($10–50). Tickets are completely non-refundable. Passes are cheaper if your international flight is with the relevant national airline.

The most popular **single-country airpasses** cover the region's largest countries, Argentina and Brazil. In Argentina, both LAPA and Aerolineas Argentina airpasses currently cost $339 for three flights, with extra flights (up to nine in total) available for $105 each. Brazilian airpasses with Varig and TAM currently cost $530 for five flights (extra flights cost $100). The sheer size of Brazil means that two connecting internal flights to your planned destination only count as one flight – for instance, if you fly from Rio to Brasilia via São Paulo. Other single-country airpasses cover Mexico, Colombia, Peru and Chile.

Perhaps more useful than single-country airpasses are **regional airpasses**. The Mexipass International is particularly good, taking in all the Latin American cities served by the domestic Mexican airlines AeroMéxico and Mexicana. Prices start at $120 for two flights in Mexico, rising to $600 for the longest distances, such as from Mexico to Buenos Aires. The Mexipass also takes in American cities and makes particular sense if you're flying through Latin America from the US. Similar deals are offered by both Grupo Taca, based in Costa Rica (minimum three flights, with prices starting at $246), and Copa Airlines, Panamá's national carrier (minimum two flights, starting at $264). In South America, the Mercosur airpass covers Argentina, Brazil, Uruguay, Paraguay and Chile (prices vary depending on how far you fly). For more information, contact a good travel agent (see pp.320–22).

# Buying a ticket

The most obvious, though often also the most expensive, way of buying a plane ticket is to contact the relevant airline directly. In most cases the airline will just quote you their standard scheduled fares, although they do occasionally have special offers which are worth checking for. In general, however, it's cheaper to go via a **discount ticket agent** – known as "bucket shops" in the UK and flight consolidators in North America. Discounted tickets are sold in blocks by airlines to these travel agents, who pass on most of the discount to their customers. What you actually pay depends on the mark-up added by the travel agents, as well as the price they originally paid for the tickets (you'll invariably find the person on the plane beside you has paid a different price to you).

Discount agencies are often listed in the classified ads of newspapers' travel sections, and in free or listings magazines. These include, in the UK, the *Sunday Times* travel section, the *Evening Standard* or, best of all, London's *Time Out;* in the US, there's the *Village Voice* in New York, the *Chicago Tribune* and the *Los Angeles Times;* in Australia, try the *Sydney Morning Herald* or *TNT* magazine. Ring around as many as you can and compare prices, which can vary dramatically. If you do decide to buy your ticket from a bucket shop, check that they're bonded with ATOL (ⓦwww.atoldata.org.uk) or ABTA (ⓦwww.abtanet.com) in the UK, or with AFTA (ⓦwww.afta.com.au) in Australia. This means that if the company goes bust you'll be refunded in full – it also tends to indicate a decently run and professional operation. There is no such organization in the US, but you can protect yourself by paying with a credit card (this applies worldwide); again, you'll be refunded in full if your ticket agent goes bust.

Even better is to find a **specialist travel agency** with expertise in Latin America (see the list in Basics on pp.323–24). Most of these have expert staff with first-hand experience of the region, and they can often match the cheapest flights found in bucket shops – as well as giving you the lowdown on airpasses, visas and perhaps even inoculation requirements.

Although booking airline tickets on the **internet** can turn up some great bargains, it has the disadvantage that you'll need to specify both outward and return dates, even though you might be looking for an open-ended departure date. See pp.320–22 for a list of discount agents, most of which have websites.

On the whole, you'll get a better price if you book your ticket several months in advance, since cheaper seats usually go before more expensive ones. If you book your ticket less than two weeks before departure, you may end up paying over the odds, unless you're lucky enough to find a special last-minute flight deal (more likely in low season). In addition, unlikely as it sounds, it's worth trying to bargain, particularly with bucket shops. Discounted ticket prices are not fixed, and if you tell the person you're speaking to that you've been quoted a lower price by another agent you may find that price being matched or even undercut.

When you find the right ticket, remember that discounted tickets are nearly always non-refundable and non-transferable. Check that you can alter your return date should you need to, and find out exactly how much you'll be charged for doing so. On some airlines your travel agent can reserve you a seat and on all of them you can request special meals (vegetarian, halal, kosher) in advance. Very few now permit smoking – if won't be able to last a long flight without lighting up, ask your agent which carriers still take smokers, or stock up on nicotine gum. Finally, pay for your ticket as soon as you can. A small deposit ($75) will usually hold a reservation, but won't guarantee the price you've been quoted.

## Insurance

Having some form of **travel insurance** is absolutely essential. Although the vast majority of travellers to Latin America return home safe and sound, accidents do happen, and without insurance you could be faced with huge medical or legal bills that you can't possibly pay for. As with airfares, it's worth doing a little research on travel insurance before you buy a policy.

Insurance is a very lucrative – and hence highly competitive – business, which helps keep prices low. Premiums vary depending on the level of coverage selected, ranging from around £50/$75 to £100/$150 for six weeks, and approximately £220/$350 to £375/$550 for six months. Some travel agents will try and sell you their own insurance policy when you buy your ticket – these are usually as good as any you can find yourself, but check the details before you sign up. The specialist travel agencies listed in Basics (see pp.323–24) also offer insurance. Other insurers advertise in the travel sections of the publications listed in "Buying a ticket" on p.133, and on the internet.

## Choosing a policy

All insurance policies provide slightly different types of cover, though all include some form of medical coverage and some protection against loss of personal effects (unless you choose to go without this part of the policy – see below). Other standard things covered by travel insurance policies are unavoidable missed flights or cancelled trips, legal expenses, hijack and kidnap, though you won't be covered in the event of a natural disaster or the outbreak of war. The following are the things you should think about before you buy your travel insurance:

- Every policy is slightly different, both in the cover it offers and the way it's written, and it's important to read every last detail. The small print (usually "conditions and exclusions") will tell you exactly what you can and can't claim for – there are virtually as many exclusions as inclusions on most insurance policies.
- Almost all travel insurance policies are one hundred percent refundable within a week of purchase, provided you haven't set off yet. If you decide you're not happy with yours, send it back.
- Dangerous sports, such as rock climbing, skiing, scuba diving and whitewater rafting, often aren't covered by insurance policies unless you pay an additional premium – even fairly innocuous activities like horse-trekking are sometimes not covered. Pay particular attention to the small print in this section to see what's included and what's not.
- Check that you're able to extend your policy from abroad if you decide to extend your trip – this usually just takes a phone call.

Once you've bought insurance, it's essential to make a note of your policy number and the emergency 24-hour telephone helpline (most travellers take their insurance certificates with them, although this isn't usually strictly necessary). You'll have to quote your policy number in any contact you have with your insurance company. If something does happen to you, hold on to copies of all medical bills, receipts or other official documents – without them you won't have a claim.

Finally, remember that insurance companies are notoriously reluctant to pay out; if you do make a claim, the onus will be on you to prove that whatever happened was unavoidable and in no way caused by your own actions. In other words, being insured doesn't give you a licence to jump off cliffs, get into fights or leave your possessions lying around. Take the same amount of care of yourself and your things as if you weren't insured.

## Medical coverage

By far the most important part of your travel insurance is the **medical** coverage. In a worst-case scenario, you may have to be airlifted to hospital and perhaps even repatriated with a trained medical team. Very few people could afford the vast cost of doing this, which is where your insurance company steps in. Less dramatic expenses – medicines and doctor's fees – are also covered. The exception is if you have any existing medical condition which leads to you being treated or hospitalized abroad, in which case you will not be able to make a claim.

Check what the procedure is should you need emergency medical treatment: some companies require you to pay first and then reclaim the costs on your return; others will pay your bill directly to the relevant hospital or doctor. You may also be required to phone (collect call) first to speak to a company-approved doctor to check that you're being offered the correct treatment.

## Personal effects

Although the medical component of your insurance is the most important part, the most common cause of insurance claims is theft – most insurers now offer a discount of around twenty percent if you choose to leave out this area of cover and take your chances. Coverage for personal effects usually includes the loss of a certain amount of cash, passports and other essential documents, but there's usually a maximum amount you can claim for any one item – roughly $250–500 – meaning that you may not be able to claim for the full value of expensive items like cameras which exceed this limit. You might need to invest in a household insurance policy which covers them outside the home or get specialist insurance – camera insurers sometimes advertise in photographic magazines.

## Rough Guides Travel Insurance

**Rough Guides** offers its own travel insurance, customized for our readers by a leading UK broker and backed by a Lloyd's underwriter. It's available for anyone, of any nationality and any age, travelling anywhere in the world. There are two main Rough Guide insurance plans: **Essential**, for basic, no-frills cover; and **Premier** – with more generous and extensive benefits. Alternatively, you can take out **annual multi-trip insurance**, which covers you for any number of trips throughout the year (with a maximum of 60 days for any one trip). Unlike many policies, the Rough Guides schemes are calculated by the day, so if you're travelling for 27 days rather than a month, that's all you pay for. If you intend to be away for the whole year, the **Adventurer** policy will cover you for 365 days. Each plan can be supplemented with a "Hazardous Activities Premium" if you plan to indulge in sports considered dangerous, such as skiing, scuba diving or trekking.

For a policy quote, call the Rough Guide Insurance Line on UK freefone ☎0800/015 0906; US toll-free ☎1-866/220 5588; or, if you're calling from elsewhere ☎+44 1243/621 046. Alternatively, get an online quote or buy online at ⓦwww.roughguidesinsurance.com.

# 3

# When to go

Obviously, planning **when to go** to Latin America is largely dependent on your own circumstances, and when you're able to find the time and the money to get away. These constraints aside, it's important to have an idea of what the **weather** will be like in the areas of Latin America you're planning on visiting, and to understand how seasonal variations in climate are likely to affect your travels – with a little planning, it's possible to organize an extended itinerary through the region that makes the best of the weather conditions in each country you're visiting.

However, it's also worth bearing in mind that, in any particular region, the time of year which enjoys the best weather will almost inevitably also be the **peak tourist season**, particularly if it coincides with the December-to-January, Easter, and June-to-August holiday periods in the US and Europe. Prices for everything from international airline tickets to accommodation are at their highest at these times, and popular destinations can get uncomfortably crowded. If you're prepared to put up with a little rain and visit outside these periods, you'll often be rewarded by lower costs and fewer crowds.

Weather aside, you may also want to arrange your visit around one of Latin America's major **fiestas**. These extravagant festivals encapsulate the heart of Latin American culture and are amongst the most colourful and exciting experiences the region has to offer, so it's well worth making the effort to coincide with one of these, as it's likely to prove one of the highlights of your travels.

If you're travelling for a few months or so, bear in mind that it's also a lot more pleasant to be away during the winter and to return home in the spring or summer.

## Climate in Latin America

Most of Latin America lies within the **tropics**, the zone on either side of the equator between the Tropic of Capricorn in the south and the Tropic of Cancer in the north. There's no real difference between winter and summer in the tropics, and seasonal variations in temperature are minimal – Belize City, for example, is 27°C in January and 31°C in July. Despite the relatively stable temperature, there are considerable seasonal variations in rainfall and humidity which may affect your plans. Most tropical regions have **wet seasons**, when heavy rain can make travel difficult and uncomfortable.

However, despite the fact that most tropical regions receive extremely high annual rainfall, even in the rainy seasons this tends to be concentrated in torrential bursts lasting a few hours or so (in some places, afternoon downpours are so predictable you can almost set your watch by them), after which the skies clear and the sun comes out. In some tropical lowland regions – particularly in the rainforests of the Amazon and the Colombian Pacific coast – it can rain almost every day (it's not called rainforest for nothing), so the occasional soaking just goes with the territory and will only really spoil your trip if roads are washed out, making bus travel impossible.

That's not to say tropical Latin America is uniformly hot, however: **altitude** is a huge factor in determining local climate, particularly in the Andean countries, which sit astride the highest tropical mountain range in the world. Temperatures decrease by about 6–7°C with every 1000m you ascend, so that in the Ecuadorian capital Quito, for example, which is set at an altitude of 2800m, the year-round daytime temperature never really exceeds a spring-like 20°C (with much cooler nights), even though the city sits almost directly on the equator. In mountainous countries you can take advantage of local differences in climate caused by altitude: if you can't stand the heat and humidity of the lowlands, you can always escape to the comparatively cooler highlands (it's no coincidence that many Spanish colonial cities were founded at higher altitudes), while if the bitterly cold nights in one of the cities of the high Andes get too much to bear, you can always jump on a bus and head down into the sweltering lowlands for a day or two.

South of Latin America's tropics, the temperate "**Southern Cone**" region – comprising Argentina, Chile, Uruguay and southern Brazil – experiences far greater annual variations in temperature, with seasons similar (but in reverse) to those of the northern hemisphere. However, it's only in the far south of the Southern Cone that the cold weather and short days of the southern-hemisphere winter (June–Sept) can limit your options and make travel unpleasant.

Whilst taking seasonal variations into account, you shouldn't let the prospect of very wet or cold weather put you off altogether, so long as you're prepared for travel arrangements to be less reliable and for certain outdoor activities, such as trekking, to be less enjoyable.

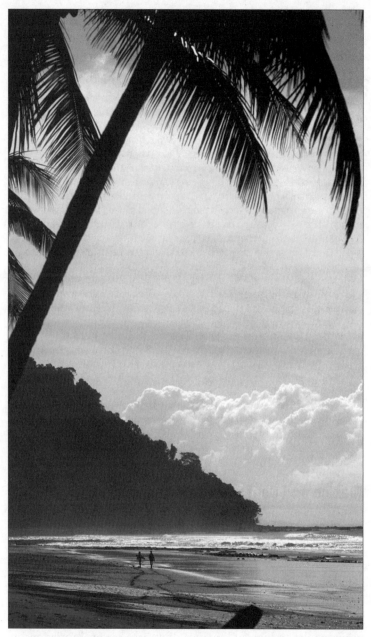

△ Pacific Coast beach, Costa Rica

## El Niño

Every two to seven years, weather patterns across much of Latin America and beyond are transformed by a natural phenomenon known as **El Niño**, with devastating results. The phenomenon was first recognized by Peruvian fishermen in the nineteenth century, when the appearance of unusually warm waters off the coast of Peru, displacing the colder, nutrient-rich Humboldt Current, had catastrophic effects on fish catches. They christened the phenomenon El Niño – meaning "Little Boy" or "Christ Child" – because it usually appears around Christmas time.

This shift in Pacific Ocean currents is caused by a slackening of the trade winds and resultant warming of the surface layer of water in the eastern and central Pacific, accompanied by sharp swings in atmospheric pressure. As well as disrupting vital fisheries, El Niño provokes sudden and often disastrous changes in weather patterns, bringing sudden floods to some parts of Latin America and drought to others. The last time El Niño struck, in 1997–98, it wrought havoc throughout Latin America, particularly in Peru and Ecuador, where massive floods killed hundreds, devastating crops and infrastructure and inflicting many millions of dollars worth of damage. Nor is El Niño's impact limited to Latin America: scientists now believe it also changes weather patterns worldwide, and may be responsible for droughts and floods in places as far apart as the US, Australia and East Africa, as well as for increasing the strength and frequency of hurricanes in the Caribbean. Scientists are also becoming more concerned that the frequency and severity of El Niño may be growing as global temperatures rise, possibly as a result of human activity. If so, the consequences for millions of people in Latin America could be dire indeed. As a traveller to Latin America, it's worth keeping an eye on news reports to see if your visit coincides with a possible El Niño year. If it does, be prepared for freak weather conditions and severe disruption. For a wealth of information on El Niño, including the latest predictions, check out the US National Oceanic and Atmospheric Administration website at Ⓦ www.elnino.noaa.gov.

# Mexico and Central America

**Northern Mexico** is the only part of Latin America north of the tropics, but the region is so hot and arid that rain and the northern hemisphere winter are no real impediment to travel, though it can get pretty cold at higher altitudes between December and February. **Southern Mexico** lies within the tropics and shares the same seasonal climate patterns as the countries of **Central America**, which are generally hot and humid year-round (though, again, cooler in highland regions), but have seasonal variations in rainfall and humidity. The best time to visit southern Mexico and Central America is during the dry season, which runs roughly from November to March. The rainy season runs from around May to October, but even then it doesn't rain all the time, and you'll often get a fine sunny morning followed by a few hours of rain in the afternoon. Along the **Caribbean coastline** of Central America, rain and humidity continue year-round with only slight seasonal variations.

## The tropical Andean countries

Running the length of the western side of South America, the Andes are the second-biggest mountain range in the world, and the highest range in tropical latitudes. In the five tropical countries the Andes pass through – **Venezuela, Colombia, Ecuador, Peru** and **Bolivia** – the extreme variations in altitude created by the mountains produce an astonishing number of different climatic zones within a surprisingly small area. The eastern slopes of the Andes, in particular, are so steep that it's possible to experience both sub-zero conditions and extreme tropical heat in the same afternoon, even if you're travelling on foot. Colombia is home to so many different microclimates as to make generalization almost impossible, while Peru embraces perhaps the greatest extremes of climate of any country on earth, ranging from the world's driest desert on its Pacific coast to the glacial peaks of the high Andes and the hot and humid lowlands of the world's largest tropical rainforest in the Amazon basin. This enormous variety means that whatever time of the year you happen to be in one of these countries, the weather conditions are likely to be ideal in at least some regions (though it's equally likely to be pouring with rain elsewhere).

However, there are also some broad seasonal differences that you should be aware of when planning your trip. In so far as it's possible to generalize, **Venezuela** and **Colombia** broadly share the same dry season as Central America, particularly along the Caribbean coast, so November to March is the best time to visit. The rest of the year tends to be much wetter (though rain falls throughout the year in the lowland rainforest regions in both countries and along Colombia's Pacific coast). Further south, the Andean countries of **Ecuador, Peru** and **Bolivia** experience more defined seasonal differences. In the **highlands**, the dry season runs between May and October, with bright, dry, sunny days, though nights can be cold, particularly at higher altitudes. This is obviously the best time to visit, particularly if you want to do any trekking or mountaineering, though it also coincides with the peak tourist season from June to August. The rainy season runs roughly from November to April, with the wettest weather in January and February, and is generally a less favourable time to visit, particularly for trekking in the mountains: rain makes hiking pretty miserable and cloud can obscure the best views, while some high-altitude routes become cut off by snow. However, trekking aside it rarely rains so much as to spoil your day, and the landscape is arguably more beautiful than during the dry season, with crops high in the fields and the mountainsides green with vegetation, rather than parched and brown. The main drawback is that heavy rains can cause floods and landslides that damage or completely block the generally poor mountain roads, causing frequent travel delays.

Though the **Amazon Basin** is pretty wet all year round, along its western edge in Peru and Bolivia it is also affected by the Andean rainy season, so between November and April the Amazon regions of both countries see heavy rain and can be impossible to visit, as roads are washed away and large areas are flooded (though, conversely, river transport can be easier). The **Pacific coast** of Ecuador and Peru is affected by a very different set of seasonal variations. The period from around December to March generally sees hot, sunny days along the coast (in comparison to the rains that affect the highlands), but for most of the rest of the year the region is covered by low coastal cloud or mist known as *garúa*, which makes for grey days and cold swimming, even though it rarely ever rains along the entire length of the Peruvian coast.

## Brazil

Given its vast size, it's no surprise that **Brazil**'s climate varies considerably between different parts of the country. The entire country lies within the tropics, so it's generally hot and humid year-round, and in most areas rain can fall at any time of the year, though rarely for long enough to affect your travel plans – in general, most of the country can be visited at any time. The main exception to this is the **far south** of the country, where the climate is more temperate and seasonal variations are more marked; here, the southern-hemisphere winter months from June to August see cooler temperatures and heavy rains which can make travelling miserable, while the peak summer months of January and February are particularly hot and humid and coincide with the main holiday period for Brazilians.

## The Southern Cone

South America's **Southern Cone**, comprising Argentina, Chile and Uruguay, lies almost completely outside the tropics and enjoys a temperate climate with more marked seasonal differences in climate between the winter (June–Aug) and summer (Nov–Feb) – the fact that these seasons are the exact opposite of those in the northern hemisphere means that if you time your trip right you can

### The Best Time to Visit

What follows is a very broad guide to the best times of year for travelling to each country in Latin America ("best" meaning the driest and mildest conditions). This summary is meant only as a general introduction to help you plan your route; for more detail, check the relevant guidebooks, tourist offices and other sources of information.

| | |
|---|---|
| **Argentina** | Dec–May |
| **Belize** | Late Dec to March |
| **Bolivia** | May–Sept |
| **Brazil** | Feb–June |
| **Chile** | Nov–March in the south; year-round elsewhere |
| **Colombia** | Nov–March |
| **Costa Rica** | Nov, April & May |
| **Ecuador** | June–Aug in the highlands; Dec–April on the coast |
| **El Salvador** | Nov–April |
| **Guatemala** | Feb–May |
| **The Guianas** | Feb & March, July–Nov |
| **Honduras** | March–May |
| **Mexico** | Nov–Feb |
| **Nicaragua** | Dec–March |
| **Panamá** | Dec–April (the dry season) |
| **Paraguay** | May–Sept (the cooler winter months) |
| **Peru** | May–Sept in the highlands and Amazon (the dry season) and Dec–March on the coast |
| **Uruguay** | Sept–April |
| **Venezuela** | Nov–June (the dry season) |

enjoy two summers in one year. Uruguay and the northern parts of Chile and Argentina can be comfortably visited at any time of the year, though the winter months are cooler and drier than the summer, which can be unpleasantly hot: the optimum times are spring (Sept & Oct) and autumn (March & April). The further south you travel in Chile and Argentina, however, the better it is to avoid the winter months, when the days become short and it gets very cold and wet; in addition, heavy snow can prevent access to mountainous national parks and block some passes between Chile and Argentina (though, of course, this is the perfect time to go skiing). In the far south, the summer offers the added advantage of long summer evenings, allowing far more time to enjoy the sights.

## Fiestas

Latin Americans welcome any excuse for a party, and most countries host a large number of national, regional and local **fiestas**. These are amongst the most vibrant and exciting spectacles Latin America has to offer, and are often worth planning your trip around. For many Latin Americans, fiestas are the most important events of the year and are taken very seriously, often involving lengthy preparation and considerable expense, with the largest featuring thousands of costumed dancers, massed bands, fireworks, copious food and drink, and unrestrained revelry that can continue for a week or more.

The most famous fiesta is without doubt the **Carnaval** in Rio de Janeiro, one of the biggest parties in the world. It's worth remembering that Carnival (originally a religious festival marking the start of Lent) is also celebrated throughout Brazil and the rest of Latin America, albeit on a less spectacular scale, and smaller celebrations can often have a more intimate and authentic and less commercial feel.

Like Carnival, many of the major fiestas mark important dates in the Roman Catholic **religious calendar**, so the dates they're held on can vary from year to year – tourist offices should be able to give you precise details of major events. As well as religious occasions like Carnival and Semana Santa (Easter), many national and regional public holidays mark significant events in Latin America's post-conquest **history**, such as the gaining of independence, famous battles or the foundation of particular cities – although still treated as an excuse for a party, these tend to be somewhat stuffier affairs, involving interminable civic and military parades.

During major fiestas, **transport and accommodation** can be very difficult to come by and prices increase dramatically, so it's worth booking well in advance. Even when they don't coincide with an official public holiday, major fiestas tend to result in pretty much everything shutting down for at least a day or two, so they're not a good time to buy an airline ticket, change money in a bank, or get a visa extension. The same is true of national public holidays, particularly the Christmas and New Year period, when buses and trains get very crowded as people travel to visit relations, and international flights are often booked up months ahead by expatriate Latin Americans returning home for the holidays.

As well as major national and regional celebrations, most towns and villages have their own annual **local fiesta** (some have several), usually held on the day of its patron saint. These celebrations can be much more fun to visit than major fiestas in larger towns, particularly in rural areas of countries with a large indigenous population such as Guatemala, Peru and Bolivia, where they can last over a week and involve traditional music and colourful costumed folkloric dances. Be prepared to change your itinerary at short notice if you hear of a good local fiesta going on anywhere near where you are – it's an opportunity not to be missed.

We've listed some of our favourite fiestas below; any guidebook or local tourist office will suggest many others. It's also worth looking at *Wild Planet! 1001 Extraordinary Events for the Inspired Traveller* by Tom Clynes (Visible Ink Press), which has details of dozens of celebrations throughout Latin America and the rest of the world, or check out the websites ⓦwww.whatsonwhen.com and ⓦwww.worldparty.co .uk, which list hundreds of events by country and by month.

● **Feria de Alasitas** La Paz, Bolivia (last week of Jan). This unusual festival sees the streets of central La Paz filled with stalls selling miniature models of items as varied as cars, houses, livestock, wads of dollar bills, and even computers and university degree certificates. Locals buy these to offer to Ekeko, the household god of abundance (portrayed as a diminutive, smiling, moustached man), in the belief that whatever they give him in miniature will be given back to them for real before the year is out.

- **Carnival** (late Feb or early March). Beginning on the Friday before Ash Wednesday, the pre-Lenten *Carnaval* in Rio de Janeiro is without doubt the world's most famous party, a five-day extravaganza that attracts over a quarter of a million foreign visitors each year. The highlights are the processions of the samba schools, each made up of thousands of costumed dancers and myriad decorated floats, who parade along the main avenues and around the purpose-built Sambódromo, competing both to impress the *Carnaval* judges and the huge crowds. The manic celebrations continue through the night at numerous themed *Carnaval* balls, unrestrained parties that start a week before the main event.

    Carnival is also celebrated throughout the rest of Brazil and Latin America, albeit on a smaller and less dramatic scale than in Rio, though usually involving the same ingredients of music, dance and licentiousness. If the sheer scale and commercialism of the Rio *Carnaval* puts you off, you may be better off joining a smaller but arguably more authentic celebration somewhere else – many people rate the celebrations in Salvador de Bahia, with its strong Afro-Brazilian traditions, more highly than Rio. Elsewhere, the Carnival in Baranquilla, on the Colombian Caribbean coast, is renowned for its raucousness, while Carnival in the bleak Bolivian mining city of Oruro is amongst the most colourful folkloric fiestas in all Latin America.

- **International Caribbean Music Festival** Cartagena, Colombia (March). For two weeks in March the beautiful colonial port city of Cartagena, on Colombia's north coast, is taken over by bands and musicians from all over the Caribbean who come to take part in one of Latin America's best live-music events. All the region's rich musical heritage is featured, including reggae, soca, salsa, merengue and vallenato.

- **Semana Santa** (March or April) Semana Santa – the Easter Holy Week – is marked throughout Latin America with colourful religious processions. The celebrations in the city of Ayacucho in Peru and in Antigua in Guatemala are particularly fervent and dramatic. For more on Semana Santa, see the box on p.VIII.

- **Qoyllur Riti** Peru (May or June). Held at the foot of a glacier in an isolated valley in the Andes south of Cuzco in the week before Corpus Christi, this is one of the most exciting fiestas in Latin America, a celebration of ancient Andean beliefs centred on mountain gods and the Pleiades constellation and covered only by the thinnest veneer of Catholicism. Thousands of indigenous peasants make the pilgrimage to a bleak spot at over 4000m, many of them marching through the night, and costumed dances, accompanied by traditional music and dynamite explosions, continue for three days and nights. On the last night, young men dressed in ritual costumes of the Ukuku – a half-bear, half-human hero figure from Andean mythology – stay up on the high glacier, marching down at first light bearing hunks of ice on their backs (which are melted down and taken to their home communities to improve fertility) as well as the bodies of those who have died during the night either from hypothermia or as a result of falling into crevasses – there are usually several deaths annually, which are considered at once a personal tragedy and an auspicious occurrence which is an essential part of the fertility rite. This is primarily an indigenous fiesta and though a few Cuzco tour agencies take groups, it's only for the adventurous, as you'll have to hike there and camp out at high altitude.

● **Inti Raymi and Corpus Christi** Cusco, Peru (June). Inti Raymi (June 24) is a popular and commercial re-enactment of the Inca Festival of the Sun, performed by costumed actors in Sacsayhuaman, the massive Inca fortress that towers above Cuzco. The fiesta draws thousands of tourists to the city, and hotels and flights fill up, but it's far from the most authentic of Cuzco's many fiestas: Corpus Christi, which takes place nine weeks after Maundy Thursday (usually in mid-June), is a more traditional event, involving mass processions of saints' effigies (a practice which replaced the Inca tradition of parading the mummies of former emperors) accompanied by costumed dancers, traditional music, and street markets selling traditional food.

● **Day of the Dead** Mexico (Nov 1 & 2). Fervently celebrated throughout Mexico on All Saint's Day, and through the night into the following day (All Soul's Day, the Day of the Dead proper), the Day of the Dead is a time of remembrance which is at once sombre and festive. People converge on cemeteries with food and drink to party with their deceased loved ones and ancestors. In the run-up to the event throughout the country shops and market stalls sell special foods and macabre decorations in the shape of skulls, coffins and the like, which are used to adorn graves, and ceremonial offerings arranged in honour of the dead, who are believed to return to the land of the living and visit their former homes for the day. Precise customs vary from region to region within Mexico – one of the most dramatic places to witness the occasion is on the Lago de Pátzcuaro, about 200km east of Mexico City, where locals converge on an island cemetery in canoes carrying candles and floral offerings. The Day of the Dead is also celebrated in similar fashion in Guatemala (where the fiesta at

Santiago Sacatapéquez involves the flying of massive kites to release the souls of the dead) and – though on a more restrained scale and without the bizarre ritual paraphernalia – throughout the Andes.

- **Día de la Tradición** Argentina (around Nov 10). Also known as the Fiesta del Gaucho, this is a celebration of Argentina's most powerful cultural icon, the gauchos (cowboys) of the pampas grasslands. Centred on the town of Santiago de Areco, the festival involves traditional gaucho folk music and dance, rodeos and horse-riding displays, and the consumption of large quantities of the finest beef in the world, much of it cooked in the traditional gaucho style: roasted on a spit over an open fire.
- **Día de la Virgen de Guadalupe** Mexico (Dec 12). Mexico's patron saint's day is celebrated with extravagant processions and a mass pilgrimage to the Basilica de Guadalupe, outside Mexico City, with many of the thousands of celebrants advancing to the shrine on their knees.

# 4

# How much will it cost?

The cost of travelling in Latin America varies wildly: from ultra-cheap countries like Nicaragua or Bolivia to places like Chile or Costa Rica, where living costs can be similar to those in Europe or North America. Overall, though, travelling in Latin America is much less expensive than travelling in your own country. Having said this, you're going to come across the kind of opportunities on your trip that you don't normally come across – staying in a remote eco-lodge in the Amazon, hang-gliding over Rio, riding with gauchos in Argentina – and these opportunities all have a price tag. While you might baulk at the cost of all this, actually doing any of these things will give you memories which will last well beyond the pain caused by prising open your wallet. Just accept, even before you set off, that visiting Latin America is going to cost you – if this really is the trip of a lifetime, then it's worth doing it properly.

Obviously, your budget is vital in determining what kind of trip you have, and it's important before you set out to have at least a rough idea of how much you'll need. If you do have a very limited budget, then think about taking a shorter but more satisfying trip. Nothing is more frustrating than not having enough cash to really enjoy your holiday. Imagine getting all the way to Venezuela and not being able to afford the flight to the Angel Falls, or going to the Caribbean islands of Mexico, Belize or Honduras and sitting forlornly on the beach while everyone else goes snorkelling or scuba diving.

However tedious it sounds, once on the road, it really does help to keep a record of your expenses so that you always know how much money you have to play with. It's all too easy to run out of cash well before the end of your trip, or (much less likely) forgo a special outing because you're saving money when actually you don't need to. Don't be alarmed if you spend a lot of money in your first few days, however – it's well worth the investment just to feel safe and properly acclimatized. If you're on a tight budget, consider flying into one of the cheaper Latin American countries and then taking on the more expensive ones once you're an old hand at cutting corners.

If you're planning to get involved in voluntary, ecology or community projects whilst away, you may be eligible for some kind of grant or sponsorship – check the *Directory of Grant Making Trusts, The Grants Register* or *The Australian Grants Register* in your local library. These publications list businesses which regularly give funds to or sponsor all kinds of projects and individuals, including small-scale schemes which involve travelling abroad.

## Cost of living

It's difficult to generalize about the cost of living in Latin America, which can vary wildly even between adjacent countries – travelling in Costa Rica costs two or three times more than in neighbouring Nicaragua, for example, whilst crossing the border from Bolivia into Chile will immediately double your expenses. In general, the richer, more westernized Latin American countries are significantly more expensive to travel in than the poorer, less developed ones, and knowing roughly how much you'll need in each one will allow you to prepare for sudden changes in living expenses. For more details, see the box overleaf.

Bear in mind that parts of Latin America have been – and may again be – subject to periods of economic meltdown and hyper-inflation, as demonstrated by recent fiscal woes in Argentina, which have had a topsy-turvy effect on that nation's cost of living.

# Making savings before you go

With a little careful planning, you can start cutting the cost of your trip immediately.

- Begin planning well in advance of your departure date – if you leave everything to the last minute you'll invariably pay over the odds. Do some research on basic expenses like airfares and insurance so you know, before you start, how much you should be paying.
- Wait for the sales to buy your equipment or surf the net for special deals. Alternatively, borrow gear from friends and family – rucksacks, in particular, are often bought, used and then thrown into the back of the wardrobe – and consider buying secondhand stuff (although you should check important pieces of equipment like rucksacks or boots carefully), such as clothes, which you can then ditch on your way home. Alternatively, you could wait to buy basic clothing until you arrive in Latin America, where it's invariably cheaper than at home.
- Make sure you buy those day-to-day items which cost considerably more abroad before you go – these are usually things that the locals don't use as much, such as camera film, batteries, suntan lotion, moisturising cream and tampons.

# Making savings on the road

Obviously there are unavoidable expenses, mainly consisting of the big three: lodging, eating, transport. The following tips will help you to minimize expenses.

- The slower you travel the cheaper your trip will be. Not only will you cut down on transport costs, which in some countries can be considerable, but with each day you spend in one place you'll be discovering new budget restaurants, and you should also be able to get a reduced rate on accommodation if you're staying more than a few days – always ask.
- Travel during the low season, when hotel and tour prices drop (sometimes dramatically) and when the relative lack of tourists gives you more bargaining power. Conversely if you're staying in a holiday resort or popular spot over a local holiday period you'll pay premium rates – if you don't mind missing the party avoid going to the beach or the UNESCO World Heritage Site at weekends or on public holidays.

## Sample budgets

Listed below are **minimum** daily living expenses in Latin America (which cover staying in cheap hotels/hostels, eating *comida corriente* and travelling by local bus).

**Cheap – less than $15**
Bolivia
Colombia
Guatemala
Nicaragua

**Moderate – $15–25**
Argentina
Brazil
Ecuador (excluding trips to the
   Galápagos Islands)
El Salvador
Guyana
Honduras

Mexico (excluding the more
   expensive Caribbean coast)
Paraguay
Peru
Suriname
Uruguay
Venezuela

**Expensive – over $25**
Belize
Chile
Costa Rica
French Guiana
Panamá

## Sample budgets

The following sample budgets are linked to a few of the itineraries suggested on pp.105–13.

**Three weeks on South America's Caribbean coast** Though both Venezuela and particularly Colombia are inexpensive to visit, anywhere on the Caribbean tends to cost more than inland destinations. Still, $600 will cover your expenses and include a couple of snorkelling or boat trips, the odd night in a decent hotel and an occasional posh meal.

**One month on the Ruta Maya** Ten days in Mexico and Belize will be fairly expensive, though the rest of this trip – twenty days in Guatemala, Honduras and El Salvador – will cost much less. Altogether, count on spending $700 for the month.

**Three months in the Andean highlands** While Chile is one of the priciest countries in South America, the other places on this itinerary – Peru, Ecuador and particularly Bolivia – are among its cheapest. For this trip reckon on a minimum budget of $1000.

- Form groups with other travellers for arranging tours, hiring transport and even getting good deals on accommodation. The more there are of you, the cheaper things get. Once you've got your bargain, you can always split up into your original smaller units.
- Always ask the price of things before you start. Be very wary of menus with no prices, agree fares with taxi drivers before you get in (and get the driver to repeat it back to you so there can be no confusion).
- Do as the locals do. Take local buses, eat in markets or informal cafés and choose the daily set meal.
- Travel at night. In the larger countries of South America, many journeys can be taken at night, saving you the cost of a night's accommodation (but check before you go that the journey isn't prey to thieves or guerrillas – some, unfortunately, are).
- Stay in hostel dormitories. They're often the cheapest accommodation available, and most also have kitchens where you can cook your own meals. You might even want to take a tent – you can often camp in the gardens of hostels or cheap hotels, or in national parks – or buy a hammock, which you can sling up on a willing hotel proprietor's porch for a very small fee.
- Take a water filter or some other method of purifying unclean water. Tap water in Latin America is usually not safe, and bottled water, not something the locals buy, can cost as much as other drinks including beer, sometimes more – buying several litres every day will hike up your daily budget.
- Home stays – staying with a local family – are good for practising your Spanish or Portuguese, a great way to get involved in the community and, above all, cheap.

## Tourist prices

You may as well accept right from the start that you'll be paying more for most things than the locals – annoying as you might find this, there's very little you can do about it. In some parts of Latin America, tourists are officially charged more than nationals for things like entrance fees to museums and art galleries, national parks and sites of historic and archeological interest. Arguing until you're blue in the face won't make any difference. If you want to visit these places then you'll have to pay the extra.

Much more widespread is the unofficial hike in prices that happens when a tourist comes to town. Market food, taxi fares and perhaps even hotel rooms and meals will invariably cost more. However, you should refuse to pay anything that seems outrageous, not only for the sake of your own funds, but also because tourists who pay silly money push up the cost of living for the locals – after all, why sell something to a local when you can get five times its value from a rich visitor? Very soon locals become second-class citizens – which naturally fuels resentment, making things even worse for visitors.

Having said that, as a tourist you'll always pay a bit extra, so you may as well accept it – always bear in mind that what is small change to you might be a lot more important to the seller. There is nothing uglier than a tourist with a thousand-dollar camera round his neck quibbling with a *campesino* over the price of an orange.

For more on spending money responsibly, see the section on ethical tourism on pp.328–29.

## Bargaining

One way to cut costs and reduce the effect of tourist prices is to master the fine art of bargaining. Latin America's more developed countries tend to be relatively closed to bargaining, whereas those with a large indigenous population have a long tradition of flexible pricing. Markets are the best place to start, since virtually all prices in these are open to negotiation. The quoted cost of hotel rooms, tours and private transport (including taxis and boats) can also sometimes be lowered. Don't assume, however, that all prices are open to negotiation in every country – they're not, and there will be much rolling of eyes if you pick the wrong place to have a go. Places where bargaining is off limits are fairly obvious: supermarkets, smart clothes shops and chemists all have fixed prices; equally, you can't bargain for airline or bus tickets, or reduce the cost of items on restaurant menus.

Before buying anything, have a look around and compare prices to give yourself an idea of prices. When bargaining, retain a sense of humour at all times and be as charming as you can; be complimentary, polite and patient, and bear in mind that this is not a matter of life or death – at least, not to you. If you think your chosen stallholder is trying to rip you off or you're just not happy with the way things are going then walk away – the simple act of leaving might trigger a better offer. If you're planning on buying a lot of last-minute presents or souvenirs you might save some money by buying them all in the same place. Don't appear too keen when bargaining, and if you've almost sealed the deal, get out the relevant cash: the sight of your money might encourage the seller to close out the deal at a slightly lower price.

## Splashing out

In Latin America, quite possibly for the first time in your life, you'll be considered rich. And, like it or not, by most Latin American standards, you are – compare the cost of your return airfare with wages in the poorer parts of the continent of as little as $15 a week (coupled with 75 percent unemployment rates) and you begin to get the picture. Instead of fighting this and irritating the locals by continuing to insist that actually you're an impoverished student struggling to make ends meet, why not make the most of your temporary wealth?

In some parts of Latin America, $30 will buy you a night in a plush hotel room with all the frills. On the Atlantic coast of Nicaragua you'll pay less than $7 for a slap-up meal of freshly caught lobster. You can learn to scuba dive in the Bay Islands of Honduras for as little as a third of what it would cost elsewhere – and the same holds for learning Spanish in Guatemala, whitewater rafting in Peru or mountain-climbing in Bolivia.

Occasionally there may be times on the road when you need to indulge yourself. Long bumpy bus rides; lack of sleep caused by poor hotels; bad food; mosquito bites; extremes of heat and cold – all these can take their toll and leave you exhausted. Instead of staggering on until you grind to a halt or fall ill, it's a good idea to take time out by paying more than normal for a decent night's sleep and a proper hot meal. And when it comes to your personal safety, no price is too high to pay. If the only budget hotel in town is down a dark alleyway, don't book in; if the cheapest local guide is clearly a bit of a cowboy, don't hire him; and if the third-class boat you're planning to board looks like it might sink, don't get on it. You'll feel very foolish if something awful happens simply because you were cutting corners.

# How to take your money

The best way to keep your money safe is to take it in as many different forms as possible – cash, travellers' cheques, credit cards. In addition, be sure to check exchange rates on the internet (Ⓦwww.oanda.com or Ⓦwww.xe.com/ucc) or in a newspaper before you go so that you'll know roughly what you should be getting.

## Dollars and dollarization

The US dollar rules supreme in Latin America, and you should never be without some. It's actually the official currency of both Panamá and Ecuador, in Panamá's case since independence in 1904, and in Ecuador as recently as 2000; in addition, in 2003 both El Salvador and Guatemala will be adopting the dollar as national currency. This process of using the US dollar as the official currency – known as "dollarization" – is increasingly prevalent in Latin America. Costa Rica, Argentina and Mexico are the next likely candidates for full dollarization, and have all held high-level talks on the subject.

Dollarization is popular because the US dollar has a great track record as a stable currency, and adopting it puts an end to sudden spells of devaluation and hyperinflation. Trade between Latin America and the US costs less without currency conversion and, at a grassroots level, local people feel confident that their savings are safe. It does, however, mean a loss of economic independence – an important political hurdle, especially given that relations between the US and Latin America are uneasy at the best of times. This is perhaps why Mexico, an obvious candidate for dollarization, has resisted the process thus far and is still hotly debating the subject. The bad news for visitors is that countries which have adopted full dollarization have generally become more expensive than previously to visit.

Much more to the point, however, is unofficial dollarization – dollars still have a kind of mystique in some parts of Latin America, and some traders prefer them to local currency. Every country in Latin America accepts US dollars as payment as well as its own currency – according to the IMF, eighty percent of the money supply in Bolivia is made up of dollars, while in Argentina, Costa Rica,

Nicaragua, Peru and Uruguay, it's more than thirty percent. Generally speaking, the more expensive the service or goods you're buying, the greater the chance that you'll be able to pay in dollars, while the further away you get from tourist areas, the slimmer your chances of paying in dollars become.

Buying dollars before you leave home is the same as for any other foreign currency. In case you run short, you can also get dollars from ATMs in some parts of Latin America – this is easiest in Mexico.

## Cash

The easiest and cheapest – though least secure – way to take your money is as cash, either in local currency or as US dollars. Don't change too much cash all in one go, though. You'll miss out on local currency fluctuations, which often favour established hard currencies like the dollar and the pound. More importantly, you won't get cash back if it's stolen unless you've invested in a more comprehensive insurance scheme.

## Travellers' cheques

Travellers' cheques (*cheques de viaje*) are by far the safest way of carrying cash abroad, and come with a guarantee that they'll be swiftly replaced in full should they be stolen (assuming you've kept a record of the lost cheque numbers). The price for this security is the commission you pay to buy them (usually 1–1.5%), as well as a possible commission when you change them and, in many cases, a lower exchange rate.

For Latin America, you should always buy travellers' cheques issued in US dollars; any other currency renders them virtually useless. Also ask for a variety of different denominations: larger ones will save you commission fees and endless visits to the bank, while smaller ones are good for changing in places where you'd rather not carry heaps of cash. American Express travellers' cheque are recognized almost everywhere, while Thomas Cook cheques are also well known – other types of cheque may not be accepted.

The standard procedure for using travellers' cheques will be explained to you in full when you buy them. You'll also be given a record of purchase as well as a list of the serial number of each cheque you've bought. Keep both these documents safe and separate from the cheques themselves – a record of purchase is sometimes requested by the bank changing your money as a security check, and if you do have travellers' cheques stolen you'll have to quote the numbers of those missing. Tick off each number on your list as you change them.

If your cheques are stolen, you'll have to make your way to the nearest American Express or Thomas Cook agent. If you ring in advance your replacement cheques may well be waiting for you when you arrive – make sure you carry the free hotline number on you at all times. You will be expected to take the necessary precautions to avoid being robbed and, if you are, to have a plausible explanation of the circumstances.

## Credit and debit cards

Credit and debit cards are the most convenient, if not necessarily the cheapest, way to carry funds in Latin America. Most banks will give you an advance on your card, and there are increasing numbers of ATMs across Latin America where you can withdraw the local currency (and sometimes even dollars) – you can check the location of ATMs in Latin America at Ⓦwww.visa.com or Ⓦwww.mastercard.com. In lots of places, you can also pay for higher-end hotel rooms, meals, airline tickets and other large purchases using plastic.

It's worth remembering, however, that using a credit or debit card is far from cheap. When it comes to **withdrawing money** from an ATM, the average cost for using both types of card includes a 1.5% handling charge plus a further 2.75% commission on foreign exchange – in total, a whopping 4.25% (on the plus side, however, ATMs often offer far better exchange rates than local banks or *casas de cambio*). With credit cards, you'll also be paying interest on any money withdrawn from the moment you take it out. Additionally, if you're paying for a room or a meal with plastic you may be stung with an additional charge levied by the hotel or restaurant owner to cover the commission that the proprietor will have to pay to the card issuer – such additional charges are completely unregulated, and can potentially be as high as fifteen percent. Always check in advance if you're intending to pay by card. In terms of security, avoid withdrawing cash from an ATM at night and exercise due caution at all times – choose machines in busy public places and don't hang around after your transaction. If your card is stolen, ring the emergency phone number (which you should always carry with you) as soon as possible to cancel it. Assuming you report the theft promptly, you won't be liable for a thief's spending spree.

The most popular credit cards in Latin America are Visa and Mastercard – Visa is the more widely accepted of the two, though it's worth carrying both. If you're travelling for a while, you'll need either to set up a direct debit or ask a friend to pay off your account. It's also possible to get Visa debit cards: these work in most Latin American ATMs (as do other debit cards linked to the Cirrus or Plus networks). Don't take a debit card issued by your bank unless it carries a Visa, Mastercard, Cirrus or Plus symbol, or it will probably prove useless.

An alternative way of carrying funds is **Visa TravelMoney**. This is a disposable debit card which you can use in any ATM which accepts Visa cards. You can buy cards loaded with prepaid funds from most branches of Thomas Cook and Citicorp. Once the funds you've loaded on to the card run out, you simply throw it away. You can also request up to nine cards to access the same funds – very useful for couples or groups travelling with a common kitty.

## Changing money

The easiest form of money to change is dollars: in many parts of Latin America virtually everyone you come across – hoteliers, restaurateurs, shopkeepers, local business people, market traders – will be more than happy to change them for you at the going rate. There are also moneychangers (*coyotes*) on the streets in most Latin American countries who'll change dollars for rates slightly better than banks, and without commission. They normally hang out in commercial areas, like shopping malls or around markets – you'll recognize them by the wads of cash they flick through and wave in your face. Some are licensed, while some are unofficial – be very careful if you decide to deal with the latter, who are adept at all kinds of scams. By contrast, official licensed moneychangers (look for the badge) are often trustworthy, though it's worth checking locally first.

You can also change money at banks and *casas de cambio* (exchange bureaux, usually street booths); some will also change

△ Money-changers

First-Time Latin America | how much will it cost?

travellers' cheques and give advances on credit cards. In some places, banks offer better rates than *casas de cambio*, while in others, the reverse applies. Whatever the case, banks are potentially much more frustrating places than *casas de cambio*, with long queues (although tourists are sometimes ushered to the front) and inflexible set hours for changing money. *Casas de cambio* are generally more user-friendly, with many opening late and over weekends.

Change is in very short supply in many Latin American countries so whenever you're changing money always ask for small-denomination notes and check that they're in fairly good condition – torn or even just grubby notes may be refused by traders (this goes for dollars too). Once you've completed your transaction, be it with a moneychanger, *casa de cambio* or bank, count your money carefully. You might prefer to go straight back to your hotel, just to be on the safe side, rather than wandering around with a pile of money.

## Emergency funds

The easiest and fastest way of getting emergency funds is to have someone wire money. The two main operators are Western Union (Ⓦwww.westernunion.com) and Moneygram (Ⓦwww.moneygram .com), both of which have branches all over the world – even quite modest-sized towns in Latin America have an office of one or other (Western Union is more prevalent). Someone at home will have to take the money to the local branch, which is then wired immediately (taking no more than fifteen minutes) to the office you have specified. Remember, though, that wiring money is hugely expensive – costing anything up to fourteen percent of the sum being wired – and should be considered a last resort.

# Finding work

If you run out of cash and don't want to return home you could always try looking for a job. Bear in mind, though, that unemployment runs as high as eighty percent in some parts of Latin America and if there aren't jobs for the locals, chances are there won't be jobs for foreigners.

Obviously, if you speak Spanish or Portuguese you'll massively improve your chances of employment. That said, most job opportunities exist in one of two areas: TEFL or tourism. TEFL (Teaching English as a Foreign Language) is the most widespread work available for foreigners in Latin America. More and more locals are keen to learn English and every capital city will have scores of English schools as well as private classes held at large businesses or in individual's homes. Generally the hourly rate of pay is quite reasonable, although your hours (usually before and after the working day) won't be convenient. Although it's not mandatory, having a TEFL qualification will greatly improve your chances of employment and increase your status and wages. The best qualification to go for is the RSA/Cambridge Certificate in English Language Teaching to Adults; the course takes a month to complete and is recognized worldwide. Courses are widely available in the UK, US and Australia and cost around $2500 (see Basics for details); once qualified you can work anywhere in the world. Alternatively you could try just turning up at an English-language school on spec – particularly in places less popular with tourists, there might well be vacancies for English teachers, and all you may be asked for in terms of qualifications is to be a native speaker.

Additionally, you may find work in tourist resorts, especially if you have a special skill or qualification in something like scuba diving, sailing, whitewater rafting or mountain-climbing – ask around at likely spots. Otherwise, you might find a job in a hotel as a chambermaid, waiter or even receptionist. Backpacker hostels, especially those run by gringos, often hire broke guests to help serve food and drinks or clean in exchange for board and lodging, although this won't be of much use if you've already run out of cash and need to earn more money, rather than just having a place to stay. Whatever sort of work you find, however, it's likely to be of an unofficial nature. Work visas for Latin America are difficult to obtain: you'll need a contract of employment and endless patience to negotiate the relevant bureaucratic hurdles. Fortunately, many employers will turn a blind eye to your lack of papers.

# 5

# Guidebooks and other resources

Whatever the nature of your trip, the chances are that the more you know about Latin America, the more you'll enjoy your trip. Having some idea about the history, politics and culture of the countries you'll be visiting will whet your appetite for travelling and place what you see in some kind of larger context.

There are lots of ways of learning about Latin America. The **internet** is a huge and growing resource; use a good search engine like Google (Ⓦwww.google.com), type in the subject or place you're interested in and you'll get hundreds of useful links to websites, online articles and photo-essays (see p.330 in Basics and the individual country profiles for some recommended websites). Cities with large Latin American populations in North America, Europe and Australasia all have specialist **resource centres** with libraries and collections of useful videos; they also run courses, lectures and publish useful leaflets and magazines (see p.332 for details). Their staff are often experts in Latin America. Specialist travel agencies (see pp.323–24 and national tourist boards (see pp.315–16) should also be able to advise you, particularly on the practical aspects of your trip.

# Guidebooks

A decent **guidebook** is an essential tool in planning your trip – not only is it a source of all kinds of practical information, from how to buy a plane ticket to how to ask for a cup of tea in Portuguese – but it will also give you a reasonable grasp of a country's or region's culture and history. Bear in mind, though, that it's impossible for guidebooks to be one hundred percent accurate – prices change constantly, restaurants open and hotels shut down every week. Guidebooks also, inevitably, reflect their authors' bias, and though decent editing should ensure a degree of objectivity, your own opinions will inevitably clash at some point with those in your book. The other disadvantage of slavishly following a guidebook, especially a popular one, is that you'll constantly bump into other readers following the exact same route as you. Places given an endorsement by best-selling guidebooks can become overpriced and rest on their laurels, leading to a decline in standards. Conversely, places not listed may be perfectly decent, and actually make more of an effort to provide a good service.

When it comes to **choosing a guidebook**, go to a large bookshop and browse through all the relevant titles; compare the way different guidebooks write up a particular destination, and see what sort of hotels and restaurants they list to work out how relevant they're likely to be to your budget. And don't leave getting a guidebook till the last minute – good guides are full of useful pre-trip advice. Compendium volumes which cover several different countries in one area (the *Rough Guide to Central America* or Lonely Planet's *South America on a Shoestring*, for example) are obviously popular, since most travellers to Latin America will visit more than one country – bear in mind, though, that tight editing means that they contain much less information than single-country guides. If you're planning to go to just two or three countries it might be worth taking a separate guidebook for each one – any more than that and you should opt for a compendium. You might be able to sell guidebooks you've no further use for while travelling, or even swap them for books on the region you're heading to – check the noticeboard in backpackers' hostels and book exchanges. If you've planned your trip round a particular theme or activity – whether scuba diving, bird-spotting or trekking – you might want to also take a **specialist guidebook**; the best of these are detailed in Chapter 1 under the relevant theme or itinerary.

The following, listed in alphabetical order, are the most popular general guidebooks to Latin America.

## Cadogan

**Cadogan** guidebooks (⊛www.cadoganguides.com) are text-driven, with a strong focus on culture, history and ecology. There are currently only two Cadogan guidebooks to areas in Latin America – *The Amazon* and *Yucatán and Southern Mexico* – which might be useful if you're planning on spending a lot of time in one of these regions. *The Amazon* is a compendium volume covering the entire Amazon basin including Colombia, Venezuela, the Guianas, Brazil, Ecuador, Peru and Bolivia, with guest essays written by experts on flora and fauna, ecotourism and indigenous peoples.

## Footprint

The UK-based **Footprint Handbooks** (⊛www.footprintbooks .com) publish the *South American Handbook*, which first appeared in 1921 and has been updated over seventy times since. Still sometimes referred to as "The Bible" amongst travellers to South America, the *Handbook* is densely packed with information – over 1600 pages – though some people find the writing dry and the book difficult to use, with perfunctory listings and poor maps. Footprint also publish a compendium *Central American Handbook* as well as individual country guides to most Latin American countries, including lesser-visited destinations like El Salvador, Colombia and Nicaragua.

## Let's Go

Researched, written and produced exclusively by Harvard University students, **Let's Go** (⊛www.letsgo.com) guidebooks focus solely on budget travel for students and claim to be updated annually – as you'd expect, the emphasis is on low-cost, high-adrenaline pursuits like camping, hitchhiking and adventure sports rather than history, culture and sights. The book's text is clearly laid out, and each title includes a useful list of suggested routes and itineraries. There are Let's Go guides to *Mexico*, *Central America*, and *Peru, Ecuador and Bolivia*.

## Lonely Planet

**Lonely Planet** (www.lonelyplanet.com) publish two main compendium guides to Latin America: *Central America on a Shoestring* and *South America on a Shoestring*, both of which are aimed fairly and squarely at the backpacker market, with their main focus on detailed listings of cheap hostels and hotels – the popularity of Lonely Planet books means that there's a well-trodden trail of readers moving from one recommended place to another. The books' strength lies in their ease of use, with clear layout and good maps, although there's little background description of places and sites. Lonely Planet also publish individual guides to most countries in Latin America – including five on Mexico alone – plus a series of diving and snorkelling guides to Baja California, Cozumel, Panamá and Honduras and the Bay Islands.

## Moon

**Moon Handbooks** (www.moon.com) are published in California and aimed at independent travellers of all means, though their main focus tends to be middle-income and middle-aged tourists. Moon handbooks are clearly laid out, with particularly detailed hotel listings (pages and pages in some cases), though there's sometimes a lack of background information on specific places, while some people find the text irritatingly folksy. Still, the introductory essays on society, politics and ecology make interesting reading, as do the factboxes on little-known aspects of each country's culture. Moon Handbooks specialize in Mexico – there are no fewer than eleven individual books on the country including *Archaelogical Mexico* and *Colonial Mexico* – as well as guides to Belize, Costa Rica, Guatemala and Honduras. Ecuador is their only South American country guide.

## Rough Guides

**Rough Guides** (www.roughguides.com) are based in the UK and US and cover independent travel for all budgets and age ranges. Rough Guide authors pride themselves on their educated approach to travel – readers are not patronized, and featured places have comprehensive background information on history, architecture and ecology. A recent redesign means that guidebooks now have a full-colour photo-essay introducing each destination's major attractions, which makes a good starting point for planning an itinerary. There are currently two Rough Guide compendium guides – *Central America* and *The Maya World* – plus individual guides to Argentina, Bolivia, Brazil, Chile, Ecuador, Peru, Belize, Costa Rica, Guatemala and Mexico. A brand-new compendium volume covering the whole of South America is due for publication in early 2004.

# Maps

Although your guidebook should have **maps** of cities and particular regions, these will inevitably be fairly basic, given the constraints of book format. Although it's not strictly necessary (unless you're travelling under your own steam), it's worth thinking about taking a proper map with you. This will give you a much better overview of where you're going, with enhanced road details and contour markings, so you'll get a much clearer picture of the land through which you're travelling. For a list of good map shops, see pp.329–30.

The best travel maps of Latin America are published by International Travel Map Productions, Vancouver, Canada (@www.itmp), who are specialists in the region. Their maps are renowned for their accuracy, for being regularly updated, and for their wealth of detail (including symbols for caves, lighthouses and even oil pipelines). ITMP have the largest-scale maps for most countries in Latin America, including less-visited destinations like French Guiana and Uruguay, as well as maps of particular regions, such as the Amazon Basin and the Galápagos Islands. Those produced by Berndtson and Berndtson (@www.berndtson.com) – which are laminated for extra durability – and GeoCenter (@www.geocenter.de) are also good. If you're planning on trekking, most Latin American capital cities have an Instituto Geográfico Nacional or Militar which sells detailed topographical maps of the country.

# Background reading

While your guidebook is a good starting point for learning about Latin America, to really flesh out your knowledge of the region's history, geography, politics, society and people, you'll need to consult other sources.

## Magazines

There are a whole range of **travel magazines**, which run the gamut from very chic (*Condé Nast Traveller*) to very serious (*National Geographic*). These have articles on Latin America on a regular basis. Most feature general information on travelling as well as reviews of the latest equipment and books, plus current travel news. Published in the UK (but available worldwide on subscription), *Wanderlust* (@www.wanderlust.co.uk), *Traveller* and *Global Adventure* feature off-the-beaten-track destinations with great photographs and well-written articles. Comprehensive sections in all three list websites, road-test new equipment and review the latest travelogues and guidebooks. *Wanderlust* also has a useful classified sections with adverts for travelling companions. *Adventure Travel* (@www.at.co.uk) is written with hikers and mountain climbers in mind, though it too has a wealth of more general travel information. *Geographical* (@www.geographical.co.uk), the magazine of the Royal Geographical Society, has special features on exploration and ecological/environmental issues. In North America, the best magazines on adventurous, independent travel are *Outside* (@www.outsidemag.com), *Escape* (@www.escapemag.com) and *Big World* (@www.bigworld.com); in Australia, *Backpacker Essentials* (@www.backpackeressentials.com.au), the magazine of the Australian Youth Hostel Association, is packed with useful travel tips plus features written by backpackers; *TNT* (@www.tntmagazine.com.au) runs articles on budget travel and is a good source of practical information on cheap flights and insurance policies.

There are a number of magazines devoted to Latin American society and politics, which are available to read in specialist libraries (see p.332) and on subscription. The best of these are printed in the US: the bimonthly *Americas* (@www.americasmagazine.oas.org) is published by the Organization of American States and has clearly written features on history, film and food; *Report on the Americas* (@www.nacla.org), published by the left-wing North American Congress on Latin America, is more highbrow, though still highly readable. The *Latin American Weekly Report* (available on subscription – and online – from Latin American Newsletters, 61 Old

Street, London EC1V 9HW; ⓦwww.latinnews.com) offers a useful overview of political, economic and financial happenings in the region.

# Books

Although Latin America is not as widely visited or written about as Europe or Asia, there are still dozens of good **books** on all aspects of the region which will whet your appetite for the countries you're going to visit – if you don't get time to read them before you go you might want to take some of them with you. Recommended bookshops with comprehensive travel sections are listed in Basics. Detailed below are a few of the best books on Latin America, as well as some of our particular favourites.

## Travel writing

- Sybille Bedford: *A Visit to Don Octavio*. Wonderfully idiosyncratic and vivid account of a visit to Mexico in the 1950s. While some of the book portrays a Mexico long since gone, other passages feature scenes of everyday life – chickens on buses, colourful markets – which are still familiar sights today.
- Bruce Chatwin: *In Patagonia*. Inspired by tales of his grandmother's cousin, a sailor who settled in Punta Arenas after his ship sank in the Straits of Magellan, Bruce Chatwin set off in 1975 to explore the strange and wild plains of southernmost Latin America – this award-winning travelogue, with its unerring eye for human and historical eccentricity, was the result.
- Peter Ford: *Tekkin' A Waalk*. Taking a break from city life in Managua, journalist Peter Ford walked the length of the wild and swampy Caribbean coast from Belize to Panamá in the mid-1980s, describing aspects of the unique Garífuna and Miskito cultures he came across along the way.
- Charles Nicholl: *The Fruit Palace*. A humorous and thrilling investigation into the 1970s cocaine trade, exposing the ubiquitous corruption and craziness which underscore Colombian life and business.
- Salman Rushdie: *The Jaguar Smile: a Nicaraguan Journey*. Invited to Nicaragua by the Sandinista Association of Cultural Workers, writer Salman Rushdie spent three weeks in the country in 1986 and returned to write this thought-provoking account of his brief stay.

- John Lloyd Stephens: *Incidents of Travel in Central America, Chiapas and Yucatán*. Classic account of two trips made by the American ambassador to Central America and keen amateur archeologist, John Lloyd Stephens, in search of the lost cities of the Maya. Together with draughtsman Frederick Catherwood, whose elegant drawings illustrate some editions of the book, Stephens provided the outside world with the first detailed descriptions of Uxmal, Palenque, Copán and Chichén Itzá, as well as vivid scenes of everyday life in the Maya villages of the region.
- Paul Theroux: *The Old Patagonian Express*. A decidedly bad-tempered, misanthropic but keenly observant Paul Theroux leaves his native Boston and travels all the way through Latin America to its southernmost tip by train – a journey made particularly poignant because, with the abandonment of almost all train networks on the continent, it's no longer possible to follow in his footsteps.

## Politics and social sciences

- *In Focus Guides*. Published by the Latin American Bureau in London, this excellent series of individual country profiles covers more than half of the countries in Latin America, each consisting of a collection of short and clearly written essays organized by theme – history, politics, environment and society.
- Eduardo Galeano: *Open Veins of Latin America: Five Centuries of the Pillage of a Continent*. Written some 25 years ago by Uruguayan journalist Eduardo Galeano, this groundbreaking treatise lays the blame for Latin America's ills squarely on its sixteenth-century European colonizers and, more recently, on the creeping globalization initiated by the USA.
- Duncan Green: *Faces of Latin America*. Comprehensive and lively introduction to Latin American politics, economics and society, illustrated with deftly chosen accounts drawn from personal experiences.
- Joe Kane: *Savages*. Deeply depressing but excellently researched tale of the environmental destruction of parts of the Ecuadorian Amazon by US oil companies and the attempt to fight back by the forest's Huaorani people.
- Claude Lévi-Strauss: *Tristes Tropiques*. Seminal work by the legendary French anthropologist describing a working trip to Brazil in the 1930s to study the Nambikwara and Tupi-Kawahib Indians, describing with wit and insight the ups and downs of travelling in a strange culture.

- Gabriel García Márquez: *News of a Kidnapping*. Using interviews and diary entries, Márquez skilfully recreates the stories of several brutal kidnappings (Colombia is the kidnap centre of the world, with over a thousand annually) by infamous drugs lord Pablo Escobar – by turns gripping and grimly illuminating.

## History and culture

- John Hemming: *The Conquest of the Incas*. Clear and easily digestible history of the Spanish victory over the Incas, using a vivid narrative style woven together from original accounts from both sides of the battle.
- Michael D. Coe: *The Maya*. Celebrated general introduction from a renowned Maya expert to one of Latin America's most sophisticated indigenous cultures.
- Charles Darwin: *Voyage of the Beagle*. The journal of young naturalist Charles Darwin recording his five-year trip around the southern end of South America (1831–36), a journey which inspired his evolutionary theories, with an obvious – though not exclusive – focus on flora and fauna.
- Bartolomé de Las Casas: *A short account of the Destruction of the Indies*. Written by a Dominican cleric and "Defender of the Indians" in 1542, this furious letter (addressed to the then king of Spain, Philip II) records Las Casas' horror at his fellow Spanish colonists' appalling treatment of the native people of Cuba and other parts of the New World.
- *Salsa: Musical Heartbeat of Latin America*. Attractively presented and illustrated history of the ubiquitous Latin American dance-music style and its offshoots – rumba, mambo, cumbia and merengue.
- Chris Taylor: *The Beautiful Game*. Fascinating and thoroughly researched history of Latin American football along with an examination of the vital role football plays in the region's culture, politics and society.

## Latin American fiction

Latin American literature is known principally for its evolution of a literary style which has influenced writers worldwide: **magic realism**. A seamless blend of fact and fantasy, magic realism often takes as its themes the absurdity of murderous dictatorships, brutal regimes and eccentric family life. Latin American writers also have a particularly strong political commitment – both Mario Vargas

Llosa (see below) and Chilean poet Pablo Neruda ran for the presidencies of their respective countries. Detailed below are some of the most celebrated Latin American novelists.

- The literature of Nobel prize winner **Gabriel García Márquez** (1936–) is one of Colombia's most famous exports. *One Hundred Years of Solitude* is the seminal work of magic realism, telling the story of the pioneering Buendía family and the history of their strange little town, Macondo, in the South American outback. *Love in the Time of Cholera* is the romantic and humorous love story set on the steamy Caribbean coast. *The General in his Labyrinth* is the spare and wonderfully poetic story of the tragic dying days of Simón Bolívar, El Libertador.

- Peru's most famous author and former presidential candidate, **Mario Vargas Llosa** (1936–) is a ubiquitous figure in Peruvian society. *Aunt Julia and the Scriptwriter* is a partly autobiographical and very amusing account of a young radio soap writer's life in which fact and fiction become marvellously confused. Set in the Brazilian backlands in 1897, *The War of the End of the World* is a fictionalized account of the charismatic leader Antonio Conselheiro, his short-lived utopian commune at Canudos, and the brutal suppression of his followers, which left thousands dead.

- Niece of assasinated Chilean president Salvador Allende, **Isabel Allende** (1942–) is the author of several of the most recent popular examples of Latin American magic realism. *House of the Spirits* is a fantastical saga of the wealthy Trueba family which follows the lives of matriarch Clara and her eccentric, unusual children and grandchildren. *Of Love and Shadows* is set against the background of a brutal military dictatorship whose unexplained disappearances mirror those in Chile under Pinochet.

- **Jorge Amado** (1912–2001) was a lavish chronicler of life and culture in the colourful tropical state of Bahia, northeast Brazil. In *Dona Flor and her Two Husbands*, Dona Flor marries a sensible pharmacist after her roguish husband drops dead at *Carnaval*, only to find her previous husband returning as a ghost. When *Gabriela, Clove and Cinnamon* was made into a TV film in Brazil, the entire country, including the government, downed tools to tune in. Here Amado chronicles the growing prosperity of the Bahian town of Ilheus in the 1920s, thanks to the creation of vast cocoa plantations as seen through the eyes of a young mulatto girl, Gabriela.

- **Jorge Luis Borges**'s (1899–1986) *Labyrinths,* a collection of short stories and essays, is a compact introduction to the inventive and philosophical world of Argentina's – and perhaps Latin America's – most esteemed writer. With his original style, comprising an erudite mixture of wild fantasy and intellectual rigour, Borges has often been called the father of magic realism.

- The work of Guatemalan **Miguel Angel Asturias** (1899–1974) interweaves the past, present and future and is often seen as a precursor of magic realism. Asturias's main theme was the deep-rooted and continuing value of indigenous Latin American traditions. In *Men of Maize* he tells the story of a backlash by the Maya against the intended cultivation of maize – a crop woven into their culture and folklore - for profit by outsiders. *The President* chronicles the machinations of a ruthless dictator who plans to rid himself of a political opponent in an unnamed country generally considered to be Guatemala.

## Fiction set in Latin America

- Joseph Conrad: *Nostromo.* Conrad's 1904 masterpiece records the story of a silver mine in the imaginary South American republic of Costaguana, brilliantly depicting the damage done by corrupt Latin American politicians and big business, as well as the continuing North American obsession with controlling the rest of the continent.

- Malcolm Lowry: *Under the Volcano.* Set in Cuernavaca, Mexico, over the course of a single day in 1938, this wonderfully written novel painstakingly unravels the last hours of alcoholic British Consul Geoffrey Firmin's life through a haze of mescal and the macabre celebrations of the Day of the Dead.

- Graham Greene: *The Power and the Glory.* Based on Greene's own travels in Chiapas (described in his travelogue, *The Lawless Roads*), *The Power and the Glory* takes as its theme the anti-clerical purges in the southern states of Mexico during the 1930s. It tells the story of an outlawed priest on the run, a drunken anti-hero who redeems himself through a dogged sense of duty and eventual martyrdom, and wonderfully evokes the tropical torpor of Mexico's backwaters.

## Memoirs

- Diego Rivera: *My Art, my Life.* Between 1944 and 1957, Mexican painter Rivera dictated over two thousand pages of idiosyncratic recollections and opinions on the three things that mattered most to him – art, sex and politics. This vivid "autobiography" – an edited transcription of Rivera's choicest sayings, complete with black-and-white photos of his work, wives and colleagues – is the result.

- Rigoberta Menchú: *Rigoberta Menchú – An Indian Woman in Guatemala*. "This is my testimony. I didn't learn it from a book and I didn't learn it alone . . . My personal experience is the reality of a whole people." So begins the story of a young Quiché woman as told to a French anthropologist in 1983, which details the atrocities of Guatemala's civil war and the complex culture of the Quiché, one of 23 Maya groups in the country. When her brothers and parents were murdered by paramilitaries, Menchú became the leader of her community and went on to win the Nobel Peace Prize. These memoirs brought her international fame and are a fascinating social document, though some writers have attempted to discredit them as being riddled with inconsistencies.
- Subcomandante Insurgente Marcos: *Our Word is our Weapon*. A collection of writings from Subcomandante Marcos, the famously erudite and poetic leader of the Mexican revolutionary movement, the Zapatistas, who are fighting for land rights for the indigenous peoples of southern Mexico.

# Film

Three countries have long dominated **Latin American cinema**: Argentina, Brazil and Mexico. Brazil's *cinema novo* was one of the world's most vibrant film movements in the 1960s. After quieter years – which coincided, not surprisingly, with military dictatorships in both Argentina and Brazil – all three countries are currently undergoing a cinema revival with slick modern films which have attracted critical acclaim and are being shown in mainstream cinemas.

An annual Latin American **film festival** is held in London every September (@www.latinamericanfilmfestival.com), while there are numerous festivals in the US, including ones in New England (@www.latin-americanfilmfestival.org); Austin, Texas (@www.cinelasamericas.org); Chicago (@www.latinoculturalcenter.com); and Miami (@www.hispanicfilm.com), among others. If you become seriously interested in Latin American films, *Mediating Two Worlds: Cinematic Encounters in the Americas* and *South American Cinema: A Critical Filmography* are both recommended.

# Latin American films

The following films are a selction of those made in Latin America in either Spanish or Portuguese.

- *Black Orpheus/Orfeu Negro* (1958). Set amidst the Rio *Carnaval*, this is a vivid reworking of the ancient Greek legend of Orpheus and Eurydice, a fatalistic love story with a tragic ending. The city's dramatic setting is beautifully though rather sentimentally filmed – Rio's *favelas* (slums) look almost pretty – and is accompanied by a best-selling soundtrack by Antonio (Tom) Jobim and Luís Bonfá which ushered in a new type of Brazilian music: bossa nova.
- *Central Station/Central do Brasil* (1998). This colourful and heart-rending film tells the story of Dora, a lonely and cynical older woman who spends her days writing letters for illiterate customers at Rio de Janeiro's Central Station. Things begin to change when she reluctantly befriends a homeless orphan and agrees to help him search for the father he's never known. Features a wonderful performance by acclaimed Brazilian actress Fernanda Montenegro.
- *Like Water for Chocolate/Como Agua para Chocolate* (1992). Set during the Mexican revolution, this award-winning film, adapted from a best-selling novel by Laura Esquivel, follows the story of three sisters and their separate but entwined destinies. Tita is denied the man she loves who marries her sister instead and, stuck in the kitchen, uses food to vent her anger and frustrated passion – with magical results.
- *Nine Queens* (2000). An ingenious con-man comedy set in Buenos Aires over the course of 24 hours, *Nine Queens* also reflects the cynicism and suspicion of Argentines towards their thoroughly corrupt institutions. A remarkably prescient film, made shortly before the country's economic meltdown in 2001.
- *Pixote* (1981). The story of a homeless urchin in São Paulo, *Pixote* is a fictionalized account of the appalling lives of Brazil's numerous street children and won many awards for its affecting and graphic depiction of a world which, lamentably, still very much exists.

## Films set in Latin America

Predictably many films set in Latin America are made in the US and tend to focus on cowboys, lost-in-the-jungle action movies or civil war. The following include some more critically acclaimed offerings, as well as a couple of documentaries.

- *Aguirre, Wrath of God* (1972). Werner Herzog's crazed masterpiece tells the story of a band of Spanish conquistadors who go up the Amazon in search of El Dorado, the fabled city of gold. Led by the megalomaniac Aguirre, self-styled "Wrath of God", the trip rapidly descends into chaos and death as the group travel from the high Andes into primeval forest.
- *Missing* (1981). Based on true events during the Chilean coup of 1973, *Missing* tells the story of an American journalist who "disappears" and of his family's subsequent search for him, taking a dark look at the human tragedy of murderous dictatorships like Pinochet's, and evocatively portraying a society coming apart at the seams.
- *Salvador* (1986). Arguably Oliver Stone's best film, *Salvador* features James Woods as washed-up American journalist Richard Boyle, who travelled to El Salvador in 1980 in search of a story and instead found himself in the middle of a civil war. Co-written by Boyle himself, the film has brilliant action sequences underpinned by a forceful and sometimes moving polemic.
- *Carla's Song* (1996). Left-wing filmmaker Ken Loach's examination of the civil war in Nicaragua centres around the love affair of a Glaswegian bus driver (played by Robert Carlyle) and a Nicaraguan refugee – the film's witty depiction of the Nicaraguan's humour and playful language had the audience at its Managuan premiere in fits of laughter.
- *The Battle of Chile* (1973). Patricio Guzman's three-part documentary on Allende and the Chilean coup d'état is widely feted as among the best documentaries ever made. The three films cover events in chronological order, mixing trenchant political analysis with revealing interviews with some of those who took part in the events described.
- *Señorita Extravida/Missing Young Woman* (2001). Moving and lyrical documentary made by Chicano film-maker Lourdes Portillo about the more than two hundred young women who have been kidnapped, raped and murdered in the border town of Cuidad Juárez. Portillo has also made films about the Day of the Dead and the women who march weekly in Buenos Aires for their "disappeared" children.

# Learning Spanish or Portuguese

One of the advantages of going to Latin America rather than Asia or Africa is the ubiquity of **Spanish** – it's an official language in all but

## Castellano confusion

I found doing a Spanish course before I went to Latin America a top investment of time and money but once over there I soon learnt to tell people that I spoke "Castellano", as in some places they don't like the Spanish colonial thing at all. Having a grasp of the language helped me to meet people and also got me out of all sorts of fixes, but there are some semantic differences from country to country that can give rise to comical situations. Like an innocent abroad, I went to Mexico secure in the knowledge that *coger* meant "to take" or "catch" as in "catch a bus", so it was somewhat surprising when I discovered that I had been going around asking people where I could "have sexual intercourse with a bus to Mérida" – only it wasn't intercourse but something considerably ruder. Similarly, in the Andean countries *pico*, a bird's beak, is slang for "penis", but in Spain and Central America they use it to mean "a bit"; when a Chilean asks you the time, tell them "son las tres y pico" (it's just after three o'clock) and they'll roll on the floor laughing. In Chile I was taught to call a baby a *guagua* (which is pronounced "wow-wa" and is supposed to sound like one crying) but in Venezuela and around the Caribbean I found it means "bus". You can imagine how worried I was that I might be arrested for asking where I could "catch a bus" in certain countries and just how useful my Castellano would be in explaining myself!

Mary Green

four of Latin America's twenty-one mainland countries (Guyana, French Guiana, Suriname and Brazil) – and being able to speak even a little Spanish will make your trip much easier and more interesting. Although English is understood in some popular tourist resorts, especially in Mexico and Costa Rica, you'll have trouble communicating if you go off the beaten track unless you speak Spanish. It really is worth learning the basics of the language before you set off; once on the road you'll find plenty of opportunity to improve on what you already know.

Spanish is a Latin language, which means it has similar grammatical structure and vocabulary to Portuguese, Italian and (to a lesser extent) French – if you speak any of these languages already you'll find learning Spanish easy. Unlike English, it's also phonetic, which means that vowel sounds follow strict rules, making Spanish words relatively easy to pronounce. **Latin American Spanish** differs surprisingly little from the Spanish spoken in Spain – the chief difference is the omission of the lisping '*th*' sound that northern Spaniards use to pronounce soft '*c*'s and '*z*'s. Obviously accents vary enormously and each country has its own slang – Nicaraguans, for example, are notorious for inventing new words or playing with old ones, while Hondurans have a particularly thick accent and speak very fast.

Spanish classes are easily found – it's the world's most widely spoken language after English. **Evening classes** and **part-time**

**courses** are run by night schools, colleges and specialist language schools (check the resource centres listed in Basics on pp.332–33), and you can also find details on the internet (ⓦwww.learnspanish.com or ⓦwww.spanishstudies.com); if you do enrol on a language course try to find one which specializes in Latin American rather than European Spanish. You can also teach yourself with a book/tape course, although this requires self-discipline and there's no one to correct you if you get things wrong. You might also consider buying a small dictionary and phrasebook: both Lonely Planet and Berlitz publish pocket phrasebooks on Latin American Spanish, and you can also find phrasebooks covering Mexican Spanish (Rough Guides), Costa Rica Spanish and Brazilian Portuguese (Lonely Planet). **Learning Spanish in Latin America** is increasingly popular and usually works out as much cheaper than studying at home, with the added advantage that you'll be surrounded by Spanish speakers with whom to practise. See p.333 for more details.

Though they look very similar, Spanish and **Portuguese** are very different in actual sound. It shouldn't take long, however, to learn the basics of one if you've already got a good grounding in the other. Portuguese is also still readily available as a language course – try to find one that specializes in Brazilian Portuguese, since this is markedly different from the language spoken in Portugal.

# 6

# What to take

The short answer to the all-important question "what shall I take?" is as little as possible. If there's one piece of indispensable advice when embarking on a long journey it's to travel light. And once you realize just how often and how far you're going to have to lug your gear around, you'll understand why it's a very good idea to reduce your packing to the bare minimum. There's nothing like an hour wandering with all your stuff around a hot and unfamiliar town looking for a hotel to make you curse your rucksack and everything in it. Remember too that public transport in most Latin American cities and towns consists of a motley collection of beaten-up tin buses, vans and trucks. These are invariably crammed to the gills, and in many cases there literally may not be room for you and your enormous rucksack. In addition, the larger your pack, the more likely you are to be marked out as a gringo no matter how well you know the country or how good your Spanish or Portuguese. The size of your luggage will signal the fact that you've just arrived, making you a sitting target for every wide boy, conartist and thief in town.

Having said that, there is a certain amount of travel kit that you will need to take, unless you want the hassle of having to constantly buy stuff as you go along (or, worse still, scrounge off fellow travellers). Travelling light is smart; travelling with too little is not smart.

# Rucksacks

Your rucksack is the single most important piece of kit that you'll take – if you've got any money to spend on equipment, this is the time to splash out. Rucksacks vary in price from £50/$75 to £200/$300, and generally you get what you pay for. Shop around various specialist travel, camping or adventure-sport shops – the best shops have knowledgeable staff who have travelled widely themselves (see pp.334–35 for listings of recommended retailers).

Backpack **sizes** are measured in litres (since their actual weight depends on what you put in them). A medium-sized, 50-litre pack is the most popular size, and you'd be mad to carry anything bigger than 65 litres, even if you're taking camping gear. If you're a really ruthless packer, you might manage with 25–30 litres, the size of a largish daypack. Experts recommend that the total weight of your pack doesn't exceed one-fifth to a quarter of your body weight. In practical terms, this means that most men shouldn't try to carry more than 18–22 kilos, whilst women ought to stick to 13–17 kilos.

The most important element of a backpack is its **harness**. The best harnesses are fully adjustable and have padded shoulder straps, a wide hip belt (essential for transferring weight from your back) and compression straps on the side of the pack which push its contents tightly into your back. If your backpack doesn't come with a built-in harness cover (rucksacks usually don't; travel packs usually do – see below), you should consider buying one – this is very useful for airplane holds and other luggage racks because it avoids straps being torn and damaged by baggage handlers (the most frequent source of backpack damage); following complaints, airlines now sometimes insist that backpack straps are tidied away with a harness cover or outer sack; alternatively, they may charge you to wrap it properly themselves.

The way the pack is divided into **compartments** is also important. Outer pockets are useful for quick access to essential items, though these are hard to secure properly. Too many outer pockets will make your backpack bulky – the narrower your pack, the easier it will be to manoeuvre while wearing it, and to store it in tight spaces when you're not.

It's esssential to try on a backpack before you buy it to check that it fits properly and feels comfortable. First, though, find a knowledgeable shop assistant who will measure your back length (from the top of your hip bone to the seventh vertebra) – this is vital in determining the right size of pack. Backpacks should never be tried on empty – get a shop assistant to fill it with a suitable weight – and you should then walk around the shop to ensure that the pack is stable. A properly fitting pack has a good harness (see above) with shoulder straps and a hip belt which fits snugly and doesn't dig. Other features to look for are a ventilated or mesh back system which will help reduce sweating, long-lasting and tightly woven fabrics, and triple-sewn seams (stress points should have five lines of stitching). Most manufacturers make rucksacks specially designed for women; these have straps which are closer together to fit narrower shoulders, making them significantly more comfortable.

## Toploader and travel packs

There are two basic types of backpack: choosing the right one depends on what kind of trip you're planning. A **toploader** or traditional rucksack opens principally at the top, though most brands also have side pockets and a bottom compartment. The long, narrow shape of toploaders gives them an effective weight distribution and makes them particularly comfortable to carry – useful if you're planning on doing any serious trekking, mountain-climbing, or even if you just expect to have to lug your pack around a lot.

The newer type of backpacks, known as **travel packs**, are wider than traditional toploaders, with horseshoe-shaped zips, meaning that almost all the pack can be easily accessed (although this does mean that it's less secure), whilst clothes can be packed flat as in a traditional suitcase. Most travel packs also come with a zip-on daypack (see below) and built-in harness covers. If you're not planning to carry your pack around a great deal, a decent travel pack will suffice.

## Weatherproofing

Surprisingly, backpacks aren't entirely rainproof. You can remedy this by **waterproofing** your backpacks with a can of waterproofing spray; these can be bought at most camping and outdoor shops. Use the spray outside, however, and apply it well before you leave – it smells horrible at first and gives off toxic fumes (though these

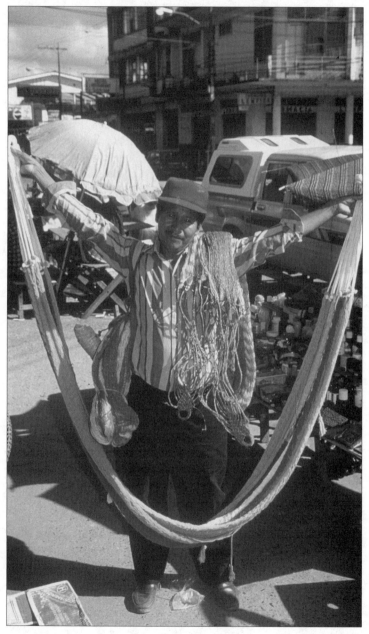

△ Maya hammock vendor

wear off after the first few days). Alternatively, you could buy an elasticated rucksack raincover or a waterproof backpack liner. If you're on a really tight budget you can either line your pack with a binliner or simply pack your stuff in a series of plastic bags before putting it in your pack.

## Security

Keeping your rucksack and its contents **safe** is a major concern. Essentially, it's impossible to completely secure a pack against a determined thief, and the best way to avoid losing valuables while travelling is not to take them in the first place. That said, most thieves are opportunists, and any attempt to make their job harder and slower will probably encourage them to look elsewhere.

One traditional way of stopping thieves slashing your pack open is to line it with **chickenwire**, which is cheap and fairly tough and can be bought at most hardware shops. It's still a good deterrent – try to get wire with the smallest holes. There are several other ways of making your pack more secure. You can now buy something called PacSafe, which works on the chickenwire principle – it's a sheet of very strong metal mesh which fits over the outside of a backpack; it also comes with a padlock so that you can attach your pack to a luggage ruck or other fixed object. Although PacSafe is heavy and not totally foolproof (it can be cut with wirecutters), it does at the very least make getting into your rucksack a job for professional rather than amateur thieves.

A further option is a **cable lock**: a long length of thick wire which can be used to lock your pack to fixed objects. Some cable locks come with sturdy combination locks and a built-in alarm which goes off if someone touches or tries to move your pack – particularly useful if you're travelling alone and have no one to help keep an eye on your stuff. Finally, you could also take small padlocks to slot through backpack zips and secure openings, but their size and limited strength make it relatively easy to snap them open.

# Daypacks and shoulder bags

Once you've arrived at your destination, found a hotel and dumped your backpack, you'll still need a **daypack** to carry essential items

– guidebook, water, camera, extra clothing – in. Daypacks are essentially just smaller versions of a backpack (between 15 and 30 litres). Most travel packs now come with matching daypacks zipped onto the front. If you're buying one of these, make sure you unzip the daypack and examine it properly before you buy it – some are sturdier than others.

If you're buying a daypack separately it's as important to choose it as carefully as a backpack. You're likely to use your daypack on a daily basis, and it needs to be tough, with strong padded straps and sturdy zips. Some travellers prefer to take a different kind of day bag. This has the advantage of making you look less like a tourist when you're strolling round town. A good choice is a nylon shoulder bag (which can be worn across the body for extra safety) or a local bag, something that the locals use to carry their shopping in – all over Latin America you can buy extremely tough, brightly coloured, very cheap nylon mesh bags from the market; they weigh almost nothing and last forever. Anything made of leather is obviously much bulkier and weighs more, as is anything woven (although hand-woven bags are also widely available in Latin America and make great souvenirs). None of these options, though, will be as comfortable to carry or as secure as a proper daypack.

## Money belts

You need somewhere safe to carry your documents and money – don't under any circumstances keep valuables in your back pocket or in an outside compartment on a pack. Many tourists still carry their cash in a bumbag (fannypack), worn around the waist outside clothes, but there really couldn't be a less discreet way of carrying your stuff. If you must wear one, don't use it for valuables.

Most travellers nowadays keep their documents and cash in a slim **money belt** with two zipped compartments (one the size of a passport, the other big enough for credit cards), which is tucked away underneath your clothing. The most popular type of money belt goes round your waist; other types can be found which hang round your neck; which are strapped under your arm or round your calf; or which hang from your regular belt inside your trousers. Another recent innovation is an apparently ordinary buckled belt with a narrow, zipped pocket inside where you can hide folded banknotes (though obviously it's no use for larger items like passports).

Obviously, wearing your belt around your waist makes it more accessible, though sweat can be a problem (it's a good idea to keep documents, travellers' cheques and notes wrapped in plastic to avoid them getting soggy). Choose a belt made from cotton to keep as cool as possible – it's amazing how much hotter something light round your waist can make you feel. Additionally, a skin-coloured or beige belt is far more discreet. Bear in mind also that thieves in Latin America are all too aware now that foreigners carry their valuables in hidden money belts, although on the positive side they take too long to remove to be regularly stolen.

If you're travelling alone, something else to consider is a **water-safe** or plastic container to keep money and keys in if you want to go for a swim without leaving them lying on the beach. These are worn round the neck and range from fairly bulky containers to slim, wallet-shaped affairs with watertight zip locks.

# Documents

It's a good idea to take photocopies of important **documents**, such as your plane ticket and the personal pages of your passport, with you. Keep these copies with you but separate from the originals (it's also worth leaving another copy with a friend back home); having a copy of the information-bearing pages in your passport hugely speeds up the process of getting it replaced if it's stolen. Alternatively, as a further precaution you could email a scan of them to your on-the-road email address (see p.281) to download in case of emergency. Other useful documents to take with you include your driving licence and an international student card, which entitles you to various discounts. Passport photos are handy for visa extensions or any permits or passes that you might need.

# Clothes

Before packing, lay out all the **clothes** you think you'll need, and then halve the amount – remember that you can buy much of what you'll need (and generally more cheaply) in Latin America itself. Trainers/sneakers, T-shirts and trousers are sold everywhere, while in Andean countries like Ecuador, Peru and Bolivia you can buy very cheap and wonderfully warm alpaca sweaters, gloves and socks. It's also worth leaving your favourite clothes at home: if they're not lost or stolen, they'll likely be reduced to shreds by the wear and tear of constant travelling. Instead, pick up bargain bits and pieces at cheap chain stores, charity shops or jumble sales, which can be dumped when they've worn out or you no longer need them.

Remember when you're packing to allow for Latin America's extremes of **temperature**, from the high Andes to sizzling Caribbean beaches. Unless you're only going to one region in one country you'll probably need clothes for both hot and cold weather, and it's always worth erring on the side of caution – even in the warmest climates, you might find yourself on overnight buses with freezing air-conditioning. If you're heading into the Andean highlands or Patagonia in winter you'll need to have adequate clothing to deal with temperatures that can fall well below freezing. Don't assume that because these places suffer freezing temperatures they have indoor heating systems – most parts of Bolivia, for example, don't. Conversely, in a city like Manaus in Amazonian Brazil, where it's too hot to move by 10.30 in the morning, even cotton can seem too warm and clothes need to be light and loose.

For more on Latin American **dress codes**, see p.210.

- **Dress** A cool loose sundress is an excellent piece of all-round clothing: they're generally light, easy to pack and can do service both for more formal occasions and also as party gear.
- **Fleece** Fleece jackets are an absolute godsend: they weigh nothing and are very cosy, so you won't need to take another jacket or jumper. Although the best are expensive ($90–200), they're worth every penny. High-street stores sell fleeces in all shapes and sizes, though they're not as effective as those made by adventure sports manufacturers (see Basics).
- **Hat** A small, foldable hat is a great idea, both for keeping the sun off your head when it's hot and helping retain body heat when it's cold (when a fleece or woolly hat is invaluable).
- **Raincoat** Unless you can afford an expensive breathable Gore-tex jacket, raincoats are too sweaty to be comfortable in Latin America. If you're planning on doing some serious trekking in the

rainy season, however, you will need a decent waterproof jacket. Tropical rain can be torrential, and you'll be wasting your money if you buy anything that's not hardy enough.

- **Socks** Take several different thicknesses – lightweight for deterring mosquitoes in the tropics and a thermal pair for the mountains and long, chilly bus rides.
- **Shirts and trousers** Avoid taking jeans: they're bulky, heavy, difficult to wash and take forever to dry. Much better to take something like cargo pants, which are lightweight, tough and comfortable, although be careful with combat trousers – the soldier-boy look doesn't always go down well in countries which have suffered brutal military dictatorships or, like Colombia, are still in the throes of civil war. Specialist manufacturers make practical travelling trousers which are made from breathable showerproof fabric, dry out very quickly and zip apart to make a pair of shorts. A pair of loose drawstring trousers, cool in the heat and doubling up as pyjamas (recommended if you're sleeping outside in a hammock) is also a good idea. Shirts should also be loose and lightweight – a loose shirt can be much cooler than a T-shirt. Take one with long sleeves for protection against mosquitoes, in case you get sunburnt or need to cover up.
- **Tights** If it gets cold, a pair of tights worn under trousers can add a valuable extra layer of insulation.
- **T-shirts** Take two different thicknesses. A long-sleeved T-shirt is a good idea for chilly nights. Bear in mind, if you're a woman, that wearing very tight or low-cut T-shirts will attract ogling men.

## Checklist

- Three or four pairs of underwear
- Swimwear
- Two or three pairs of socks
- One pair of longish shorts
- Two T-shirts (one long and one short-sleeved)
- Two shirts (one long and one short-sleeved)
- Two pairs of trousers
- One or two dresses
- One lightweight jumper
- Fleece jacket
- One pair of trainers or walking boots
- One pair of sandals
- Hat
- Waterproof raincoat

# Footwear

Shoes and boots are obviously a vital part of your kit, but don't take more than two pairs because that's all you'll need and they take up lots of room. A pair of sturdy **walking boots** is essential if you're planning on doing some serious trekking, and recommended even if you're not. Modern brands are incredibly lightweight and last forever, and a good pair is a great investment. The best come with special gripping soles, supported sides (to protect your ankles) and waterproof lining so that your feet don't get wet. Specialist shops (see Basics) sell a wide range of walking boots, but you won't find them on sale in many places in Latin America, so buy them before you leave. Many travellers take a pair of trainers or sneakers instead – these are cheaper, do pretty well on the road and are easily replaced.

Your other pair of shoes should be **sandals** – most popular are Tevas (or similar brands), which are hard-wearing and waterproof. Again, they're most easily found in adventure sport shops. Leather sandals are sold everywhere in Latin America – in fact shoes of every kind are a Latin American fetish – and are cheap and attractive. Flip-flops in every shape and colour are also available absolutely everywhere.

# Essentials

Below is an alphabetical list of items (apart from documents and clothes) that you're likely to need.

- **Alarm clock** Take the smallest one you can find and make sure it has a light.
- **Batteries** Standard batteries are available everywhere (though they're often expensive), but you may have difficulty finding more obscure camera or watch batteries – take spares with you.
- **Cable lock** More useful than a padlock: with a good cable lock you can attach your rucksack to fixed objects; fancier models come sealed into a natty hardwearing case with combination lock and with a 100-decibel alarm. You can hang them from hotel doors and windows – particularly useful if you're a lone woman traveller – so that you'll know if someone is trying to get into your room while you're sleeping.
- **Cigarette lighter** Surprisingly useful even if you don't smoke, and much better than matches (which are sometimes so flimsy that

they're virtually useless) for lighting mosquito coils, camp fires and candles during power cuts.

- **Contact-lens solution and glasses** Contact-lens solution can be difficult to find outside big cities; take supplies with you. If you wear glasses, take a spare pair and your prescription.
- **Contraceptives** Condoms are available pretty much everywhere, but may not reach the same rigorous standards as those at home. If you're on the Pill, take a supply with you – you may not be able to find your prescription in Latin America.
- **First-aid kit** See p.263 for details.
- **Flashlight (torch)** An important piece of kit, since there are still large parts of Latin America without any electricity, while power cuts are also common.
- **Guidebook** See pp.167–70.
- **Liquid soap** Special, all-purpose liquid soap (available in specialist adventure shops) can be used to wash yourself, your hair, your clothes and even fruit and vegetables.
- **Penknife** Take a good penknife with a sharp blade, bottle opener and corkscrew (and remember not to fly with it in your hand luggage).
- **Sarong** A sarong is extremely versatile and can be used as an emergency towel, a bedcover, a scarf, a skirt, and so on. They're widely available in beach resorts, though you might prefer to bring one with you.
- **Sheet sleeping bag** Useful in hostels where they don't provide sheets and in cheap hotels (if you first spray it with a solution of Permethrin) to ward off fleas, lice and bed bugs. You can easily make one yourself from a folded sheet sewn across the bottom and down the side.
- **Sunglasses** Vital for protecting your eyes from the sun (and also from snow-glare in the mountains). Make sure you get proper UV-resistant lenses – a pair of cheap sunglasses is worse than useless.
- **Sunscreen** Sunscreen is available in big cities and tourist resorts, but the locals don't use it, so it's expensive and sometimes not of the best quality. You'll need at least factor 15 to start with.
- **Tampons** Not available in every country in Latin America (the less industrialized the country, the less chance of finding them), although most capital cities and, especially, large tourist resorts and gringo hangouts have them.
- **Toiletries** Keep your washbag supplies to a minimum and transfer things like shampoo and moisturizing cream into smaller travel bottles which you can buy at chemists or in camping shops. Avoid bottles with pop-tops which tend to open in depressurized environments (such as aircraft holds) and will then leak every-

where. The heat and fierce sun mean that one thing you will need loads of is moisturizing lotion; in some parts of Latin America this will cost more than your lunch.

# Non-essentials

- **Binoculars** Great for bird- and wildlife-spotting. The latest models are tiny and very light; you ought to be able to get a decent pair for $30.
- **Books** Although there are innumerable book exchanges at backpacker's hostels and cafés across the continent, the quality of books on offer is often pretty dire, so you'll probably want to bring plenty of reading matter of your own.
- **Camera** Most people take an auto-focus ("point and shoot") camera; these are small, light and virtually idiot-proof, and cost no more than $150 for a good-quality model. More serious photographers will probably want to take an SLR (single lens reflex) camera – but bear in mind that camera equipment is easily damaged and stolen, as well as being a pain to carry around. Other useful equipment for committed photographers includes filters, additional lenses and perhaps a lightweight, fold-away tripod. Make sure you carry spare camera batteries. Standard camera film is widely available (though prices vary widely), but you should take a supply of slide and/or black-and-white film if you use these, since they're not always easy to get hold of in Latin America. It's also worth taking plenty of high-speed film (400 ASA), which is best for naturally dark environments like the rainforest.
- **Camping gear** Obviously, taking camping gear opens up lots of extra possibilities in terms of trekking and saving on hotel costs, although it also means you'll have to say goodbye to travelling light and carry a much larger pack.
- **Compass** Important if you're planning on trekking, and useful anywhere to get your bearings.
- **Earplugs** Latin Americans love noise and scarcely seem to notice it, but you might not: a decent pair of earplugs is a godsend if you find yourself in a hotel next to an all-night bar or sitting beside the sound-system on a bus.
- **Games** A pack of cards or a travel chess or backgammon set can help while away the hours waiting for buses, on buses or sitting indoors during rainy season days.
- **Map** A decent map can add hugely to your appreciation of the country you're travelling through, both as a guide during long journeys and as an aid in planning itineraries.

- **Mosquito net** Even if your hotel does have mosquito nets, they may well have holes in them, which makes them pretty useless. Take your own. Some come impregnated with repellent; if not, you can treat it yourself with Permethrin.
- **Neck cushion** An inflatable neck cushion is great for long bus and plane journeys.
- **Needle and thread** Useful for mending clothes and sewing buttons back on.
- **Notebook** Most people keep some kind of diary of their trip – very valuable years after the event when you've forgotten the small details of life on the road that once seemed so crucial.
- **Padlock** Handy for hostel lockers and for locking the door of your room in cheap hotels.
- **Personal stereo** Great for lazy days in a hammock and long boring bus journeys. If your personal stereo has a record feature you can tape live music, local sounds and your own audio diary.
- **Plug adaptor** Sockets in Latin America are the same as those in North America (i.e. they take two flat prongs); if you're from anywhere else you'll need an adaptor, available from camping shops or at the airport.
- **Photos and postcards** Photos of your family and home town are a great way of breaking the ice with curious locals. Postcards from your home country make good presents – children, in particular, love them.
- **Plug** A universal plug is useful, since most sinks and baths in cheaper hotels have lost their plugs.
- **Radio** Lets you tune into local radio stations and sounds; with a short wave radio you can get the BBC World Service/Voice of America and keep up with news back home.
- **String** Often useful for running repairs, and can also serve as an emergency washing line.
- **Toilet paper** Although toilet paper is sold everywhere in Latin America, it's often not supplied in toilets, so carry your own roll.
- **Towel** If you'd like something more absorbent than a sarong to dry yourself, don't take an ordinary bath towel – they rot easily, smell horrible and take up far too much room. Instead take a special travel towel which looks more like a duster, folds away to almost nothing, is made from incredibly absorbent fabric and can be packed when damp.
- **Water bottle** Take a sturdy water bottle (with a carrying strap) if you're planning on camping, trekking or exploring the wilderness.
- **Water sterilizing kit** A valuable money-saving device - see Staying Healthy for details.

# 7

# Your first night

E ven for seasoned travellers, arriving in Latin America after a long flight is a daunting prospect. The noisy and chaotic scene that is likely to greet you is hardly an ideal situation when you're feeling exhausted and vulnerable, and it's often difficult to retain a positive attitude and a sense of humour. With just a small amount of organization, however, you can make sure your introduction to Latin America is as painless as possible.

## Booking hotels in advance

Chances are that you'll be flying into one of Latin America's capital cities, some of which – such as Mexico City and São Paulo – are vast. It will take you days to orient yourself, and half an hour after flying in is not the time to start. **Booking a hotel in advance** is quite possibly the best five minutes you'll spend on planning your trip, and will stop you fretting all the way through the flight (it might even make your mother fret less, too). Your guidebook should list the phone number and fax or email details of a wide range of hotels, as should the relevant tourist board and a host of internet sites (see Basics for details). When choosing a hotel, consider the following:

- Decide on the part of the city you want to stay in, as well as a particular hotel. Most cities have two distinct hotel areas – expensive and budget. While expensive hotels are often located in leafy suburbs adjacent to the city centre, budget hotels and hostels are frequently right in the heart of the city or, alternatively, near bus stations and/or markets. It's also best to pick a hotel close to several others so that you can swap easily should you want to. And try to avoid choosing a hotel miles out of the centre.
- This is the time to spend more than your allotted daily budget. After a lengthy flight you'll be in need of a comfortable bed and a hot shower, two facilities missing from the very cheapest hostels. Also, a hotel which serves breakfast and has a bar and restaurant will save you wandering the streets of a strange city unnecessarily.
- Consider booking not just your first but also your second night's accommodation. Otherwise, if you arrive late in the day, you'll have to get up early (checkout time is usually noon) and spend your first morning looking for another hotel – sounds fine now, but you might not want to do it with jet lag or altitude sickness.

When it comes to booking a room by phone, you'll find that even small hotels in Latin America often have a staff member who understands English – assuming, that is, you don't speak enough Spanish or Portuguese to make yourself understood. Easiest of all, choose a hotel with a fax number or an email address. Alternatively, some travel agents (see pp.320–22) have a hotel-booking service and can book hotels for you – if you're booking your flights through them, they might do this for free, although the hotels on their lists will probably be three-star or better and cost at least $50 a night. You can also book a bed through various international youth hostelling associations (see Basics).

## Long-haul flights and how to survive them

Unless you're flying from the southern US to Mexico or Central America, to reach Latin America you'll have to endure a long-haul flight – up to twelve hours – even before stopovers. Even if you love flying, hours and hours spent in a cramped pressurized container is bound to take its toll. There are lots of ways of avoiding feeling utterly dreadful on arrival, though.

First, arrive as early as possible at your departure airport. Most international carriers ask that you be at the check-in desk at least two hours before take-off, although in practice they often begin checking in passengers an hour before that. The earlier you arrive, the better choice of seats you'll get, unless you've been able to reserve them in advance through your travel agent or personally by phone to the relevant airline (see "Buying a ticket", p.133) – otherwise you'll have to take potluck at check-in. The position of your seat is very important in determining how comfortable your flight is. A window seat gives you a great view during take-off and landing, and you'll have somewhere solid to lean your head if you want to sleep, and a little more privacy. If you think you're going to want to get up and move around during the flight, then choose an aisle seat. Later arrivals at check-in are invariably given middle seats, which are the most cramped and have no benefits at all. You can also ask your check-in official if there are any seats available by the emergency exits – these have loads more leg room (understandably, these seats are often given to particularly tall people, if they haven't already been snapped up). In addition, the so-called "bulkhead" seats, situated in the front row of each section of the plane, have significantly more leg room – you could try asking for one of these, though they're often reserved for families with babies. It's also worth checking in early if you're travelling with a bicycle or surfboard.

During check-in, the official dealing with you will tear out the outward vouchers of your ticket. Very occasionally a careless offical will tear out the return portions as well – when your ticket is given back to you, check that these are still there or you'll find yourself in big trouble. If you're taking several different flights you may either be checked in to all of these or just the first. Ask your official to explain which is relevant to you – if you're "checked through", your luggage will automatically be sent on with you to your final destination. If not (most likely if you're travelling with several different airlines), you'll have to collect your luggage at your next port of call and then check in again.

Once you've checked in you'll be given a boarding card for your flight (plus additional boarding cards for any connecting flights you've been checked on to). Hold on to these: they have your designated seat number as well as your boarding time (approximately half an hour before take-off). In large airports these are often a fair way from check-in – give yourself plenty of time to get there.

Secondly, pack your piece of **hand luggage** very carefully. You'll have to lug this around the airport so don't make it too heavy, but do think about taking the following:

- Your guidebook, so that you can bone up on the city you're flying into.
- Novels and magazines help pass the time, as does listening to a personal stereo.
- A jumper and possibly socks: long-haul flights can be surprisingly chilly (on the other hand, your destination may well be very hot, so you'll need to dress in removable layers).
- A toothbrush and toothpaste – cleaning your teeth really does make you feel better – while moisturising cream helps combat dry plane cabins. Take some aspirin both to combat headaches and to guard against deep-vein thrombosis – and any other drugs you need to take regularly. If you wear contact lenses you'll want to take them out – dry air will make your eyes sore – so carry your glasses with you.
- Any documents you'll need on arrival, plus foreign currency, hotel address and telephone number, and booking confirmation.
- Anything valuable and/or fragile, like your camera or sunglasses.
- A large bottle of mineral water – air stewards will offer you drinks from time to time, but it's often not enough, and though you're perfectly entitled to ask for extra drinks, it's easier to take your own.

## Post-September 11 security

Following the terrorist attacks of September 11, 2001, both airport and airline security have been dramatically increased. Passengers are no longer allowed to carry any sharp or potentially dangerous objects in their hand luggage (these include Swiss Army knives, scissors and nail files). If you're taking anything of this kind, pack it in your hold luggage or be prepared to have it confiscated. You'll need official clarification if you're carrying needles or a syringe. Generally speaking, checking in is now more thorough, as are boarding procedures – you might well be frisked and/or have to open up your hand luggage. If you're concerned for any reason, ring your travel agent or the relevant airline to check current procedures before you fly.

## Deep-vein thrombosis

**Deep-vein thrombosis**, or DVT, is caused by blood clots forming in a vein in the leg. DVT can be fatal if the blood clots break away and travel through the bloodstream to the heart, causing pulmonary embolism – this may happen anytime up to three weeks after the initial clotting. DVT can be caused by lengthy bouts of inactivity, such as sitting in a tiny seat on a plane for hours on end (hence its nickname, "economy class syndrome"). Despite all the publicity surrounding the condition, your chances of developing DVT during a long flight remain minuscule, at around one in several million. There are also certain preventative measures: take an aspirin just before you fly; wear "flight socks" (special support stockings) which are widely available from chemists and at the airport; drink loads of water; move around as much as possible; wiggle your toes and ankles to keep circulation going; and don't cross your legs when sitting (which is virtually impossible on a plane, in any case). In most cases people who suffer from DVT already have circulation problems, although smoking and being on the Pill also increase the risks. If you're worried, talk to your doctor before flying.

Once on board, there are several things you can do to give yourself a head start on arrival. Drink as much liquid as possible, preferably water, and try to avoid alcohol, which has much more effect at high altitude and exacerbates the effects of jet lag. Get up and move around every few hours to avoid stiffness and DVT (see box). Use the time to prepare yourself mentally by reading your guidebook or learning a few words of Spanish or Portuguese. An hour or so before landing, go and wash your face and clean your teeth, which will make you feel much more alert and prepared for the challenge of arriving in a strange country.

# Arrival

Once off the plane you follow the signs – and everyone else – through immigration, baggage reclaim, customs and the arrivals hall (always in that order) and then out onto Latin American soil. This is where culture shock kicks in: you'll probably be jet lagged, and as a tourist you'll be prey to every hustler in the building. Don't let anyone bully you into something you don't want to do or distract you – instead, try to keep focused on getting out of the airport, and at least look as though you know what you're doing.

## Immigration

You shouldn't have any problems at immigration, assuming you've filled in all the forms correctly (these may well have been given to you on the plane) and have all the relevant documents to hand, including your passport, return ticket and proof of funds. Your entry stamp will have a number of days written on it by the official dealing with you – make sure you get the days you need for your stay; if you don't, point this out very politely and ask for the right amount. Most immigration officials speak a little English, but will always appreciate the effort if you speak even just a few words of Spanish or Portuguese. Remember there's no absolute guarantee that you'll be allowed into your chosen country, even if you have a visa. The decision to let you enter rests with whichever immigration official deals with you upon your arrival. Although it's pretty much unheard of for anyone to be refused entry without a very good reason, it doesn't hurt to be on your best behaviour.

## Baggage reclaim

Baggage reclaim is usually where the chaos begins – this may be the moment to start getting used to Latin American spontaneity and disorder. Keep your eyes peeled for your backpack, and once it arrives don't ever leave it unattended until you reach the safety of your hotel room. Beware of any distractions, particularly strangers rushing up to you and shouting in your face – this is a well-known ruse to distract you while a thief makes off with your stuff.

## Customs

Unless you're travelling with specialized equipment, you won't need to declare anything at customs – obviously, it's not recommended that you bring in weapons, large amounts of alcohol and recreational drugs (unless you relish the prospect of being locked up in squalor for a very long time). In all likelihood you'll be allowed to walk straight through customs past a couple of bored officials; if you've been given a customs declaration to fill in on the plane, this is where you hand it in, having presumably ticked no to every question – are you bringing in contaminated liquids? Explosives? Infected meat? No, no and no.

## Arrivals hall

This is where your journey finally begins. Once you've emerged into the arrivals hall – usually not as grand as it sounds – you're now officially on Latin American soil and what you do next is entirely up to you. You might have first to wade through an excited throng waiting for long-lost relatives to emerge, followed by an unholy scrum of airport hustlers pressing in on all sides. Ignore them, and head for a relatively quiet space to orientate yourself and work out where what you need is situated. This is likely to be a *casa de cambio* and the taxi rank. You might also want to make a phone call, book a hotel, use the bathroom to tidy yourself up or buy a drink. Don't spend more time in the arrivals hall than you need to, however – like any transport hub anywhere in the world, airports are a favorite hangout for all kinds of unsavoury characters who prey on the vulnerability of new arrivals.

Airports always have somewhere to **change money**, although if you arrive at night this might be closed. It's a good idea to have a rough idea of the exchange rate before you change your money, and bear in mind that airport facilities often offer a poorer rate than elsewhere, so only change enough to tide you over until the next day, unless you're arriving at the weekend, in which case you'll obviously have to change a bit more. Make sure that the notes you're given are in good condition (politely ask for them to be replaced if they're not), and check you've been given the correct amount before you walk away. Ask for some coins if you want to make a phone call. Once you've counted your cash, put it away safely in your money belt apart from whatever small amount you might need immediately. If the *casa de cambio* is closed, don't despair – there can't be an airport taxi driver in Latin America who doesn't accept dollars, and all you really need to pay for at this stage is a ride to your hotel.

Some airports also have **ATMs**: these offer better exchange rates than the *casas de cambio* and you won't have to speak a foreign language to get your cash. Be careful when using them though, especially if there are no security guards or policemen nearby. There's also likely to be some kind of **tourist information booth** at the airport. Though these are often fairly useless, staff do usually speak some English and can tell you how much you should pay for a taxi ride into the city. They should also be able to recommend a hotel (though these will be mid- or top-range places) if you haven't already got a reservation, and might even book a room for you. Some might even have a basic city map.

Some travellers arriving in the middle of the night prefer to wait in the airport until daybreak. Note, though, that some airports close after the last arrival; at others, security guards might ask you to move on. If you do spend the night in the airport, pick a well-lit, secure spot and tie your luggage onto something solid. Having said all this, it really is much easier to fork out for a taxi to take you to a hotel where you can dump your bags and get a much-needed first night's sleep.

# Getting into town

Your next challenge is to find a way of getting from the airport to your hotel, whether in a taxi, *colectivo* or bus. **Airport taxi** runs are extremely lucrative and are usually controlled by hard-nosed taxi unions who seemingly set the fare by thinking of a reasonable price and then trebling it; their members are the only drivers licensed to take you directly from the airport taxi rank. If you want a safe ride there's little you can do about this – take consolation from the fact that in almost all cases, the ride from the city back to the airport with a regular cabbie will be half or less the price you paid on arrival. Most Latin American airport taxi ranks are at least properly regulated. You'll first have to pay your fare at a ticket booth in the airport (you'll be given a receipt or coupon to hand to your taxi driver) and then have to wait in line at the taxi rank. You can pay in dollars, though prices are fixed and not open to negotiation.

Many taxi drivers speak a little English, and are generally friendly and honest, but there are a few things to watch out for. The most common is that your driver, after asking you where you're staying, will tell you that the hotel or area you're going to is dangerous and that he knows somewhere much safer. Always stick to your guns – this is a well-rehearsed ploy to take you to his aunty/mother-in-law/good friend Miguel's hotel, or indeed anywhere where he'll get a slice of your money. Secondly, if you haven't bought a coupon at the airport, always agree the price of your journey first even if the taxi is metered (meters are often doctored) and absolutely refuse to pay any more if your driver tries it on. Thirdly, don't get in any cab if there's someone else riding up front, and never get out of the taxi until you arrive at your destination for whatever reason (in Bogotá, taxi drivers claim that the engine has stopped and that they need your help pushing the car, which then miraculously springs back into life leaving you standing in the middle of the road without your luggage). Be careful, too, that taxi drivers don't drive off with your luggage at the end of your trip when you get out of the vehicle.

As well as private taxis, you may well find **shared taxis** or **colectivos**. These are usually minibuses which, once full, drive round town dropping everyone off at their various destinations. *Colectivos* are much cheaper than private taxis, stringently regulated and more secure – in sum, a much better option. Again you'll purchase a coupon from an official booth in the airport.

Another alternative (but only if you arrive in daylight) is to walk out of the airport to the nearest main thoroughfare and hail a **regular taxi**; these will charge you much less than the airport taxi service. A decent guidebook will tell you where to head for, but don't wander aimlessly, and try to make sure you get into a licensed cab (identified by a certain make of car in a certain colour, such as the green Volkswagen Beetles used in Mexico City). A riskier alternative is to go with one of the touts in the airport to his own vehicle, which will be parked outside the jurisdiction of the official airport taxi union. These unlicensed taxi drivers are often perfectly decent citizens trying to make a living – but who's to say if they're not? You could be mugged, dumped somewhere dangerous or worse – if you do take a ride with a tout you have only your instincts to decide whether he's honest or not.

## The taxista assault course

Just what you need after eighteen hours flying from London – to run an assault course of *taxistas* at San José international airport. It used to be that the taxi drivers would rush the entrance of the terminal, wrest your bag from your hand, and absolutely insist on taking you to the city, whether you had a ride lined up or not. Usually they would charge you the right fare – give or take a couple of dollars. Now the *taxistas* are crowded outside, prevented by airport officials from entering the terminal, so that your first view of Costa Rica might well be a phalanx of slightly hysterical-looking men, all yelling "taxi" of course. It's just like those wildly stereotypical American films where the fresh-faced Yankee hero goes to Latin America and steps from the airport into a cesspit of chaos and corruption. That said, airport taxis are regulated, and pirate cabs can no longer operate freely. So take a deep breath and choose your *taxista*.

Jean McNeil

If you arrive in daylight, you might find a **bus** which goes into town from the airport or close by, but you'll need to have a good idea of where you're going and some small change to pay your fare. Local buses are frequently rife with pickpockets, and if you have a huge backpack they may refuse to take you or simply not have enough room. In general airports which don't run a *colectivo* service will instead run airport shuttle buses. These take you on a set route, usually to the city centre or to hotel districts. Shuttle services are more expensive than ordinary local buses but are also safer, and frequently come equipped with air-conditioning and comfortable seats.

# Jet lag

To those who have never suffered it, **jet lag** might appear to be nothing more than a rich kid's whinge, but unfortunately it's all too real, as you're likely to discover for yourself after your arrival in Latin America, unless you've flown from North America. The condition affects a whopping 94 percent of all long-distance travellers, and unless you're one of the lucky few who are immune, it's an inevitable hazard of flying long distances. Jet lag results from the disruption of the human body clock which is caused by rapidly crossing world time zones. Our body clock runs according to a complex 24-hour cycle which governs our heartbeat, temperature and blood pressure, biological functions, periods of alertness and lethargy and the timing of both hunger and tiredness. If you cross more than three time zones (i.e. if the time in your departure city is more than three hours different from that at your destination), you can expect a bout of jet lag. You're likely to suffer less from jet lag when travelling west rather than east, so Europeans have it easier on the way out to Latin America, while Australasians will have less jet lag going home. The good news for North Americans is that if you're flying directly south from the US or Canada to Latin America you may not even cross a single time zone, thus avoiding jet lag altogether.

**Symptoms** of jet lag include extreme fatigue, disorientation, lack of concentration, disrupted sleep and dehydration. In the days following your arrival you're likely to feel light-headed and unable to go to sleep and wake up at the appropriate times. Sitting bolt upright in bed at 4am and falling asleep in your breakfast may sound amusing, but disrupted sleep patterns can wreak havoc on your health and wellbeing. According to NASA, for each time zone crossed, you'll need a day before your body clock is properly adjusted – this means that if you're flying from London to Santiago, for example, it'll take six days. And jet lag doesn't really kick in until the second day of your arrival, so don't congratulate yourself on avoiding it prematurely.

There are all kinds of bizarre **jet lag treatments** available on the market. Some, like melatonin, a synthetic version of the hormone which is secreted into the bloodstream when it's time to sleep, have large followings (though its effectiveness is doubted by as many others, and there's no standard dose) – it's available in health-food stores in the US but not Europe. A herbal remedy from New Zealand called No-Jet-Lag (ⓦwww.nojetlag.com) is said to work, as is intensive light therapy (ⓦwww.bodyclock.com). In general, though, the best way to minimize the effects of jet lag is to follow the points below:

- Try to avoid 24-hour partying the night before you leave and last-minute panicking – stress and hangovers will only exacerbate jet lag. It's possible to "save up" sleep by having several decent nights of it before you fly, which will help you to deal with the loss of sleep that comes with jet lag.
- Once on board, set your watch immediately to your destination time zone and start to adjust to the new time. Try to stay awake and sleep at the relevant hours.
- Drink loads of water, avoid alcohol and eat light, carbohydrate-based meals. Don't take conventional sleeping pills, which are dehydrating.
- Once you've arrived, continue to follow the local time even if your body is desperate for sleep. Go to bed when the locals do, eat meals at the right time and avoid sleeping during the day.
- Get out into the fresh air and spend as much time in bright natural light as possible – daylight alleviates jet lag by helping to reset your body clock.
- Take some gentle exercise as soon as possible – swimming or walking will combat the stiffness which results from sitting in one place for a long time and may also alleviate symptoms of jet lag such as disrupted sleeping patterns.
- Take it easy for your first few days – put off any non-urgent decisions, since your mental processes will be impaired by jet lag. Now is the perfect time to go to the beach, where the sunshine will aid your recovery.

# 8

# Culture shock

Don't worry if you find you don't much enjoy your first few days in Latin America. You may well find the change in climate and food and the sheer strangeness of the place overwhelms you, leaving you feeling anxious, disoriented, paranoid, self-conscious or simply exhausted. You may even find yourself wishing you'd never come, shocked by the poverty, appalled by the pollution, confused by the language and disconcerted by the apparent chaos all around you. These are all common symptoms of **culture shock**, a perfectly normal reaction that almost every traveller experiences to some degree. Even experienced travellers often undergo the same feelings of anxiety and alienation when they return to the region after some time away; in many ways, these feelings are part of the exhilaration of travel – if it didn't feel slightly dangerous, alien and exotic, it wouldn't be an adventure.

Culture shock often goes hand in hand with homesickness, and some people find it comes and goes in waves during long trips, so that the very same things which one week you find exciting about the country you're travelling through – be it the food, the local culture, the pace of life – can the next week seem deeply frustrating and annoying, making you wish you were back home surrounded by the safe and familiar. Fortunately, though, culture shock usually fades very quickly after arrival, generally giving way to excitement as you settle in and begin to enjoy all that Latin America has to offer. The following tips should help you overcome any initial culture shock and get through the confusion and strangeness of the first few days.

- If you're gong on a long trip taking in several different countries, consider starting in a country that's relatively easy to travel in, such as Chile, Argentina or Costa Rica, before taking on somewhere more challenging, such as Peru or Colombia.
- Take it easy for the first few days after arrival: you may well be jet-lagged after a long flight, exhausted and struggling to cope with a very different climate.
- Start exploring gradually rather than diving into your travels head-first. Take time to get your bearings and visit a few easy and accessible places before heading off to more remote and adventurous destinations.
- Try and speak a few words of the local language, even if you only know enough to order a beer: this will make you feel less of an alien and make the locals much more approachable.
- Call or write home about your initial experiences – often just telling someone about what you're adjusting to can make it feel much more manageable.
- Chat to other travellers, as they've invariably been through the same thing and can offer useful support and advice, and help you see the funny side of things you might otherwise find exasperating.
- Don't feel obliged to have a completely "authentic" experience right from the start, no matter what other travellers tell you. If you want to stay close to your hotel and eat only familiar food for the first few days, then go ahead – there will be plenty of time to explore further afield and eat more adventurously once you've settled in.

## Blockbuster movies

When you're travelling, cumulative cultural dislocation can make you take a sudden dive for the nearest Burger King, blockbuster movie, or other culturally familiar things you might never consider doing at home. I never see American blockbuster films at home, of course, being a snob. But it's quite entertaining, not to mention instructive, seeing *Speed III* or *Godzilla* in a Central American cinema, surrounded by the increasingly Americanophile teenage sons and daughters of the local scions (cinemas are sometimes too pricey for the average family). The parking lot is full of four-wheel drives, and the foyer stuffed with girls admiring each other's outfits (*Que chivo!, que barbaro!* – roughly, Cool!). You can learn a lot of Spanish by reading the subtitles and comparing them with what comes out of Keanu Reeves' mouth – or perhaps that's not such a good example . . .

Jean McNeil

- If after a few days the symptoms of culture shock don't go away, it may simply be that you don't like your first port of call. Try moving to another city or region where the climate or culture make you feel more comfortable.

# Different countries, different customs

Though when you first arrive in a Latin American capital it may seem disappointingly familiar, with its high-rise business district, rushing commuters and international corporate advertising hoardings, it won't be long before you realize that the Coca-colonization of the region is only skin deep. Beneath the sometimes banal globalized veneer, traditional Latin American culture runs deep, and it will quickly become clear that you are in the midst of a society with a very different approach to life and view of the world to what you're used to back home. Religion – above all Roman Catholicism – and extended families play a far greater role in Latin American culture than you're probably used to, and you may find many of the attitudes you encounter surprising in comparison to those commonly held in Europe or the US. Traditional Latin American values, especially those related to gender roles, inequality and social conformity, may seem stiflingly conservative or even outrageously oppressive. Many Latin Americans will find your behaviour equally strange – the very fact of your travelling to faraway countries simply for pleasure may be viewed as an irresponsible eccentricity, while to be unmarried and childless in your midtwenties will strike many as at best bizarre or at worst indicative of some underlying misfortune.

Though there have been important steps towards more equal rights in recent decades, **machismo** – a traditional culture of gender stereotyping whereby men are seen as strong and dominant and women weak and subservient – is alive and well in Latin America, and for women, dealing with this can be the most challenging aspect of travel in Latin America. Advice on coping with sexual harassment is given on pp.301–2, but you should also be prepared to cope with more general gender prejudices. If you're a woman travelling with a man – be it a husband, partner or friend – most conversation will be addressed to him, even if you're the one who speaks the local language; if you're a woman travelling alone, meanwhile, many Latin American men will assume it's because you can't find a man back home, and act accordingly.

Other aspects of Latin American culture that you may well find frustrating include a near-complete disregard for timekeeping, widespread corruption, shocking levels of poverty and inequality and interminable bureaucracy. However infuriating these aspects of Latin American culture can be, there's almost nothing you can do to change them, so railing against them is a waste of time and energy that can really spoil your trip. It's much better to accept such traits as part and parcel of what you came to experience, and adapt accordingly; keeping a sense of humour and perspective about things also helps.

## On your best behaviour

However much you may dislike the idea of being an ambassador for your country, this is how many Latin Americans will see you, just as your view of their country will be shaped by how the locals treat you, so it's important to act with respect towards the cultural and social norms of the country you're in. No one expects you to transform yourself overnight into a Latin American, but adapting your behaviour to the country you're visiting is polite and generally makes travel easier and more enjoyable and makes local people more receptive. Mastering the full range of social niceties in any country takes considerable time, but there are a few general behaviour codes you should definitely try to follow.

Even if you're only travelling for a few weeks, it's essential to learn at least a few basic words of Spanish or Portuguese. As well as being practical, making an effort to **speak the local language** makes locals react more favourably towards you, even if it's no more than basic greetings. Although few Latin Americans speak good English, many understand enough to know if you're talking about them, and certainly recognize common English obscenities, so be careful what you say.

Though it varies in degree from country to country, Latin Americans generally attach considerable importance to **politeness and formality**. It's normal to shake hands and use a formal greeting such as "good morning" or "good afternoon" before engaging someone in conversation – failure to do so will make you appear rude and can cause offence, or at least make people less helpful. It's also a good idea to use formal titles like *señor/señora* or *don/doña* and, if speaking Spanish, to use the formal *usted* rather than *tú* when addressing older people or those in authority. Politeness is particularly important when dealing with officials such as police officers, for whom the respect accorded their uniform or position is one of the few compensations for low pay and poor conditions. If you're rude or disrespectful, they can make things very difficult for you.

Though you're likely to see a few locals doing it, **getting angry** and raising your voice will seldom produce results, and is more likely to cause further antagonism, particularly when dealing with people in authority. This doesn't mean you can't be firm and assertive – just do it in as calm and civil a manner as you can manage. Getting involved in any kind of fight is a very bad idea, as the use of fists can easily provoke a reaction with a knife or gun.

# Dressing the part

Latin Americans also attach considerable importance to **appearance**. Even if they are so poor they only have one set of clothes, they're still likely to be clean and relatively smart. Although the prejudice against people perceived as hippies is not as strong as it once was, dressing in scruffy or dirty clothes is usually viewed unfavourably, whilst having at least one set of reasonably smart attire can get you into places where scruffier backpackers wouldn't be admitted.

It's a good idea to observe local **dress codes** as much as possible. Short shorts, sleeveless shirts and bikinis are fine on the beach, but in towns and cities they are usually frowned upon, and in some isolated rural communities can cause serious offence and even provoke stone-throwing. Wearing part or all of the traditional costumes of local indigenous groups, on the other hand, provokes ridicule at best and grave offence at worst, so save them until you get home. Military clothing, particularly anything camouflaged, is also a bad idea, especially in countries with recent experience of armed conflict.

The Roman Catholic religion is taken seriously across Latin America, so it's particularly important to dress appropriately and behave respectfully when **visiting churches** or attending religious ceremonies or fiestas.

△ Aymara women in traditional dress

# Harsh realities

Unless you've travelled to other developing countries before, the thing you'll find most shocking when you arrive in Latin America is likely to be the extreme **poverty** endured by much of the region's population. Most major cities are ringed by slums and shanty towns which lack even basic amenities such as water, electricity and sewerage, and whose populations are constantly increasing as a result of migration from rural areas where poverty is even more desperate and rates of malnutrition and infant mortality are appallingly high. Unemployment levels are very high, and wages so low that even those who do have jobs (including professionals such as teachers) often struggle to make ends meet. This poverty is even more shocking in comparison with the extreme wealth enjoyed by small sections of the population: many Latin American countries are amongst the most unequal societies in the world, and the gap between rich and poor is distressingly pronounced.

The most visible manifestation of poverty you'll come across is undoubtedly the large number of **beggars** on the streets of almost every city. Many Latin Americans of all social classes give generously to beggars, particularly to the old and sick, and their donations act as an informal welfare system in countries where generally there is no universal health provision or financial support for the unemployed. Many tourists are unsure how to deal with beggars in Latin America, and you wouldn't be the first to mask your discomfort by averting your gaze while marching by. Obviously, giving is a personal decision, and you may prefer to give to a charity instead, or even to get actively involved in a local charity for a while. If you do decide to give money, you may want to follow the example of most locals by targeting the old, disabled and sick rather than those beggars who could otherwise be working for a living. There are also other ways of giving to the poor: the locals you see paying for the services of the countless shoe-shine boys and girls in every city centre do so not just because they want immaculate footwear; paying for small services like this is also an informal way of giving money to the poor whilst encouraging hard work and self-reliance in street children who might otherwise turn to begging or crime. Having your shoes shined will also deflect the often annoying pestering to which the shoe-shiners will subject you, at least until the next day.

# Mañana, mañana

One of the most striking cultural differences between Latin America and countries in the developed world is in their attitude to **time**. Whereas back home turning up fifteen minutes late is considered at best thoughtless and at worst rude and unprofessional (if you do it persistently, it can even lose you your job), in most of Latin America arriving hours or even days late for a meeting barely warrants an explanation, never mind an apology. This relaxed attitude to time, whereby almost anything can be put off until tomorrow (*mañana*) and punctuality is considered of little or no importance, is one of the aspects of Latin America that most tourists and travellers find most frustrating. In part, dictionaries are to blame. Take a look in an English–Spanish dictionary and you'll probably read that *ahora* means "now". Though technically correct, in practice this translation is way off the mark: in Latin America *ahora* means sometime in the future, possibly today; the diminutive *ahorita* (literally "right now") means fairly soon; only when you start using terms like *inmediatamente* (immediately) or *ahoritita/ahorita mismo* (absolutely right away) is any sense of urgency communicated – and even then, it's likely to be ignored. Latin Americans are usually aware of this trait (though that doesn't stop them setting very exact agendas which they've no hope of meeting) and often rather bemused by gringos' bizarre obsession with punctuality. Indeed, when they really, truly mean an exact time, they'll emphasize it by using the expression *hora inglés* ("English time").

## Yesterday's train

After five days hard trekking in the high Peruvian Andes, we arrived in the tiny hamlet of Santa Teresa, on the railway line that runs between Cuzco and the jungle town of Quilabamba. With little in the way of food or drink available, we were anxious to catch the next train out. The stationmaster told us it was scheduled to arrive at 8 o'clock the next morning. Though it sometimes ran late, he assured us it never left early. We made camp beside the hot springs outside town, cooking the last of our meagre supplies and dreaming of cold beer and huge steaks that awaited us at the end of the line. We were woken at 7 o'clock the next morning by the whistle of the train as it arrived, and rushed down to the station just in time to see it move off down the valley.

Outraged, we confronted the stationmaster. "You told us the train never departed early!" we cried. "That's right, señores," he replied gravely, "it never does." He then paused for a moment as we pointed at our watches and gesticulated at the disappearing engine before adding: ". . . you see, that was yesterday's train."

James Read

That they're aware of it, however, doesn't mean they're going to change just for you, and the bottom line is that there's nothing you can do about it. Getting angry because a bus leaves a few hours after the official departure time isn't going to make things happen any faster, so to avoid frustration it's best to allow extra time for every journey and leave enough space and flexibility in your travel plans to accommodate the inevitable delays. It also helps if you can adopt the same laid-back approach to time as the locals, and enjoy the relaxed unpredictability it adds to life: after all, if you want to travel in a country where the trains run on time, you'd be better off going to Switzerland. Finally, it's worth bearing in mind that, according to Latin American travellers' lore, the only time a bus or train does leave on time is when you arrive at the terminal five minutes late.

# Being a gringo (what they think of you)

Wherever you go in Latin America, it won't be long before you hear locals refer to you as **gringo** or (if you're female) gringa. The origins of the word are thought to lie in the nineteenth-century US–Mexican War, either drawn from a slogan shouted at the invading green-uniformed US troops ("Green Go Home!"), or derived from the song "Green Grow the Rushes, Oh!" to which those same troops apparently marched. Strictly speaking, the term originally only applied to people from the US, and this meaning is still retained in most of Mexico, but elsewhere in Latin America "gringo" is used to describe anyone from rich, developed and largely white countries in Europe, North America and Australasia – in parts of the Peruvian Andes, it's even used to refer to lighter-skinned people from elsewhere in the country. Though it can have negative connotations – in Colombia, for example, the expression *hacerse el gringo* ("to act like a gringo") is used to mean "play the fool" – generally speaking though it's not an insult, just a description of which ethnic or cultural group you belong to in Latin American eyes, so it's not worth getting upset about. Latin Americans are equally blunt in describing people of Chinese, African and indigenous descent as *Chino*, *Negro* and *Indio*, and while there is a degree of racism in this system of categorization, with the exception of *Indio*

Latin American attitudes to **people from the US** – often referred to as *Yanquis* (Yankees) no matter what part of the States they're from – are a complex mixture of love and hate. On one hand, Latin Americans generally admire the wealth, dynamism and material success of the US. Millions have friends and relatives who live, work and study in the US, and millions more would like to join them and live the "American dream" in what's seen as a land of milk and honey. However, this admiration is tempered by widespread political resentment of the US government's longstanding support for brutal military regimes in Latin America, its ongoing political and military interventions in the region, and its deeply hypocritical approach to the so-called "war on drugs". The US is also widely blamed (not without some reason) for the poor economic situation in many Latin American countries, especially where the Washington-based International Monetary Fund and World Bank have insisted on swingeing government spending cuts that have crippled social services. In addition, there are few political crises that are not blamed in some quarters on supposed CIA conspiracies and US "imperialism". These resentments are particularly strong in countries that have borne the brunt of US intervention in recent years, such as Nicaragua, Bolivia and Colombia. Some US citizens go so far as telling casual acquaintances they are Canadian when travelling in Latin America, but in fact these political resentments are rarely directed towards individual travellers and are unlikely to affect you as long as you stay out of heated political discussions and keep a relatively low profile in countries and regions where tension is high. The one glorious exception to this is the indigenous territory of Kuna Yala on Panama's Caribbean coast, where people from the US are referred to respectfully as *Merki* (from American), a prestigious term that dates back to US intervention in the early twentieth century in support of Kuna autonomy.

these terms are not generally considered racist in themselves – it depends on the tone and context. If you're black or of Asian descent but from a gringo country you'll find Latin Americans have some difficulty categorizing you, but generally speaking you'll suffer less discrimination than local members of these ethnic groups can face in Latin America.

While gringo is not in itself a derogatory term, you will find that Latin Americans are prone to making assumptions about foreign travellers, just as Latin Americans are often stereotyped in the media back home as superstitious, shiftless, corrupt and prone to thieving and drug-trafficking. Gringos in Latin America are in turn often stereotyped as being ignorant, clumsy, arrogant, rude, naive, sexual-

Searching for the immigration office in downtown Medellin, I soon realized the map in my guidebook was hopelessly out of date. Aware that walking a few blocks in the wrong direction could land me in a very dangerous neighbourhood, I stopped to ask directions from a respectable-looking man. "Where are you from?" he asked in return, and when I told him I was British, he said, "Well in that case, head two blocks down this street, and turn left at the traffic lights." I thanked him politely for his help, but before I continued on my way I couldn't resist asking him why he'd first enquired about my nationality. "Well," he said, "if you'd said you were from the United States, I'd have told you it was in the opposite direction."

James Read

ly promiscuous, obsessively uptight about time, unable to string two words of Spanish or Portuguese together, and, above all, as inordinately wealthy (see opposite). However, like all stereotypes, these are easily broken by engaging in a little direct human contact. Often, just making an effort to speak the local language, eating the local food, sharing a drink or a joke, revealing a little about your real life and showing a modicum of interest in local culture or respect for local social norms is enough to shatter these clichés and make local people realize you're not some ugly stereotype that's stepped out of the latest Hollywood movie, but an ordinary person much like themselves, albeit from a different country and with different experiences of life.

Making that contact is also pretty easy, as generally speaking Latin Americans are just as fascinated by you as you are by them, and wherever you go you're likely be engaged in conversation and bombarded with questions. "Where are you from?", "Where are you going?", "What do you think of my country?", "How much did it cost to fly here?", "How many children do you have?" (and, if you have none, why not) – the same enquiries will come again and again, but though the constant repetition and the assumptions that underlie these questions can be irritating, they're usually just conversational openers. Particularly in areas that see little tourism, a foreign traveller passing through can be an exciting event for the locals, an opportunity to practise their English and satisfy some of their curiosity about the outside world, something few Latin Americans are able to do by travelling themselves. Some travellers like to carry photos of their friends and family to show curious locals, and coins or postcards of typical scenes back home to give as presents as a good way of making friends and giving a clearer picture of what their life back home is really like.

# Being a wealthy tourist

All over Latin America, the most common assumption you'll confront is that as a gringo you are, by definition, extremely **wealthy**. You'll find people constantly asking you how much your flight cost and what the minimum wage is in your home country, then gasping in amazement as their preconceived view of your inordinate personal wealth is apparently confirmed. What makes this stereotype almost impossible to dispel is the fact that it is, by and large, entirely accurate. However low your economic position may be back home and however tight your budget, compared to the average Latin American earning just a few dollars a day you're very rich. Not only do you come from a wealthy country, you can even afford to take time off work and travel long distances for pleasure, something most locals can only dream about. Small wonder that many Latin Americans can't understand why so many travellers dress in scruffy clothing – surely if you can afford a flashy camera and a long-distance air ticket, you can stretch to a decent set of clothes? You can counter this assumption of endless wealth to a certain extent by explaining how long you had to work to raise the money for the trip, or how prices back home are much higher, but in the end you're unlikely to convince anyone that you're not comparatively rich, because all the evidence points in the other direction.

And why bother, when this comparatively wealthy status, however unusual you find it at first, was probably one of the reasons you chose to go to Latin America in the first place (just as wealthy Japanese or Arabs choose to do their shopping in Europe). After all, unless you're used to being relatively rich back home, it can be very enjoyable suddenly to be able to take a taxi whenever you want rather than waiting for a bus, to eat in restaurants every day, and to take part in all kinds of activities that would be too expensive to contemplate back home. Whilst enjoying the freedom wealth allows, however, you should be aware that your (probably newfound) wealth involves some responsibilities, too. As a person with cash to spend you can drive up local prices just by paying over the odds for a taxi fare or a beer – and many locals will encourage you to do this – as traders may then overcharge future customers, driving inflation up. In the worst cases, goods and services in popular tourist destinations can become so expensive that locals can no longer afford them. Ask locals about prices before buying and try to pay a reasonable price, but conversely don't worry too much about being slightly overcharged: as a relatively rich person in a poor country you can afford to be slightly magnanimous, and getting angry and frustrated over a few cents really isn't worth the energy. In some countries and regions local traders operate an informal two-tier price system whereby foreign tourists are charged more than locals – some buses in Guatemala, for example, or hotels in Nicaragua. This can be quite annoying, but there's usually not much you can do about it, so it's not worth getting upset about – think of it as an unofficial subsidy for the locals who struggle to afford the same service.

For more on tourist prices and **bargaining**, see pp.153–57.

# Food and drink

Getting used to the local food and drink can be one of the trickiest cultural transitions to deal with while travelling, but in comparison to Asia or Africa, Latin American food and drink isn't so very different to what you find at home, and there are only a handful of dishes – such as iguana eggs, guinea pigs or the dried ants popular in eastern Colombia – which you're likely to find totally alien. In cities and towns you'll find that familiar foods like pizza, burgers and fried chicken are widely available, and in areas popular with budget travellers you'll find restaurants and cafés specializing in the kind of food backpackers eat the world over – muesli, banana pancakes and the like. If you're travelling on a tight budget, you're better off sticking to local food, particularly the very good-value set lunch and dinner menus available in most countries, though you may find you eventually tire of regional staples like rice and beans, maize tortillas, or starchy soups. However, you'll be really missing out on one of the great pleasures of travel in Latin America if you don't sample the local specialities in the countries you visit: from Peruvian *ceviche* (a cool, spicy dish of raw fish marinated in lime juice, chilli and onions) and Mexican *chipotle* (a spicy bitter chocolate sauce served with turkey or chicken) to Argentine steaks (the best in the world) and Brazilian *feijoada* (a stew of black beans, beef and sausage), the region is a cornucopia of culinary delights.

The one thing to be wary of is the fondness of people in some countries (above all Mexico and Peru) for particularly **spicy food**

– Latin America is, after all, the original home of the red-hot chilli pepper. Fortunately for those without the fire-eating habit, chilli is usually served in a side dish, either chopped raw or blended into sauces with all kinds of other ingredients. Be cautious in applying this to your food, as it could well be hotter than anything you've tasted back home; the best remedy if your mouth is on fire is bread or something sweet rather than cold water. In addition, always wash your hands after handling chillies, as otherwise touching your eyes or other more sensitive parts of your body can give you a culture shock of a particularly agonizing kind.

The only reason you're likely to have difficulty with food is if you are a **vegetarian**. Latin America is very much a meat-eating society, and most Latin Americans who can afford to do so eat meat with pretty much every meal. All kinds of fruit and vegetables are of course available, but outside tourist areas they rarely make it onto menus as main dishes. Telling a waiter you're a vegetarian is quite likely to produce a blank stare, while insisting you don't eat meat will probably be interpreted as meaning you don't eat beef, but pork or chicken is okay. If you're a strict vegetarian, be warned that ostensibly vegetarian dishes such as beans are often cooked in pork fat for extra flavour. With a little persistence and determination, however, it is possible to be a vegetarian in Latin America. Most large towns and cities have at least one vegetarian or health-food restaurant (often run by Hare Krishnas), and tourist restaurants usually have several vegetarian options. If you stick to local places, however, you may well find yourself consuming a lot of eggs. Shopping for fruit and vegetables in the local market – where a huge range of both is almost always available – and cooking or preparing it yourself is one way to supplement the rather meagre fare available to vegetarians on the road.

# Taking photos

For many people, taking photographs or video footage is one of the great joys of travel and one of the best ways of preserving memories, and the sheer visual magnificence of so much of Latin America makes it an excellent place for photographers, whether you're fully kitted out with state-of-the-art professional equipment or snapping away with a cheap point-and-shoot. However, not all Latin Americans are happy to have their photo taken by tourists, and there are certain situations where you should be cautious about who or what you photograph. The following guidelines should help you get the picture you want without causing offence or getting into trouble.

- Always ask permission before taking pictures of people, as failure to do so is at best rude and at worst deeply offensive. Remember that you're not in a theme park, and think how you would feel if strange foreigners began taking your picture without so much as a by-your-leave. Be particularly cautious in isolated indigenous communities, where taking people's picture is sometimes considered akin to theft.
- Sometimes you may find people ask you to pay them a small fee in return for allowing you to take their photo. Some travellers view such demands with outrage, but in fact they represent a perfectly reasonable exchange – you get the picture, the usually poor subject earns a little money which may make him or her more receptive to tourists in the future, and locals are encouraged to maintain the colourful and unique costumes and traditions which are probably the main reason you wanted to photograph them anyway.
- Locals will often ask you for copies of the pictures you take of them or their families, as many can't afford cameras or development costs themselves. Though the quality of prints is usually not as good as back home, getting your film developed locally and giving away a few copies to the people you've photographed makes the whole process a much more equal exchange, and the delight a few pictures can bring to people who have perhaps never seen a photo of themselves can be very satisfying. However, don't promise to send people photos if you're not going to follow through, as this will make them less receptive to future photo requests.
- Always ask before taking pictures in churches and during religious processions and fiestas, as it may be considered disrespectful. Flash photography is often banned in churches as it can damage ageing oil paintings and other decorations.
- Don't take pictures of border posts or any kind of military installation, as this can result in you having your film or camera confiscated or even in your being arrested by paranoid military personnel. Always ask permission before taking photographs of police or soldiers or, better still, avoid doing so altogether.

# Responsible tourism

Culture shock works both ways, and with the number of tourists visiting Latin America increasing all the time, it's important not to underestimate the impact the tourism industry has on local cultures, particularly in popular destinations. One of the most alarming aspects of reverse culture shock is the tendency for big businesses to take over local enterprises in resort areas, preventing the economic dividends of tourism from reaching local communities. As a first-time traveller you'll probably be on a fairly tight budget and so unlikely to be patronizing international hotel chains, but you may well be tempted to stop off at familiar multinational takeaway food outlets. Where possible, it's much better (as well as cheaper, more enjoyable and more authentic) to support local shops, restaurants and hotels instead. That way, the money you spend stays within the community and local residents retain control over their own neighbourhood, ensuring that the place keeps its original character – which is, after all, what you travelled so far to experience. In this way, budget travellers can have a beneficial effect on the countries they visit: though they spend less money than wealthier tourists on short, all-inclusive tours, most of the money they do spend tends to go to small local businesses, and so has a far more positive impact on local economies than the major tourism developments beloved of bankers and government officials.

It's also important to **support local initiatives** when it comes to visiting traditional indigenous communities, so that the people you go to see – be it Quechua-speaking llama-herders in the Andes or semi-nomadic tribes in the Amazon – see some economic benefit from your curiosity. All too many tour companies sell trips to visit isolated indigenous groups without giving travellers any chance to communicate with them, turning communities into little more than human zoos and exotic photo opportunities where traditional culture is parodied rather than respected. Where possible, try to organize a tour with a tour guide or agency from within the community you wish to visit, or at least endeavour to actually meet and interact with the people you've travelled so far to see. Tourism can have a dramatic negative impact on remote communities, in some cases plunging them suddenly into an unfamiliar market economy and materialist society. However, if conducted in a sensitive manner, tourism can have a positive effect, reviving local economies and keeping local traditions alive. A growing number of community-based guides and tour operators are springing up all over Latin America, offering a far more authentic and positive experience of traditional societies than you'll get with many more mainstream tour agencies. If you can't find any useful leads in guidebooks or the websites listed on pp.330–31, check out the *Good Alternative Tourism Guide*, published by Earthscan for the campaigning organization Tourism Concern, which lists a selection of successful local tourism initiatives in Latin America and the rest of the world. Tourism Concern also have a website at ⓦ www.tourismconcern.org.uk.

As a **responsible tourist**, you should also try to reduce your impact on the environment, particularly in national parks and other protected wilderness areas, where you otherwise risk damaging the pristine natural beauty you've travelled so far to see. In practice, this can mean everything from being careful about rubbish disposal to following strict national park rules. Even if the locals appear unconcerned about litter, it doesn't mean you should be. In particular, don't dump non-biodegradable stuff like plastic, cigarette ends and dead batteries in rural areas: if you can manage to carry it in with you, you can certainly take it out again. Don't buy souvenirs made from endangered species such as black coral, and avoid eating endangered species such as turtle, which often make it onto tourist menus. When visiting protected natural areas, try and follow the mantra: "leave nothing but footprints and take nothing but memories (and photographs)".

In recent years Latin America has seen an explosion in **eco-tourism**, which in theory involves tourists visiting fragile natural environments such as rainforests and coral reefs whilst minimizing the negative impact their visit has on them and their inhabitants. In the best cases, ecotourism can even have a positive impact, encouraging environmental protection by allowing local communities to make a living through conserving rather than exploiting natural resources. In many cases, however, tour agencies claim to practice ecotourism to attract clients but in fact do little or nothing to reduce the negative impact of their tours, a process known as "greenwashing". Where possible, you should treat such claims with caution. Advice on getting involved in **nature conservation** work in Latin America is given in Chapter 1, and you'll find a list of relevant organizations in Basics on pp.324–26. You'll also find plenty of information and advice on ecotourism on the websites ⓦ www.planeta.com and ⓦ www.ecotour.org.

# Getting around

Travelling in Latin America can be wonderful and frustrating, often at the same time. The extremes of terrain, poor infrastructure and the enormous distances involved mean that simply getting people from one place to the other is an enormous challenge, but it's one that Latin American transport operators overcome every day, moving millions of passengers around using the wide range of transport including planes, trains, passenger ships, river boats, motorized dugout canoes, tourist buses, local buses, open-top lorries, pick-up trucks and shared taxis.

**Road transport** is the main way of getting around throughout the region, though the quality of this varies enormously. In relatively rich and developed countries such as Argentina and Venezuela, most main roads are well paved and buses are often modern and reliable. In poorer countries, however – and particularly in sparsely populated regions with swampy or mountainous terrain – most roads are unpaved dirt highways in very poor condition which are only kept open by constant labour against floods and landslides, and by the determination, skill and sheer bloody-mindedness of bus and lorry drivers.

Throughout the vast, rainforest-covered basins of the Amazon and Orinoco, meanwhile, roads are few and far between and the mighty river systems form the main highways, served by a variety of **boats** ranging from large ships to canoes hewn from single tree trunks. In many coastal regions, too, ferries and fast launches are the main means of hopping along the shore or reaching nearby islands. Throughout the region local **flights**, whether in airliners shuttling between major cities or light aircraft skimming over the treetops, offer a quick and easy way of getting around, saving many hours or even days of hard overland travel at a relatively reasonable price.

All this exciting variety must be set against discomfort, poor safety conditions and often appalling driving, delays and sometimes unbelievable **unreliability**, all of which are enduring characteristics of travel in Latin America. While back home a five-hour bus ride in a comfortable seat may seem interminable, and a fifteen-minute delay a serious inconvenience, if you want to travel in Latin America for any length of time you'll find yourself making a lot of twelve-hour bus journeys in cramped seats and confronting delays of many hours, often for no apparent reason. If you look on the travel itself as part of the adventure, you'll have a better chance of keeping things in perspective. The twelve-hour bus journey that turns into a three-day marathon may be a gruelling experience at the time, but when you get home you'll probably look back on it as one of the most memorable adventures of your trip. On most journeys, too, the spectacular scenery you'll pass through and the colourful antics of your fellow passengers are usually compensation for the arduousness of the trip.

# Planes

Almost all countries in Latin America have an internal air network of some sort, and **flying** is by far the fastest way to get around. It's also by far the most expensive, and only a very small proportion of Latin Americans can afford to travel this way. However, the prices of flights are generally a lot cheaper than in Europe or North America, and flying is an excellent way of avoiding exhausting overland journeys and saving time if you're trying to fit a lot into a relatively short trip – a one-hour flight between Lima and Cuzco in Peru, for example, can cost as little as $60, not much when you consider that the alternative is an exhausting bus journey lasting at least thirty hours. And although you'll miss out on many of the scenic views at ground level, many flights – especially those passing over the high peaks of the Andes or across the endless green carpet of the Amazon rainforest – offer breathtaking bird's-eye views.

You can often book **internal flights** from home when you book your outward flight (see p.132): though this will cost more than booking in Latin America itself, it's worth doing if

## Hitching a ride in a Cessna

In Central America it can be quite cheap to hire a small plane and its pilot, if there are four or five of you – although it's best to ask around for recommendations and to press for credentials, as light aircraft accidents are distressingly common. But for those who like to fly, it can be literally awesome, flying above volcanoes (perfect views of the craters and the lagoons) and over carpets of low rainforest, mangroves and the lazy rivers and man-made canals that dot much of the east coast in the isthmus. I used to hitch rides with a pilot friend of mine in his Cessna, and we'd fly quite low, so that we could see fishermen out for their morning catch, or even herons lazily launching themselves from the riverside, and arrive at small hamlets with an airstrip and little else. In countries like Costa Rica and Nicaragua, flying is the fastest way by a long chalk to get to the Caribbean coast, and small planes can be a revelation after travelling in commercial jets. You see much more of the wildlife and landscape, and it's pleasant, rather than scary, to feel the various updrafts and air currents.

Jean McNeil

Tourism is still very much in its infancy throughout Nicaragua, so getting around can require a lot of patience and a good sense of humour, as my friend and I discovered when we flew from Managua to the ramshackle Caribbean town of Bluefields, named after seventeenth-century pirate Abraham Blauwveld.

The Bluefields Express was the name of a passenger ferry that used to make its way from the town of Rama (96km away) until it was found in a forest after Hurricane Joan in 1988. You can still travel this journey by boat, or you can fly on one of the most un-aerodynamic aeroplanes you are ever likely to see, also called the Bluefields Express.

My friend's aversion to small planes became apparent as soon as we saw the "flying box". He tried to pluck up some Dutch courage with the aid of Nicaragua's lifeblood Flor de Cana rum. Meanwhile, the rum seller had donned his DJ hat and was playing an old Sandinista favourite, aptly titled "Come Take a Ride on The Bluefields Express". The locals literally danced onto the aircraft. I sensed my friend was not in a dancing mood, so I handed him a copy of the local paper to help keep his mind off the flight ahead. It might have worked, had the leading article not been about a man who had taken this same flight one week previously and covered himself in gasoline. Threatening to set himself alight, he demanded to be taken to Costa Rica and then proclaimed to be a "saviour, sent by the Lord". Luckily all passengers survived and the man was arrested, but it did take a while for my friend to see the humour behind the irony.

Rafe Stone

you're short on time and want to travel on popular routes, which may be booked up well in advance. Several airlines offer internal **airpasses** at good rates to tourists, which can be worthwhile if you're intending to cover a huge amount of ground in as short a time as possible (for more on airpasses, see p.132).

As well as domestic commercial carriers, in some countries the airforce also operates passenger services as a means of subsidizing the maintenance of their aircraft and connecting isolated regions. These military flights are usually slightly cheaper than commercial flights. In some remote regions like the Amazon you can also travel in small light aircraft that carry only five to twelve passengers. Though expensive, this is an exciting way to travel and can save days of arduous overland travel; in some cases it's also the only way to reach the most remote (and therefore most pristine) national parks and wilderness regions.

When using Latin American airlines, the following tips should make your trip easier:

● Some of the airlines flying internal routes are small operators with minimal back-up both on and off the ground, so don't expect them to be as efficient or punctual as airlines back home.

- Not all Latin American airlines have the same safety standards as at home, and some have poor records: if in doubt, check with your embassy before you book, or visit Ⓦwww.airsafe.com, which lists the safety records of many Latin American airlines.
- It's often easier to book air tickets through a reliable local travel agent for a small fee.
- Having booked a seat, you often need to reconfirm with the airline before travel. Check before you book, and make a careful note of the number you'll need to ring to reconfirm.
- Flights are often cancelled or delayed at short notice due to weather conditions or due to technical problems or lack of aircraft. Build as much flexibility into your itinerary as you can, and, if possible, avoid relying on an internal flight to get you back to the capital on the day your international flight home departs.
- Overbooking – where more tickets are sold than there are seats on the plane – is also often a problem, so make sure you reconfirm, and check in as early as possible as boarding passes are usually issued on a first-come-first-served-basis.
- Follow the advice on hand baggage on p.198 – just because a flight is internal doesn't mean you can't get delayed or they won't lose your baggage.
- In most countries you have to pay a domestic airport tax before flying. This is often payable only in cash, so make sure you have enough with you before heading to the airport.

## Long-distance buses

Most Latin Americans rely on **long-distance buses** when it comes to making extended journeys, and travelling this way is one of the most enjoyable (and also sometimes the most exasperating and exhausting) experiences the region has to offer – all of human life is jammed together, often with a few chickens or pigs thrown in for good measure, travelling at a pace slow enough to really appreciate that landscape you're passing through. The buses are often a sight in themselves, painted with bright slogans and designs and with lavish handmade consoles around the driver complete with statues of Christ or the Virgin Mary that light up when the brakes are applied. Bus travel is also extremely good value – for example, travelling from one end of Peru to the other, a distance of about two thousand kilometres, will cost you less than $30. In some countries there's an annoying custom of charging foreign tourists slightly more for bus travel, although this is only a small amount and not worth getting angry about – just think of it as a subsidy for poor locals, for whom that $4 bus fare is a major expense.

The quality of buses varies enormously both within and between countries. The best ones – variously described as *Pullman, primera clase* or *de lujo* – are modern vehicles with air-conditioning or heating, comfortable reclining seats, plenty of leg-room, chemical toilets, television and video, and even waitresses serving drinks to passengers. These are more common on major inter-city routes and in wealthier, more developed countries. They tend to be fairly punctual, particularly in more developed countries like Chile or Argentina, and also make fewer stops, meaning that they're faster. Obviously, these types of buses cost a bit more than slower and less comfortable vehicles.

At the other extreme are ageing buses with dodgy engines, cracked windscreens, ripped seats and balding tyres; many are old school buses from the US, or even flat-bed lorries fitted with seats. When there are a number of different bus companies operating the same route, it's worth trying to get a look at the bus before buying a ticket and choosing the one that looks in best condition. These buses tend to stop frequently en route to pick up passengers, who are crammed into every available space, both on extra benches or folding seats which fill the aisles or standing (or even hanging) out of the door or perched on the roof – this latter option should be avoided if at all possible; if you do sit on the roof, keep a careful lookout for overhanging branches. A popular joke asks: "How many passengers fit in a Peruvian [or Bolivian, etc] bus?", with the inevitable answer, *unito mas* – "just one more!"

Seats at the back are always the bumpiest, while those at the front afford the best view of the driver's technique and an earful of his favourite music. Frustratingly, while you will want to enjoy the views, the Latin American sitting beside you will likely want to draw the curtains to block out the sun and the (to him or her) mundane scenery and concentrate on the trashy B-movie on the video at the front of the bus. Latin American buses are generally designed for smaller physiques – many are made in Japan but refitted with smaller seats to allow for extra passengers – so don't underestimate the stamina required for long journeys, particularly if you're relatively large.

Any journey over four hours or so is likely to involve a **meal stop** at a roadside restaurant. You'll rarely be told how long this will last, so watch what the driver and other passengers order and keep an eye on the bus lest it leaves without you. Unless you're on a luxury bus with a chemical toilet, these meal stops are usually the only opportunity you'll get to relieve yourself, so think carefully before drinking that extra beer or cup of coffee. Anywhere the bus stops it's likely to be boarded by people selling drinks, snacks, sweets, complete meals and whatever is the local speciality or produce of the region you're passing through, as well as hawkers of miracle cures, poets, musicians, beggars and even magicians hoping to entertain the passengers in return for a few cents – this can often be an enjoyable part of the whole experience. It's worth carrying some food and drink with you on long journeys, however, as you may not like or trust what's on offer at the roadside and never know when a breakdown or other delay might leave you stranded and hungry. It's also worth keeping some warm clothing or even a sleeping bag or blanket with you on the bus, even if it's extremely hot when you set off – nightfall or a climb in altitude can send temperatures plunging, and in luxury buses powerful air-conditioning can leave you shivering even as the temperature climbs above 30°C outside.

Generally speaking, journeys are measured in time rather than geographical distance. On well-paved roads between major cities and in more developed countries, buses make good time, but elsewhere roads are often simply rough tracks or mud and rock, and mountainous terrain often means that what looks like a short distance on your map actually takes far longer to cover than a much greater distance on a good road through flat country. **Punctuality** varies greatly between different countries – Chilean buses almost always leave on time, for example, whereas buses in rural Peru often leave hours after the man who sells you the ticket tells you they will. Often buses will leave only after hours of futile driving around town hooting loudly to conjure up nonexistent passengers. Sometimes it can appear that buses leave on time only if you arrive five minutes after the official departure time written on your ticket, and if they're full of passengers they may even leave early.

Once underway, further delays can be caused by poor **road conditions**, landslides, police or customs searches, or simply by the driver's desire to spend an hour with his girlfriend in a town en route. All this can be very frustrating, of course, but if you can it's best to take delays with the calm, fatalistic approach adopted by many Latin Americans – if you always expect journeys to take longer than expected, it's a pleasant surprise when you arrive as scheduled; if you really want to travel in a country where the buses always run on time, you're better off going somewhere like Switzerland.

On long inter-city routes you'll often have the option of **travelling overnight**. Many travellers favour this as a way of saving money on accommodation and making extra time for sightseeing at their next destination. Latin Americans often prefer it too, as it means they can travel to the city, spend a day conducting their business, then travel home the next night without splashing out on a hotel. However, travelling by night does mean that you'll miss out on the scenery, and unless you're in a luxury sleeper bus with fully reclining seats, it can be difficult to sleep in cramped conditions and on bumpy roads, leaving you tired and washed-out when you arrive. In addition, you're more vulnerable to theft, whether by bandits stopping the bus or sneak thieves filching your bag while you sleep, and drivers are far more prone to potentially fatal accidents when travelling by night.

△ Copper Canyon Train, Mexico

On more luxurious intercity buses, your **luggage** will usually be put in a locked compartment under the bus, and you'll be given a ticket with which to claim it at the end of the journey; the compensation this ticket entitles you to if your bag goes missing is paltry, but the system is usually pretty safe. On more basic buses in poorer countries or more remote regions, your bag will often be slung on the roof. If you like, you can climb up and padlock it to the roof rack yourself; otherwise, it's worth keeping an eye out of the windows when the bus stops to make sure no one takes it accidentally or on purpose. It's not a bad idea to cover your backpack with a sack (available in any market) to protect it from dust, rain, oil and prying fingers, and to disguise it from potential thieves, though you should mark the sack to avoid it being mistaken for someone else's potatoes. If you're travelling light, you can keep your luggage with you on your seat, and it's worth keeping valuable or fragile items with you in your hand luggage in any case. Be sure to keep it within sight, ideally with a strap looped around your leg, as otherwise it may disappear while you sleep, or you may unpack later to find someone has removed your camera and carefully closed the bag again afterwards. For more on rucksack security, see p.186.

Most larger towns and cities have one or more **bus terminals** for long-distance buses (*Terminal de Buses* or *Terminal Terrestre* in Spanish, *Rodoviária* in Brazil), though in some places buses depart from various offices scattered around town. These are often on the outskirts of town, and worth taking a taxi to if you have heavy luggage; taxi drivers are also good people to ask if you're confused as to where you need to go to catch a bus to a particular destination. Bus terminals tend to have an information desk of some kind, as well as left-luggage offices, restaurants, and cheap (though usually insalubrious) accommodation close by. You'll often have to pay a small terminal tax on departure.

Generally speaking it's a good idea to **book a seat** in advance if you can, though on busy routes served by frequent buses this isn't always necessary – just turn up and buy a ticket for the next departure. On most bus trips you'll be allocated a numbered seat when you buy your ticket, so if you can it's worth having a look at the bus to choose a seat with a good view or more leg room. If you're travelling from a small town between major destinations or in a remote region where traffic is scarce, your best bet is often to flag down anything passing in the right direction, even though this may involve standing up for some time until a seat becomes available. During **public holidays and fiestas** people travel in great numbers, and bus tickets can be hard to come by even though prices are often higher.

In countries and regions where the tourist infrastructure is more developed, private companies operate special **tourist bus** services exclusively for foreign visitors. On these buses there's usually more space for luggage, and the vehicles are usually in better condition, but in other respects they are not much different from regular public buses. However, they do offer a direct, hassle-free and usually faster service between main tourist destinations. The downside is they're more expensive and they deprive you of the colourful (if sometimes infuriating) experience of sharing your journey with ordinary Latin Americans.

## Lorries

In remote areas, and particularly in poorer countries, passengers often travel in heavy goods **lorries** rather than buses. Sometimes these are specially converted for passengers and fitted with basic seats, but usually you'll simply be standing in the back or sitting on top of the cargo or on a wooden plank placed across the top. On a good day, travelling in the back of an open-top truck with the wind in your face and 360-degree views is a fantastic experience – for the first hour at least. After that the dust, hard wooden seats (when there are any seats at all), exposure to the elements and extremely bumpy ride start to take their toll. Lorries are also slower and generally more dangerous than buses, and stop more frequently. Still, travelling by lorry is a quintessential Latin American experience that's worth trying at least once. For shorter journeys in remote areas, smaller pick-up trucks, known as *camionetas* in Spanish, also carry passengers; these share the same drawbacks and pleasures as lorries, but are slightly faster and less bumpy.

## Is it safe?

There is no escaping the fact that road travel in Latin America is often a hair-raising experience. Buses and other vehicles often travel far too fast for the conditions – overtaking on blind corners is a

## Best bus rides

**The World's Most Dangerous Road** Descending more than 3500m over a distance of just 64km, the perilous highway linking La Paz with Coroico in Bolivia (dubbed the "World's Most Dangerous Road" by the Inter-American Bank due to the number of vehicles which plunge over the edge) is amongst the most spectacular roads in the world, plunging from the frozen high Andes down through dense cloudforest into the lush subtropical valleys of the Yungas.

**Cusco to Puerto Maldonado** Linking Cusco, the ancient mountain capital of the Incas, with the remote jungle town of Puerto Maldonado, this route crosses stunning high Andean passes before plunging down into the dense rainforests of the Upper Amazon. In good weather the journey takes about two days, but rain can turn it into a week-long odyssey.

**The Chilean Carretera Austral** Stretching over 1000km south from Puerto Montt to the remote settlement of Yungay, the Carretera Austral carves its way through great tracts of untouched wilderness, taking in soaring snow-capped mountains, ancient glaciers, narrow fjords, emerald rivers and swathes of temperate rainforest.

regular occurrence – and drivers are often poorly trained and work long hours without sufficient sleep. Road conditions can be appalling, and vehicles poorly maintained, so not surprisingly, accidents do happen – you only need to look out for the white crosses beside the road that mark where the victims of previous accidents have died to realize that bus travel involves a greater degree of danger in Latin America than it does at home. Statistically, however, the risk remains small, and you should remember that even after buying a ticket you can still choose not to climb on board the bus – if it looks too dangerous or the driver appears drunk, it's best to follow your instinct and stay put or travel in a different vehicle.

# Trains

Travelling by **train** is often the safest and most memorable way of getting around Latin America, and usually considerably more comfortable than travel by bus. Unfortunately, however, railway travel is very much in decline across Latin America, and many networks have been abandoned, partly as a result of privatization and the withdrawal of government subsidies, partly because the industries like mining that once sustained them have fallen on hard times, but mostly because bus travel along the ever-increasing road network is generally cheaper and faster. Only rarely does rail offer a serious alternative for moving from one destination to another, but fortunately governments and tourist boards are waking up to the fact that many foreign visitors prefer to travel by train, and in many countries the most spectacular stretches of line have been preserved as tourist attractions even though most local cargo and passenger traffic now goes by road.

Though they vary between countries and lines, **ticketing systems** usually involve two or more classes: the most luxurious and expensive are tourist-only carriages featuring comfortable seats,

## Top train rides

**Cusco to Machu Picchu** This train is the only way to reach the fabled Lost City of the Incas without walking the Inca Trail and is a spectacular journey in its own right, climbing up switchbacks from the city of Cusco and passing high Andean peaks that flank the Sacred Valley before plunging down the deep, narrow ravine of the rushing Río Urubamba to the foot of the ruins at Aguas Calientes.

**Uyuni to Calama** Running from the railway junction of Uyuni in Bolivia, this route runs across the dramatic, bleak lunar landscape of the high Altiplano, passing the southern edge of the Salar de Uyuni, the world's largest salt lake and between snow-capped volcanic peaks before crossing the border and descending to the Chilean town of Calama.

**Panamá Railroad** The Panamá or Trans-Isthmian railroad was the first railway to cross the American continent between the Atlantic and Pacific oceans when it was completed in 1855 at great financial and human cost. It now runs through pristine rainforests alongside the Panama Canal and has recently reopened as a tourist attraction, making it one of the best ways to experience that most impressive of waterways.

**Copper Canyon Railway** Starting on the Mexican Pacific coast at Los Mochis, this line clings to the wall of the dramatic 2000-metre-deep canyon of the Río Urique, known as the Copper Canyon, as it climbs up to cross the continental divide amongst the peaks of the Sierra Madre before reaching the city of Chihuahua.

**The Old Patagonia Express** A narrow-gauge steam train made famous by Paul Theroux's (rather disparaging) book of the same name, the Old Patagonia Express is a classic South American train journey, lurching across the arid steppe of northern Patagonia for a 1650-kilometre stretch between Esquel and El Maitén.

heating or air-conditioning, restaurant cars, waiter service and additional security; at the other extreme are second-class carriages with hard seats and few facilities which are usually packed to the seams with local passengers sitting, standing and hanging off the sides or on the roof. Buying tickets for the former is usually easy and can also be done through tour agencies as well, while getting tickets for the latter can involve arriving at the station before the ticket office opens and lengthy queuing to get a seat, especially at small intermediary stations. Security issues on trains are fairly similar to those on long-distance buses, except that you'll usually have your **luggage** in the compartment with you, in which case it's worth locking your backpack to the luggage rack and keeping small bags away from windows at stations.

# Boats

Latin America offers a range of spectacular **boat journeys**, some of which are amongst the highlights of a visit to the region. Boat travel is also sometimes a cheaper alternative to flying, and in some regions – particularly amongst the many offshore archipelagos along the Pacific and Atlantic coasts and throughout the Amazon Basin – it's often the only other way of getting around. There's a huge range of memorable boat journeys you can make in vessels ranging from the modest motorized dug-out canoes which ply the Amazon backwaters to luxury tourist yachts and ships which cruise around the Galápagos Islands and the glaciers of Patagonia. Whatever kind of boat trip you take, however, bear the following points in mind:

- Be sure to take a sun hat, sunscreen and sunglasses, as reflected light off the water increases the effect of the sun while cool breezes can disguise its intensity.
- It gets cold at sea, so keep warm clothing close at hand. Waterproof clothing is also a good idea on sea, lake and river trips, as even if it's not raining, you can easily get soaked by spray.
- It's a good idea to take seasickness pills with you for sea voyages, even if you've never suffered before.
- Even if you're a strong swimmer, it is best to make sure life jackets are available before you depart. As with other forms of transport, boats are often overloaded, and accidents do happen.

Providing life jackets is a legal requirement for public carriers in most countries, but one that is sometimes ignored.

- Put cameras and other valuables in plastic bags or other waterproof containers to protect them.

- On longer trips, take your own food and water, as the quality of what's available on board can be poor. Boats sometimes break down or get delayed by bad weather or other factors, so your journey may take longer than expected.

- On long river trips in the Amazon, you should take along your own hammock for sleeping in, ideally fitted with a mosquito net – both are available in most river ports. Most boat captains will let you sleep on board for a day or two while waiting for departure – a good way to save money on hotels.

## Best boat trips

**The River Amazon** Whether in a cabin of a luxury tourist cruiser or slung in a hammock on a slow cargo boat, taking a boat trip along the world's mightiest river is a quintessential South American experience – even if at times you can't see either bank.

**Amazon canoe trips** For a closer look at Amazonian wildlife, you can't beat a trip in a motorized dug-out canoe along one of the minor tributaries in the Upper Amazon – you can do this either by travelling in a canoe used for local transport, as part of an organized rainforest tour, or by hiring a boat yourself (though the high fuel consumption of outboard motors means this is expensive unless you're sharing the cost with several other travellers). The trip down the Alto Madre de Dios and up the Río Manu into the pristine Manu National Park in southern Peru is one of the most spectacular of these trips.

**Panamá Canal** Taking a half- or one-day cruise along the Panamá Canal is the best way of appreciating the magnitude and surprisingly rugged beauty of one of the greatest engineering feats of all time. With a little luck you might even get taken on as a line handler on a yacht and be paid for the privilege of sailing down the canal.

**Galápagos cruise** A week-long cruise exploring the unique and astonishing wildlife of the Galápagos Islands, 900km off the coast of Ecuador, is one of the world's finest boat trips, though the cost may stretch your budget to breaking point.

**San Rafael Glacier** The 200-kilometre boat trip from the port of Chacabuco through the spectacular fjords and islands of southern Chile and along the seemingly unnavigable Río Tempranos into the iceberg-choked Laguna San Rafael, at the foot of the giant glacier of the same name, is one of South America's most magical boat journeys.

- For Amazon river trips you may have to wait around a day or two (or longer in remote towns) for a departure. The naval port authority office can usually tell you which boat is likely to leave first.

# City transport

Getting around the teeming cities of Latin America can be an intimidating experience. Most have grown incredibly quickly in recent decades, and under funded and overloaded public transport systems struggle to cope with the near-impossible task of moving millions of people around every day. The capitals of more developed countries like Buenos Aires or Mexico City boast modern subway systems, but in most Latin American cities urban transport is dominated by a seemingly chaotic array of buses and minibuses.

However, despite the sense of bewilderment which you'll probably initially feel, after a few days you'll most likely be able to work out which routes will take you where you need to go. Indeed the process of finding your way around by public transport can be a great way of exploring a new city, even if it means getting on the wrong bus a few times. If all this seems too daunting, or you're short on time or concerned about security, you'll be better off relying on taxis. These are generally plentiful and inexpensive, particularly if you are sharing the fare with one or more other travellers.

## Local buses

Most Latin American cities are served by a mixture of large and small **buses** – often former US school buses or ageing colossuses which lumber around belching diesel fumes as they ferry people in and out of town from outlying suburbs. These are supplemented by an ever-increasing number of minibuses and vans known as **combis**, **micros** or **colectivos**, which race around shorter fixed routes, picking up passengers at every street corner.

Fares on all these vehicles are extremely low, but finding out which one will take you where you want to go can be very difficult – official bus stops are rare, and even then they're unlikely to display details of which buses stop there; bus timetables or maps of local services are even harder to come by, if they exist at all. Details of transport to popular tourist destinations, however, should be fairly easy to come by – ask at the local tourist office or in your hotel, or check your guidebook. Many buses have their main destinations written on the windscreen, while their conductors or fare collectors (often children) hang out of the open door at every stop shouting their destinations at the top of their voices. Drivers, conductors and other passengers are generally helpful, though rush-hour commuters around the world aren't known for their patience and Latin America is no exception. The following tips should help you survive the chaos:

- Before you set off, find out the fare system and how to pay.
- Carry plenty of small-denomination coins or notes, as getting change can be a nightmare.
- Give yourself as much time as you can and keep calm and you'll soon be nipping around town like a local. Don't worry too much about getting lost, as this is often part of learning to find your way around.
- Be wary of pickpockets and thieves who use razors or sharp knives to cut luggage straps and bags. Keep your valuables hidden away.
- Most buses and minibuses don't have room for any luggage: if you occupy space that could be filled by another passenger you'll be expected to pay double. If you're travelling with large bags you're better off taking a taxi for security reasons anyway.

## Taxis

**Taxis** are plentiful and relatively inexpensive throughout Latin America – prices vary between cities and countries, but generally speaking a taxi ride in a city centre never costs more than a few dollars, offering a fast, convenient and relatively safe way of getting around, particularly if you're sharing the cost with one or more other passenger. In wealthier countries and larger cities taxis are licensed and marked as such, and have radio controllers, but in many places anyone with a car can become a taxi driver simply by putting a sign in the windscreen of their private car – often, in fact, the two types of cab operate alongside each other. These informal taxis tend to be cheaper but less reliable. Many Latin Americans from all walks of life moonlight as taxi drivers in their private cars to supplement their meagre incomes, which can make for far more interesting conversation than you usually get from taxi drivers at home. The Peruvian capital Lima, in particular, lays claim to having the best-educated taxi drivers in the world, and it's not unusual to find a doctor or university professor behind the wheel of your cab.

If you're travelling with heavy luggage, particularly when you've first arrived – and above all at night – it's a good idea to take a taxi straight to your hotel and dump your bags rather than risking public transport – think of the fare as an insurance policy. It's not unknown for taxis to be used by criminals as a means of robbing unwary passengers, but you can reduce the risk of this by telephoning for a cab from a reputable company. If your luggage is in the boot, it's best not to get out of the car until the driver does, as he or she may be tempted to drive away with your bags. In some cities taxis are equipped with meters, but otherwise **fares** are based on distance or a zone system, though they're generally negotiable. There's a strong tendency to overcharge foreign tourists, so it's best to agree the fare before you set off. You can get an idea of how much it should cost by asking other travellers or at your hotel. Fares tend to increase late at night and during public holidays, and taxis to or from international airports (see pp.202–3) usually charge fixed and relatively high fares. In some cities, special **tourist taxis** congregate outside upmarket hotels and major tourist attractions; these tend to charge far more than ordinary taxis.

If you want to see a lot of sights in a short time, it can be a good idea to hire a taxi for a few hours or a day (or even longer; see below) to take you around town – you can usually negotiate a reasonable rate, especially where business is slow, and with luck you may even find that your driver acts as a good impromptu tour guide.

In some countries taxis are treated almost as a form of public transport: fares are charged per person, and you may be asked to share your cab with a stranger, though you can always refuse this if it makes you uncomfortable. In some places you'll also find **collective taxis** (*colectivos*), which run along fixed routes picking up and dropping off passengers rather like a bus.

## Motorbike taxis

In some cities and towns – especially in towns in the Amazon with poor or no road connections to the outside world – motorbikes operate as taxis, offering an exciting but risky way of getting around. These are always cheaper than cars and often faster, and are a good option if you're travelling alone. Obviously they can't carry much luggage, though that rarely stops them trying – if you have a backpack you may have to carry it on your back while riding pillion, which is uncomfortable and precarious. Always negotiate the fare before you get on, as with conventional taxis, and always use a helmet if one is available.

## Vehicle rental

**Renting a car** is relatively expensive in Latin America but does offer the freedom to visit areas which are otherwise difficult or impossible to reach by public transport. **Costs** vary between countries and regions, but generally speaking you'll be looking at around $30–50 per day for a small car; much more for a large car or four-wheel drive (4WD). Most capitals have branches of international rental companies such as Hertz, Budget and Avis, which means you can book your vehicle in advance from home, but these places are usually more expensive than local companies. As with pretty much everything in Latin America, prices are flexible, so shop around for a good deal and be prepared to negotiate. Obviously sharing the cost and the driving with one or more other travellers makes hiring a car cheaper and more attractive. To hire a car you'll need to be over 25 and to have an international driving licence. You'll also need a credit card or large quantity of cash as a deposit. Many companies require you to take out additional vehicle insurance as well as third party, so make sure you read the small print and know exactly what is covered and what you may be liable for in case of an accident.

**Buying a car** is only really a worthwhile option if you're staying in one country for a long time, ideally as a resident rather than on a tourist visa, and even then it involves considerable hassle, especially when you come to sell it at the end of your stay. It's possible to **drive from the US** into Mexico (beyond the immediate border area) and on into Central America, but this involves considerable expense and bureaucratic hassle; shipping a car to Latin America entails even more trouble and expense, and really isn't worth it unless you absolutely must have your own vehicle.

If you do want to travel by car, consider hiring a local taxi driver to take you around for a daily rate rather than hiring and driving yourself. This doesn't usually cost much more than hiring a car, even though you'll have to pay for the driver's meals and accommodation costs on longer trips, and it means you can sit back and enjoy the scenery rather than concentrate on driving and worry about insurance and additional costs if anything goes wrong. A local driver will probably know the way (or be better at asking if he or she doesn't), and will often have good suggestions about side trips; with any luck, the driver will also offer a useful insight into the local area and people. If you do decide to drive yourself, the following tips should help:

- Make sure you know the legal speed limits and other requirements, and be aware that many local drivers regularly ignore road signs and traffic regulations, and may not even have driving licences, never mind insurance.
- Find out the local rules of the road. Your guidebook should have some information about these, although be aware that Latin American drivers often show scant regard for official rules – watch how people drive before attempting it yourself.
- Inspect the rental vehicle carefully before you accept it and make a note, signed by the owner, of any scratches or dents, as otherwise you may get charged for these when you return it.
- Check things you would take for granted on a rental vehicle at home: the lights, horn, windscreen wipers, door locks, petrol cap, seatbelts, and so on.
- Make sure you know how to open the bonnet (hood) and check the spare tyre, jack and tool kit.
- Read the small print on the contract carefully, checking what the insurance covers and what the excess is – the amount you'll have to pay in case of an accident.
- Carry your passport, licence and all documents related to the vehicle with you at all times, as you'll often have to show them to police at roadblocks and impromptu checks. Failure to do so can lead to a bureaucratic nightmare, or at least having to pay a bribe.
- Make sure the rental agency gives you a 24-hour emergency telephone number.
- Secure parking is often a problem, so stay in hotels with garages or car parks. Don't leave a parked vehicle unattended for long, and never leave anything valuable in it. In many cities street children offer to watch over cars in return for a small tip, a service that's well worth taking up.
- Pay close attention when you buy gas, and make particularly sure that the pump gauge has returned to zero before you're served.

## Motorbikes

**Motorbikes** are rarely available for rent in Latin America, and when they are it's usually on an informal basis, often from the same people who act as motorbike taxi drivers. All the tips for driving a car in Latin America also apply to motorbikes, with the added proviso that driver and passenger should always wear helmets and cover up, even if not required to by law. Pillion passengers also need to be careful to avoid leg burns from the exhaust pipe. Be aware that unpaved roads are difficult to ride on and can be very unpredictable, turning from dust to mud depending on weather conditions. Riding a motorbike in Latin America is not for beginners.

## Bicycles

**Bicycles** are available to rent in a growing number of tourist centres in Latin America, with the emphasis particularly on **downhill mountain-biking**, which involves taking a bus or truck ride up to a high pass on a mountain road and riding down the other side. This is easiest to do on a guided excursion with a tour agency, but you can easily do it yourself by renting the bike and using public transport. Unsurprisingly the Andean countries – Ecuador, Peru, Bolivia, Chile and Argentina – are the best and most popular places to do this, as they feature innumerable downhill rides, including some of the longest, most exciting and most scenic descents in the world.

For **longer trips** you're better off bringing your own bike from home, as buying a good-quality bike or renting one for long periods is likely to end up costing you more. Most airlines are happy to carry a bike, often for no extra fee, if you ask them in advance and pack the bike in a bike box. You should bring the best machine you can afford, plus extras like panniers, lights and a strong lock; make sure you also bring plenty of spare parts, and ensure that you're capable of carrying out minor repairs yourself. Though dust, wind, rain, heat, high altitude and unpaved roads mean bicycle touring is often hard work, it is nonetheless one of the most enjoyable ways of travelling around at a slow pace, giving plenty of contact with local people and allowing you to go pretty much at your own pace. If the going gets too hard, you can always stick your bike on top of a bus and relax for a while. For more information, see *Latin America by Bike, A Complete Touring Guide*, by Walter Sienko (Mountaineers Books, US, 1993).

Though common in smaller towns, suburbs and rural areas, bicycles are rarely used as a means of getting around in larger towns or cities, as almost no provision is made for cyclists and the snarling traffic makes riding very dangerous. If you do decide to ride a bike, whether for a day's easy riding, for a hardcore downhill run or for some long-distance touring, bear the following in mind:

- If you rent a bike, try it out before parting with your money, carefully checking the wheels, brakes and gears, and making sure the seat is set at the right height.
- Most rental bikes come without lights, so be sure to get back before nightfall.
- Protect yourself from the sun and carry plenty of water – cycling is thirsty work.
- Ride defensively, as most drivers will behave as if you don't exist.
- Carry a pump and a puncture-repair kit or spare inner tubes.
- Local mechanics are usually masters of improvisation when it comes to fixing bikes, but spare parts are difficult to come by, so if you're bringing a bike from home, bring plenty of spares.

## Hitchhiking

The cost of transport in Latin America is so low that **hitching** isn't really necessary for tourists, though in out-of-the-way places when the last bus has gone, no taxis are available and there's still a long way to go to your hotel it can become the only option. In such circumstances, local drivers who pick you up will anyway expect you to pay something close to what the bus fare would have been – the distinction between public and private transport is a hazy one in Latin America, and in remote regions private vehicles often carry paying passengers. Hitchhiking on roads where public transport is also available is unlikely to get you far for free and involves a greater degree of risk than doing the same thing at home. If you must hitch, never do so alone and, if you're a woman, never do so unaccompanied by a man. Don't suspend the instincts that keep you safe at home, and if you are in any way suspicious of a person offering you a lift, don't get into the vehicle.

# Walking

With all these different means of transport available, don't forget the simplest and cheapest way of all – whether it's a short stroll around a city centre or a long hike in the mountains, **walking** is one of the best ways to enjoy Latin America and take in the sights. If you are planning to do much walking it's a good idea to bring hiking boots or at least robust walking shoes with you. When walking around in towns and cities, be very cautious when crossing roads, as Latin American drivers show scant regard for pedestrians and often ignore road signals. For longer walks in rural areas – even for just a few hours – it's important to be properly equipped with warm clothing, rain gear and/or sun protection, as well as food and plenty of water.

# Organized tours

Throughout Latin America there are an ever-increasing number of national and local tour companies and travel agents offering all manner of **organized trips**, from brief city tours to hardcore wilderness adventures. You may leave home swearing to do everything independently, but once you're in Latin America you'll often find it's easy, convenient and relatively inexpensive to go on an organized trip. They're a particularly good way of visiting remote attractions that are otherwise difficult to reach – indeed, many of Latin America's finest attractions can only realistically be reached on a guided tour. Going with a local guide who knows the area and speaks the language can also make it far easier to visit regions where foreigners might otherwise be treated with suspicion or worse, and by acting as a mediator a good guide can give a much better insight into the lives of local people than you'll get travelling on your own.

Many tour companies also offer a range of excellent activities that are very difficult to do on your own or which require specialist equipment that you're unlikely to be carrying in your backpack, such as climbing, trekking, mountain biking, kayaking and whitewater rafting. If you're contemplating taking an organized tour, bear the following in mind:

- A day or half-day city tour can be a very good way of orienting yourself in a place before setting out to explore on your own, and allows you to see far more than you'd manage in the same time travelling by public transport.

- Unless you have abundant cash, experience and equipment, an organized tour is often the only way to reach many of Latin America's most beautiful national parks and other remote wilderness areas.
- Not all tours are luxurious (and therefore expensive) – indeed many are budget trips aimed squarely at backpackers with limited cash.
- Going on an organized tour means you get to share the expense of things like local guides and boat or jeep hire which would end up costing you a fortune of you tried to do it on your own.
- With longer trips, be sure to find out the full details of the itinerary and exactly what's included before you sign up – make sure, for instance, that a "four-day trip" doesn't leave after lunch on the first day and return early in the morning on the fourth.
- In popular tourist centres, tour agencies tend to be very competitive, so shopping around can get you a good deal. The best way to find out which agencies are reliable and have good guides is by asking other travellers who have just returned from a similar trip to the one you want to go on.

# 10

# Accommodation

S ome of your best and worst memories will be of the hotels or hostels you stayed in – these aren't just places to sleep, but also where you'll make contact with other travellers, where you'll hang out whilst recovering from long journeys or bouts of illness, or where you'll retreat to if you simply can't face the outside world or it's pouring with rain. Finding somewhere good to stay is a real bonus and might even shape your itinerary: it can be difficult to leave a place if you've made friends, if the hotel café has food you've been craving or you have a room with a great view for almost nothing. Conversely, if you've heard that a place has nowhere decent to stay, you'll probably be tempted to drop it from your plans.

Accommodation in Latin America ranges in price from a few dollars a night in a basic Guatemalan or Bolivian hostel up to several hundred in one of Mexico's chic *haciendas* or a flash hotel in Rio or Buenos Aires. However, it doesn't always follow that the cheapest countries to travel in have the best-value hotels: in general, the lack of demand and competition means that rooms in less-visited places will often be less keenly priced and often of a lower standard than places in popular tourist centres, which are usually packed with affordable and attractive hostels and hotels.

Accommodation costs will be a major part of your expenditure if you're on a tight budget. Even so, in Latin America you'll have the chance to stay in some amazing places for a fraction of the price you'd pay back home, and it would be a shame to miss out. Not only that, but there's nothing more guaranteed to restore the spirits after a few days of rough travelling than a decent hotel room with comfortable beds and an en-suite bathroom – try and factor the occasional posh hotel into your budget before you set out. If you're on a moderate budget you'll have a lot more choice, obviously – the difference between a $10 room and a $20 can be surprisingly large, although the downside of staying in mid-range hotels is that you might find yourself rather cut off from other travellers. At over $20 per day, you can expect something very comfortable indeed, with all the mod-cons, including air-conditioning, television and phone.

# Finding somewhere to stay

The last thing you'll feel like doing when you stumble off a plane or bus at the end of a long journey is finding somewhere to stay. This is where a bit of pre-planning can save you unnecessary hassle, and where a good guidebook is at its most useful. Study the town map in your guidebook first and choose an area which has several likely-sounding hotels close together so that if your first choice isn't right you can easily check out others – hotel accommodation is often clustered conveniently either around the major bus station or in the town centre.

It's important to remember, though, that guidebooks aren't infallible, since they rarely have enough space to list every hotel in town and inevitably go out of date between new editions. Once you get on the road, the travellers' network is the most up-to-date source of information about good accommodation. In addition, noticeboards and visitors' books in gringo hangouts like hostels and internet cafés also often have personal recommendations of places to stay.

At popular tourist destinations, you might be met by touts at the bus station. These will often be boys, and in most cases they're genuine and helpful, either taking you to a relative's hotel or to a hotel where the patron will give them a small fee for each guest checked in. Don't be instantly suspicious – many of the places you'll be shown will be fine, and if you don't like the place, you shouldn't be under any pressure to stay – and if you're lucky they might take you to an excellent local guesthouse not listed in any guidebook which

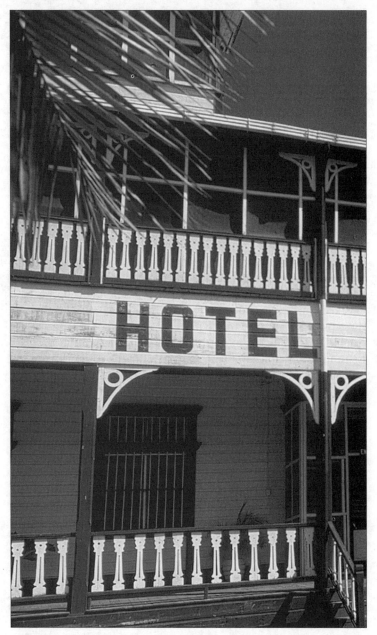

△ Caribbean coast accommodation, Guatemala

you wouldn't otherwise have found. In addition, touts can also save you the bother of reading a map and finding your way around an unfamiliar town (although of course you should always try to keep your wits about you and retain some sense of where you are). The usual common sense applies when deciding whether or not to go with a tout: if it's the middle of the night, if you're on your own or if you just don't like the look of the tout, then politely refuse their services. You should be more wary of airport cab drivers in large cities, however, who are notorious for telling tourists that the place they're going to doesn't exist or is dangerous, and then suggesting other hotels, many of which are overpriced or miles out of the way (but which pay commission to the driver).

However you intend to find a hotel, it's best to arrive as early as possible at your destination – this will give you plenty of time to orientate yourself and find somewhere you like. Arriving early will also enhance your chances of getting into the better places – popular backpackers' hostels, particularly those in areas with little competition, often fill up as soon as the previous night's occupants have checked out, often around 11am or midday. It's worth phoning these places in advance to see if there's room before you go to the trouble of turning up in person. Looking for a hotel in the dark isn't much fun either – if your bus arrives in the early hours of the morning it might be safer to wait until daylight in the bus station (many stay open all night) before you begin your search. It's also worth waiting since if you check in before the dawn (usually 5-6am) you may have to pay for a whole night.

There are also times in certain towns during big festivals or public holidays (see pp.146–50) when every room gets booked out months in advance. If you're planning on visiting during these times, try to sort out accommodation as far in advance as you can. If you haven't done this, however, don't despair: enterprising locals often respond to tourist influxes by offering visitors rooms in their homes or turning their gardens into campsites.

# Types of accommodation

Accommodation in Latin America covers the entire spectrum of different places to stay, from five-star hotels to backpacker dormitories; these are detailed below, in roughly descending order of expense.

# Five-star hotels and boutique hotels

Latin America's **five-star hotels** tend to be part of international hotel chains and are usually located in the hotel zones of capital cities and expensive tourist resorts such as Cancún in Mexico. Often looking like large tower blocks with hundreds of rooms, they have every creature comfort but little in the way of identifiable Latin American personality – you could be anywhere in the world.

**Boutique hotels** are a more attractive option, though rarely within the budget traveller's price range (many cost $150 or over a night). These are always small, beautifully decorated – some by famous interior designers – and elegantly luxurious. Most boutique hotels are located in well-known beauty spots, classy seaside resorts and quiet colonial towns. Some of the loveliest are restored *haciendas* in Mexico's Yucatán peninsula.

# Eco-lodges and estancias

There's a well-established network of **eco-lodges** in Latin America, generally situated in private wilderness reserves and offering full board plus guided walks and other outdoor activities. Many are situated in places of great natural beauty, and the best really are worth splashing out for. Their remoteness means that you'll be expected to book in advance, partly so that you can be given a lift to the lodge. In theory, eco-lodges are environmentally friendly, though this is not always the case in practice – look out for those personally run by conservationists and ecologists. Eco-lodges tend to be on the expensive side, although some have a range of accommodation with much cheaper options, often in dormitories.

Another way of getting off the beaten track – and a distinctively Latin American one at that – is to stay at an **estancia** in Uruguay, Argentina and Chile. These are working cattle ranches where you can join in the daily life of the farm, riding round on horses and seeing the local gauchos (cowboys) at work. Although not cheap, *estancias* are usually fairly posh (often similar in style to a big farmhouse), and all meals are included in the price – you may also get treated to an *asado* (barbecue), with delicious beef roasted on a spit over an open fire.

# Some favourite hotels

## Affordable

- *Cabinas Guarana* in the **Costa Rican** party town of Puerto Viejo has very friendly Italian owners, a treehouse in the garden with wonderful views over the village and sea and pretty rooms, each one individually decorated.

- In the peaceful walled city of Campeche on **Mexico's** Yucatán peninsula, the *Colonial* has a tranquil central patio and immaculately clean and simple rooms with original tiles and other features.

- At one end of Little Corn Island, off the Caribbean coast of **Nicaragua**, the individual cabins of the *Hotel Casa Iguana* perch on the cliffs – most rooms are spacious and have porches with hammocks. Evening meals, held family-style in the hotel's reception lodge, are a great way to meet other travellers and swap stories.

- Some travellers end up staying for several weeks rather than days at the *Platypus* hostel in Bogotá, **Colombia.** The dormitory rooms are basic but the hostel's owner, German Escobar, is a mine of valuable information about the whole country, which makes this place an essential port of call if you're going to Colombia.

- The *Residencial Sorata* in Sorata, **Bolivia**, was once a grand mansion and is now a popular hotel with pleasant rooms, several flower-filled courtyards and bags of charm.

- *Finca Ixobal* is a working farm, set in cool pine forest in the foothills of **Guatemala's** Maya mountains. Friendly staff take energetic visitors out riding, walking or rafting – if you're feeling less active you could just relax by the pool in the beautiful grounds. There's a range of accommodation from bungalows to dorms, hammock space and even treehouses.

- The *Pole House* in Vilcabamba, **Ecuador**, is a pretty wooden cabin, surrounded by orange and passionfruit trees, on the banks of the Río Chambo. Further up the hill but still within the privately owned forest reserve are a couple of simple adobe huts.

- Aguas Calientes, in **Peru**, is the closest village to the Inca site of Machu Picchu, and at *Hospedaje Rupa Wasi* you can stay in a cabin with a view of the ruins. The hostel terrace overlooks the Urubamba valley, the café's food is wonderful, and alternative therapies are available on site.

## Eco-lodges worth saving up for

- *Albergue Ecologico Chalalán*, Parque Nacional Madidi, **Bolivia**, was established as part of a sustainable living project for local people and is owned and managed by the Quechua-Tacana community of the Tuichi river. Rooms are in traditional Tacana style, with thatched wooden cabins and solar-powered energy, and the lodge overlooks a lake teeming with birdlife.

- Bizarrely situated in the metallic tower of a former US radar station, *Canopy Lodge* in central **Panamá** sits high above the forest with bright comfortable rooms and superb bird-watching. The *Lodge* is especially popular in March and October, the migrating seasons of hawks and vultures, who pass over in their thousands.

- *Reserva Selva Bananito* on the Caribbean coast of **Costa Rica,** between Puerto Limón and Cahuita Costa Rica, is a private rainforest reserve run by a family determined to protect their piece of the forest from loggers. With nothing but trees and dense vegetation as far as the eye can see, there's not much to do but swim, ride, climb trees, hike, or simply kick back and enjoy the green peace.

- Set up as a conservation project with public access, the 3000 square kilometres of virgin cloudforest that make up *Parque Pumalín* in southern **Chile** have seven beautifully furnished cabañas for visitors and a welcoming café with an open fire serving freshly caught fish and organic roast lamb. For budget travellers, there are simple camping and barbecue facilities.

- *Chan Chich* is an award-winning world-class eco-lodge in western **Belize** with its own Maya ruin in the grounds. Large thatched cabañas are set amid the jungle, and expert staff take guests on superb guided walks, with jaguar sightings not uncommon.

- There are numerous eco-lodges in **Brazil**'s Pantanal but *Réfugio Ecológico Caiman* is the most luxurious. Vast grounds host its own air strip and numerous activities for guests – nocturnal safaris, boat-trips and cattle-drives.

- Close to the gaucho stronghold of San Antonio de Areco in **Argentina**'s pampas is one of the country's loveliest *estancias* (cattle ranches), *La Bamba*. The main building is a classic example of early eighteenth-century rural architecture and one of the rooms for visitors is in an adjoining watchtower. The Río Areco runs through the grounds, so that guests can fish if they're bored of riding, and there's also a large swimming pool.

# Pensiones, residenciales and hospedajes

Latin America's mid-range and cheap hotels go under a bewildering variety of names: *pensión*, *posada*, *albergue*, *residenciale* and *hospedaje*. These names are often fairly meaningless, however – *hospedajes* (see below), for example, are usually fairly basic, though you'll also fine some rather fancy examples. If you're using a guidebook to select a hotel, room rates are a much more useful indication of the type of service you should expect. The most commonly used name for this sort of cheap to mid-range accommodation is **pensión** (in Brazil, *pensão*) – these are usually small, reasonably priced guesthouses run by local families; they invariably have a lot more character than bigger hotels. Rooms vary enormously in quality, though you should get your own bathroom, towels and soap and have your room cleaned daily. Rates sometimes include breakfast.

**Residenciales** and **hospedajes** are generally cheap hotels with a range of accommodation in dormitories and double and single rooms. Many have shared bathrooms only, fairly basic facilities and desultory cleaning. Guests are usually a mixture of budget travellers and young locals on holiday.

## Backpacker hostels

It's likely that you'll end up staying at least some of the time in a **backpacker hostel** – a place geared to the needs of foreign travellers on a budget (though they're not nearly as common in Latin America as they are in Asia, and as soon as you leave established tourist routes they are few and far between). As well as having some of the most competitively priced accommodation in town (usually a mixture of singles, doubles and dormitories), they're also a major source of information, with English-speaking staff, travellers' noticeboards and internet access.

In general, backpacker hostels offer a good way to ease your way into Latin America – or to retreat to if the going gets tough. Almost all offer good value for money and have staff who are used to dealing with budget travellers. Many also have lively on-site cafés with all the things you've been missing from home on the menu – bacon sandwiches, proper vegetarian food, pasta (even if you're staying elsewhere you'll usually be welcome to come in and check the noticeboard or visit the café). Don't assume, however, that these places are automatically cleaner or more comfortable than other hotels, and in terms of security you should look after your possessions as you would in any other hotel, and with particular care if you're sharing a dormitory.

## Youth hostels

**Youth hostels** (*albergues juveniles* or *albergues de la juventad*) exist in Mexico, Costa Rica, Argentina, Uruguay and Chile, which all have youth hostels affiliated to the International Youth Hostel Association (⊛www.iyha.org); if you have an IYHA card you'll be entitled to a discount. Standards vary, but most youth hostels are similar to those worldwide, with bunk beds in dormitories, shared cooking facilities and cheap rates (under \$10 a night). Many travellers eschew youth hostels in favour of backpacker hostels (see above), though the former are just as good value and a better place to meet young Latin Americans.

## Dormitorios

Virtually every town in Latin America has one cheap hotel or *dormitorió* – these are often semi-permanent homes to migrant (male) workers who share rooms, string their washing through the corridors and stomp noisily off to work at four in the morning. Although you'll be welcome and rates will be very low, you might feel intimidated if you're female and you shouldn't expect high standards of hygiene – particularly in the shared bathroom. Occasionally, the town *dormitorió* is not just unsalubrious but also dangerous – in all cases, inspect the premises, management and clientele if possible before you check in, and if you don't feel safe, don't stay.

## Rooms in private houses

**Home stays** – staying with a local family in their own home (*casas privadas*) – are popular in some parts of Latin America, particularly Guatemala and Nicaragua. This is a relatively cheap option (approximately \$10 for full board and lodging, or less than \$5 for room only), which contributes directly to local communities and – depending on the family set-up, of course, and how long you stay for – gives an insight into daily family life that you might not otherwise get.

Home stays are usually arranged in combination with a **language course**, so that you can practise what you've learnt outside the classroom, though it's also possible to arrange a home stay for a night or two without studying – either contact a language school in the area you're interested in, ask at the local tourist office for a list of local home stays, or look out for signs on private homes which say *hay cuartos, cuartos para alquilar, se alquila cuartos* (rooms to rent). Some home stays are formal arrangements where you'll get a room and have little or no contact with the family involved while in others, particularly those used by language schools, you'll eat three meals a day with your family, have your clothes washed and even go on outings with family members. In most cases, rooms in private homes are simple but scrupulously clean.

In various parts of Latin America without accommodation for tourists (such as the Solentiname Archipelego in Nicaragua) there might be an informal network of home stays. In this case you'll be met on arrival by family members, often children, who'll take you to their home – and if not, you could try asking around. You should-n't assume, however, that families will always be willing to take in tourists if you offer to pay – where this is not the norm don't insist or you'll risk causing offence.

## Short-stay hotels

**Short-stay hotels**, which charge by the hour and are euphemisti-cally called "love hotels" or *motels*, exist all over Latin America. They're usually found on the outskirts of towns and advertise them-selves with gaudy neon signs and lurid names. If you get stuck with nowhere to stay, don't rule out motels – the staff won't turn you away, and while they won't have the cheapest rates in town, rooms are often good value for money, with en-suite bathrooms and (not surprisingly) comfortable double beds.

Other hotels in Latin America used for short-stays include cheap hotels, particularly those situated around bus stations or the local market, which double up as informal brothels – this should be fair-ly obvious when you walk in though, again, you're unlikely to be turned away if you want to stay for the whole night. While some of these places are deeply unsalubrious, others are clean and safe, if rather noisy.

## Camping and sleeping in a hammock

Camping is obviously one of the cheapest forms of accommoda-tion, although the inevitable hassle of having to carry a tent, sleep-ing bags, mats and cooking equipment might outweigh the savings you make. Remember too that organized campsites only exist in significant numbers in Costa Rica and the countries of southern South America (Brazil, Uruguay, Argentina, Chile). In these coun-tries, where accommodation is relatively expensive and camping is popular with young locals as well as tourists, it's worth considering – although also bear in mind that the south of Argentina and Chile are freezing cold in the winter (June–Sept). If, on the other hand, you're only going to the region's cheaper Andean countries like Bolivia or Peru, then it's only really worth taking a tent if you're planning on doing a lot of trekking, given the cheapness of accom-modation, the lack of proper campsites, and the challenging moun-tain temperatures. Likely locations for campsites are seaside resorts,

By mid-afternoon, on the first full day of my boat journey from Iquitos to Yurimaguas, the air was still and the deck had become uncomfortably hot. I tried to sleep because I couldn't bear to do anything else, but the children in the hammock "next door" had become restless. The baby was cranky, and in trying to cheer her up her older siblings had become rambunctious, banging me every so often, starting the domino effect; I banged my travelling companion, and he banged the next person, and so on. With so many hammocks crammed into such a small deck area, there was a lot of banging going on. Once in a while a little foot would pop over into my hammock, then an arm. Then I felt tiny little hands below me – the baby was underfoot, with her hair in a ponytail straight up on her head. Suddenly she was swept up and put in the hammock and covered up as if in a cocoon, where she squealed with delight, content with her game of hide-and-seek. Meanwhile her father slept beneath me on his plastic tarp, his head resting on my backpack. It was a lesson in patience, typical of Amazon journeys. Everyone pokes and prods and everyone gets poked and prodded, and people are amazingly tolerant. At bedtime, I realized my neighbours had shifted in such a way that their hammock (holding four of them) was practically on top of me. They were fast asleep, and I could feel the weight of their bodies no matter which way I turned. There was nowhere to go but up, so I raised my hammock and happily drifted off to sleep, no matter that I was completely lopsided.

Julie Feiner

national parks and popular beauty spots. Backpacker or youth hostels (see above) with gardens often keep some space free for tents.

Camping in the wild isn't recommended, since you risk upsetting local landowners (unless you specifically ask permission) and you put yourself at risk of robbery or attack. Never camp on a beach unless it's standard practice to do so. The exception is if you're on a guided trek, since you'll have safety in numbers and your guide should be able to find a good secure base for the night.

Even cheaper than camping is using a **hammock**. These are ubiquitous in many parts of Latin America – and if you're planning any long river trips you'll need to take your own. Hostels and other cheap hotels sometimes have a dedicated space for travellers to hang their hammocks or will be happy to let you hang it in a corridor, yard or garden for a few dollars a night. Laid-back beach resorts like Tulum in Mexico will have sets of bamboo huts or *cabañas* on the beach furnished with nothing but a pair of hammock hooks. Remember that you'll need to sleep diagonally across a hammock rather than along it if you want to avoid backache, so you'll need one that's a decent size – ask for a *matrimonial* (or couple-sized) hammock.

# Inspecting the facilities

Never take a room without inspecting it first. Obviously, if you don't like any rooms you're shown you're under no obligation to stay, but try to avoid being rude when you leave in case, for any reason, you have to come back.

- Ask if the room you're being shown is the best room they have available. Hotel staff will often show potential guests the worst or most expensive room available first in the hope of getting rid of it. If you don't like the room you're being offered or can't afford the rate, ask to see another one – it's surprising how much rooms in the same hotel can vary in size and price.
- Try to avoid rooms next to shared bathrooms or communal areas unless you fancy spending your entire time listening to the sound of flushing toilets or blaring televisions.
- Check if the bathroom is clean, particularly if it's shared – some are filthy enough to put you off immediately. Also ask if there's hot water and for how long each day, and find out whether towels, soap and toilet paper are provided.
- Sit on the bed to see how comfortable it is – beds in cheap hotels often have thin foam mattresses which sag terribly and give you chronic backache if you stay for several nights.
- If there's a fan or air-conditioning (fairly essential in a hot climate), turn it on to see that it works without sounding like a traction engine.
- Is the room secure? Make sure the windows close properly, particularly if you're on the ground floor, and that the room can be properly locked.
- Check whether there's a curfew: if you're out on the town, you might not be able to get back in until morning.

# Room rates and checking in

Although **room rates** vary enormously, you ought to be able to find a bed in a hostel dormitory for $10 per night in the most expensive countries in Latin America, while in the cheapest, the same sum will get you a comfortable en-suite room in a small hotel with breakfast included. Don't assume that room rates are standard across a country (sometimes a popular seaside resort will charge twice as much for its rooms as a small mountain village, or vice versa), and don't be surprised if the rates quoted in your guidebook no longer exist – waving your book at a bemused hotel owner won't usually get you anywhere. Having said that, rates are pretty flexible. If you're travelling in low season, if the hotel is almost empty or if you're planning to stay for several nights it's always worth **bargaining**; this may save you a dollar or so, although you won't get a huge discount unless you're staying for weeks.

Check-in procedure is fairly standard. If the hotel is full and you arrive before midday you'll have to wait until guests vacate the rooms before you can check in (Latin American hotels almost never operate the 24-hour checkout system favoured in some other parts of the world). Usually you'll be welcome to dump your bags so you can go for lunch while your room is cleaned. Otherwise it's simply a question of filling in a basic form with your name, address, nationality and passport number and, in most cases, paying in advance for the room. You shouldn't surrender your passport to hotel reception, and it's unlikely that you'll be asked to do so, unless you choose to put it in the hotel safe for security (for more on hotel security, see pp.291–94).

## Showers and toilets

There are a few differences between the showers and toilets you'll be used to at home and those in Latin America. There's no hot water of any kind in many parts of Latin America, partly because of the climate, partly because hot running water is perceived as an unnecessary luxury. If you're staying in a cheap hotel in a warm part of Latin America your shower will invariably only have cold water, and although it's a shock to the system at first you'll quickly get used to it. Take showers during the heat of the day if it's too cool in the evenings or upgrade yourself to a more expensive hotel if you really can't bear it. Water pressure is often inadequate too, and hotels almost never have bathtubs.

In colder parts of the continent, cheaper hotels and hostels have come up with a device known to travellers as the "killer" (or "suicide") shower. This involves attaching a small electric unit to the top of the shower which heats the water as it passes through. Most are controlled by water pressure – the slower the flow of water, the hotter it will be. In most cases they're pretty unsatisfactory and provide a thin trickle of lukewarm water at best, and because they consist of a combination of water and electricity they're also highly dangerous and electric shocks are not uncommon. Be very careful when using them and if possible wear a pair of flip-flops or rubber-soled shoes – never fiddle with the electric unit while standing in the shower with the water on.

The other thing to know about Latin American plumbing is that it's pretty basic and you can't throw anything into the toilet bowl without risking it getting blocked. It's standard practice in virtually every country to put toilet paper, sanitary towels and tampons into a basket beside the toilet (these should be emptied regularly). Don't ignore this custom even if you find it distasteful – the other option, a blocked and overflowing toilet, is far worse.

# 11

# Staying healthy

D espite dramatic extremes of climate, unclean drinking water and often poor standards of hygiene, visitors to Latin America are unlikely to suffer from anything more serious than a bout of diarrhoea or a touch of sunburn. All the same, it helps if, before setting off, you get yourself in as good shape as possible, and take care to get lots of sleep, good food and exercise.

Having said that, it's also worth remembering that the majority of travellers to Latin America inevitably suffer from the change in environment, usually manifesting itself as diarrhoea and/or nausea and vomiting – both can be very unpleasant, though far from life-threatening (if symptoms persist beyond a few days, though, they could be indicative of something more serious and you should see a doctor). Resign yourself to the fact that you may well lose a few days of your trip to illness, and make sure there's enough flexibility in your itinerary to ensure you don't have to travel when you're feeling awful. And just in case you have the misfortune to suffer a serious health problem, make sure you get a comprehensive insurance policy which covers all medical expenses in an emergency, including repatriation – see pp.134–37 for more details.

## First-aid kits

Travel clinics, adventure sports shops and large pharmacies all now sell comprehensive travel health kits with a combination of the following – alternatively, it's easy enough to put together your own:

- Anti-diarrhoeals, for emergencies only, such as unavoidable journeys
- Antihistamines, for itchy bites, rashes and allergic reactions
- Antiseptic cream, very important for the tropics where strong humidity exacerbates the infection of wounds
- Antiseptic liquid soap, the best way to ensure you're really clean
- Insect repellent with DEET
- Painkillers (Ibuprofen, for example)
- Band-aids/plasters in several sizes, and a length of bandage plus scissors
- Rehydration salts, for coping with the dehydrating effects of diarrhoea and sickness
- Sun block (SPF 15+)
- Sterile needles
- Tweezers, for removing splinters and sea-urchin spines

### Antibiotics

Available only on prescription at home, though you may be able to persuade your doctor to give you a course of general antibiotics such as metronidazole or ciprofloxacin (both of which kill diarrhoea-causing bacteria) in advance. Or you could just buy them over the counter in Latin America if and when you need to (see overleaf). Remember that with antibiotics it's vital to take the whole course, and make sure you get your illness diagnosed before starting treatment.

### Alternative medicine

Increasingly popular, alternative medicine offers effective natural cures – consult your local health food store or homeopath for detailed information. Particularly useful remedies to take include arnica or calendula cream for bruises and bites; echinacea to boost your immune system; citronella, eucalyptus or lavender oils to ward off mosquitoes and other nasty bugs; tea tree oil, which acts as an antiseptic; tiger balm for heachaches; and Rescue Remedy, a Bach Flower Remedy which calms the nerves in stressful situations. Additionally, if you're planning on wilderness trekking or going into the jungle for a lengthy period, vitamin supplements, particularly vitamins B and C, will help to keep you healthy.

- Although most countries in Latin America don't have free or subsidized health care, private health clinics of all kinds abound in large cities and are frequently very good indeed. And even the most expensive will be more affordable than their equivalent at home.
- The prescription system doesn't exist in Latin America, which means you can buy any drug over the counter. Locals frequently don't bother consulting a doctor but instead go straight to the pharmacy, where staff are often very knowledgeable and are used to offering informal diagnoses. If you're not convinced, shop around for the best pharmacist locally – even small towns usually have several. It's also worth memorizing the generic names of useful general antibiotics (such as metronidazole, trade name Flagyl), so that you can get the right drug fast.
- Latin Americans love discussing medical problems in gory detail. If you do get ill, the staff at your hotel will all have an opinion on what you have, who you should consult and what to take. Most locals, particularly in the countryside, have some idea of natural or indigenous cures (usually an infusion made from local plants) – these often work wonderfully well.
- That said, it's important that you don't self-diagnose if you're feeling very sick – you must consult a professional doctor. Local medical services – public or private – in Latin America will be aware of the diseases listed in this chapter and should be able to treat them adequately.
- Before you set off, it's a good idea to have a dental check-up.
- There are lots of excellent sources of information on travellers' health (see Basics for websites). Books include the handy, pocket-sized *Rough Guide to Travel Health*; *Bugs, Bites and Bowels*; and *Where There is no Doctor*, which is particularly good if you're planning to stray far from accessible medical care.

## Vaccinations

Unless you're a frequent traveller to the tropics, you'll inevitably need several vaccinations before you set off. Don't leave them to the last minute – some require more than one dose, others need to be given a few days apart from each other so that they don't cancel each other out or cause reactions, and all vaccinations need several weeks for full immunity to develop; it's best to start getting inoculated around three months before you depart. And don't freak out if you feel slightly unwell after your jabs – they do, after all, work by giving you a mild dose of the disease which spurs your immune system into action.

You will probably have been inoculated as a child against certain diseases, including **diphtheria**, **polio** and **tetanus**; in these cases you'll require only a booster jab, if that. Other diseases that you'll need to be vaccinated against are **typhoid** and **hepatitis**. Combined injections now exist (ask your doctor about them), which lessen the ordeal. Two more vaccinations you might consider having are **yellow fever** and **rabies**.

If your home country has some kind of public health service, you may be able to get some of your vaccinations (tetanus, for example) free or at a greatly reduced cost from your local doctor. Less commonly requested jabs (such as yellow fever) are not always available and will cost as much as going to one of the many **private travel clinics** (see Basics, pp.326–27, which deal exclusively with vaccinations and information about tropical diseases. The clinics have expert staff and generally offer much more rapid and convenient consultations, although prices for ordinary jabs can be much higher than your doctor charges. Additionally, there are several premium-rate phone lines in the UK, North America and Australasia that give specific health advice for travellers, plus various websites where you can pay for an online consultation (see pp.326–28 for details).

# Diseases you should know about

- **Chagas' disease** (aka American trypanosomiasis) Transmitted by reduviid beetles, also known as "assassin bugs", Chagas' disease is rife in some parts of Latin America (particularly northeastern Brazil) and, though you're unlikely to be affected, can be fatal if left untreated. Try to avoid staying in the adobe or mud huts that the reduviid beetle lives in (if you can't, then be sure to sleep well away from the walls), and if you are bitten, disinfect the bite with antiseptic and don't scratch it. Should a fever develop within ten days, get a blood test as soon as possible – if you have the disease you'll need to be hospitalized. Other symptoms are localized swelling around the bite, swelling of the lymph glands and an itchy rash.
- **Cholera** Cholera is spread by contaminated water or by eating contaminated shellfish and manifests itself as a particularly nasty

## Tropical acne

Spending a night in the Belizean rainforest is an incredible experience. As the light fades the air is filled with the shrill screeches of insects and the croaking and booming of frogs and toads. At dusk the biting insects increase their attacks, forcing you to cover up, burn leaves to create smoke or retreat into the tent.

Later, after dinner, the insect swarms gradually thinned and I rolled out my sleeping pad under a tree. Closer to the natural world here than in my tent, I thought. Indeed I was, because that's when the sandflies strike. These tiny insects can't fly or jump far, so you're most at risk when sleeping outdoors. I didn't feel anything biting so slept outside for a few more nights.

At home a month later, I noticed some tiny spots on my face, a bit like acne. A couple of weeks later they'd grown bigger and were clearly active. In Belize and Guatemala leishmaniasis was a disease that the *chicleros* – the men who tapped the latex of chicle trees to gather the base ingredient of chewing gum – caught, but it was extremely rare for outsiders to catch it. By the time I'd got an appointment with a dermatologist, the spots were about the size of a penny, like miniature red volcanoes, erupting with serum and turning green. Small children were staring and pointing, asking their mums what was wrong with that man. I now knew what it felt like to be a social leper – or perhaps even a real leper.

Strangers stared and colleagues were shocked. Telling them what the treatment involved horrified them further: for twenty days I had to go to hospital for a very strong dose of antibiotic delivered by drip. My whole body ached and at times I could barely move; I was on massive doses of painkillers. Today, more than a year later, the red lesions are still visible on my face and it will be several more months before they disappear entirely.

Peter Eltringham

bout of diarrhoea and/or vomiting. There's currently no effective vaccine – the best way to avoid catching cholera is by being careful about the water you drink. Diagnosis is by stool sample and treatment is with antibiotics such as doxycycline.

● **Dengue fever** A virus spread by the Aedes mosquito, which bites in the early morning or late afternoon. Initial symptoms (similar to those of malaria) typically appear five to eight days after being bitten and include fever, headache, joint pains and backache, as well as short-lived but severe diarrhoea and a fine rash. Diagnosis is made by blood test; you should check for malaria at the same time if you have this particular collection of symptoms. Dengue fever has no specific cure and is usually treated with bed rest. More seriously (though rare – it most commonly affects children aged 15 and under) the disease can develop into dengue haemorrhagic fever, which is life threatening – seek immediate medical attention if you go into shock (characterized by clammy skin, a weak pulse and shallow breathing) or start to bleed from any orifices.

● **Hepatitis** Hepatitis (an inflammation of the liver)

exists in several different forms. Hepatitis A is a virus spread by contaminated water or intimate contact; symptoms include nausea, loss of appetite, weight loss, fatigue and abdominal pain and, most distinctively, jaundice, which turns the patient's skin and eyeballs yellow. Hepatitis B is a more severe and longer-lasting form of the disease; it's spread by blood through sexual contact, sharing needles or blood transfusions. Both forms are usually treated with several weeks of bed rest. Effective vaccinations for both hepatitis A and B exist and can be given in one combined shot. Immunization is recommended.

● **Leishmaniasis** Found in many parts of Central and South America, leishmaniasis is transmitted by sandflies and exists in several forms. Most common in Latin America are the cutaneous and mucocutaneous strains: these cause the sandfly bites to develop into itchy red skin ulcers which can leave severe and permanent scarring. Diagnosis is made by a skin biopsy and treated with a ten-day intravenous course of drugs. There is no vaccine, although sandflies are low-flying, and sleeping above ground level will lessen your chances of being bitten, as will using an insect repellent. Mosquito nets, however, will not protect you, since sandflies are small enough to pass through the mesh.

● **Malaria** See overleaf.

● **Rabies** Rabies is spread by the bite of an infected animal (usually a dog) and is a serious paralyzing and potentially fatal disease which rapidly becomes incurable. Symptoms initially include fever, nausea and loss of appetite, muscle aches and sore throat; they may also include unpredictable or aggressive behaviour followed by muscle spasms, fear of water and paralysis. A three-dose vaccine exists which will partly protect you against the disease developing, but if you're bitten, even if you've been immunized, you must seek urgent medical attention. Treatment consists of a further course of injections. Thorough cleaning of the wound also helps to reduce the chances of becoming infected.

● **Tetanus** Tetanus spores live in soil, dust and manure and infect humans through open wounds. Symptoms develop following an incubation period of between five and twenty days and include headache, fever, irritability and jaw-muscle spasms which spread to the neck, limbs and torso and may result in breathing difficulties. Tetanus is potentially fatal, with various complications including blood clots, pneumonia and heart problems; treatment requires hospitalization. Most people in the developed world are vaccinated as children, though you'll need a booster if it's been over ten years since your last immunization.

- **Typhoid** Typhoid is carried in contaminated water or food and, like cholera, is fairly widespread in unsanitary areas. Symptoms are similar to cholera and include fever, headache, lethargy and stomach pains. In some cases, coughing, temporary deafness and pink spots on the torso also occur, and what begin as mild symptoms may deteriorate over two weeks into serious illness. Diagnosis is through a blood or stool test, and the disease can usually be treated with antibiotics such as ciprofloxacin. An effective typhoid vaccine exists, and immunization is recommended.
- **Yellow fever** The yellow fever virus is spread by mosquito bites and is found throughout the Amazon region. Mild though sudden symptoms of fever, abdominal pain and vomiting often disappear rapidly, only to recur in fifteen percent of cases along with jaundice, kidney failure, bleeding and shock. This secondary yellow fever is potentially fatal and there's no specific treatment. There is a vaccine, however, and in various parts of Latin America (specifically Brazil, and in Amazonian areas in general – check with a travel clinic) you may be asked to produce an International Certificate of Vaccination proving that you've been immunized. If you can't, you run the risk of being immunized on the spot in potentially less than sanitary conditions. Immunization lasts for ten years and is recommended.

## Mosquitoes and malaria

**Malaria**, a potentially fatal disease spread by the bite of the female Anopheles mosquito, is one of the world's most widespread diseases, with an estimated 300 to 500 million cases every year and over a million deaths. Although outbreak patterns change from year to year, parts of Latin America, particularly the Amazon region, are generally considered high-risk. There's currently no vaccine, although scientists continue to work on one, and anyone going to tropical or subtropical Latin America should take a course of preventative drugs and try to avoid being bitten.

The initial **symptoms** of malaria are worryingly similar to flu or more general fever. Typically, sufferers start feeling very cold and shiver, then develop a very high temperature and finally begin to sweat – these three stages continue in one- to three-day cycles. There are four different strains of the malaria parasite; the most dangerous, *p.falciparum*, can become potentially fatal in a matter of hours.

Your local doctor and specialized travel clinics, phone lines and websites (see pp.326–28) will have up-to-date advice on **malarial areas** and **anti-malarial drugs**. There is some controversy about anti-malarial drugs because of their side effects and efficacy (none is one-hundred percent effective), but all offer at least some (and usually much more) protection against contracting the disease.

There are several anti-malarial drugs on the market; which one you take will depend on your medical history, where exactly you're going and for how long. The longest established anti-malarial, chloroquine, is also the most widely available, the cheapest and has no significant side effects (it can be taken continuously over a five-year period). However, its heavy use over the years has led to *p.falciparum* (see opposite) mutating to become **chloroquine-resistant** and thus rendering chloroquine ineffective in certain areas. In Latin America, *p.falciparum* exists throughout the Amazon Basin (which covers every country in South America apart from Paraguay, Uruguay, Argentina and Chile), and if you're travelling in this region you'll need another anti-malarial.

Of the other drugs currently available, mefloquine (Larium) is the most effective, can be taken for up to a year and works well against most strains of malaria – although strains are starting to become resistant to it. However, there have been reports of disturbing side effects, including hallucinations and psychosis, as a result of taking Larium – be aware of the risks if you decide to take it. It's also the most expensive anti-malarial. Doxycycline is effective against *p.falciparum* only, can be taken for three months though its side effects include increased risk of sunburn, nausea, and vaginal yeast infections. It's not easily available in the USA. Malarone is the newest anti-malarial on the market, is effective against all strains of malaria and has few side effects – though it shouldn't be taken for more than 28 days.

All anti-malarial courses must be started before you reach the malarial zone, from two days for doxycycline to one to three weeks for mefloquine, and continued for up to a month after you've left. You'll have to pay full price for anti-malarial drugs (and most aren't cheap), but buying them before you set off is recommended since their availability and quality in Latin America can't be guaranteed.

In terms of alternative medicine, a Chinese remedy, *quinhaosu* (sweet wormwood), has attracted much interest from the tropical medicine community and is being thoroughly researched although it's still in the experimental phase.

The best way to **avoid getting malaria** is to avoid being bitten (and bear in mind that as well as transmitting malaria, mosquitoes may also carry dengue and yellow fever). The following precautions will help when in malarial areas:

- Mosquitoes are mainly nocturnal – and malaria-carrying ones particularly love dusk, which is when you're most likely to be bitten. Cover up as much as possible, wearing long-sleeved shirts and trousers tucked into socks. Mosquitoes are drawn to strong dark colours – white is your best bet for keeping them at a distance.

- Buy an effective insect repellent and use it diligently. The best repellents contain varying levels of DEET (from 15 to 100 percent), and although it smells nasty, can sting sensitive skin, and actually melts plastic, it does work (but try not to apply it in a closed environment or near other people, unless you want to asphyxiate them). If you want to use natural repellents, citronella, eucalyptus and lavender essential oils (mixed into a base of oil or water) are effective for several hours. Bizarrely, Avon's Skin-So-Soft moisturizing lotion, available from drugstores in North America (and parts of Latin America), is one of the best repellents of both mosquitoes and sandflies. It's also claimed that mosquitoes love perfume, pregnant women and sweat, but hate the smell of garlic and vitamin B.

- Sleep under a mosquito net – it's best to take your own (those in hotels invariably have holes); good ones roll up into a small and virtually weightless pouch. In addition, soak your net in permethrin before you set off or choose one that's already been treated. You can also impregnate your travelling clothes with permethrin, which will act as a further line of defence.

- Burn mosquito coils in your room – they're the most popular local form of repellent and so are usually cheap and readily available.

- If you're not on a tight budget, choose a hotel room with mesh screens over the windows. Both air-conditioning and powerful ceiling fans prevent mosquitoes from getting near you because they find it hard to fly in circulating air currents.

- Even if you're not in a malarial area, mosquito bites can be distressing. If you are bitten, try not to scratch the bite – this only spreads any infection further. Calamine lotion, tea-tree oil or an antiseptic cream may help to soothe the irritation; if the itching becomes unbearable, antihistamine tablets or cream will calm it considerably.

- The website ⓦwww.malaria.org is a good source of information on the disease – otherwise check the general travellers' health websites.

# Heat and cold

Apart from stomach upsets, you're most likely to fall ill during your trip as a result of **exposure to the sun**. Remember that the sun is at its hottest between 11am and 3pm, and you should try to avoid being outside in direct sunlight for too long during these hours. You'll notice the locals keeping a low profile – copy them and have lunch in the shade or take a siesta. Bear in mind also that the effect of sun is stronger at high altitudes and anywhere where light is reflected, such as snowscapes, or in and on the water; if you're on a boat, cooling breezes may mask the strength of the sun. Be extra careful in both these environments and cover up in a lightweight shirt and long trousers.

When you do venture out into the sun, always use a **sunscreen**, which will help protect you against skin cancer and premature age-ing – however much you want to return from your trip with a healthy-looking tan, you could be seriously damaging your long-term health if you're not properly protected from the sun's ultravi-olet rays. Use a sunscreen with at least SPF 15 and choose one that protects against both UVA and UVB rays and is waterproof. Apply it twenty minutes before you go out and reapply it diligently every couple of hours. Take a large bottle of sunscreen with you from home – it's often very expensive in Latin America – and once on the road, stock up in big cities since smaller places often don't have anything suitable. Also take a sunscreen stick for your lips – these are often neglected and burn or blister easily.

The other important item to take is a decent pair of **sunglasses** – cheap shades are little more than coloured sheets of plastic and can do more harm than good; get a pair of sunglasses with polaroid or UV-resistant lenses. You may also want to take a hat to stop your head getting burnt. If you do get burnt, there's little you can do about it except slather yourself in a soothing after-sun lotion (any-thing with aloe vera in it is wonderfully cooling), increase your fluid intake (but avoid alcohol) and stay in the shade until the red-ness and soreness have gone.

As well as direct exposure to the sun, you'll also probably have to deal with the overall **heat and humidity**. Acclimatizing to these takes a while – weeks rather than days – so don't rush around or undertake strenuous exercise immediately after you've arrived. You should also increase your fluid intake, and if you do start to feel you're overheating, bathe frequently in tepid or cool water. Prickly heat or heat rash results from inflamed sweat glands, caused by over-exposure or over-exertion in high temperatures, and manifests itself as small itchy pink/red spots on the head, neck, shoulders and other sweaty parts of the body. As well as taking cool showers, treat heat rash by wearing loose lightweight clothing, using talc to keep dry and soothing aftersun creams to stop the itching. Heat stroke, by contrast, is a potentially life-threatening condition. If your body temperature rises significantly (above 41°C) and you experience nausea, sensitivity to light, rapid breathing and, most significantly, stop sweating, you need urgent medical attention.

At the other end of the scale, in the Andes the temperature can fall well below freezing. It may be hot during the daytime in the mountains, but as soon as the sun sets the temperature drops alarmingly fast – if you're out hiking, take layers of warm clothes with you. At worst, severe cold can lead to **hypothermia** (when the human body temperature drops beneath 35°C). Symptoms include slurred speech, stumbling and shallow breathing; if untreated, hypothermia can lead to coma and then death. If you do get very cold, you can warm yourself up by consuming high-energy foods like chocolate and hot, sugary drinks (alcohol should be avoided because it dilates blood vessels near the surface of the skin, meaning you actually lose heat). Sharing your companion's body heat (and/or sleeping bag) is another highly effective way of increasing your own body temperature.

## Water

Probably the biggest single health hazard travellers to Latin America face is **contaminated water**, the cause not only of travellers' diarrhoea and dysentery, but also of much more serious diseases like cholera, hepatitis and typhoid. Avoiding contaminated water, however, isn't that easy. With a very few exceptions (most of Argentina, Chile, Costa Rica), tap water in Latin America isn't safe to drink. Obviously, you should only drink and clean your teeth with bottled or purified water, as well as avoiding swimming in fresh water and (although it sounds stupid) taking a shower with your mouth open. In addition, avoid ice, fruit juices (*jugos*, *licuados* or *batidas*) and salads, which in most restaurants are either made with or washed in tap water.

Bottled water is widely available and inexpensive; alternatively, if you're on a very tight budget, in a remote area or camping, you can purify local water yourself with either chlorine or iodine drops which can be purchased back home in camping shops. Iodine can only be used for up to six weeks continuously although it has the advantage of killing the giardia parasite (see p.275), which chlorine doesn't. Both make water taste unpleasant, although you can add neutralizing crystals which mask most – but not all – of the taste (iodine tablets are available with neutralizers already added). Your other options are portable water filters or, better, purifying kits which both filter and sterilize water – although water filters won't get rid of every nasty organism, water purifiers clean water to a high level. They range vastly in price ($25–100) and come in several sizes; consider weight, efficacy and ease and speed of use before you buy one. If you're carrying a camping stove it's easier to just boil water (for at least five minutes; longer at higher altitudes) to rid it of any harmful bacteria.

# Food

Food that isn't properly cooked or is unhygienically prepared is another source of diarrhoea and sickness. When choosing where and what to eat, bear the following points in mind:

- Look at hygiene standards: if the floor is swept, tables wiped and ashtrays emptied regularly, chances are the same attitude extends to the kitchen.
- You don't have to completely avoid eating street food – some stalls are scrupulously maintained, with ingredients covered and food freshly cooked. Look around for the busiest places – often the best way to tell if somewhere is worth going to.
- Conversely, don't assume that gringo cafés will be more hygienic than local places – they may not be.
- Choose places where food is cooked to order – food that's been left sitting around attracts flies and harmful bacteria.
- Undercooked meat and reheated rice could give you serious food poisoning and salad is often washed in unclean tap water – you should avoid all three. Be particularly careful with shellfish, which is prone to contamination because of the large amounts of polluted seawater they filter while feeding. Additionally a handful of people die every year in Chile from eating shellfish contaminated by the

*marea roja* ("red tide"), a very poisonous algae – although the government does issue warnings when it's present. Also avoid fruit that you haven't peeled yourself, and unpasteurized milk and cheese.

# Diarrhoea, dysentery and giardia

However careful you are, chances are that at some stage in your travels you'll come down with some kind of **stomach bug** or bout of diarrhoea/vomiting – often shortly after arriving. This may be as much to do with a dramatic change in environment as anything, and the good news is that most cases of even severe diarrhoea and sickness clear up within days and can be easily treated without a visit to the doctor.

If you do come down with something, try to rest for a few days until you feel better – you'll also make the experience less unpleasant for yourself (and other guests) if you check into a hotel with a private bathroom. You probably won't feel like eating if you're sick, and cutting back on food intake will give your guts a much-needed break, although the latest thinking is that it's best to eat at least something. Avoid anything spicy or strongly flavoured – stick to plain, freshly boiled rice, bananas and dry biscuits. Unless you have to travel, don't take anti-diarrhoea medication, which works by blocking you up, thus preventing your body from expelling the bacteria which caused your illness in the first place.

The most important thing, if you're suffering from diarrhoea and vomiting, is to ensure that you don't become **dehydrated**, since your body will be losing vital fluids. If you have a dry mouth and tongue, a loss of skin elasticity (you can test this by pinching the skin on the back of your hand: if it takes a while to return to its initial state then you're dehydrated), dark urine, headaches and backache, then you've already become seriously dehydrated and need to start rehydrating immediately – try to avoid reaching this stage by increasing your fluid intake as soon as diarrhoea and vomiting start. Adults need to take in 2–3 litres of liquid a day (not including alcohol, coffee or tea, which further dehydrate your system) – more in particularly hot or humid climates. Although in the worst stages of a particularly bad bout you may not be able to keep down anything at all, it's important to keep trying. Take sips of bottled water at frequent intervals; even better, add oral rehydration salts to boiled or bottled water to replace lost salt and sugar. If you don't have any in your medical kit you can prepare your own by adding half a level teaspoon of salt and eight level teaspoons of sugar to a litre of clean water. Alternatively, if you're feeling up to it, try drinking something fizzy (rather bizarrely, Coca-Cola is thought to soothe stomach upsets) and eating salty crackers. If more than three or four days pass without you being able to keep down liquids, or if you stop urinating altogether and start to feel drowsy, you may need an intravenous drip and should go to a hospital for treatment.

There are several **homeopathic remedies** for diarrhoea – *arsenicum album*, *china officinalis* and *veratrum album*. Ginger helps to alleviate feelings of nausea, while live yoghurt (not easily found in Latin America) or acidophilus tablets will repopulate your intestines with good bacteria after a serious bout of sickness. Locals may also have some ideas – this may well involve a herbal tea of some kind, usually foul tasting but often effective.

While most cases of diarrhoea and vomiting clear up within a few days, there are several more serious gastrointestinal illnesses which have similar causes and symptoms. The most notable of these are **amoebiasis (amoebic dysentery)** and **giardia**. Both are caused by parasites which enter the gut via contaminated water or food and are characterized by abdominal cramps, fever, nausea and weight loss. If you have amoebic dysentery, you may also be passing blood and in severe cases, where the parasite has reached the liver and caused an abscess, suffer intermittent pain on the upper right-hand side of the abdomen; **giardia** is very distinctive, with sulphurous or eggy burping and farts and a bloated stomach. Both can cause long-term intestinal damage (including lactose intolerance) if left untreated; treatment is with antibiotics (metronidazole).

Still more serious illnesses with similar symptoms to travellers' diarrhoea are hepatitis, cholera and yellow fever, amongst others – if you continue to feel ill after five days, have a high fever (above 39°C) or severe abdominal pain, seek medical advice.

# Wildlife and parasites

You'll probably have the jitters about creepy-crawlies if you've never been to Latin America, and particularly if you're planning to visit the rainforest, but in truth you're extremely unlikely to be bitten by any poisonous creatures – they'll be avoiding you harder than you them. That said, there are many species of poisonous snakes and other unpleasant insects and parasites in the region, particularly in the Amazon, and it's worth following the points below to minimize the risk of being bitten:

- Tread carefully in jungle terrain and make as much noise as possible – which gives snakes, rarely aggressive, the chance to slither away. If you are bitten by a snake, get to a doctor as soon as possible and try to stay calm since panicking will pump the venom faster around your body. If you're able to kill the snake and take it to be identified, you may hasten the process of diagnosis and treatment. Attempting to suck out venom is not recommended.
- Avoid swimming in rivers, lakes and lagoons, particularly in tropical South America, where cayman (alligators), electric eels and piranha fish make their home. Although cayman aren't generally aggressive, they have been known to attack if protecting young or just plain hungry. The *candiru* fish is native to the Amazon and swims up the uretha and lodges there or in the bladder, which results in severe blood loss and infection and may be fatal; removal is by surgery. Other nasty parasites also live in tropical freshwater, such as those that cause schistosomiasis (also known as bilharzia), now the second most prevalent tropical disease worldwide after malaria. Minute larvae penetrate human skin, grow in the liver, mate and then release their eggs via faeces or

## Footworms in Brazil

When you've finally reached that perfect beach – powdery white sand and palm trees – one of the first things you want to do is kick off your shoes and walk barefoot along the shore. So when I found my beach on an island in Brazil, that's exactly what I did. Two days later I had an itchy big toe and, on examination, a small swelling right by my toenail – it wasn't an insect bite, though. Jose, the man who ran my hotel, knew what it was as soon as he saw me scratching furiously – "Ah," he said phlegmatically – "you have a *bicho de pé*", which he went on to explain was a footworm, a small maggotty insect fond of crawling into the cracks between human toes and toenails and then moving into the bloodstream. Once I'd recovered from the shock, Jose explained that I'd have to remove it as soon as possible. "Oh God," I said, "and how do I do that?" Footworms, it appeared, have to be dug out with a thorn from a lemon tree – the native way – or with a sewing needle – the gringo method. However I did it, it wasn't the first and last footworm I dug out of my toe – every evening as sun set, examining my feet for the telltale signs became a nightly ritual – I could, of course, have just worn shoes on the beach like the locals did…

Polly Rodger Brown

urine. An initial itchy rash may be the only specific symptom of schistosomiasis, which can cause kidney failure and damage to the heart, lungs and central nervous system.

- Shake out your shoes every morning – they're a favourite habitat of scorpions and spiders. If you are stung by either (which is highly unlikely, and rarely fatal), apply ice or cold compresses to the bite and take antihistamines and pain relievers. Seek urgent medical advice if you show an allergic reaction to the bite.

- Avoid walking barefoot, especially on beaches or any other area where dogs roam freely (ie most of rural Latin America), no matter how tempting. Jiggers are small fleas that penetrate the skin, normally around the toenails, and lay their eggs. The only way of getting rid of them is to pick them out with a sterilized needle – not much fun. If you see and feel a dark itchy bump on one of your toes you must remove the flea or risk gangrene and septicaemia. Bathing your feet in hot water after walking in an infested area may help dislodge the fleas before they've become firmly attached, while the liberal use of insect repellent is

## A close encounter

Sitting around the campfire in the midst of the pristine Amazonian rainforest of Peru's Manu National Park, our tour guide, Barry, had warned us to watch out for the bushmaster. He said the most venomous snake in the Americas was also extremely aggressive, and had been known to pursue those who disturbed it, using infrared vision to track them down before delivering a lethal bite with its fangs. According to the locals, Barry said, the person walking third in line on a jungle trail was most at risk from the bushmaster: the first person passing by would disturb it, the second annoy it, and the third would pay the ultimate price. And so I was slightly concerned when, as we set out on a night walk through the forest an hour or so later, I found myself walking up a narrow trail with only Barry and one other ecotourist ahead of me. Within minutes, Barry suddenly stopped and took a step back, shining his torch at what looked like a stick lying across the path. "Bushmaster", he whispered, and I watched as one end of the stick rose vertically into the air, revealing it as a two-metre-long snake, angry and ready to strike. Even Barry seemed pretty unsettled at the sight, lighting a cigarette and puffing nervously as we peered over his shoulder. When asked what the striking range of the snake was, however, he was still cool enough to reply "Oh, he could get me from there." We waited at a safe distance until the bushmaster slithered into the forest and we could continue along the trail. I didn't realize quite how fortunate we'd been until a year later, when I ran into Barry in a Cusco bar. A few weeks after our trip, he told me, another tour group had run into a bushmaster in the same region. The snake had pursued one ecotourist and bitten him on the ankle. "What happened to him?" I asked, and Barry said he'd been lucky: after being airlifted to a Lima hospital, he'd lived to tell the tale, though only after having his leg amputated.

James Read

sometimes effective. Locals will be able to keep you up to date about the prevalence of jiggers in their area – be wary if you see a lot of locals sitting around picking their feet.

● If a tick – which looks like an eight-legged woodlouse and can carry nasty diseases – attaches itself to you, remove it carefully using tweezers so that you don't leave part of it embedded in your flesh.

● Leeches are not dangerous and will drop off once they've satiated themselves on your blood, though if you'd rather not wait, applying a lit cigarette usually persuades them to leave sharpish. As with ticks (see above), don't pull them off.

● Try not to sleep in mud or adobe buildings. These harbour the assassin bugs which cause potentially fatal Chagas' disease (see p.265).

# Altitude

**Altitude sickness**, known as *soroche* in Spanish, is caused by insufficient acclimatization to high altitudes (over 2500m) and the body's inability to cope with reduced levels of oxygen. You should be particularly wary of altitude sickness if you fly into La Paz in Bolivia (3636m), Cusco (3500m), Quito (2800m), Bogotá (2650m) or Mexico City (2400m) – arriving at any of these cities from a low altitude, you should take things easy for the first few days after your arrival. Symptoms of altitude sickness include persistent headache, vomiting, dizziness and breathlessness. Drinking lots of water will help enormously; in Bolivia, the local coca tea (*mate de coca*) is an effective remedy. There is also a homeopathic remedy, *coca*.

At very high altitudes (3000m or more, for example when climbing in the Andes) altitude sickness can worsen to become **acute mountain sickness** (AMS), which is much more serious and potentially fatal. Symptoms of AMS, caused by increased fluid and swelling on the brain and lungs, include lethargy and confusion, coughing and a bluish tinge to lips, nails and skin. If you're planning to climb in high altitudes you should be in good physical shape. Spend several days acclimatizing before you set off, limit your ascent to no more than 300m each day and keep hydrated by drinking at least three litres of non-alcoholic fluids a day. The only effective cure for AMS is to descend immediately – even several hundred metres will instantly make you feel better – although the drugs dexamethasone, frusemide and nifedipine (which should only be used under medical supervision) might buy you some time while you descend.

# Aids, HIV and contraception

**AIDS** (*sida*) is just as common in Latin America as in Europe, the US and Australasia – indeed Brazil has one of the world's highest number of infected people. All the usual precautions apply: never have unprotected sex or share needles. If you're planning on being sexually active, take a supply of condoms (*preservativos*) with you – the quality of those in Latin America may not be as good as you'd hope.

If you're on **the Pill**, take supplies with you, since your particular brand may be hard to find. Bear in mind that prolonged periods of diarrhoea and vomiting will affect the efficacy of the Pill, so take extra precautions following any gastrointestinal upset. Also be aware that taking the pill does increase your risk of thrombosis, as does travelling at high altitudes – if you're planning on trekking above 4000m you should seriously consider coming off the Pill during this period (consult your doctor for advice). Alternatively, if you're planning some kind of adventure holiday and would rather not have to deal with periods, it's possible to prevent bleeding for up to three months with no problems by taking the Pill continuously and ignoring the monthly Pill-free week. If you're at all concerned, discuss your trip with your doctor before you leave.

# 12

# Keeping in touch

**K**eeping in touch with home during your travels in Latin America is now relatively inexpensive and uncomplicated, largely thanks to the Internet, which has revolutionized communications in Latin America just as it has done everywhere else. Postal and phone networks too, though much less used by tourists nowadays, have been largely privatized and are now fairly reliable. There are obviously regional variations in communication networks – for specific details on keeping in touch check your guidebook, which should have a section covering the relevant issues in the country you're visiting. A few general points apply wherever you are, however. To begin with, don't fall into the trap of setting fixed times and dates in advance for ringing home or sending an email, since it's unlikely that you'll be able to stick to them – a

## Dear Mom,

Glad you're enjoying my stories. Not much to report at the moment. Spent Christmas Eve on top of a *Coca-Cola* truck driving around Iquitos with Santa Claus, and Christmas Day morning with a monkey on my head. The night before Christmas Eve, I went to an Evangelical church dinner with a Brazilian boat captain who once worked with Jacques Cousteau. During the meal I talked with a (female) judge who fights drug trafficking in the Amazon.

That's about it.

Hope you had a great Christmas.

Love,

Julie

Julie Feiner

delay in your itinerary, a power cut (frequent in some parts of Latin America) or a public holiday might all mean you can't send an email or get to a phone. However, if you find yourself anywhere near a natural disaster, airplane crash or political coup, get in touch with your family as soon as possible. Inevitably they'll have seen the details on the news, sometimes days before you, and will want to know that you're safe.

# Email and the Internet

**Internet access** is widely available in Latin America. Every city and decent-sized town in even the poorest or least touristed of countries now has at least one Internet café – in fact, because many Latin Americans still don't have access to a computer at home or work, Internet cafés are far more popular with the locals than in the US or Europe. In addition, post offices, telephone centres, universities and libraries also often offer cheap Internet access – it's always worth asking at these places. Don't, however, assume that you can access the Internet everywhere. Many places in Latin America still lack electricity and phone lines. And the further off the beaten track you go, the more expensive using the Internet is likely to be.

If you don't already have an email account, there are now dozens of companies which offer **free Web-based email accounts** which can be accessed from anywhere in the world. Two of the most popular are Hotmail (🌐www.hotmail.com) and Yahoo! (🌐www.yahoo.com), which are both reliable, although with millions of subscribers using the service at any one time, logging on can be slow. Other recommended free servers are Fastmail (🌐www.fastmail.fm) and Planet Access (🌐www.planetaccess.com), which are among the fastest services available (though in terms of speed, it's worth remembering that the emptier your inbox, the faster you'll be able to log on to your account). Virgin (🌐www.virgin.net) offer twice as much storage space (10MB) as many other free servers, so that you can keep more emails in your account. The Website 🌐www.emailaddresses.com has reviews of more than a hundred free email accounts, with useful comments and information on how to choose one which suits you.

**Costs** for Internet access in Latin America vary enormously – from $0.50 in Ecuador to $12 a hour in the Bay Islands of Honduras – though they usually average $4–5 per hour; there's usually a minimum charge of ten or fifteen minutes. You may have to be patient, though – particularly in poorer countries and rural areas, connection times can be very slow, and occasionally you may not be able to get through at all. If you get stuck, many staff in places with Internet access speak some English. It's also worth knowing that the @ symbol (*arrobá* in Spanish) is not on many Latin American keyboards – you have to hold down the "Alt" key and then type 64.

To find out the locations of Internet cafés in Latin America, visit the comprehensive ⓦwww.netcafeguide.com, ⓦwww.latinworld.com or ⓦwww.planeta.com, or check your guidebook, which should have listings. In general the best areas to find Internet cafés are around universities and in heavily touristed towns; in addition, many backpacker hostels now have Internet access. If you get stuck in the middle of nowhere and need to use the Internet, you could always try asking around at local business-es or hotels (assuming there are any).

In some places you can also now make **Web calls**. These are effectively phone calls made through the Internet, and cost the same per minute as being online (which is to say they're consider-ably cheaper than a standard international phone call). Bear in mind that there's little privacy in most Internet cafés and the Web-call process is still in its early experimental days – you may have badly echoing or crackling lines and long delays in getting through.

# Phoning home

Phoning home from Latin America is usually a fairly straightforward procedure, although you have several choices in how to make your call. All cities and towns in Latin America (and, nowadays, even some villages) have a **telephone centre** (*centro de llamadas* or *caseta de teléfono*; *posto telefônico* in Brazil) – generally a branch of the national telecom company. These usually have a series of numbered booths and an operator. You give the number you wish to call (preferably written in full with all the relevant codes) to the operator, who will dial it for you and then point you to a booth where you can make your call in private. You'll be charged by the minute, although there may be a minimum charge. Telephone centres vary enormously when it comes to rates – some charge no more than the cost of a call made in a public phone, while others hike up the prices substantially. Always check the **prices** of international calls first, since they can be exorbitant, and are always more than the cost of an international call from your home country. Generally, though, it costs about $1–2 per minute to phone the US, $3–4 to phone Europe, and $6–8 to phone Australasia. Telephone centres may not always have the cheapest rates available (see below), but are often the simplest (and most private) way of making a phone call. In addition, telephone centres in larger towns and cities often offer a **fax service** and, increasingly, also provide Internet access.

You can also make international calls directly from certain **phones** on the street; this is sometimes cheaper than using a telephone centre, although access to international phone lines is erratic at the best of times. You'll need to buy a phonecard (*tarjeta telefónica*) – these are now used in most public phones in Latin America rather than coins, and are sold widely in grocery stores, pharmacies and newsstands (buy the highest-value card available if you're making international calls). The drawback is that public phones in Latin America are often situated in noisy public places, so if you do get through, you may not be able to hear anything.

Another option is to sign up for an **international calling card** before you leave home. Hundreds of telecom companies now offer this service: the best-established include AT&T, MCI and Sprint in the US and Canada; BT and Mercury in the UK; Telstra in Australia; and Telecom in New Zealand. American Express also do a prepaid card, and it's also possible to use a Visa credit card (⊛www.visa.com).

△ Phoning home

E-kit (◍www.ekit.com) offer an advanced calling card service with voicemail, so that your friends and family can leave messages which you later pick up. With so many services to choose from, you should compare rates – US-based calling cards are often the best value and are increasingly available in Europe and Australasia. You can sign up for most calling cards via the relevant website. Once payment is agreed, you'll be given details of how to use the service and a PIN number, which you should keep secure at all times.

Calling cards have lots of advantages: they're often cheaper to use than calling from a public phone or telephone centre, and can also be used when calling from private phones – including those in hotels – at no extra charge. While some calling card services are prepaid (such as American Express), the majority are now charged to a credit card account or home phone number, and you can top up the service as you go. The procedure is fairly straightforward – you dial a specified operator, quote your PIN number and then the number you wish to call. It's not always plain sailing though – sometimes lines are engaged or faulty and occasionally you may even be cut off.

Finally, note that **phones in hotel rooms** should be treated with caution, since rates for ringing from these are notoriously exorbitant (if you use a calling card you shouldn't be charged, although hotel staff don't always understand the system or might try to impose a surcharge). In dire emergencies you can always attempt a **collect (reverse-charge) call** (*llamada a cobrar*) through the international operator, and in some cases it may actually be cheaper to pay for the call when you arrive home than dialling directly from Latin America. Collect/reverse-charge calls can be made from telephone centres, the street or your hotel, although the country you're calling from will need to have a reciprocal agreement with the country you're phoning, and these don't always exist.

## Post

Unlike an email, a **letter or postcard** can be written anywhere and is a great way of whiling away long evenings. Postal services in Latin America are fairly reliable but slow (up to three weeks to Europe and longer to Australasia, although post to the US usually arrives within a week): always send letters airmail.

There aren't many **mailboxes** in Latin America; it's easiest to send mail from post offices. It's also best not to post mail from remote areas, where it may be collected only sporadically; wait instead until you reach a big town or city where post is sorted every day – your post home might arrive weeks earlier as a result. Stamps (*estampillas* in Spanish or *sellos* in Brazil) are available in general stores as well as post offices and are relatively expensive.

If you're having letters sent to you via **poste restante**, you can collect them at any post office: mail should bear your name followed by the words "Lista de Correos" (Posta Restante in Brazil; General Delivery in Belize), Correo Centrale, and then the town and country name. Every main post office will have a Lista de Correos section where they keep mail for at least a month. Letters are often filed erratically, however: ask the clerk to check under both your first name and surname. You'll have to present some form of ID (preferably your passport) when collecting post, and in some countries you'll also have to pay a small fee. It's also possible to pick up post from American Express offices – all big Latin American cities have them – though in theory you should be using an Amex credit card or travellers' cheques to qualify for this service. In practice this is often not necessary, though you might then be charged a few dollars to collect your post.

While letters usually get through safely, **packages** are likely to be tampered with or go missing – it's best to avoid having these sent to you at all via national postal networks. If you really need something sent to you, use a worldwide courier service (see below). To send a parcel, you'll need to find a large central post office, preferably in a capital city, where there'll be a special section. Take the contents of your parcel unwrapped – they'll have to be inspected by a customs official and you may then have to wrap them a certain way. Fortunately, all the materials necessary will be conveniently on sale, either in the post office or on the streets outside. Be aware, though, that parcels leaving Latin America are equally prone to disappear.

Alternatively, you can send anything home via an international **courier** company – both Fedex and DHL have offices all over Latin America and offer an expensive but efficient service. In some very touristy places, such as Antigua in Guatemala or San Miguel de Allende in Mexico, **private shipping companies** exist who will send home your souvenirs safely – for a price.

# The media

As well as speaking or writing to your friends and family you might want to know what is happening in the news back home. If you're from North America, keeping in touch with the news is relatively easy, particularly in Mexico and Central America. Europeans and Australasians, however, may have a hard time finding newspapers and TV stations carrying news from home.

The most commonly found **foreign newspapers** in Latin America are all from the US and include the *Miami Herald*, the *International Herald Tribune* and the *New York Times*, which can be bought at newsstands in capital cities throughout Latin America. The news magazines *Time* and *Newsweek* and *The Economist* are also widely available, though expensive. If you're really desperate to know the news you're better off logging onto the website of your favourite newspaper back home. Alternatively, foreign embassies and consulates sometimes keep newspapers and magazines which you can go in and read.

Most countries also have an **English-language weekly** of some kind, usually found in capital cities and places with large expat communities who provide a ready market for English-language news, as well as contributing articles and columns. These papers tend to concentrate on local community issues and have little foreign news. The *Mexico City Times* is a notable exception and includes pieces extracted from the *New York Times* and the UK's *Independent* and *Guardian*. The Cuzco-based weekly, *New World News*, is also good, with news gathered from the whole of South America as well as the rest of the world.

If your Spanish or Portuguese is up to it, you could try reading **national newspapers**, some of which are very decent, with foreign reportage, serious political analysis and commentary. The *Buenos Aires Herald*, the *Folha de São Paulo* and Mexico's *La Jornada* are some of the best-regarded Latin American papers.

**Television** is something of an obsession in Latin America, and increasingly numbers of Latin Americans are now subscribing to North American cable and satellite services, meaning that if you have a TV in your hotel room you'll probably have access to CNN, at the very least. In backpacker centres and big resorts you'll also find bars with sports channels, MTV and (if they're run by Europeans) the international BBC news channel, all in English.

**Radio** is also a good way of keeping up with news from home via the Voice of America or the BBC World Service, but you'll need a good shortwave radio to pick them up. It's also worth checking out frequencies in advance, since these change with baffling rapidity from region to region and at different times of the day.

# 13

# Crime, safety and sleaze

From what you read about Latin America in newspapers back home, it's easy to get the impression that the entire region is dominated by earthquakes, floods, violent crime, drug-trafficking and civil disorder. In reality, although such problems do exist, they're unlikely to affect you – instead, you're much more likely to experience more mundane hassles like petty theft and con-tricks of one kind or another. The information in this chapter should help you avoid the pitfalls that await the unwary and ensure you join the great majority of those who visit Latin America without experiencing any problems with crime or personal safety.

It's worth reiterating that on no account should you set foot in Latin America without adequate insurance; see pp.134–37 for more information on this.

## Avoiding trouble

In most of Latin America the threat of crime is not that much greater than in North America or Europe. The difference is that, whereas back home you blend in and can spot potential danger signs much more easily, in Latin America you probably stand out like a sore thumb – a very wealthy sore thumb, moreover, at least in the eyes of most Latin Americans. The most important rule is not to suspend the instincts that keep you safe at home. It's better to become slightly paranoid than to wander around oblivious to potential dangers: just because you're on holiday, it doesn't mean the crooks are. Once you get used to local cultural norms and, ideally, pick up some of the local language, you'll find you can judge whether or not to trust people just as effectively as you can at home. Latin Americans aren't all angels, but they're not all villains either, and you shouldn't let one bad encounter put you off the entire population.

It's also important to **stay informed**. Supplement what's in your guidebook with up-to-date information from newspapers, magazines and websites. Natural disasters, civil wars and the like don't make it into the pages of guidebooks until months or years after the event, but they'll be all over the international news media within hours. Travellers' newsgroups and bulletin boards on the internet are also an excellent resource (see pp.330–31 for a list of some of the most useful), and most governments have a department to advise on safety abroad (see p.328) – contact them or check their website to find out the current situation in countries you're planning to visit. In the event of an emergency while you're travelling, contact your nearest embassy or consulate (see pp.304–5 for details on how they can help you); the address should be listed in your guidebook. It's important to keep such information in perspective, however. If you hear about a guerrilla uprising or natural disaster in a country you're about to visit, be sure to check it out, but be aware that the problem may well be limited to a remote region hundreds of kilometres from anywhere you're intending to go – an outbreak of fighting in the southern Mexican state of Chiapas, for example, isn't going to affect your plans for a beach holiday in Cancún.

Once you're travelling, always heed **advice** from locals and other travellers, whether it's about a region affected by bandits, an area of a city affected by crime, a hotel where rooms are frequently robbed or a dodgy tour company. Such advice is often much more reliable and up-to-date than what's in your guidebook, though always be aware that some locals may themselves have an ulterior motive – telling you that a hotel has closed down, for instance, and directing you to their cousin's place instead.

# Passports

In most Latin American countries you are legally required to carry your **passport** with you at all times; failure to produce identification when asked for by a policeman can result in arrest or lay you open to a bribe. A photocopy of the personalized pages of your passport makes it easier to replace if lost or stolen, and in some countries you can have the copy authorized by a public notary for use as a temporary form of identification if you leave your passport in safe-keeping. If you're staying in the same country for a while, consider registering with your embassy; this can also save lots of time if you have to replace a lost or stolen passport.

# Theft

Opportunistic **theft** of one kind or another is the most common crime tourists face. More often than not it's simply the result of carelessness, and by using common sense, staying alert and taking some simple precautions you can greatly reduce the chances of becoming a victim. The following guidelines should help reduce your chances of being robbed – or make it easier to deal with the consequences if you are.

- Keep a separate stash of emergency cash hidden some-

## A trained eye

Travelling through Bolivia in a freezing cold, uncomfortable, third-class train carriage, we slept intermittently, marking time by the stations that came and went, and with them encounters with the local kids – burnt cheeks, snotty noses and matted pigtails. We bought alpaca bobble-hats and traded pens and fruit for photos. Finally, we pulled into Oruro, our final destination, 37 long hours after our journey began. As happened at every other station, our arrival caused widespread excitement and much clambering on and off the train. In retrospect the clambering on should have seemed strange, as this was where the train terminated. But so eager were we to get off the train that the constant watch over our bags faltered for a brief moment and my daysack was whipped away in the fervour. As quickly as it happened – whilst I was hoisting my large rucksack on my back – all three of us leaped off the train and scoured the crowded platform. On the advice of a local man I rushed outside and in my best Spanish yelled at all departing taxis to stop and please open their boots. Needless to say the next few hours were spent in the police station making a report of the theft. I didn't lose my passport, tickets, money or travellers' cheques as they were tucked away in an under-garment money belt, but I did lose letters and photos, which to me were priceless. I did learn from the experience, though – sometimes it's worth paying a bit more to get some sleep and arrive in a new place with your wits about you.

Claire Southern

where about your person for use if your main money belt gets stolen.

- Make a careful note of your plane ticket numbers, the phone numbers you'll need if you have to cancel your credit cards, travellers' cheque numbers (always keep the purchase receipt separately) and insurance details, and keep all these separate from your valuables.

- Carry money, credit cards and vital documents like your passport and airline ticket close to your body and concealed under your clothes at all times. Money belts (see p.187) are good for this, but you can also buy secure wallets that hang under your shirt or from a loop on your belt under your trousers; a hidden pocket sewn inside your trousers, a leg pouch or a belt with a secret zip for cash are even more difficult for thieves to find. Some Latin American women hide cash inside their bras.

- Keep your day's cash separate from your main stash, so your hidden money belt isn't revealed every time you buy a cup of coffee. It's also good to have some cash to hand over in case of armed robbery, so the muggers don't start looking for your main money belt.

- You are at your most vulnerable, and have the most to lose, when you're on the move or arriving in a new town and have all your luggage with you. Bus stations are a favourite hunting ground of thieves the world over: try not to arrive after dark, keep a close eye and hand on your bags at all times, and consider taking a taxi from the bus terminal to your hotel as a security precaution.

- Mugging and violent robbery usually occur at night, so try to avoid having to walk down empty or poorly lit streets in the early hours, particularly on your own. ATMs are an obvious target for robbers – don't use them at night, if possible. If the robbers are armed, do not resist.

- Unless you travel very light, when moving around by bus or train you'll often have to put your backpack into a luggage compartment or on the roof. This is usually safe, and some bus companies will give you a baggage reclaim ticket, but it's still worth keeping an eye out when the vehicle stops to make sure no one carries your bag off either by mistake or on purpose. It's also worth covering your backpack with a sack (available in any market) to make it less conspicuous – though mark it so you can distinguish it from others.

- Some travellers like to chain their bags together or onto an immovable object when waiting around transport terminals, and onto the roof of the bus or train luggage rack when travelling. You can also buy lockable lightweight metal meshes to fit over your pack for extra security – though this may be a little excessive.

- Transport terminals, markets, city centres, fiestas and other crowded public places are favoured by pickpockets and thieves. If you're carrying a daypack, keep it in front of you where you can see it to avoid having it slashed; when you stop and sit down, loop a strap around your leg to make it more difficult for someone to grab.
- Better hotels often have a safe or strongbox at reception where you can deposit valuables. This is usually safe, though it's best to leave stuff in a tamper-proof holder (anything with zips which can be padlocked will do) or a signed and sealed envelope. In addition, make sure you get an itemized receipt for whatever you leave, and count cash carefully before and after. Leaving credit cards isn't a good idea – you may return home to find your card has been used up to its limit while you were off on an expedition and you thought it was safely locked away.
- A small padlock is useful for replacing or supplementing the one on your hotel room door if you're worried about security.
- Never leave cameras or other valuables lying around in your hotel room, and be cautious if sharing a room with people you don't know well – other travellers can be thieves too.
- Never leave valuables on the beach when you swim. Most travel shops sell waterproof canisters which you can wear in the water; alternatively, just take enough cash for your immediate needs and keep it in a small plastic bag in a pocket in your swimming trunks or tucked into your swimsuit.
- Don't flaunt your wealth. Avoid wearing expensive jewellery, use a cheap watch and carry your camera concealed in your daypack rather than round your neck.
- Never carry important stuff in the pockets of your backpack: they're especially vulnerable to theft. You can always carry a small daypack on your front where you can see it.
- Beware of accepting food, drink or cigarettes from fellow passengers on journeys. Some thieves use these to drug their victims, making off with everything they own while they sleep it off. A variant on this, found particularly in Colombia, involves the use of a substance called Burundanga, which can make victims susceptible to hypnotic suggestion. Rather than just rob you, thieves may take you to a bank to withdraw cash on your credit card, or worse. When you come to hours or days later, you may have no recollection at all of what has happened.
- Though usually safer than walking, taxis can also carry an element of risk, since they're usually poorly regulated and drivers can be criminals too. If travelling alone, don't sit in the front seat, where you're vulnerable to attack from behind, lock passenger doors to

stop people jumping in beside you, and be wary of cabs driving away with your bags – if your luggage is in the boot, wait for the driver to get out first. Where possible, it's better to order a cab by phone rather than flagging one down in the street.

● Don't automatically trust other travellers – a small minority fund their travels by ripping off others.

● Some travellers are tempted to make false claims of theft so as to claim money from insurance companies for items that have not, in fact, been lost. As well as being a criminal offence back home, fraudulent insurance claims can get you in a lot of trouble in Latin America. In popular tourist areas local police are often wise to this scam, and may well march you round to your hotel room to find your "stolen" camera.

## Common scams

The common scams practised on tourists in Latin America change, evolve and become ever more elaborate, but never really go away. The best source of information about all the latest cheats and tricks is other travellers, so talk to other people on the road and learn from their mistakes. Here are a few classic scams you should watch out for:

● Thieves pose as plainclothes police officers, complete with fake documents, and ask to see your documents or check for fake currency, often calling on a "passer-by" (read accomplice) to verify their identity. Don't show them your valuables or get in a car with them, and insist on going to a genuine police station.

● Criminals pose as tour guides with the intention of robbing and/or raping you once they get you out in the middle of nowhere. Only go on trips with reputable tour companies and – particularly for trips to remote areas – with other travellers you trust.

● Your bag or clothing is mysteriously sprayed with mustard or the like. A "friendly passer-by" points this out and offers to help you clean it while his accomplice (who sprayed it there in the first place) picks your pockets or grabs your bag. If you are sprayed, walk away quickly and refuse his or her "help" – you can always clean up later.

● Something valuable – cash, a credit card – is dropped at your feet. A passer-by spots it and asks you to check your wallet to see if it's yours, or offers to share it with you. The story ends either with your own money disappearing by sleight of hand or with you being accused of theft. Ignore anything dropped at your feet and walk away as quickly as possible.

- Someone asks you to carry a package or letter to their friend or relative in another town or country – they may be smugglers and the contents could well be drugs. With this in mind, don't carry packages for other people.

- Some street moneychangers are adept at ripping you off by sleight of hand while counting notes, or of passing you forged notes; some even have specially rigged calculators. If you can, change money or travellers' cheques at a bank or *casa de cambio* – rates aren't much different these days anyway.

# Hazards of nature

Latin America is home to pretty much the full range of dangerous natural phenomena, including lava-spewing volcanoes, catastrophic floods, landslides and earthquakes, not to mention deadly venomous snakes. However scary these might all sound, the chance of you experiencing any of them is remote.

If you're the sort of person who likes to prepare for any eventuality, *The Worst Case Scenario Survival Handbook*, by Joshua Piven and David Borgenicht, has detailed tips on everything from surviving a shark attack to wrestling an alligator.

## Earthquakes and volcanoes

The western edge of Central and South America runs along the Pacific Rim, at the meeting point of two of the earth's major tectonic plates, meaning that it experiences an unusually high level of volcanic and seismic activity. El Salvador, Colombia, Mexico and Peru have all experienced major **earthquakes** in recent decades, while the capitals of both Mexico and Ecuador, as well as many smaller cities and towns in the region, live in the shadow of highly active **volcanoes**. Seismologists are notoriously poor at predicting when earthquakes will strike, and while major volcanic eruptions are usually detectable some time in advance – and you should check the state of alert before travelling near active volcanoes – they can also strike with frightening suddenness. Realistically, however, the chances of you being caught up in a major natural disaster are very small.

If you are unlucky enough to be caught in a major earthquake, it's best to stay inside unless you're close to a large open space, as falling debris from buildings is a major cause of fatalities. Stay away from windows to avoid splintering glass, and shelter under a doorway or strong table if the building looks like it might collapse. Although phone lines are usually damaged by major quakes, try to contact friends or relatives at home as soon as possible to let them know you're safe.

## Hurricanes and floods

The **hurricane** season in Mexico and Central America runs from roughly October to November and affects both the Atlantic and (to a lesser extent) Pacific coasts. Hurricanes are usually predicted well in advance (you can check the latest forecasts in the local media or on the US National Hurricane Center website at ⓦwww.nhc.noaa.gov), but they can change course fairly quickly. If you're in the path of a hurricane, get out of the area if you can. If you can't, stay indoors away from windows, preferably on high ground to avoid the risk of flooding, taking plenty of food and water with you. As well as loss of life, hurricanes can cause massive damage to transport and other infrastructure, and drinking water may become contaminated: if a region you're planning to visit is hit by a major hurricane, think seriously about revising your itinerary.

Hurricanes often cause substantial **flooding**, which can also occur following heavy rain anywhere throughout tropical Latin America. Flooding in mountainous regions often wipes out bridges and causes landslides which block roads. Never camp in creeks or dry riverbeds in mountainous areas, as sudden rain can bring devastating flash floods. In addition, don't camp on small islands in rivers in rainforest regions like the Amazon, and be wary of camping on river beaches, as water levels can rise very quickly, even if it isn't raining where you are.

## Snakes and other dangerous creatures

The chances of encountering venomous **snakes** – such as the lethal and aggressive bushmaster, which uses infrared vision to track its prey – is obviously greater in, say, the Amazonian rainforest than in most places back home (the same goes for other dangerous creatures like spiders and scorpions). But though the thought of a snake in your sleeping bag or a tarantula in your trousers might make you wish you never thought of visiting Latin America, in reality you're highly unlikely to suffer anything worse than a few mosquito bites, especially if you listen to local advice and take sensible precautions.

- Trek with local guides who know the terrain and potential hazards.
- Give snakes a wide birth, and don't ever antagonize them. Most snakes are usually as scared of you as you are of them, and they tend to avoid humans as far as possible, although they will strike if they feel threatened. Wearing thick boots and long trousers, watching where you step and making plenty of noise all reduce the chances of getting bitten.
- If you are bitten by a snake, the chances are it won't have injected enough venom to be dangerous, so try to remain calm. Clean the wound, immobilize the limb and avoid all movement to slow the progress of any venom through your bloodstream, and seek medical help immediately. If possible, kill the snake for identification.
- Shake your shoes or boots out every morning: spiders and, especially, scorpions sometimes sleep inside. It's also a good idea to look before you place your hand on the ground or a branch in outdoor areas – arachnids won't look to attack you, but if you disturb or threaten them they will bite or sting, and some species are extremely dangerous.
- Though fairly rare, rabies does exist in Latin America and does kill people, so give dogs a wide berth. Even if not rabid, dogs are often aggressive and can be dangerous, though you can usually dissuade them from matching their bark with a bite by waving a stick or throwing a few stones in their general direction (for more on rabies see p.267).

## Hazardous activities

Activities like whitewater rafting, kayaking, mountain climbing, and skiing are not known as **dangerous sports** for nothing, and though the degree of risk is minimal, safety standards in Latin America are not generally as high as they are back home. Many of the companies that offer such activities may not even be licensed or insured, their "expert" guides may not be properly trained, and their equipment may be shoddy or even dangerous. Don't suspend your usual criteria for judging danger just because you're travelling, check your insurance covers you for specific activities before you undertake them, and always go with a recommended and reputable company, even if it means paying more – dangerous sports are one area where it's really not a good idea to go for the cheapest option.

## Swimming

**Swimming** in the sea can be hazardous due to sharks, poisonous creatures such as sea snakes and jellyfish, heavy surf that can batter you unconscious, and dangerous currents that can drag you out to sea (riptides) or drag you under the water (undertows). Only the most popular resort beaches have lifeguards, so if you do get into difficulties in the water you shouldn't count on getting rescued, so it's best to exercise caution before going for a swim. The best guide is to ask locals whether it's safe to swim before getting in the water: if no one else is swimming, you should definitely ask why before doing so yourself. **Riptides** are formed when two currents running parallel to the shore meet, forcing one current out to sea in a powerful stream. They are usually found on beaches with heavy surf or near river estuaries. Some are permanent, while others "migrate" up and down the beach. If you get caught in one and find yourself being dragged out to sea, don't panic or exhaust yourself by trying to fight it and swim back to shore. Instead, try to attract the attention of people on land, and when the current slackens after taking you away from the shore, swim back in at a 45-degree angle so as to avoid being caught in the current again. **Undertows**, which drag you beneath the surface of the water, are more difficult to escape: the best thing is to avoid getting in the water in the first place, so always check if the beach is safe before swimming. The same goes for **dangerous sea creatures** such as sharks and jellyfish: ask local people if it is safe to swim before getting in the water, and get out quick if you see a shark or other hazard.

Swimming in freshwater can also be hazardous. River and lake currents can be deceptive, while buoyancy in fresh water is less than in saltwater – a dangerous combination that increases the risk of drowning. **Piranha fish**, found in tropical South American rivers, are far less dangerous than books and films would have you believe (most eat fruit rather than humans), but they pack a painful bite and do sometimes attack in shoals, especially when concentrated in small pools at the end of the dry season, or if their victim is already bleeding. **Cayman crocodiles** rarely attack humans, but you should still avoid swimming in waters where they are present. Other freshwater hazards include **electric eels**, which pack a powerful shock equivalent to 500 volts, and the infamous **candiru**, a small, parasitic eel-like fish with a penchant for swimming up the urethra to feed on blood and lodging there using its sharp barbs, an extremely painful – and even fatal – condition which can only be cured by surgery; always wear swimming trunks or a costume and don't urinate in the water while swimming. Always check with locals before swimming in tropical rivers and lakes. Freshwater **stingrays** also pose a risk, so wear shoes or boots and probe sandy riverbeds with a stick before wading across them. Finally, though many of the **volcanic hotsprings** scattered around Latin America are safe to bathe in, it's always a good idea to check the temperature before plunging in, as this can vary from day to day, and some unfortunate travellers have been badly scalded by springs which were generally considered perfectly safe.

## Guerrillas, bandits and civil unrest

Until the early 1990s, many countries in Latin America were riven by bloody **civil wars** and other armed conflicts, usually between Marxist guerrillas and oppressive military regimes. Fortunately, most of these have now been resolved, and democracy (albeit often of a limited kind) is now the rule across the region. A notable exception to all this is **Colombia**, large areas of which remain off-limits to travellers because of ever-fiercer fighting – the risk of being kidnapped or caught in the crossfire between left-wing rebels, right-wing paramilitaries and the security forces is very real. Research the current situation carefully before visiting Colombia, and take local advice on which areas are safe when there. This conflict sometimes spills over into the border areas of neighbouring countries, and the Darién Gap between Colombia and Panamá in particular should be avoided. Some remote parts of **Peru** are still off-limits because of the presence of remnant bands of the Shining Path (*Sendero Luminoso*) rebel group, and parts of the southern Mexican state of **Chiapas**, where the stand-off between the Zapatista rebels and the Mexican army continues, should also be avoided.

The end of the region's armed conflicts has left many countries awash with arms and with former combatants who have few prospects and little to lose; some of these have turned to **banditry** (itself a long-standing Latin American tradition), holding up cars and buses on isolated roads. However, this is usually confined to very localized areas and the risk of encountering bandits is small, and can be further reduced by taking local advice on which regions or roads are dangerous and avoiding travelling by night where possible.

Though the era of armed conflicts and brutal dictatorships has largely passed, many Latin American countries – including in recent years Argentina, Peru, Bolivia, Ecuador, Venezuela, Nicaragua and Guatemala – are still subject to periods of serious **political and economic upheaval**. This very much goes with the territory in Latin America, and will

## A revolutionary encounter

Being pulled over at impromptu police and military road blocks is not an uncommon experience when travelling by road in Colombia, but it was only after the bus drew to a halt that I realized that the armed figures in camouflaged fatigues that had emerged from the forest on either side of the road were not members of the security forces but battle-hardened guerrillas from the ELN – the National Liberation Army. Fears of kidnap, robbery or worse immediately flashed through my mind, but to my surprise we were instead treated to a long speech on Colombian politics, Marxist theory and the justifications for armed struggle, delivered by an earnest young woman carrying an assault rifle. She ended by asking for donations to the revolutionary cause, an invitation that in the circumstances seemed foolish to refuse. Along with the other passengers, I handed over the equivalent of a few dollars. The bus moved on, and for weeks to come I was able to entertain other backpackers with the story of my brush with the guerrillas, turning what was probably a lucky escape into an archetypal Latin American travellers' tale.

James Read

usually have little effect on your travel plans, though strikes, roadblocks or protests can sometimes paralyse cities or entire countries, so it's worth keeping an eye on local and international news sources (check ⓦwww.bbc.co.uk or ⓦwww.cnn.com). It's best to steer clear of political demonstrations: these can spiral out of control very quickly and police responses are often extreme. Elections, too, sometimes involve considerable tension, and even when they don't, extra security measures and travel restrictions may prove a problem. If you get caught up in any major political upheaval it's best to sit tight in your hotel and wait until things blow over – everything's likely to be shut anyway.

You should also be wary of **discussing politics** in public and with strangers, as tempers can get very heated, and be cautious about getting directly involved in local politics – a recent vogue for so-called "guerrilla tourism" in the southern Mexican state of Chiapas has seen many young travellers expelled from the country.

## Sexual harassment

Though it varies in degree between countries and regions (it's generally weaker in areas where indigenous culture is strong) **machismo** – the cultural stereotype that characterizes women as weak and submissive, and men as strong and dominant – is alive and well in Latin America, and attitudes to gender equality and the rights of women are a long way behind those you're probably used to at home. Under traditional machismo stereotypes, women are viewed either as virgins or whores – foreign women in particular are widely considered to fall into the latter camp, an attitude which is reinforced by films and magazines. The local perception of female travellers is often one of sexual availability and promiscuity (the very fact that you have the freedom to travel the world is seen as confirming this), so as a female traveller you're likely to face some degree of verbal or physical harassment, something many Latin American women suffer from as well. Having said that, most female travellers to Latin America don't experience any serious problems, even when travelling alone, and if you rely on the instincts you use to avoid sexual harassment at home, you should be able to prevent it from spoiling your trip. The following tips may help:

- Exercise at least the same degree of caution as you do at home: don't walk alone down dark streets at night; avoid hiking or camping alone or in small groups; avoid taking taxis alone at night and, if you do, try to call a radio taxi rather than flag one down on the street.
- Always carry enough cash on you in case you need to take a taxi back to your hotel.
- Make sure your hotel room is secure, taking care to check door and window locks. You may want to use your own padlock.
- Harassment usually takes the form of whistling or cat-calling: the best way to deal with it is to ignore it.
- Be aware of the different interpretations that may be placed on your behaviour in Latin America: what may pass for simple flirta-

tion or even just friendly conversation back home may be seen as a direct come-on by Latin American men.

- Be assertive: if you find yourself the subject of unwanted male attention don't be afraid to politely but firmly tell them where to go. Men who grope or harrass you can be shamed into leaving you alone if you draw public attention to their actions.
- Observe how local women dress. While skimpy bikinis and figure-hugging lycra may be all the rage in some coastal resorts, in remote areas they can cause deep offence and may even get you chased out of town.
- Many Latin American bars are pretty much men-only and should be avoided: if you want to go out for a drink, choose more upmarket places or those frequented by other travellers.
- If you're not married, invent a mythical husband: some unmarried women travellers wear a wedding ring to ward off potential pests.
- Don't automatically trust male travellers just because of cultural familiarity or shared language.
- Remember that sexual harassment can work both ways: many men can feel extremely uncomfortable with the direct approach of Latin American prostitutes in some areas. Latin American attitudes to homosexuality are also generally conservative. Though some countries (especially Brazil) and cities have thriving gay communities, in much of the region homosexuality is frowned upon and kept under wraps. Gay travellers are unlikely to suffer any direct abuse, but it's best to be discreet and avoid public displays of affection.

# Drugs

The production and trafficking of illegal **drugs** – particularly cocaine, but also marijuana and heroin – is a major industry in many countries in Latin America, and despite what governments in the region would have you believe, local consumption is also on the increase. However, though drugs are widely available in many areas, penalties for possession – never mind trafficking – are very severe. Under heavy pressure from the US to stamp out the drug trade, local authorities are particularly happy to throw the book at foreign offenders, and being caught with even small amounts of an illegal substance can get you a long sentence in a Latin American jail, as many travellers have found to their cost.

If this doesn't put you off, be warned that in tourist areas, set-ups by dealers and the police are commonly used as a way of extorting money from unwary travellers. Areas where drugs are produced – particularly the coca-growing regions of Bolivia, Colombia and Peru – should be given a wide birth, as you're likely to be taken either for a trafficker or a foreign drug-enforcement agent. Coca leaf itself – the raw material from which cocaine is produced – is legal in Peru and Bolivia, where it has been used for thousands of years by local indigenous people as a mild stimulant and a key ingredient in traditional rituals and medicine (it's also used to make a herbal tea which is useful in combating altitude sickness). It's illegal in other Latin American countries and the rest of the world, however, so if you buy some be sure to get rid of it before you cross any borders or get on a plane home.

# Corruption and the police

In general, the **police** rarely trouble tourists, and with any luck, your contact with them will be limited to frontiers and road checkpoints. Even so, it's important to be polite in any dealings you have with them, as they can easily make problems for you if you're not. Bear in

## Official encounters

We drove slowly to the gate marking the border of Mexico, and stopped at the fumigation office. While I fended off the moneychangers, a man sprayed the car inside and out. When the fumes subsided, the border gate was lifted, and we entered Guatemala. We pulled over and went into the immigration office. The border officials were amazingly friendly. They took our information, stamped our passports, and we handed over 30 pesos (just over US$3), laughing as we recalled horror stories we'd read about having to bribe border officials with exorbitant amounts of cash. The customs officials were even friendlier. They looked in the car, fingered a few things, asked us what they were, and filled out a form or two.

An hour after we'd arrived at the border, we were on our way, still laughing about how nervous we had been. But we weren't in the clear yet. We began snaking our way along a valley set below incredible mountains, and not thirty minutes into Guatemala, we found ourselves driving behind a police vehicle. I saw someone in the back seat turn around and look at us, and seconds later the lights went on. "Oh please, not already," I thought. Sure enough, I saw a hand poke out of the passenger side window and motion for us to pull over. We did, and out of the vehicle came three policemen with enormous machine guns. I smiled my best "oh my god, look at those guns" smile, and said "Buenas tardes". "Buenos dias" they responded. Thinking that perhaps we'd entered a new time zone when we crossed the border, I asked them what time it was. They told me it was midday, and smiling, they said "Si, buenas tardes". Then they asked where we were from and where we were going, took a glance around the car, smiled again, and wished us a good trip. Even before they'd walked away, we began to laugh in disbelief – yet again. It seemed they just wanted to say hello!

Julie Feiner

mind that police officers are invariably armed, and may well shoot you if you run away from them. Anyone claiming to be an undercover policeman is probably a thief or confidence trickster (see p.294); don't get in a car with them or show them your documents or valuables, and insist on the presence of a uniformed officer. If you do need to contact the police, it's best to go to the **tourist police**, where they exist; they'll probably have a better understanding of your problem, and are more likely to speak English.

Latin American police are generally very poorly paid, and in many countries graft has become an accepted part of the job. It's not unusual to be offered an opportunity to **bribe** a policeman even if you've done nothing wrong. Often they're just trying it on, and there's no need to pay if you're innocent of any misdemeanour: refusing politely or acting like you don't understand is usually enough. In some circumstances, however, it can work to the advantage of both parties – if you've committed an offence, paying a small bribe is certainly preferable to going to jail. Beware of initiating a bribe unless you're very sure of your footing and speak the language reasonably well, however, as doing so can sometimes cause offence and make the situation worse; in Chile, for instance, the police have a scrupulous reputation for honesty and won't take kindly to being offered a bribe.

Corruption is by no means limited to the police: throughout much of Latin America it's very much a normal part of everyday life that involves everyone from presidents down to minor officials – there may be times when you're invited to pay a bribe or a "tip" to ensure you get a seat on that plane or get through border formalities without hassle·or delays. Once again, there's no need to pay if you don't want to – asking for a receipt is a good way of avoiding irregular payments to officials – but there may be occasions when it's easier just to hand over a small sum and be on your way. If you choose to do so, however, bear in mind that you're oiling the wheels of a system that many Latin Americans feel is one of the main causes of the region's poverty and under-development (even as they themselves pay up).

# If disaster strikes

If disaster strikes and you're robbed or find yourself in trouble with the authorities, your embassy or consulate abroad can:

- Issue emergency passports – having a photocopy of the original will speed this up immediately.
- Contact friends and family and ask them for help with money or tickets.
- Put you in touch with local doctors and lawyers.
- Contact or visit you in prison.
- Inform next-of-kin in case of serious illness.
- Evacuate you from the country in the event of major political upheaval or civil war.

However, your embassy or consulate cannot:

- Give you money (though they may give an emergency loan under very strict criteria).
- Pay to fly you home, other than in very exceptional circumstances.
- Get you out of prison. You won't get much sympathy or help if you're on a drugs charge.

You may also need to:

- Contact the police if you have been the victim of a crime, and to get a written report for insurance purposes if you've been robbed.
- Contact your insurance company. You should carry your policy number and emergency contact details with you and leave a copy at home. Be aware of the procedures you

## In at the deep end

Matthew arrived in Bogotá shortly after his eighteenth birthday at the start of a nine-month circuit of South America with an overland tour truck company. He wasn't due to meet up with his group until the next morning, so he headed out onto the streets to do some sightseeing, revelling in the excitement of his first day in Latin America. Within minutes of stepping out of his hotel, however, he was held up at knife-point by a gang of youths. They took his passport, camera, travellers' cheques, daypack, even the jacket off his back. Deeply shocked, he returned to his hotel, wishing he'd never even thought of setting foot in what seemed a benighted continent. The next day, however, with the help of his tour guide, he was able to arrange a new passport and new travellers' cheques. He picked up a secondhand camera (probably stolen from some other tourist, he said) in the market, and replaced the jacket and bag with local equivalents during the course of his travels. When I met up with him months later in Peru, he said that while at the time the robbery had been frightening and deeply disheartening, on reflection he actually felt it had liberated him from much of his anxiety about travel in Latin America. Everything he'd lost that he hadn't been able to replace locally now seemed to him unnecessary encumbrances he was better off without. And once you've been robbed, he said, you realize it's not the end of the trip, much less the end of the world, so you don't live in fear of it happening again.

James Read

need to follow in the event of robbery or illness, as failure to do so could invalidate your claim. In the case of theft or loss of possessions, you can usually wait until you get home, but in the event of serious medical emergencies you'll need to contact your insurer promptly, especially if you need them to cover hospital or air-evacuation costs.

● Cancel your credit cards if they're stolen – make sure you have an international 24-hour hotline number for doing this. If your travellers' cheques are lost or stolen you'll need to contact the issuer with full details to order replacements.

# 14

# Coming home

E veryone expects to experience culture shock when they travel to Latin America, but culture shock works both ways, and after a long period away you may find returning home a surprisingly difficult transition to make. Even though it's initially exciting to be surrounded once again by familiar things and people, normal life back home may soon seem tedious and banal compared to the excitement of travel, and friends and relatives may not be able to relate to experiences of life on the road. You may find that your outlook on life has been transformed by your travels, even while those closest to you hope you've "got it out of your system" and are now ready to settle down. At worst, exchanging the freedom of travel and the joy of experiencing new things every day for the sometimes humdrum realities of work and life back home can be very depressing. Short of immediately setting off on further travels, there's no real antidote for the homecoming blues. However, the following tips should make it easier to cope with:

● Before you go away, try to set aside some money as your coming-home fund – returning home is bad enough, never mind doing so without a penny to your name.
● While you're still on the road make some plans – however basic – for the immediate future after you get home. Returning home with nothing to look forward to is the worst possible scenario;

having a job, university place or some other project lined up makes the transition much easier to deal with.

- Make sure you keep in touch with people back home who are important to you, so they're aware of your experiences and thoughts. That way, they won't be too surprised by how you may have changed while you've been away.

- Don't expect everyone at home to be enthralled by your traveller's tales and photographs. Some people may find your experiences boring or difficult to relate to, while others may simply feel envious that you've been off having an adventurous time while they've been stuck in the same old routine.

- Get in touch with other travellers you've met on the road, and with friends and relatives who've been travelling themselves: they will probably understand what you're going through and will be much more interested in hearing about your trip.

- Keep in touch with locals you've met during your travels, and send out those photos you promised them.

- If you live in a large city with a Latin American community, seek out their bars, restaurants and cultural events where you can relive some of your favourite experiences. Taking salsa classes, learning to cook some classic Latin American dishes, reading books and watching films about Latin America are also all good ways of keeping the experience alive.

- If the worse comes to the worst, start planning and saving money for your next trip. If that's not possible, remember Latin America will always be there, so you will be able to go back one day.

# Getting involved

However much you enjoy travelling in Latin America, the chances are you will have found some aspects of life there depressing and shocking, such as the extreme poverty faced by most of the population, the corruption and political oppression, the dearth of basic public services and lack of opportunities. You may also have been dismayed by the rate at which many of the beautiful natural environments you've experienced are being destroyed in the name of economic development. If so, getting involved with some of these issues when you return is a good way of maintaining your interest in Latin America; it's also a positive way of using your experiences and of making sense of all that you saw and did while you were there. The following are some of the major organizations which campaign about issues in Latin America and make a contribution towards tackling some of the problems you may feel strongly about.

- **Amnesty International** (🌐www.amnesty.org) Leading international human rights organization which publishes reports on political oppression in countries around the world, including many in Latin America. Their website has a huge amount of information (including much which governments would prefer you didn't see) as well as excellent links to other human rights-related sites.
- **Brazil Network** (🌐www.brazilnetwork.org) A London-based campaign group that provides information on social, environmental and cultural issues in Brazil that rarely make it into the mainstream media. They stage frequent cultural events and have a good website with a wide range of information on Brazil.
- **Greenpeace** (🌐www.greenpeace.org) An international environmental group best known for its dramatic direct-action protests, Greenpeace campaigns on many issues relevant to Latin America, including climate change, genetically modified crops, tropical rainforest conservation and biodiversity protection.
- **Latin America Bureau** (🌐www.lab.org.uk) London-based independent research and publishing organization working to broaden public understanding of issues of human rights and social and economic justice in Latin America and the Caribbean. Publishes a huge range of non-specialist books and is the main point of reference in the UK for people interested in Latin America, with a website full of information and a list of organizations sending voluntary workers to Latin America.
- **One World** (🌐www.oneworld.org) One of many international organizations campaigning for the cancellation of the crippling international debts of poor countries in Latin America and elsewhere. Their website has a plethora of information on Latin America, excellent links to other campaigning organizations, as well as lists of job vacancies and volunteering opportunities.
- **Rainforest action network** (🌐www.ran.org) International campaign network working to prevent rainforest destruction and protect the human rights of forest peoples, with a website full of information on Latin America's dwindling forests and links to other relevant sites.
- **Survival International** (🌐www.survival-international.org) Campaigns for the rights of tribal people all over the world and against governments, armies, corporations, banks, missionaries and anyone else who threatens their future.

# Making your trip work for you

After your travels you may be looking for work, either at home or overseas. Your prospects with future employers will be better if you can not only describe your trip as an enjoyable adventure but also show that you developed useful abilities or experiences while travelling. Doing some kind of voluntary work during part of your trip always looks good on a CV. Speaking Spanish or Portuguese is a valuable skill, so you might want to polish what you picked up while travelling by taking further language tuition.

In the longer term, your experiences in Latin America can help prepare you for work in the travel industry, either working for a travel agency at home or as a guide back in Latin America. To get work as a **tour guide** you'll need to speak pretty good Spanish and/or Portuguese and convince the tour operator that you have the necessary background knowledge, social skills and ability to take responsibility before they entrust a group of paying clients to your care. Look out for job adverts in the travel press and don't be afraid to approach tour operators if you think you've got what they need. When you are travelling you may well run into people working in the industry who you can ask about what the work is like, and what potential employers are looking for. Back home, travel fairs are a good place to find out more.

If you've taken good photographs or written about your travels you may be able to make some money out of it when you return, or even turn it into a career. If you want to **sell photos or travel stories**, it's worth having a good look at the kind of material different newspapers and magazines favour before you go. Unless you have good contacts or previously published work you're unlikely to elicit much interest before you set off on your trip, and you'll have to submit articles and photos to publications on spec when you get back. Obviously, travel magazines with small circulations or which are distributed free are much more likely to look at your work than national newspapers and major magazine titles. They don't pay much, but the first step is to get something into print, which you can then use to approach other publishers. In several Latin American countries there are small English-language newspapers which can be a good place to get your picture or stories published. Most national newspapers and travel magazines run annual travel-writing competitions for young people, which are an excellent way of getting into the industry – even if you don't win, a good entry can get you noticed and bring future commissions. Photographers are better off approaching picture agencies and libraries rather than magazines – remember, if you're hoping to sell your photos, you'll really need to take slides or high-resolution digital images rather than colour prints. Both travel writing and photography are difficult areas to break into, and even if you succeed you still may well struggle to make a living, but it's a big industry that always has room for new talent. Have a look at Guy Marks' very useful *Travel Writing and Photography, All You Need to Know to Make it Pay* or Louise Purwin Zobel's *The Travel Writers Handbook, How to Write and Sell Your Own Travel Experiences* for further advice.

# Basics

# National tourist offices

Many Latin American countries do not have a national tourist organization with overseas offices (often in the US only) – those that do are listed below. Unfortunately, information given by tourist offices abroad is generally not geared to independent travellers, particularly those on a budget – neither is it very imaginative nor always accurate. Most countries have an official tourism website which may prove more useful. Embassies and consulates (see pp.316–20) provide tourist information for those countries which do not have an overseas tourist organization. The website ⓦ www.towd.com is an online directory of tourist offices worldwide.

## Argentina

ⓦ www.turismo.gov.ar

US 12 West 56th St, New York, NY ☎ 212/603-0443; 5055 Wilshire Blvd, Suite 210, Los Angeles, CA ☎ 213/930-0681; 2655 Le Jeune Rd, Ph 1, Miami, FL ☎ 305/442-1366

## Belize

ⓦ www.travelbelize.org
US ☎ 1-800/624-0686 (toll-free)

## Bolivia

ⓦ www.bolivia-travel.gov.bo

## Brazil

ⓦ www.embratur.gov.br

## Chile

ⓦ www.segegob.cl
ⓦ www.visitchile.org
US 9700 South Dixie Hwy, Suite PH, Miami, FL 33156 ☎ 1-800/244-5366

## Costa Rica

ⓦ www.tourism-costarica.com
US and Canada Toll-free tourist information hotline (☎ 1-800/343-6332) which is answered by English-speaking ICT (Instituto Costarricense de Turismo) staff in San José.

## Ecuador

ⓦ www.vivecuador.com

## El Salvador

ⓦ www.elsalvadorturismo.gob.sv

## French Guiana

ⓦ www.guyanetourisme.com

## Guatemala

ⓦ www.guatemala.travel.com.gt

## Honduras

US 2100 Ponce de Leon Blvd, Suite 1175, Coral Gables, FL 33134 ☎ 1-800/410-9608

## Mexico

ⓦ www.mexico-travel.com
UK Wakefield House, 41 Trinity Square, London EC3N 4DJ ☎ 020/7488 9392
US and Canada ☎ 1-800/44-MEXICO

There are dozens of SECTUR or Secretaría de Turismo offices throughout the US and Canada – here are just some:

**US** 1911 Pennsylvania Ave NW, Washington DC 20006 ☎202/728-1750; 10100 Santa Monica Blvd, Suite 224, Los Angeles, CA 90067 ☎310/203-8191; 405 Park Ave, Suite 1401, New York, NY 10022 ☎212/755-7261

**Canada** 2 Bloor St W, Suite 1801, Toronto ON M4W 3E2 ☎416/925-0704; 999 Hastings St, Suite 1610, Vancouver BC V6C 1M3 ☎604/669-2845

### Nicaragua

🌐www.intur.gob.ni

### Panamá

🌐www.ipat.gob.pa

### Peru

🌐www.peru.org.pe

### Venezuela

**US** Box 3010, Sausalito, CA 94966 ☎415/331-0100

# Embassies and consulates

### Argentina

**UK and Ireland** Embassy: 65 Brook St, London W1Y 1YE ☎020/7318 1300
Consulate: 27 Three Kings Yard, London W1Y 1FL ☎020/7318 1340

**US** Embassy: 1600 New Hampshire Ave NW, Consular section, Washington DC 20009 ☎202/238-6400
Consulates: 5055 Wilshire Blvd, Office 210, Los Angeles, CA 90036 ☎323/954-9155
800 Brickell Ave, Penthouse 1, Miami FL 33131 ☎305/373-1889
12 West 56th St, New York City, NY 10019 ☎212/603-0400
plus others in Atlanta, Houston and Chicago

**Canada** 🌐www.argentina-canada .net
Consulates: 90 Sparks St, Suite 910, Ottawa, ON KIP 5B4

☎613/236-2351
2000 Peel St, 7th Floor, Suite 710, Montréal, Québec H3A 2W5
☎514/842-6582
1 First Canadian Place, Suite 5840, Toronto, ON M5X 1K2 ☎416/955-9075

**Australia** Consulate:
Goldfields House, Level 13, Suite 1302, 1 Alfred St, Sydney NSW 2001 ☎02/9251 3402

**New Zealand** Embassy: Level 14, 142 Lambton Quay, PO Box 5430, Wellington ☎4/4728 330

### Belize

🌐www.belize.gov.bz/diplomats.html

**UK** Belize High Commission, 22 Harcourt House, 19 Cavendish Square, London W1M 9AD ☎020/7499 9728

**US** Embassy of Belize, 2535 Massachusetts Ave NW,

Washington DC 20008 ☏202/232 9636

Canada Consulate: Suite 3800, South Tower, Royal Plaza, Toronto, ON M5J 2JP ☏416/865 7000 also Québec ☏514/871-4741 and Vancouver ☏604/730 1224

Australia and New Zealand Contact the British High Commission, which represents Belize in these countries

## Bolivia

UK 106 Eaton Square, London SW1W 9AD ☏020/7235 4248

US ⓦwww.bolivia-usa.org 3014 Massachusetts Ave NW, Washington DC 20008 ☏202/483-4410 Suite 702, 211 East 43rd St, New York, NY 10017 ☏212/499-7401

Canada Suite 416, 130 Albert St, Ottawa, ON KIP SG4 ☏613/236-5730

Australia Level 6, 74 Pitt St, Sydney NSW 2000 ☏02/9235 1858

## Brazil

UK and Ireland Embassy: 32 Green St, London W1Y 4AT ☏020/7499 0877 Consulates: 6 St Alban's St, London SW1Y 4SQ ☏020/7930 9055 Europa House, Harcourt Centre, Harcourt St, Dublin 2 ☏01/475 6000

US Embassy: 3006 Massachusetts Ave NW, Washington DC 20008 ☏202/238-270 Consulates: Boston ☏617/542-4000; Chicago ☏312/464-0244; Los Angeles ☏323/651-5833; Miami ☏305/285-6200; New York

☏212/777-7777; San Francisco ☏415/981-8170; Washington DC ☏202/238-2828

Canada Embassy: 450 Wilbroad St, Sandyhill, Ottawa, ON K1V 6M8 ☏613/237-1090 Consulates: Montréal ☏514/499-0968; Toronto ☏416/922-2503

Australia Embassy: 19 Forster Crescent, Yarralumla, Canberra, ACT 2600 ☏02/6273 2372 Consulate: 31 Market St, Sydney ☏02/9267 4414

## Chile

UK 12 Devonshire St, London W1N 2DS ☏020/7580 6392

US Embassy: 1732 Massachusetts Ave, Washington DC 20036 ☏202/785-1746 Consulates: Houston ☏713/963-9066; Chicago ☏312/654-8780; Miami ☏305/373-8623; New York ☏212/355-0612; San Francisco ☏415/982-7662

Canada Embassy: 50 Connor St #1413, Ottawa, ON K1P 6L2 ☏613/235-4402 Consulates: Toronto ☏416/924-0106; Montréal ☏514/499-0405; Vancouver ☏604/681-9162

Australia Embassy: 10 Culgoa Circuit, O'Malley, ACT 2606 ☏02/6286 2430 Consulate: Level 18, National Mutual Building, 44 Market Street, Sydney 2000 ☏02/9299 2533

New Zealand 19 Bolton St, Wellington ☏04/471 6270

## Colombia

UK Embassy: 3 Hans Crescent, London SW1X OLR ☏020/7589 9177

Consulate: 15–19 Great Titchfield St, London W1P 7FB ☎020/7637 9893.

US Embassy: 2118 Leroy Place NW, Washington DC 20008 ☎202/387-8338.
Consulates in Atlanta, Boston, Chicago, Houston, Los Angeles, Miami, New Orleans, New York, San Francisco.

Canada Embassy: 360 Albert St, Suite 1130, Ottawa, ON K1R 7X7 ☎613/230-3760.
Consulates in Montréal, Toronto, Vancouver.

Australia Embassy: 2nd floor, 101 Northbourne Ave, Canberra, PO Box 2892, ACT 2601 T02/6257 2027.
Consulate in Sydney.

New Zealand 10 Brandon St, Wool House, Level 11, Wellington ☎04/721 1080.

## Costa Rica

UK 14 Lancaster Gate, London W2 3LH ☎020/7562 2855.

US 2114 S St NW, Washington, DC 20008 ☎202/234-2945, ⓦwww.costa-embassy.org.

Canada 135 York St, Suite 208, Ottawa, ON K1N 5T4 ☎613/562-2855.

Australia 11/30 Clarence St, Sydney ☎02/9261 1177.

## Ecuador

UK Flat 3b, 3 Hans Crescent, London SW1X OLS ☎020/7584 1367.

Ireland 27 Library Rd, Dun Laoghaire, Dublin ☎01/280 5917.

US 2535 15th St NW, Washington DC 20009 ☎202/234-7200.

Canada 50 O'Connor St, Office 316,

Ottawa, ON K1P 6L2 ☎613/563-8206.

Australia 1st Floor, The Law Society Building, 11 London Circuit, Canberra, ACT 2601 ☎02/6262 5282.

New Zealand Ferry Building, 2nd Floor, Quay St, Auckland ☎09/377 4321.

## El Salvador

UK Tennyson House, 159 Great Portland St, London W1N 5FD ☎020/7436 8282.

US Embassy: 2308 Calif St NW, Washington, DC 20008 ☎202/387-6511.
Consulates: New York ☎212/889-3608; San Francisco ☎415/781-7924; Miami ☎305/371-8850.

Canada 151 Bloor St, West Suite 320, Toronto, M5S 1S4, ON ☎416/975-0812; Ottawa ☎613/238-2939; Montréal ☎514/861-6515.

## French Guiana

See French embassies:

UK 58 Knightsbridge, London SW1X 7JT ☎020/7073 1000.

US 4101 Reservoir Rd NW, Washington DC 2007 ☎202/944-6000.

Canada 42 Sussex Drive, Ottawa, ON K1M 2C9 ☎613/789-1795.

Australia 6 Perth Ave, Yarralumla, ACT 2600 ☎02/6216 0100.

New Zealand 1–3 Willeston St, Wellington ☎04/472 0200.

## Guatemala

UK 13 Fawcett St, London SW10 9HN ☎020/7351 3042.

US Embassy: 2220 R St NW, Washington DC 20008 ☎202/745-4952.
Consulates: Chicago ☎312/332-1587; Houston ☎713/953-9531; Los Angeles ☎213/365-9251; Miami ☎305/443-4828; New York ☎212/686-3837; San Diego ☎415/282-8127.

Canada 130 Albert St, Suite 1010, Ottawa, ON K1P 5G4 ☎613/233-7237.

Australia and New Zealand
Contact the embassy in Japan – ☎03/3800-1830.

## Guyana

UK 3 Palace Court, Bayswater Rd, London W2 4LP ☎020/7229 7684.

US Embassy: 2490 Tracy Place, Washington DC 20008 ☎212/527-3215.
Consulate: 866 United Nations Plaza, New York NY 10017 ☎212/527-3215.

Canada 151 Slater St, Suite 309, Ottawa, ON K1P 5H3 ☎613/235-7249.

## Honduras

UK 115 Gloucester Place, London W1H 3PJ ☎020/7486 4550.

US 3007 Tilden Street NW, Washington DC 20008 ☎202/966-7702.

Canada 151 Slater St, Suite 908A, Ottawa, ON KIP 5H3 ☎613/233-8900.

Australia 19/31 Pitt St, Sydney NSW 2000 ☎02/9252 3779.

## Mexico

UK 8 Halkin St, London SW1X 8QR ☎020/7235 6393
ⓦwww.mexicanconsulate.org.uk.

Ireland 43 Ailesbury Rd, Ballsbridge, Dublin 4 ☎01/260 0699.

US 1911 Pennysylvania Ave NW, Washington DC 20006 ☎202/728-1600 and in dozens of towns across the US.

Canada 45 O'Conner St, Suite 1500 Ottawa ON K1P 1A4 ☎613/233-8988; Montréal ☎514/288-2502; Toronto ☎416/368-2875; Vancouver ☎604/684-3547.

Australia 14 Perth Ave, Yarralumla, Canberra, ACT 2600 ☎02/6273 3963; Sydney ☎02/9326 1292.

New Zealand 111–115 Customhouse Quay, 8th floor, Wellington ☎04/472 5555.

## Nicaragua

UK Vicarage House, Suite 12, 58–60 Kensington Church St, London W8 4DB ☎020/7938 2373.

US 1627 New Hampshire Ave NW, Washington DC 20009 ☎202/939-6531.

Canada 130 Albert St, Suite 407, Ottawa, ON K1P 5G4 ☎613/234-9361.

## Panamá

UK 48 Park St, London W1Y 3PD ☎020/7493 4646.

US 2862 McGill Terrace NW, Washington DC 20008 ☎202/483-1407; consulates in Miami, New York, San Francisco.

Canada 130 Albert St, Suite 300, Ottawa, Ontario ON K1P ☎613/236-7177.

## Paraguay

UK Braemar Lodge, Cornwall Gardens, London SW7 4AQ ☎020/7937 6629

US 2400 Massachusetts Ave NW, Washington DC 20008 ☎202-483-6960.

Canada 151 Slater St, Suite 401, Ottawa, ON K1P 5H3 ☎613/567-1283.

Australia 107 Gloucester St, The Rocks, Sydney NSW Z000 ☎02/9241 1802.

## Peru

UK 52 Sloane St, London SW1X 9SP ☎020/7235 1917.

US Embassy: 1700 Massachusetts Ave NW, Washington DC 20036 ☎202/462-1084. Consulates: Chicago ☎312/853-6170; Houston ☎713/355-9517; Miami ☎305/374-1305; Los Angeles ☎213/252-5910; New York ☎212/481-7410.

Canada Embassy: 130 Albert St, Suite 901, Ottawa ON K1P 5G4 ☎613/238-1777. Consulate: 10 Mary St, Suite 301, Toronto, ON M4Y 1P9 ☎416/963-9696.

Australia Embassy: 40 Brisbane Ave, Barton, Canberra ☎02/6273-8752. Consulates: Melbourne ☎03/9725-4908; Sydney ☎02/9262-6464.

New Zealand Level Eight, Cigna

House, 40 Mercer St, Wellington ☎04/499-8087.

## Suriname

US 4301 Connecticut Ave NW, Suite 108, Washington DC 2008 ☎202/244-7488.

## Uruguay

UK 2nd Floor, 140 Brompton Rd, London SW3 1HY ☎020/7584 8192.

US 2715 M St, 3rd Floor, Washington DC 20007 ☎202/331-1313.

Canada 130 Albert St, Suite 1905, Ottawa, ON K1P 5G4 ☎613/234-2937.

Australia MLC Tower, Ist Floor, Suite 107, Woden, ACT 2606 ☎02/6282 4800.

## Venezuela

UK 56 Grafton Way, London W1P 5LB ☎020/7387 6727.

US 1099 30th St NW, Washington DC 20007 ☎202/342-2214.

Canada 32 Range Road, Ottawa ON K1N 8J4 ☎613/235-5151.

Australia 1st Floor, Suite 106, MCL Tower, Woden, ACT 2606 ☎02/6282 4827.

# Discount flight agents

## UK and Ireland

Apex Travel Republic of Ireland ☎01/671 5933, ⊛www.apextravel.ie. Specialists in flights to the US.

CIE Tours International Republic

of Ireland ☎01/703 1888, ⊛www.cietours.ie. General flight and tour agent.

Co-op Travel Care Northern Ireland ☎028/9047 1717, ☏028/471

339. Flights and holidays around the world.

**Destination Group** UK ☎020/7400 7000, 🌐www.destination-group.com. Good discount airfares.

**Flightbookers** UK ☎020/7757 2444, 🌐www.ebookers.com. Low fares on an extensive selection of scheduled flights.

**Flynow** UK ☎020/7835 2000, 🌐www.flynow.com. Large range of discounted tickets.

**Joe Walsh Tours** Republic of Ireland ☎01/872 2555 or 676 3053, 🌐www.joewalshtours.ie. General budget fares agent.

**Liffey Travel** Republic of Ireland ☎01/878 8322 or 878 8063. Package tour specialists.

**London Flight Centre** UK ☎020/7244 6411, 🌐www.topdeck-travel.co.uk. Long-established discount flight agent.

**North South Travel** UK ☎01245/608291, 🌐www.north-southtravel.co.uk. Friendly and competitive travel agency offering discounted fares worldwide – profits are used to support projects in the developing world, especially the promotion of sustainable tourism.

**Quest Worldwide** UK ☎020/8547 3322, 🌐www.questtravel.com. Specialists in RTW discount fares.

**STA Travel** UK ☎0870/160 6070, 🌐www.statravel.co.uk. Worldwide specialists in low-cost flights and tours for students and under-26s, though other customers are welcome.

**Trailfinders** UK ☎020/7628 7628, Republic of Ireland ☎01/677 7888, 🌐www.trailfinders.com. One of the best-informed and most efficient agents for independent travellers; they also produce a very useful quarterly magazine worth scrutinizing for RTW routes.

**Travel Cuts** UK ☎020/7255 2082, 🌐www.travelcuts.co.uk. Canadian company specializing in budget, student and youth travel and RTW tickets.

**USIT Now** Northern Ireland ☎028/9032 7111, Republic of Ireland ☎01/602 1777 or 677 8117, 🌐www.usitnow.ie. Student and youth specialists for flights and trains.

## US and Canada

**Air Brokers International** ☎1-800/883-3273 or 415/397-1383, 🌐www.airbrokers.com. Consolidator and specialists in RTW tickets.

**Airtech** ☎212/219-7000, 🌐www.airtech.com. Standby seat broker; also deals in consolidator fares.

**Council Travel** ☎1-800/226-8624 or 617/528-2091, 🌐www.counciltravel.com. Nationwide organization specializing in student and budget travel.

**Educational Travel Center** ☎1-800/747-5551 or 608/256-5551, 🌐www.edtrav.com. Student/youth discount agent.

**High Adventure Travel** ☎1-800/350-0612 or 415/912-5600, 🌐www.airtreks.com. Specialist in RTW tickets; their website features an interactive database.

**Skylink** US ☎1-800/AIR-ONLY or 212/573-8980, Canada ☎1-800/SKY-LINK. Consolidator.

**STA Travel** ☎1-800/777-0112 or 1-800/781-4040, 🌐www.sta-travel.com. Worldwide specialists in independent travel; also sell student ID, travel insurance, car rental and rail passes.

**TFI Tours International**
℡1-800/745-8000 or 212/736-1140. Consolidator.

**Travac** ℡1-800/872-8800, Ⓦwww.thetravelsite.com. Consolidator and charter broker.

**Travel Avenue** ℡1-800/333-3335, Ⓦwww.travelavenue.com. Discount travel agent.

**Travel Cuts** Canada ℡1-800/667-2887, US ℡416/979-2406. Canadian student travel organization.

**Travelers Advantage Cendent Membership Services, Inc** ℡1-877/259-2691, Ⓦwww.travelersadvantage.com. Discount travel club; three months' trial membership costs $1.

**Worldtek Travel** ℡1-800/243-1723, Ⓦwww.worldtrek.com. Discount travel agency for worldwide travel.

**Worldwide Discount Travel Club** ℡305/534-2642. Discount travel club.

## Australia and New Zealand

**Anywhere Travel** Australia ℡02/9663 0411 or 018/401014, anywhere@ozemail.com.au. Discount flight and travel agent.

**Budget Travel** New Zealand ℡09/366 0061 or 0800/808040. Discounted flights and packages.

**Destinations Unlimited** New Zealand ℡09/373 4033. Discount fares and tours.

**Flight Centres** Australia ℡02/9235 3522 (for your nearest branch call ℡13/1600), New Zealand ℡09/358 4310, Ⓦwww.flightcentre.com.au. Competitive discounts on air fares and holidays.

**Northern Gateway** Australia ℡08/8941 1394, oztravel@norgate.com.au. Discount fares and holidays.

**STA Travel** Australia ℡13/1776 or 1300/360960 Ⓦwww.statravel.com.au, New Zealand ℡09/379 3920, Ⓦwww.statravel.com.nz. Discount fares for students and under-26s.

**Student Uni Travel** Australia ℡02/9232 8444, Australia@backpackers.net. Student/youth discounts and travel advice.

**Thomas Cook** Australia ℡13/1771 or 1800/801002, New Zealand ℡09/379 3920, Ⓦwww.thomascook.com.au. Global travel agent.

**Trailfinders** Australia ℡02/9247 7666, Ⓦwww.trailfinders.com.au. Specializes in cheap flights.

**Usit Beyond** New Zealand ℡09/379 4224 or 0800/788 336, Ⓦwww.usitbeyond.co.nz. Student/youth travel specialists.

# Courier flight agencies

## UK

International Association of Air Travel Couriers ☎0800/0746 481 or 01395/216 920, ⓦwww.aircourier.co.uk

## US

Air Courier Association ☎800/282-1202,

ⓦwww.aircourier.org or ⓦwww.cheaptrips.com

International Association of Air Travel Couriers ☎352/475-1584, ⓦwww.courier.org

Now Voyager ☎212/459-1616, ⓦwww.nowvoyagertravel.com

# Specialist tour operators

## UK and Ireland

**Audley Latin America** ☎01869/276210, ⓦwww.audleytravel.com. Classy tailor-made trips.

**Austral Tours Ltd** ☎020/7233 5384, ⓦwww.latinamerica.co.uk. Tailor-made tours to South America, plus bird-watching, photography and trekking trips.

**Condor Journeys and Adventures** ☎01422/822068, ⓦwww.condorjourneys-adventures.com. Imaginative ecotourism company with dozens of different themed tours.

**Journey Latin America** ☎020/8747 3108, ⓦwww.journeylatinamerica.co.uk. Long-established specialists in flights, packages and interesting tailor-made trips to Latin America. Also organize Spanish-language course holidays.

**Pura Aventura** ☎01273/676712, ⓦwww.pura-aventura.com. Challenging small-group adventure

holidays in Chile, Mexico and Nicaragua.

**Reef and Rainforest Tours** ☎01803/866965, ⓕ865916. Individual itineraries from a very experienced company focusing on nature reserves, research projects and diving.

**South American Experience** ☎020/7976 5511, ⓦwww.southamericanexperience.co.uk Escorted tours with experienced specialists.

**South American Safaris** ☎020/8767 9136, ⓦwww.southamericansafaris.com. Budget camping trips (3–14 weeks) in purpose-built trucks.

**Tucan Travel** ☎020/8742 8612, ⓦwww.tucantravel.com. Latin American specialists offering three-week adventure tours and overland camping expeditions.

## US and Canada

**Adventure Life** ☎1-800/344-6118,

Ⓦwww.adventure-life.com. Small personal organization with a community focus.

Andean Treks Ⓣ1-800/683-8148, Ⓦwww.andeantreks.com. Camping and trekking tours in the mountains.

Far Horizons Ⓣ1-800/552-4575, Ⓦwww.farhorizon.com. Superb yearly archeological trips to remote Maya sites led by renowned experts in the field.

Green Tortoise Adventure Travel Ⓣ1-800/867-8647, Ⓦwww .greentortoise.com. Tours through Mexico and Central America from November through April on converted buses with sleeping space.

Kon-Tiki Tours Ⓣ877/566-8454, Ⓦwww.kontikitours.com. South American tour operators with basic package and add-ons plus mountain-biking and mountaineering excursions.

Myths and Mountains Ⓣ1-800/670-6984, Ⓦwww.myth-sandmountains.com. Socially responsible cultural tours, including exploration of the medicinal heritage of the Andes and rainforest and visits to community projects.

Tropical Travel Ⓣ1-800/451-8017, Ⓦwww.tropicaltravel.com. Tailor-made trips, taking in ruins and rainforests. Diving packages also available.

## Australia and New Zealand

Adventure Associates Australia Ⓣ02/9389 7466, Ⓦwww .adventureassociates.com. Comprehensive tour company with cultural trips, city stopovers and activity holidays including mountain-biking and sports fishing.

Austral Tours Australia Ⓣ03/9600 1733, Ⓦwww.australtours.com. Central and South American specialists.

Australian Andean Adventures Australia Ⓣ02/9235 1889, Ⓦwww.andeanadventures.com.au. Trekking specialist with mountain-climbing courses in Bolivia and Peru.

Contours Australia Ⓣ03/9670 6900. Specialists in tailored city stopover packages to Central America.

Maupintour Australia Ⓣ02/9255 0899, Ⓦwww.maupintours.com. All-inclusive guided tours and cruises from the US to Central America.

Peregrine Adventures Australia Ⓣ03/9663 8611, Ⓦwww .peregrineadventures.com. Extended overland and sea adventures from Southern Mexico through Central and South America.

South American Travel Centre Australia Ⓣ1800/655051, Ⓦwww.satc.com.au. Specialists in luxury, tailor-made tours to South and Central America and Cuba.

Surf Travel Company Australia Ⓣ02/9527 4722, Ⓦwww.surftravel.com.au. Overland surfing tours from Los Angeles to Central American top wave spots.

# Voluntary work

There are hundreds of different voluntary projects based in Latin America – ⓦwww.planeta.com has well-organized links to many of them. Check your guidebook for schemes running in individual countries. Most of the organizations listed below accept volunteers from all over the world as well as national citizens.

## UK organizations

**British Council** 10 Spring Gardens, London SW1A 2BN ☎020/7930 8466, ⓦwww.britishcouncil.org. Publishes a book, "Year Between", aimed principally at gap-year students detailing volunteer programmes.

**British Trust for Conservation Volunteers (BTCV)** 36 St Mary's St, Wallingford, Oxfordshire OX10 0EU ☎01491/839766, ⓦwww.btcv.org.uk. One of the largest environmental charities in Britain with a programme of international working holidays (as a paying volunteer) in many parts of Latin America.

**I-I International Projects** 9 Blenheim Terrace, Leeds L52 9H2 ☎0870 333 2332, ⓦwww.i-to-i.com. TEFL training provider operating voluntary teaching, conservation, business and medical schemes in Bolivia, Costa Rica, Ecuador and Honduras.

**VSO (Voluntary Service Overseas)** 317 Putney Bridge Rd, London SW15 2PN ☎020/8780 7500, ⓦwww.vso.org.uk. Highly respected charity that specializes in sending qualified professionals abroad for two years or more but also operates shorter youth projects.

**World Service Enquiry Unit** 233 Bon Marché `Centre, 241–251 Ferndale Rd, London SW9 8BJ ☎020/7346 5956, ⓦwww.wse.org.uk. Umbrella organization which has contact details for jobs and short-term placements with overseas charities.

## US organizations

**Amerispan** PO Box 5812, Philadelphia, PA 19102-8129 ☎800/879-6640, ⓦwww.amerispan.com. Highly rated educational travel company which specializes in language courses but also runs volunteer programmes all over Latin America.

**Council on International Educational Exchange (CIEE)** 633 Third Ave, Twentieth Floor, New York, NY 10017 ☎888-COUNCIL, ⓦwww.ciee.org. Runs volunteer projects for students and recent graduates in 25 countries worldwide including parts of Latin America. Publishes "Work, Study, Travel Abroad" and "Volunteer! The Comprehensive Guide to Voluntary Service in the US and Abroad".

**Earthwatch Institute** 3 Clock Tower Place, Suite 100, Box 75, Maynard, MA 01754 ☎800/776-0188, ⓦwww.earthwatch.org. International non-profit organization with offices in the US, England, Australia and Japan. Volunteers work in the field with trained professionals on conservation and archeological projects.

**Global Volunteers** 375 E Little Canada Rd, St Paul, MN 55117 ☎1-800-487-1074, ⊛www.globalvolunteers.org.
Projects include working with children in Ecuador or on conservation in the Monteverde cloudforest in Costa Rica.

**Habitat for Humanity** 12 Habitat St, Americus, GA 31709 ☎229/924-6935, ⊛www.habitat.org.
Non-profit, non-denominational Christian organization which builds simple homes in impoverished areas in 83 countries worldwide. One- to three-week building trips.

**Peace Corps** 1111 20th St NW, Washington DC 20526 ☎1-800/424-8580, ⊛www.peacecorps.gov.
Places people with specialist qualifications or skills in two-year postings in developing countries.

**Volunteers for Peace** 1034 Tiffany Rd, Belmont, VT 05730 ☎802/259-2759, ⊛www.vfp.org.
Non-profit organization with links to a huge international network of "work camps", two- to four-week community-based projects.

## Australian organizations

**Australian Volunteers International** 71 Argyle St, Fitzroy, Melbourne ☎03/9279 1788, ⊛www.ozvol.org.au.
Postings for up to two years in developing countries.

# Health

## UK

**British Airways Travel Clinics** 28 regional clinics in the UK (☎01276/685 040 for the nearest or consult ⊛www.britishairways.com); in London visit 156 Regent St, W1 (☎020/7439 9584; no appointment necessary), or 101 Cheapside, EC2 (☎020/7606 2977; appointment required).
All clinics provide vaccinations, antimalarial drugs, tailored up-to-the-minute advice and a complete range of travel healthcare products.

**Communicable Diseases Unit** Brownlee Centre, Glasgow G12

OYN ☎0141/211 1062.
Travel vaccinations including yellow fever.

**Hospital for Tropical Diseases Travel Clinic** 2nd floor, Mortimer Market Centre, off Capper St, London WC1E 6AU ☎020/7388 9600. The clinic is open Mon–Fri 9am–5pm by appointment. A consultation costs £15 which is waived if you have your injections here. A recorded health line (☎09061/337 733; 50p per min) gives advice on disease prevention and appropriate immunizations.

**Liverpool School of Tropical Medicine** Pembroke Place,

Liverpool L3 5QA ☎0151/708 9393. Walk-in clinic Mon–Fri 1–4pm. An appointment is only required for yellow fever jabs.

**Nomad Pharmacy** 40 Bernard St, London WC1 and 3–4 Wellington Terrace, Turnpike Lane, London N8. Immunizations and free travel advice at clinics, open Mon–Fri 9.30am–6pm (☎020/7833 4114; appointments necessary). Telephone helpline (☎09068/633 4140) costs 60p a minute.

**MASTA (Medical Advice Service for Travellers' Abroad)** ⓦwww.masta.org. The London School of Hygiene and Tropical Medicine operates this pre-recorded 24-hour Travellers' Helpline (☎0906/822 4100 in the UK, 60p a minute; ☎01560/147 000 in Ireland, 75p a minute), giving written information tailored to your journey by return of post.

**Malaria Helpline** ☎0891/600 350; 24-hour recorded message for 60p a minute.

## Ireland

**Dun Laoghaire Medical Centre** 5 Northumberland Ave, Dun Laoghaire, Co Dublin ☎01/280 4996, ⓦwww.iol.ie/-tmb. Advice on travel medicine.

**Travel Health Centre, Department of International Health and Tropical Medicine**, Royal College of Surgeons in Ireland, Mercers Medical Centre, Lower Stephen's St, Dublin ☎01/402 2337. Expert pre-trip advice and inoculations.

**Travel Medical Services** PO Box 254, 16 College St, Belfast 1 ☎00028/9031 5220. Offers medical

advice before a trip and help afterwards.

**Tropical Medical Bureau** Grafton Buildings, 34 Grafton St, Dublin 2 ☎01/671 9200, ⓦtmb.exodus.ie

## US and Canada

**Canadian Society for International Health** 1 Nicholas St, Suite 1105, Ottawa, ON K1N 7B7 ☎613/241-5785.
Distributes a free pamphlet, "Health Information for Canadian Travellers", containing an extensive list of travel health centres in Canada.

**Centers for Disease Control** 1600 Clifton Rd NE, Atlanta, GA 30333 ☎404/639-3311, ⓦwww.cdc.gov. Publishes outbreak warnings, suggested inoculations, precautions and other background information for travellers. Excellent website and International Travellers Hotline on ☎1-877/FYI-TRIP.

**International Association for Medical Assistance to Travellers (IAMAT)** 417 Center St, Lewiston, NY 14092 ☎716/754-4883 and 40 Regal Rd, Guelph, ON N1K IB5 ☎519/836-0102, ⓦwww.sentex.net/~iamat. A non-profit organization which provides details of English-speaking doctors in the country you're going to, climate charts and leaflets on varous diseases and inoculations.

**International SOS Assistance** Eight Neshaminy Interplex Suite 207, Trevose, US 19053-6956 ☎1-800/523-8930, ⓦwww.intsos.com. Members receive pre-trip medical referral info as well as overseas emergency services designed to complement travel insurance coverage.

Travel Medicine 369 Pleasant St, Suite 312, Northampton, MA 01060 ☎1-800/872-8633, ⓦwww.travmed.com. Sells travel-related health products.

Travelers Medical Center 31 Washington Square West, New York NY 10011 ☎212/982-1600. Consultation service on immunizations and treatment of disease for travellers to developing countries.

## Australia and New Zealand

Travel-Bug Medical and Vaccination Centre 161 Ward St, North Adelaide ☎08/8267 3544.

Travellers' Medical and Vaccination Centres Branches include: in Australia, 7/428 George St, Sydney ☎02/9221 7133; 27–29 Gilbert Place, Adelaide ☎08/8212 7522; in New Zealand, 1/170 Queen St, Auckland ☎09/373 3531; Shop 15, Grand Arcade, Willis St, Wellington ☎04/473 0991, ⓦwww.tmvc.com.au. Has vaccination centres throughout

Australia and New Zealand and provides general information on travel health. Excellent website.

Travellers' Immunization Service 303 Pacific Hwy, Sydney ☎02/9416 1348.

## Travel health websites

ⓦwww.istm.org The website of the International Society for Travel Medicine, with a full list of clinics specializing in international travel health.

ⓦwww.medicineplanet.com Comprehensive website with country-by-country risks, inoculation details and customized advice according to your destination.

ⓦwww.tripprep.com Travel Health Online provides an online-only comprehensive database of necessary vaccinations for most countries, as well as destination and medical service provider information.

ⓦwww.who.int Website of the World Health Organization with useful data on disease prevalence, prevention and current outbreak trends.

# Official advice on trouble spots

British Foreign and Commonwealth Office ☎020/7238 4503, ⓦwww.fco.gov.uk.

US State Department Travel Advisory Service ☎202/647-5225, ⓦwww.travel.state.gov.

Canadian Department of Foreign Affairs ☎1-800/387-3124, ⓦwww.dfait-maeci.gc.ca.

Australian Department of Foreign Affairs ☎02/6261-9111, ⓦwww.dfat.ov.au.

New Zealand Department of Foreign Affairs ☎04/494 8500.

# Responsible tourism

## UK

**Campaign for Environmentally Responsible Tourism (CERT)** PO Box 4246, London SE21 7ZE, ⓦwww.c-e-r-t.org.
Lobbies to educate tour operators and tourists in a sensitive approach to travel, focusing on immediate practical ways in which the environment can be protected.

**Tourism Concern** Stapleton House, 277–281 Holloway Rd, London N7 8HN ⓣ020/7753 3330, ⓦwww.tourismconcern.org.uk.
Campaigns for the rights of local people to be consulted in tourism developments affecting their lives and produces a quarterly magazine of news and articles.

## US

**Global Exchange** 2017 Mission St #303, San Francisco, CA 94110 ⓣ415/255-7296, ⓦwww.globalexchange.org.
Not-for-profit organization that leads "reality tours" to developing countries which give participants the chance to learn about the country while seeing it.

**Partners in Responsible Tourism** PO Box 237, San Francisco, CA 94104-0237, ⓦwww.pirt.org.
An organization of individuals and travel companies promoting responsible tourism to minimize harm to the environment and local cultures. Their website features a "Traveler's Code for Traveling Responsibly".

## Australia

**Responsible Tourism Network** PO Box 34, Rundel Mall, Adelaide 5000 ⓣ08/8232 272, ⓦwww.caa.org.au/travel.
A non-profit travel agency which sets up sustainable-tourism projects and runs small-group tours to visit them.

## Online resources

ⓦ**www.ecotourism.about.com**
Recommended umbrella site with a wide range of discussions, articles and links on varied aspects of the relationship between tourism and the environment. Links to eco-aware travel companies.

ⓦ**www.ecotourism.org**
Website produced by the US-based International Ecotourism Society with online factsheets and reviews of eco-lodges and ecotour operators.

ⓦ**www.green-travel.com**
Hundreds of links to green companies around the world.

ⓦ**www.planeta.com**
Award-winning clearinghouse with hundreds of articles including official reports on ecotourism in Latin America and thousands of links to more general travel websites.

ⓦ**www.responsibletravel.com**
Website created by Body Shop founder Anita Roddick, which reviews hundreds of ecotours and accommodation around the world.

# Travel book and map stores

## UK and Ireland

**Blackwell's Map and Travel Shop** 50 Broad St, Oxford OX1 3BQ ☎01865/793 550, ⓦmaps.blackwell.co.uk, ⓦbooks.blackwell.co.uk

**Daunt Books** 83 Marylebone High St, London W1M 3DE ☎020/7224 2295; 193 Haverstock Hill, London NW3 4QL ☎020/7794 4006.

**Easons Bookshop** 40 O'Connell St, Dublin 1 ☎01/873 3811, ⓦwww.eason.ie.

**National Map Centre** 22–24 Caxton St, London SW1H 0QU ☎020/7222 2466, ⓦwww.mapsnmc .co.uk, ⓔinfo@mapsnmc.co.uk.

**Stanfords** 12–14 Long Acre, London WC2E 9LP ☎020/7836 1321, ⓦwww.stanfords.co.uk. Other branches within British Airways offices at 156 Regent St, London W1R 5TA ☎020/7434 4744, and 29 Corn St, Bristol BS1 1HT ☎0117/929 9966.

**The Travel Bookshop** 13–15 Blenheim Crescent, London W11 2EE ☎020/7229 5260, ⓦwww.thetravelbookshop.co.uk.

## US and Canada

**Adventurous Traveler Bookstore** 102 Lake Street, Burlington, VT 05401 ☎1-800/282-3963, ⓦwww.adventuroustraveler.com.

**Book Passage** 51 Tamal Vista Blvd, Corte Madera, CA 94925 ☎1-800/999-7909, ⓦwww.bookpassage.com.

**The Complete Traveler Bookstore** 199 Madison Ave, New York, NY 10016 ☎212/685-9007.

**Elliot Bay Book Company** 101 S Main St, Seattle, WA 98104 ☎1-800/962-5311, ⓦwww.elliotbaybook.com.

**Globe Corner Bookstore** 28 Church St, Cambridge, MA 02138 ☎1-800/358-6013, ⓦwww.globercorner.com.

**Map Link** 30 S La Patera Lane, Unit 5, Santa Barbara, CA 93117 ☎805/692-6777, ⓦwww.maplink.com.

**The Map Store Inc** 1636 1st St, Washington, DC 20006 ☎202/628-2608.

**Open Air Books and Maps** 25 Toronto St, Toronto, ON M5R 2C1 ☎416/363-0719.

**Rand McNally** ☎1-800/333-0136, ⓦwww.randmcnally.com. Around thirty stores across the US; dial ext 2111 or check the website for the nearest location.

**The Travel Bug Bookstore** 2667 W Broadway, Vancouver V6K 2G2 ☎604/737-1122, ⓦwww.swifty.com/tbug.

**World of Maps** 1235 Wellington St, Ottawa, ON K1Y 3A3 ☎1-800/214-8524, ⓦwww.worldofmaps.com.

**Ulysses Travel Bookshop** 4176 St-Denis, Montréal ☎514/843-9447, ⓦwww.ulyssesguides.com.

## Australia and New Zealand

**The Map Shop** 6–10 Peel St, Adelaide, SA 5000 ☎08/8231 2033, ⓦwww.mapshop.net.au.

Mapland 372 Little Bourke St, Melbourne, Victoria 3000, ⓣ03/9670 4383, Ⓦwww.mapland.com.au.

MapWorld 173 Gloucester St, Christchurch ⓣ0800/627 967 or 03/374 5399, Ⓦwww.mapworld.co.nz.

Perth Map Centre 1/884 Hay St, Perth, WA 6000 ⓣ08/9322 5733, Ⓦwww.perthmap.com.au.

Specialty Maps 46 Albert St, Auckland 1001 ⓣ09/307 2217, Ⓦwww.ubdonline.co.nz/maps.

Travel Bookshop Shop 3, 175 Liverpool St, Sydney ⓣ02/9261 8200.

Worldwide Maps and Guides 187 George St, Brisbane Ⓦ07/3221 4330.

# Online travel resources

## General travel websites

Ⓦwww.about.com/travel
Huge information resource with some of the best destination guides on the web and well-organized links.

Ⓦwww.bootnall.com
Travel for backpackers with good links, articles and message board.

Ⓦwww.budgetravel.com
Thousands of links from all around the world on all matter of subjects of interest to budget travellers.

Ⓦwww.gapyear.com
Comprehensive information on taking a year out with articles on fund raising, working and studying abroad as well as practical information on planning a trip.

Ⓦwww.itisnet.com
A useful source of current info for budget travellers which is reguarly updated by travellers and researchers.

Ⓦwww.journeywoman.com
Recommended site aimed at women travellers with features such as "What should I wear", travel-ogues and advice on health and travelling solo.

Ⓦwww.travel-library.com
Travel writers' website with collection of articles from well-established writers on dozens of countries and themes.

Ⓦwww.worldtravelguide.net
Destination guides with useful background and tourist information.

## Latin American websites

Ⓦlanic.utexas.edu/la
The Latin American Network Information Centre, based at the University of Texas, is easily the best online resource on Latin America. Thousands of efficiently catalogued links to cultural, political and recreation issues among others.

Ⓦwww.latinnews.com
Good selection of current news reports from all parts of Latin America.

W www.latinworld.com
Large search engine with links to hundreds of Latin American websites.

W www.planeta.com
Award-winning Latin American eco-tourism clearinghouse with links to other, lighter subjects as well as articles and official reports on the environment.

## Travellers' forums, newsgroups and bulletin board

rec.travel.latin-america and soc.travel.latin-america

Newsgroups (go to W www.groups .google.com, or use a dedicated newsreader) with thousands of messages posted.

W www.roughguides.com
Interactive site for independent travellers, with forums, bulletin boards, travel tips and features plus online travel guides.

W www.samexplo.org
Website of the South American Explorers' Club, based in Lima, Peru, which has general information on South America and a message board.

# Specialist Latin American resource centres

The following places (most connected to academic institutions) run courses and lectures on Latin American themes. They also have specialist book collections and organize film showings and exhibitions – check their websites to find out about events.

## UK

Latin America Bureau
1 Amwell St, London EC1R 1UL, W www.lab.org.uk.

Canning House
2 Belgrave Square, London SW1X 8PJ, W www.canninghouse.com.

Institute of Latin American Studies
31 Tavistock Square, London WC1H 9HA, W www.sas.ac.uk/ilas

Centre of Latin American Studies
University of Cambridge, West Road, Cambridge CB3 9EF, W www.latin-american.cam.ac.uk

## USA

There are hundreds of Latin American resource centres in the US – these are some of the best:

Center for Latin American and Caribbean Studies
53 Washington Square South, Floor 4w, New York, NY 10012, W www.nyu.edu.

Center for Latin American Studies
University of California, 2334 Bowditch St, Berkeley, CA 94720, W socrates.berkeley.edu.7001/.

Center for Latin American Studies
3520 Prospect St, Washington DC
20057-0885,
Ⓦwww.georgetown.edu.

Latin American Network
Information Center (LANIC)
Sid W Richardson Hall 1.310,
Austin, TX 8712-1284,
Ⓦwww.lanic.utexas.edu.

## Canada

Center for Research on Latin
America and the Caribbean
(CERLAC)

York University, 4700 Keele St,
North York, ON, M3J1P3,
Ⓦwww.yorku.ca/cerlac.

Latin American Research Centre
Social Sciences Bldg 714, 2500
University Drive NW, Calgary,
Alberta T2N 1N4,
Ⓦwww.ucalgary.ca

## Australia

Institute of Latin American Studies
La Trobe University, Bundorra,
Victoria 3083, Ⓦwww.latrobe.edu.au.

# Language schools and relevant associations

If you're planning to learn Spanish/Portuguese at home, find out what relevant evening classes your local authority, university or Latin American cultural centre offers.

## Online language schools

Listed below is a selection of some of the many online language courses available (from $100).

Ⓦwww.donquijote.org
Has eight language schools in Latin America, an online language course in Spanish and volunteer projects in Peru.

Ⓦwww.sonia-portuguese.com
Down-to-earth website set up by Brazilian language teacher with fourteen years of experience of teaching Brazilian Portuguese.

Ⓦwww.studyspanish.com
Combines sound language teaching methods with well-written and varied essays on cultural issues.

Ⓦwww.unforgettablespanish.com
Less formal methods of teaching languages with ideas association used to lock new vocabulary into memory.

## Language schools in Latin America

If you want to learn Spanish or Portuguese in Latin America, check your guidebook for listings of recommended language schools in individual countries. The websites below all have links to dozens of language schools in Latin America.

Ⓦ www.amerispan.com
Highly rated educational travel company with links to a variety of immersion language courses in Latin America, with home stays included.

Ⓦ www.centerforstudyabroad.com
Washington-based company offering language courses in Mexico and Costa Rica, usually as a one- to nine-week summer school.

Ⓦ www.languagesabroad.com
Toronto-based company with a wide selection of language courses ranging from two weeks to nine months.

Ⓦ www.spanishstudies.com
Comprehensive US website with links to dozens of schools teaching Spanish in Latin America.

# Travel equipment suppliers

## UK

**Cotswold Outdoor Ltd** 42–46 Uxbridge Rd, London W12 8ND ☎020/8743 2976, Ⓦ www.cotswold-outdoor.co.uk; branches countrywide. ☎01285/643434 for mail order catalogue.

**Field and Trek** 42 Maiden Lane, Covent Garden, London WC2E 7JL ☎020/7379 3793, Ⓦ www.field-trek.co.uk; branches countrywide. ☎01268/494444 for mail order catalogue.

**Nomad Pharmacy and Travellers' Store** 3 Wellington Terrace, Turnpike Lane, London N8 OPX ☎020/8889 7014; STA, 40 Bernard St, London WC1N ILJ ☎020/7833 4114; 4 Potters Rd, New Barnet, Herts EN5 5HW ☎020/8441 7208; Ⓦ www.nomad-travstore.co.uk. Specialist in travellers' medical supplies and first-aid equipment; also stocks general-purpose travel accessories.

**YHA Adventure Shops** Branches countrywide; Ⓦ www.yhaadventure.co.uk.

## US and Canada

**Campmor** PO Box 700, Saddle River, NJ 07458-0700 ☎1-800/226-7667, Ⓦ www.campmor.com. Clothing plus outdoor and camping gear.

**The North Face** Ⓦ www.thenorthface.com. Eight stores in the US and one in Canada selling camping equipment and clothing. For your nearest store, call ☎1-800/447-2333.

**Recreational Equipment Inc** PO Box 1700, Sumner, WA 98352-0001 ☎1-800/426-4840, Ⓦ www.rei.com. Sixty stores selling outdoor gear and clothing. Extensive mail-order catalogue.

**Sierra Trading Post** 5025 Campstool Rd, Cheyenne, WY 82007-1802 ☎1-800/713-4534, Ⓦ www.sierratradingpost.com. Clothes, shoes and small equipment.

**Travel Medicine** 369 Pleasant St,

Northampton, MA 01060 ☏1-800/872-8633, ⓦwww.travelmed.com. Sells first-aid kits, mosquito netting, water filters and other health-related travel products.

Travel Smith 60 Leveroni Court #1, Novato, CA 94949 ☏1-800/950-1600, ⓦwww.travelsmith.com.

## Australia and New Zealand

A-Roving 112 Toorak Rd, Toorak, VIC 3142 ☏03/9824 1714. Suppliers of travel luggage and accessories, maps and travel guides.

Bivouac 5 Fort St, Auckland 1 ☏09/366 1966. Several stores in New Zealand stocking a full range of backpacking and camping gear.

Katmandu PO Box 1191, Collingwood, VIC 3066 ☏03/9417 2480. A mail-order company with outlets in all major Australian and New Zealand cities, offering an extensive range of quality outdoor and climbing gear.

Mountain Designs 105 Albert St, Brisbane, QLD 4000 ☏07/3221 6756; branches in major Australian and New Zealand cities. Australian-designed, lightweight mountaineering and adventure equipment, specializing in sleeping bags, Gore-tex and fleeces.

Mtn Equipment Pty Ltd 491 Kent St, Sydney, NSW 2000 ☏02/9264 5888; branches in Chatswood and Hornsby. Comprehensive range of lightweight, functional gear for outdoor and sporting activities.

# Final checklist

## Documents

- ❏ Airline tickets
- ❏ Credit and debit cards
- ❏ Guidebooks
- ❏ Insurance policy
- ❏ International drivers' licence
- ❏ Maps
- ❏ Passport
- ❏ Phrasebook
- ❏ Phone card
- ❏ Photocopies of vital documents
- ❏ Travellers' cheques

## The bare essentials

- ❏ Backpack
- ❏ Clothes
- ❏ Daypack
- ❏ Fleece jacket
- ❏ Money belt
- ❏ Sarong
- ❏ Shoes
- ❏ Sun hat

## Basic odds and ends

- ❏ Alarm clock
- ❏ Batteries
- ❏ Camera equipment and film
- ❏ Contact lens stuff/glasses
- ❏ Contraceptives
- ❏ First-aid kit

- ❏ Flashlight
- ❏ Mosquito repellent
- ❏ Padlock and chain
- ❏ Penknife
- ❏ Sunglasses
- ❏ Tampons
- ❏ Toiletries
- ❏ Towel
- ❏ Wallet

## Optionals

- ❏ Books
- ❏ Cigarette lighter
- ❏ Compass
- ❏ Earplugs
- ❏ Games
- ❏ Mosquito net
- ❏ Notebook or journal and pens
- ❏ Personal stereo and tapes
- ❏ Photos/postcards of home
- ❏ Rain gear/umbrella
- ❏ Sewing kit
- ❏ Sheet sleeping bag
- ❏ Shortwave radio
- ❏ Sink plug
- ❏ String
- ❏ Water bottle, water purifier or purification tablets
- ❏ Waterproof money-holder

# First-Time
# Latin America

# Index
## and small print

# Index

map entries are in colour

## A

accommodation ..............247–261
adventure sports ......................114
AIDS .....................................279
airpasses, see flights
**airports**
   arrival .....................................199–204
   check-in ...................................197
altitude sickness .....................278
Amazon ...................vii, 24, 84, 108
Andes ...........................................111
Angel Falls (V) .............................94
Antigua (Gua) ..............................52
Arequipa (Per) ............................85
**Argentina** ...................................5–9
Argentina ..........................................6
   best time to go .........................5, 145
   costs ................................................5
   embassies .....................................316
   itineraries .......................................8–9
   online .............................................9
   routes in and out ..............................8
   tourist offices ...............................315
Asunción (Par)............................79

## B

Bahia (Br) ....................................21

Baja California (M) ......................66
Baños (Ec) ..................................44
bargaining ................................156
Bay Islands (H) ...........................61
beggars ....................................212
behaviour, appropriate ......209, 221
**Belize** ...................................10–13
Belize ..........................................11
   best time to go ........................10, 145
   costs ..............................................10
   embassies .....................................316
   itineraries .......................................13
   online .............................................13
   routes in and out ............................13
   tourist offices ...............................315
bicycles ....................................243
bird-watching ...........................117
**boats** ...............................236–238
Bocas del Toro (Pan)....................75
Bogotá (Col) ...............................36
**Bolivia**............................14–19
Bolivia ..........................................15
   best time to go ........................14, 145
   costs ..............................................14
   embassies .....................................317
   itineraries .......................................18
   online .............................................19
   routes in and out ............................17
   tourist offices ...............................315
   visas .............................................125
booking accommodation .........195

# V

# W

# Y

## Twenty Years of Rough Guides

In the summer of 1981, Mark Ellingham, Rough Guides' founder, knocked out the first guide on a typewriter, with a group of friends. Mark had been travelling in Greece after university, and couldn't find a guidebook that really answered his needs.There were heavyweight cultural guides on the one hand – good on museums and classical sites but not on beaches and tavernas – and on the other hand student manuals that were so caught up with how to save money that they lost sight of the country's significance beyond its role as a place for a cool vacation. None of the guides began to address Greece as a country, with its natural and human environment, its politics and its contemporary life.

Having no urgent reason to return home, Mark decided to write his own guide. It was a guide to Greece that tried to combine some erudition and insight with a thoroughly practical approach to travellers' needs. Scrupulously researched listings of places to stay, eat and drink were matched by careful attention to detail on everything from Homer to Greek music, from classical sites to national parks and from nude beaches to monasteries. Back in London, Mark and his friends got their Rough Guide accepted by a farsighted commissioning editor at the publisher Routledge and it came out in 1982.

The Rough Guide to Greece was a student scheme that became a publishing phenomenon. The immediate success of the book – shortlisted for the Thomas Cook award – spawned a series that rapidly covered dozens of countries. The Rough Guides found a ready market among backpackers and budget travellers, but soon acquired a much broader readership that included older and less impecunious visitors. Readers relished the guides' wit and inquisitiveness as much as the enthusiastic, critical approach that acknowledges everyone wants value for money – but not at any price.

Rough Guides soon began supplementing the "rougher" information – the hostel and low-budget listings – with the kind of detail that independent-minded travellers on any budget might expect. These days, the guides – distributed worldwide by the Penguin group – include recommendations spanning the range from shoestring to luxury, and cover more than two hundred destinations around the globe. Our growing team of authors, many of whom come to Rough Guides initially as outstandingly good letter-writers telling us about their travels, are spread all over the world, particularly in Europe, the USA and Australia. As well as the travel guides, Rough Guides publishes a series of dictionary phrasebooks covering two dozen major languages, an acclaimed series of music guides running the gamut from Classical to World Music, a series of music CDs in association with World Music Network, and a range of reference books on topics as diverse as the Internet, pregnancy and unexplained phenomena. Visit **www.roughguides.com** to see what's cooking.

## Rough Guide Credits

**Text editor**: Gavin Thomas
**Series editor**: Mark Ellingham
**Editorial**: Martin Dunford, Jonathan Buckley, Kate Berens, Ann-Marie Shaw, Helena Smith, Olivia Swift, Ruth Blackmore, Geoff Howard, Claire Saunders, Alexander Mark Rogers, Polly Thomas, Joe Staines, Richard Lim, Duncan Clark, Peter Buckley, Lucy Ratcliffe, Clifton Wilkinson, Alison Murchie, Matthew Teller, Andrew Dickson, Fran Sandham, Sally Schafer (UK); Andrew Rosenberg, Yuki Takagaki, Richard Koss, Hunter Slaton (US)
**Production**: Susanne Hillen, Andy Hilliard, Link Hall, Helen Prior, Julia Bovis, Michelle Draycott, Katie Pringle, Zoë Nobes, Rachel Holmes, Andy Turner, Dan May
**Cartography**: Maxine Repath, Melissa Baker, Ed Wright, Katie Lloyd-Jones
**Cover art direction**: Louise Boulton
**Picture research**: Sharon Martins, Mark Thomas
**Online**: Kelly Martinez, Anja Mutic-Blessing, Jennifer Gold, Audra Epstein, Suzanne Welles, Cree Lawson (US)
**Finance**: John Fisher, Gary Singh, Edward Downey, Mark Hall, Tim Bill
**Marketing & Publicity**: Richard Trillo, Niki Smith, David Wearn, Chloë Roberts, Demelza Dallow, Claire Southern (UK); Simon Carloss, David Wechsler, Megan Kennedy (US)
**Administration**: Julie Sanderson, Karoline Densley

## Publishing Information

This first edition published March 2003 by **Rough Guides Ltd**,
80 Strand, London WC2R 0RL.
Penguin Putnam, Inc., 375 Hudson Street, NY 10014, USA.
**Distributed by the Penguin Group**
Penguin Books Ltd,
80 Strand, London WC2R 0RL
Penguin Putnam, Inc.,
375 Hudson Street, NY 10014, USA
Penguin Books Australia Ltd,
487 Maroondah Highway, PO Box 257,
Ringwood, Victoria 3134, Australia
Penguin Books Canada Ltd,
10 Alcorn Avenue, Toronto, Ontario,
Canada M4V 1E4
Penguin Books (NZ) Ltd,
182–190 Wairau Road, Auckland 10,
New Zealand
Printed in Italy by LegoPrint S.p.A

368pp includes index
A catalogue record for this book is available from the British Library

ISBN 1-84353-022-8

The publishers and authors have done their best to ensure the accuracy and currency of all the information in **First-Time Latin America**; however, they can accept no responsibility for any loss, injury, or inconvenience sustained by any traveller as a result of information or advice contained in the guide.

## Help Us Update

We've gone to a lot of effort to ensure that the first edition of **First-Time Latin America** is accurate and up-to-date. However, things change – places get "discovered", opening hours are notoriously fickle, restaurants and rooms raise prices or lower standards. If you feel we've got it wrong or left something out, we'd like to know, and if you can remember the address, the price, the time, the phone number, so much the better.

We'll credit all contributions, and send a copy of the next edition (or any other Rough Guide if you prefer) for the best letters. Everyone who writes to us and isn't already a subscriber will receive a copy of our full-colour thrice-yearly newsletter. Please mark letters: **"First-Time Latin America Update"** and send to: Rough Guides, 80 Strand, London WC2R 0RL, or Rough Guides, 4th Floor, 345 Hudson St, New York, NY 10014. Or send an email to **mail@roughguides.com**

Have your questions answered and tell others about your trip at **www.roughguides.atinfopop.com**

# Acknowledgements

Polly and James would like to thank Kate Berens for seeing the project through from start to finish; Gavin Thomas for expert editing; all the Rough Guide authors and correspondents who contributed information, advice and anecdotes, including Harry Adès, Danny Aeberhard, Gary Bowerman, Peter Eltringham, Melissa Graham, Dilwyn Jenkins, Jean McNeil, Iain Stewart and Paul Whitfield; all the production team at Rough Guide, including Katie Lloyd-Jones for cartography, Katie Pringle for typesetting, Mark Thomas for picture research, Julia Bovis for keeping it all on track, and Margaret Doyle for proofreading; to Julie Feiner, Mary Green and Claire Southern; and to Rafe Stone and Miguel Vega at Journey Latin America.

James would also like to thank Matthew Read, Jonny Cohen, all those who've kept him company on the road over the years, and Emma and Freya for their love and support.

Polly would also like to thank her friends and family for their faith, encouragement and support and especially Eileen Gaughan whose idea it was to go to Latin America in the first place.

## Photo Credits

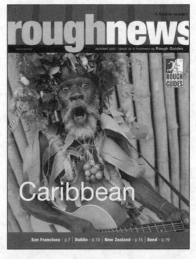

## Europe

Algarve
Amsterdam
Andalucia
Austria
Barcelona
Belgium
 & Luxembourg
Berlin
Britain
Brittany
 & Normandy
Bruges & Ghent
Brussels
Budapest
Bulgaria
Copenhagen
Corsica
Costa Brava
Crete
Croatia
Cyprus
Czech & Slovak
 Republics
Devon & Cornwall
Dodècanese
 & East Aegean
Dordogne
 & the Lot
Dublin
Edinburgh
England
Europe
First-Time Europe
Florence
France
French Hotels
 & Restaurants
Germany
Greece
Greek Islands
Holland
Hungary
Ibiza
 & Formentera
Iceland
Ionian Islands
Ireland
Italy
Lake District

Languedoc
 & Roussillon
Lisbon
London
London Mini Guide
London
 Restaurants
Madeira
Madrid
Mallorca
Malta & Gozo
Menorca
Moscow
Norway
Paris
Paris Mini Guide
Poland
Portugal
Prague
Provence & the
 Côte d'Azur
Pyrenees
Romania
Rome
Sardinia
Scandinavia
Scotland
Scottish Highlands
 & Islands
Sicily
Spain
St Petersburg
Sweden
Switzerland
Tenerife & La
 Gomera
Turkey
Tuscany & Umbria
Venice
 & The Veneto
Vienna
Wales

## Asia

Bali & Lombok
Bangkok
Beijing
Cambodia
China

First-Time Asia
Goa
Hong Kong
 & Macau
India
Indonesia
Japan
Laos
Malaysia,
 Singapore
 & Brunei
Nepal
Singapore
South India
Southeast Asia
Thailand
Thailand Beaches
 & Islands
Tokyo
Vietnam

## Australasia

Australia
Gay & Lesbian
 Australia
Melbourne
New Zealand
Sydney

## North America

Alaska
Big Island of
 Hawaii
Boston
California
Canada
Florida
Hawaii
Honolulu
Las Vegas
Los Angeles
Maui
Miami & the
 Florida Keys
Montréal
New England
New Orleans
New York City

New York City
 Mini Guide
New York
 Restaurants
Pacific Northwest
Rocky Mountains
San Francisco
San Francisco
 Restaurants
Seattle
Southwest USA
Toronto
USA
Vancouver
Washington DC
Yosemite

## Caribbean & Latin America

Antigua & Barbuda
Argentina
Bahamas
Barbados
Belize
Bolivia
Brazil
Caribbean
Central America
Chile
Costa Rica
Cuba
Dominican
 Republic
Ecuador
Guatemala
Jamaica
Maya World
Mexico
Peru
St Lucia
Trinidad & Tobago

## Africa & Middle East

Cape Town
Egypt
Israel & Palestinian
 Territories

Jerusalem
Jordan
Kenya
Morocco
South Africa,
 Lesotho
 & Swaziland
Syria
Tanzania
Tunisia
West Africa
Zanzibar
Zimbabwe

## Dictionary Phrase-books

Czech
Dutch
European
 Languages
French
German
Greek
Hungarian
Italian
Polish
Portuguese
Russian
Spanish
Turkish
Hindi & Urdu
Indonesian
Japanese
Mandarin Chinese
Thai
Vietnamese
Mexican Spanish
Egyptian Arabic
Swahili

## Maps

Amsterdam
Dublin
London
Paris
San Francisco
Venice

Rough Guides publishes new books every month:

**Rough Guides music, reference & CDs**

## Music

Acoustic Guitar
Blues: 100 Essential CDs
Cello
Clarinet
Classical Music
Classical Music: 100 Essential CDs
Country Music
Country: 100 Essential CDs
Cuban Music
Drum'n'bass
Drums
Electric Guitar & Bass Guitar
Flute
Hip-Hop
House
Irish Music
Jazz
Jazz: 100 Essential CDs
Keyboards & Digital Piano
Latin: 100 Essential CDs
Music USA: a Coast-To-Coast Tour
Opera
Opera: 100 Essential CDs
Piano
Reading Music
Reggae
Reggae: 100 Essential CDs
Rock
Rock: 100 Essential CDs
Saxophone
Soul: 100 Essential CDs
Techno
Trumpet & Trombone
Violin & Viola
World Music: 100 Essential CDs

World Music Vol1
World Music Vol2

## Reference

Children's Books, 0–5
Children's Books, 5–11
China Chronicle
Cult Movies
Cult TV
Elvis
England Chronicle
France Chronicle
India Chronicle
The Internet
Internet Radio
James Bond
Liverpool FC
Man Utd
Money Online
Personal Computers
Pregnancy & Birth
Shopping Online
Travel Health
Travel Online
Unexplained Phenomena
Videogaming
Weather
Website Directory
Women Travel

## Music CDs

Africa
Afrocuba
Afro-Peru
Ali Hussan Kuban
The Alps
Americana
The Andes
The Appalachians
Arabesque
Asian Underground
Australian Aboriginal Music
Bellydance
Bhangra
Bluegrass

Bollywood
Boogaloo
Brazil
Cajun
Cajun and Zydeco
Calypso and Soca
Cape Verde
Central America
Classic Jazz
Congolese Soukous
Cuba
Cuban Music Story
Cuban Son
Cumbia
Delta Blues
Eastern Europe
English Roots Music
Flamenco
Franco
Gospel
Global Dance
Greece
The Gypsies
Haiti
Hawaii
The Himalayas
Hip Hop
Hungary
India
India and Pakistan
Indian Ocean
Indonesia
Irish Folk
Irish Music
Italy
Jamaica
Japan
Kenya and Tanzania
Klezmer
Louisiana
Lucky Dube
Mali and Guinea
Marrabenta Mozambique
Merengue & Bachata
Mexico
Native American Music
Nigeria and Ghana
North Africa

Nusrat Fateh Ali Khan
Okinawa
Paris Café Music
Portugal
Rai
Reggae
Salsa
Salsa Dance
Samba
Scandinavia
Scottish Folk
Scottish Music
Senegal & The Gambia
Ska
Soul Brothers
South Africa
South African Gospel
South African Jazz
Spain
Sufi Music
Tango
Thailand
Tex-Mex
Wales
West African Music
World Music Vol 1: Africa, Europe and the Middle East
World Music Vol 2: Latin & North America, Caribbean, India, Asia and Pacific
World Roots
Youssou N'Dour & Etoile de Dakar
Zimbabwe

## Pocket History Series

"Solidly written, immaculately researched, Rough Guides
are as near as modern guides get to essential"
**Sunday Times, London**

www.roughguides.com

# Rough Guide Reference

NOTES

The ideas expressed in this code were developed by and for independent travellers.

### Learn About The Country You're Visiting

Start enjoying your travels before you leave by tapping into as many sources of information as you can.

### The Cost Of Your Holiday

Think about where your money goes - be fair and realistic about how cheaply you travel. Try and put money into local peoples' hands; drink local beer or fruit juice rather than imported brands and stay in locally owned accommodation. Haggle with humour and not aggressively. Pay what something is worth to you and remember how wealthy you are compared to local people.

### Embrace The Local Culture

Open your mind to new cultures and traditions - it will transform your experience. Think carefully about what's appropriate in terms of your clothes and the way you behave. You'll earn respect and be more readily welcomed by local people. Respect local laws and attitudes towards drugs and alcohol that vary in different countries and communities. Think about the impact you could have on them.

# Exploring The World – The Travellers' Code

Being sensitive to these ideas means getting more out of your travels - and giving more back to the people you meet and the places you visit.

### Minimise Your Environmental Impact

Think about what happens to your rubbish - take biodegradable products and a water filter bottle. Be sensitive to limited resources like water, fuel and electricity. Help preserve local wildlife and habitats by respecting local rules and regulations, such as sticking to footpaths and not standing on coral.

### Don't Rely On Guidebooks

Use your guidebook as a starting point, not the only source of information. Talk to local people, then discover your own adventure!

### Be Discreet With Photography

Don't treat people as part of the landscape, they may not want their picture taken. Ask first and respect their wishes.

We work with people the world over to promote tourism that benefits their communities, but we can only carry on our work with the support of people like you. For membership details or to find out how to make your travels work for local people and the environment, visit our website.

www.tourismconcern.org.uk

**TourismConcern**
Campaigning for Ethical and Fairly Traded Tourism